# Pandemics in Singapore, 1819–2022

Singapore has faced many pandemics over the centuries, from plague, small-pox and cholera to influenza and novel coronaviruses. By examining how different governments responded, this book considers what we can learn from their experiences. Public health strategies in the city-state were often affected by issues of ethnicity and class, as well as failure to take heed of key learnings from previous outbreaks. Pandemics are a recurrent and normal feature of the human experience. Alongside medical innovation and evidence-based policy-making, the study of history is also crucial in preparing for future pandemics.

**Kah Seng Loh** is a historian and director of a research consultancy.

**Li Yang Hsu** is an infectious diseases physician who is Vice-Dean of Global Health at Saw Swee Hock School of Public Health, National University of Singapore.

# Routledge Studies in the Modern History of Asia

For a full list of available titles please visit: https://www.routledge.com/Routledge-Studies-in-the-Modern-History-of-Asia/book-series/MODHISTASIA

# Pandemics in Singapore, 1819–2022

Lessons for the Age of COVID-19

**Kah Seng Loh and Li Yang Hsu**

Routledge
Taylor & Francis Group

LONDON AND NEW YORK

First published 2024
by Routledge
4 Park Square, Milton Park, Abingdon, Oxon OX14 4RN

and by Routledge
605 Third Avenue, New York, NY 10158

*Routledge is an imprint of the Taylor & Francis Group, an informa business*

*British Library Cataloguing-in-Publication Data*
A catalogue record for this book is available from the British Library

ISBN: 978-1-032-46962-1 (hbk)
ISBN: 978-1-032-46968-3 (pbk)
ISBN: 978-1-003-38401-4 (ebk)

DOI: 10.4324/9781003384014

Typeset in Times New Roman
by Taylor & Francis Books

Supported by Heritage Research Grant of the National Heritage Board,
Singapore. The views expressed here are solely those of the author(s) and do
not in any way represent the views of the National Heritage Board and/or
any government agencies.

# Contents

# List of Abbreviations

| | |
|---|---|
| AIDS | acquired immunodeficiency syndrome |
| AMRCHSS | *Annual Medical Report of the Civil Hospitals in the Straits Settlements* |
| ASEAN | Association of South East Asian Nations |
| ACE | Assurance, Care and Engagement |
| BCG | Bacille Calmette-Guérin |
| CCAR | City Council, *Annual Report* |
| CDC 2 | Communicable Disease Centre 2 |
| CDC | Communicable Disease Centre |
| COVID-19 | coronavirus disease of 2019 |
| *ENB* | *Epidemiological News Bulletin* |
| FAST | Forward Assurance and Support Teams |
| GH | General Hospital |
| HDB | Housing and Development Board |
| HIV | human immunodeficiency virus |
| HOME | Humanitarian Organisation for Migration Economics |
| LF | Labour Front |
| MDAR | Medical Department, *Annual Report* |
| MERS-CoV | Middle-East Respiratory Syndrome coronavirus |
| Mindef | Ministry of Defence |
| MOH | Ministry of Health |
| MOHAR | Ministry of Health, *Annual Report* |
| MOM | Ministry of Manpower |
| ENV | Ministry of the Environment |
| ENVAR | Ministry of the Environment, *Annual Report* |
| MPMC | *Minutes of the Proceedings of the Municipal Commissioners* |
| MTF | Multi-ministry Task Force |
| NCID | National Centre for Infectious Diseases |
| Hansard | *Official Reports of the Singapore Parliamentary Debates* |
| PAP | People's Action Party |
| PPE | personal protective equipment |
| QED | Quarantine and Epidemiology Department |
| RBDSS | *Registration of Births and Deaths in the Straits Settlements* |

| SARS-CoV-1 | Severe Acute Respiratory Syndrome coronavirus |
| SARS | Severe acute respiratory syndrome |
| SGH | Singapore General Hospital |
| SHDAR | Singapore Health Department, *Annual Report* |
| SMAR | Singapore Municipality, *Administration Report* |
| SHN | Stay Home Notice |
| SSMR | *Straits Settlements Medical Report* |
| TTSH | Tan Tock Seng Hospital |
| TWC2 | Transient Workers Count Too |
| WHO | World Health Organisation |

# Foreword

I thank Dr Kah Seng Loh and Professor Li Yang Hsu for inviting me to contribute the foreword to their path-breaking book. My only qualification for writing the foreword is that I had helped Chua Mui Hoong to write her excellent book on SARS entitled, *A Defining Moment: How Singapore Beat SARS*. I like the book for four reasons.

*First*, it is the first book on pandemics in Singapore, covering the period, 1819 to the present. It is fascinating to see how pandemics were dealt with by the British colonial government, by the Labour Front government and the PAP government.

*Second*, it is interesting to read about the interplay between medicine, science, and other factors in the making of health policy. During colonial Singapore, race, and the British prejudices against the local population, interfered with the making of good health policy. Do we have any blind spots today, for example, about our migrant workers?

There was a huge outbreak of COVID-19 in the over-crowded dormitories, housing foreign workers in Singapore. I wonder if the huge outbreak could have been avoided if the dormitories were less crowded, better ventilated, cleaner and more hygienic.

*Third*, I particularly enjoyed reading the history of vaccinations and the history of quarantine in Singapore. The opening of our world-class National Centre for Infectious Diseases (NCID) in 2019 was a game changer. NCID has a history stretching back to the first hospital for infectious diseases, at Balestier Road built in the 19th century. The locals called that hospital on Balestier Road the 'slaughter house' because of its high mortality.

*Finally*, the authors conclude that pandemics are part of human history and will always be with us. They argue that our campaign against COVID-19 was propelled by science and medicine but also political will and social support.

Compared to many other countries in the world, Singapore has done well in responding to the COVID-19 pandemic. It has listened to the advice of the WHO. It has relied on the views of experts on infectious diseases in Singapore. When the facts changed, Singapore was quick to modify its policy and approach. The transition from treating COVID-19 as a pandemic to treating it as an endemic disease was made successfully. Universal vaccination was accomplished with the support of the public.

Since pandemics will always be with us, it is a matter of time before we are hit by the next pandemic. In preparing for the next pandemic, we can usefully review the history of pandemics in Singapore. What lessons can we learn from that history? What mistakes should we avoid? This is the value of this book.

Professor Tommy Koh
Ambassador-At-Large
Ministry of Foreign Affairs
Singapore

# Preface

This book could have been shorn of its subtitle, as a historical account of Singapore's pandemics without attempting to draw lessons in light of current events. Our original research proposal did not devote much attention to the COVID-19 pandemic – the historian's common refrain to avoid stepping into the present for which the historian lacks the tools to unpack. We had wanted the research to end in 1981, when Singapore's last major typhoid outbreak occurred, thus excluding the SARS and COVID-19 epidemics. It is thanks to the insistence of the National Heritage Board and its grant reviewers that not only did we include both pandemics in the study, we did so to tremendous benefit. Thus we were able to reckon productively with the two-way relationship between past and present – that there is wisdom to be found in history that informs our current struggles, but also what we have experienced in the last few years changes the way we have written about the history of pandemics.

On reflection, the reluctance to draw historical lessons was not a strong one. One of us is an infectious disease physician with an interest in history and is a member of a public health school, for whom SARS and COVID-19 were formative experiences. The other is a historian who has left academia to become a heritage consultant and has been involved in public history as a critic and practitioner. In writing the book, we strove to combine science and history, as well as theory and praxis. The lessons we have drawn are mostly modest but crucial inquiries into why the British colonial government had constantly failed to control epidemics in Singapore. We first collaborated on a book (published in 2020, also by Routledge) on the history of tuberculosis in Singapore as part of a larger project on antimicrobial resistance in the present day. Our next project was to document the long history of the Communicable Disease Centre – Singapore's infectious diseases hospital – which had been targeted for redevelopment. We proposed that it be repurposed as a medical heritage site. Little did we know that six months after the project ended, COVID-19 would appear on the horizon. This pandemic represents our biggest challenge yet in terms of researching 'living histories'.

Our endeavour was made possible by many supportive agencies, organisations, individuals and friends from the fields of science and history. We are grateful to Ambassador Tommy Koh for writing a fitting foreword on the connections between history and current affairs. We wish to thank the National Heritage Board, Singapore, for the award of a heritage research grant on the history of pandemics in Singapore, specifically its dedicated officers Yeo Kirk Siang, John Teo, Tan Yong Jun and Sim Tng Kwang. We also thank the Saw Swee Hock School of Public Health at the National University of Singapore – in particular Sharon Lee Shi-Yun – for administering the research project.

NHB's anonymous reviewers deserve much credit for pressing us to extend the research to the present pandemic and learn from the past. We are thankful to friends who gave us ideas or platforms for the book or pointed us to useful literature, sources and interviewees: Stephanie Chok, Tim Yap Fuan, Ho Lai Peng, Melody Zaccheus, Pavin Chachavalpongpun, Hyun Bang Shin, Jean Tay, Woo Hsia Ling and Ong Biauw Chi.

Various government agencies aided our research by granting us valuable access to archival records and oral history interviewees, namely, the National Archives of Singapore (NAS), the Ministry of Health and the Ministry of the Environment; a special word of thanks must go to the facilitation efforts of Director of NAS, Julia Chee. We also record our gratitude to dormitory operator S11 Granuity Management Pte Ltd and NGO Humanitarian Organisation for Migration Economics, which arranged for us to speak to their staff and migrant workers in the midst of the COVID-19 crisis. The Lee Kong Chian School of Medicine at the Nanyang Technological University, the Saw Swee Hock Southeast Asia Centre at the London School of Economics, the *International Institute for Asian Studies (IIAS) Newsletter*, the *Kyoto Review of Southeast Asia*, and *Today* newspaper provided us platforms to share our evolving research. Early versions of three parts of the book have previously been published elsewhere:

Kah Seng Loh and Li Yang Hsu. 'The Origins of the Communicable Disease Centre, Singapore: Hanging Fire'. *Kyoto Review of Southeast Asia* Issue 26, Trendsetters, November 2019, https://kyotoreview.org/issue-26/the-origins-of-singapores-communicable-disease-centre-hanging-fire/

Kah Seng Loh and Li Yang Hsu. 'Poison in the Air: The 1890 Influenza Pandemic in Singapore'. *IIAS (International Institute for Asian Studies) Newsletter* Vol. 92, Summer 2022, www.iias.asia/the-newsletter/article/poison-air-1890-influenza-pandemic-singapore

Kah Seng Loh and Li Yang Hsu. 'Lessons of History for the Pandemic?'. *LSE Southeast Asia Blog* 21 June 2022, https://blogs.lse.ac.uk/seac/2022/06/21/lessons-of-history-for-the-pandemic/

It is often said that academics stand on the shoulders of giants; equally true is how our work depended crucially on the 'little people' who painstakingly collected and annotated our research. We have an excellent team of researchers to thank: Kymelya Sari, Mok Ly Yng, Samantha Seah, Katherine Tay, Jasmine Chin, Wang Ting Nan, Isabel Drake, Pearl Wee, Ong Shihui,

Fam Ling, Hurul Ain Binte Muhammad Reni, Madeline Gwee, Lim Xin Hwee, Nur'ain Noor Bani, Jillian Colombo, Charmaine Ang, Koh Yan En, Zuraidah Ehsan, Kirsten Thong, Zachary Tan, Chelsea Kiew, Mira Ho, Liew Shi Ping, Ly Nguyen, and Phoon Yuen Ming.

Oral history forms a major pillar of the work. We wish to thank the interviewees who shed light on the history and memory of the 110-year-old Communicable Disease Centre: Edmund Hugh Monteiro, Chew Suok Kai, David Allen, Harbhajan Singh, Akhterun Nisha, Prem Kallat, Eric Goh Wai Mun, Narindar Singh, Leong Kwai Wah, Bachan Singh, Linda Leong, Ong Quek Neo, Han Kwee Yin, Meeravathy P.S., George Yeo Poh Kee, Roy Chan, Dorothy Gomez, Vinotha Malar, Paul Toh, Ooi Peng Lim, Leo Yee Sin, Low Hong Siam, Rama bai Nathan, Iris Verghese, Cheong Yoke Ling, Joyce Arokiasamy, June Leng, and Chew Chin Hin.

Finally, we are indebted to the experts, frontliners and migrant workers who found time and mental space to speak to us during the travails of COVID-19: namely, Zakir Hossein, Salma Khalik, Paul Tambyah, Siti Mujiati, Jajala Thirupathi, Noelle Heng, Tan Chorh Chuan, Letchumanan Muralidharan, Lawrence Lee, Kenneth Mak, Ong Biauw Chi, Leo Yee Sin, Margaret Soon Chen Jing, Endah Purnamasari, Ripon Chowdhury, Lidyah Fazley, Elahi Rubel, A.K. Zilani, Teoh Yee Leong, Anonymous 1, Jayne Lim, Richard Poh, Shafiq Sahib, Phoebe Lee, Heidee Roiles, Robina Navato, Tang Zuoting, Hoe Ai Lee, Mayed R. Adducul, and Vincent Woo Kok Wah. It is due to all of them that the book is able to carry perspectives from both public health and social history.

Kah Seng and Li Yang
February 2023

# Introduction

Writing a history of infectious diseases against the backdrop of COVID-19, the coronavirus disease of 2019, offers a challenge for the historian but also an opportunity. The tone, emphasis and 'learning points' from such an endeavour would be quite different if there were no coronavirus pandemic, or if it were written before the advent of emerging infectious diseases in the last 20 years. The very idea of learning from history is a challenge because it raises questions about the role of historians that go to the heart of their discipline. But bringing pandemic disease to the study of the past is also an opportunity for historians to think long and hard about the social relevance of their research.

History is also about context and the particular: it is about this disease or that event in a specific time and place. Singapore, as a tiny developed nation-state and port city in Southeast Asia, presents both a limitation and a strength. Its experience appears to speak little to bigger countries with multiple urban settlements and large hinterlands. Its history may also seem unhelpful for states lacking the governance, infrastructure, technology or multicultural population of Singapore.

However, what Singapore, as an island of a mere 700-odd square kilometres, does offer is an excellent case of micro-history. Pandemics are by definition international events but their histories in a particular place and time are also a sum of local events, trajectories and actors. By tracing epidemiological pasts, we derive a sense of the experiences, consequences and responses of an urban population's openness to the world, including the world of boundary-passing microbes. This provides insights into how one country's pandemic history allows it to prepare for future threats.

Our book is thus more than a historical account of pandemics in Singapore. It was written during the exigent first three years of the COVID-19 pandemic, as the world transitioned to an uneasy co-existence with the disease. The book is driven by a question that surfaced at the start of the pandemic: why were so many people all over the world, including leaders and doctors, caught off-guard? We seemed disappointingly unaware of our long struggles against pandemic disease. This book does not profess easy answers or big lessons from the past. It offers an account of how pandemics unfolded in a specific time and place, how

DOI: 10.4324/9781003384014-1

well they were tackled, how they were experienced by the people and whether they were remembered in the aftermath.

### Historicism and Lessons of Pandemic History

What lessons we can draw from the past is a question that has long concerned historians. Long before the emergence of professional history, the study of the past was typically steeped in pragmatism and politics. It was the exception rather than the norm that history was studied for academic reasons. From the ancient Greeks and Chinese to the nationalists of the modern world, the past was commonly conceived as a reservoir of practical wisdom from which the arts of government could be drawn to enlighten the rulers of the day. Being doomed to repeat the mistakes of history because one didn't study the past is a common refrain by popular writers and historians.[1] The long tradition of the 'lessons of history' still casts a shadow over the discipline today. In the late 19th century, an opposing reaction took place as history became a specialised discipline, taught by professors in the universities. Leopold von Ranke was to argue that history offers no lessons and should be studied for its own sake. Our position is somewhere in between.

Let us first dispel the notion that history contains any big lessons based on simple precedents or parallels. History is notoriously unreliable as a tool for policymaking: we likely can find a historical precedent for one lesson and another for the opposite lesson. History does not provide lessons as such; it is people who draw them, which makes it a matter of methodology and motive. We refer, as John Tosh notes, to a guiding principle called 'historicism': that history can be relevant to a social issue, but its study, and not the issue, must come first.[2] While the COVID-19 pandemic is at the back of our minds, we are first and foremost concerned with the history of Singapore's pandemics. We see them as events of their times, not as precedents of a current conundrum.

Historicism comprises three elements: difference, context and process. The first means that the past is fundamentally different from the present and can be seen as an 'inventory of alternatives' to what exists today.[3] Thus, the COVID-19 pandemic and the El Tor cholera pandemic are different because they are separate events and their historical circumstances were different. This brings us to context: every pandemic is part of a set of historical conditions, which distinguishes it from other pandemics. To grasp the part we must know the whole – thus we have to study the political, economic, social and cultural aspects of the historical context. This means history never really repeats itself as is often claimed. Indeed pandemics tell us much about their times, such as conflicts that are usually concealed in society.[4] Finally, we recognise that there is a process at work. Change and continuity occur over time, so no two pandemics are identical. The 1918 influenza pandemic is a different event from the COVID-19 pandemic and we cannot apply the lessons of the former to the latter.

So the lessons are not a simple 'copy and paste' from the past. The learning points we look to draw are modest ones. As we scrutinise what was done or not done in history, we are able to consider alternatives or follow another path of inquiry with the benefit of hindsight. Why Singapore did not respond vigorously to influenza pandemics in the 20th century is something we can usefully contemplate. This does not tell us exactly what to do in the next pandemic – that is to be decided by the leaders, medical experts and the people of the country, using all the facts at their disposal, including biomedical and historical evidence. But it does offer insights into assumptions about influenza and British failure to mobilise an immigrant population.

Learning from history can also be about raising questions rather than finding simple answers. This helps to unpack popular myths and outlandish claims about the past. Diplomatic history, Ernest May observes, is a field where practitioners have looked to the past for lessons. He warns that searching for historical parallels, analogies or precedents assumes a straight line between the past and the present and can be misleading. Rather, the historian is to play a cautionary role by insisting that historical research must be thorough and rigorous.[5]

Why, we might ask, is it worth the effort to study the past for such limited gains? There are two answers. The first simply is so someone else would not draw lessons without a sound historical basis. The modesty of historicism helps prevent seductive claims from those who seek to manipulate public opinion. In this sense, the historian is not only an expert on the past but also, as Tosh notes, the guardian of a people's history and cultural heritage.[6]

The COVID-19 outbreak has produced commentaries from both historians and non-historians on the lessons of the past.[7] The venerable journal, the *History Workshop*, published two historians' blunt response that 'history has no lessons'.[8] They cautioned that looking for historical parallels is a risky endeavour. This is especially when learning from the 1918 influenza pandemic, the event with which the COVID-19 crisis has often been compared in terms of scale and virulence.

One historian who has looked to the past on a range of contemporary issues is the public intellectual Yuval Noah Harari. For him, history stimulates critical thinking and encourages the informed public to participate in the important conversations of the day. His work has drawn upon conversations with members of the public and journalists, besides other academics.[9] Harari has been accused of faulty science,[10] but historians rightly have to collaborate with and accommodate other sources of authority. This brings us to the second benefit of learning from history.

The past is an invaluable aid in our struggle against disease alongside other efforts and partners. Many critics who wholly believed in science and progress, such as during the 18th-century Enlightenment, have dismissed the utility of history. But as we can see in the present pandemic, biomedicine trailed the variants of the coronavirus for a long time, forcing us to resort to old measures such as quarantines and lockdowns that were thought to have been consigned to the ash heap of history. There is no certainty that the biomedical industry, the government or the World Health Organization (WHO) will be able to move more quickly than the microbe in the next outbreak. History is a resource available to us at all times so that we do not have to wait for the next pandemic.

Ultimately, it is a mistake to set history and science apart as opposites. In much of the developing world such as Africa, global health initiatives have long targeted specific diseases, without taking into account the political, economic, social and historical contexts in which they occurred. What is needed now more than ever is an integrated approach comprising biomedicine, the social sciences, history and the humanities.[11] Our struggles against COVID-19 have been as much social and political as biomedical and technological; it would be a mistake to think that preparing for the next pandemic consists mainly of studying viruses and making vaccines. If the past is a modest guide, it is another vital tool in our defence against infectious diseases. History can make our other weapons work better.

## Pandemics in History and Memory

Among historians, infectious diseases and pandemics are uncommon subjects, and even fewer try to draw lessons from the past. Our starting point is that pandemics are an integral part of human history and should be written into historical narratives. Like wars or depressions, they are fairly rare yet important events. Moreover, border-crossing disease outbreaks are becoming more frequent as the world becomes ever more inter-connected and humans have an increasing impact on the environment and ecosystem. While it is vital for historians of medicine to write accounts of pandemics, it is just as crucial for historians in general to consider pandemics as part of their subject matter.

Pandemics are inherently historical. We can speak of their immediate causes (catalysts or triggers), longer-term causes or a multitude of causes. George Dehner notes that influenza pandemics have become more probable over the course of human history because people have been living in dense urban communities that are increasingly connected with other such communities. As urbanisation accelerated from the 19th century, flu pandemics have also increased in frequency and severity.[12]

The same point is brought up in Mark Honigsbaum's survey of 20th-century pandemics, written in the midst of the current coronavirus crisis. He argues that it is neither possible nor desirable to predict the next pandemic. Advances in medical science have ironically locked scientists into self-limiting paradigms and theories. The last pandemic has tended to create hypervigilance about a specific disease or group of pathogens, but this can result in misdirection and error. The point is a real one: would COVID-19 trigger a similar fixation on coronaviruses? Honigsbaum maintains that it is more useful to explore the ecology of infectious diseases, to trace pandemics as the outcomes of long-term environmental and social developments such as globalisation and urbanisation.[13]

Pandemics are historical events. In Britain, the 1918 influenza pandemic unravelled major failings by the government and medical establishment, with both appearing to do little in the face of the epidemic. Senior officials were defensive, insisting that they could not have anticipated, prevented or halted the outbreak. Medical experts, too, were divided over the causal agent and the ways to arrest the epidemic. The historical context explains such confusion and inertia: Britain was undergoing a period of transition, with new emphasis on individual rights and calls for a less intrusive government.[14]

A serious disease outbreak has an immediate and broad impact on people's lives; it also disrupts trade and other forms of economic activity. A social history of a pandemic is invaluable for charting such effects and counting the costs. In her excellent book *Pandemic 1918*, Catherine Arnold retraces the influenza pandemic in the West through the eyes of those who experienced it first-hand – 'East End schoolgirls, Mayfair debutantes, Boston schoolboys and Italian immigrants'.[15] Pandemics narrated this way move historical accounts from great men (the leaders and doctors) to the little people who experienced it and bore its full brunt. By the same token, the scale of sickness and death may push communities to remember and commemorate their epidemic pasts. Social memory is a key resource in preparing for the next pandemic, because a pandemic response succeeds only if people recognise the threat.

The social history of pandemics also brings attention to their aftermaths and interludes. Long after it passed, measures to control an outbreak might change the way people lived or their relationship with the state. In East and Southeast Asia, vigorous state measures during the SARS crisis paved the way for a robust global response to the COVID-19 pandemic beyond the region. In colonial Singapore, people lived in constant fear of sickness and death from deadly diseases on the one hand and official injunctions, surveillance and punishment on the other. In yet other cases where the state's response was weak, people had to co-exist with an endemic disease such as influenza by default.

One of the questions this book tries to answer is why certain pandemics were remembered while others were pushed to the fringes of social memory. According to Peter Furtado, the 1918 influenza pandemic that ravaged much of the globe was a 'strangely private affair'; masks were worn in some public places but there was no lockdown and relatively little media coverage of the event.[16] As David Arnold notes in the case of colonial India, few lessons could be drawn from the influenza outbreak there because it also produced little noteworthy change.[17] While influenza has been called the 'Blue Death', much less attention has been paid to it than the term it derives from: the 'Black Death' or plague.

Through Niall Johnson's research on the 1918 pandemic in Britain, the medical catastrophe largely slipped away from national, local and family histories and memories afterward, overshadowed by the horrors of the First World War. Its wider historical effects on demographic trends, family formation, the healthcare system and politics also appear limited. In only a few countries like Brazil, Samoa and South Africa did the 1918 tragedy shake the government or political order.[18] With upper estimates of 50 million deaths, it is quite incredible that the flu pandemic became 'little more than a sad footnote to the more public tragedy of the Great War'.[19]

In the face of historical amnesia, we are encouraged to read mainstream accounts and official sources on pandemics more carefully. The outbreak of disease on a massive scale often reveals blind spots and triggers social faultlines. Pandemics are lived through and experienced very differently according to where people stand on categories of class, ethnicity, gender and age. When mass infection and death in a pandemic are ignored or forgotten, it tells us about whose lives mattered and to whom.[20] This has been said about the uneven impact of the COVID-19 epidemic in the US today, and it also applies to societies that were ruled by an alien power.

## Asian and Colonial Contexts

The literature on the history of pandemics is overwhelmingly Eurocentric, despite the fact that many outbreaks, including the present one, had Asian origins, trajectories, impacts, responses and contexts. Part of the reason is due to the paucity of sources in many Asian countries (including Singapore), both in the colonial and post-colonial years. When many of these countries were under imperial rule, their archives comprised colonial records written from Western vantage points, while post-colonial archives may be fragmentary or difficult to access. The challenge is to unearth Asian perspectives and narratives from available sources, while taking into account the impact of colonialism and Asian responses to the pandemic experience.

Colonial histories of medicine in Asian countries have tended to be more critically oriented towards power than most Western accounts of pandemics. Biomedicine is seen as a tool of empire and the relationship between people and the state in a colony is that between foreign rulers and subjugated natives. In his classic work, *Colonising the Body*, David Arnold views the history of biomedicine in British India as one of colonising Indian bodies, in addition to territories. The study of biomedicine cannot be detached from the colonial system. Conversely, Indian resistance to biomedicine was a response to colonial domination and not simply a rejection of modern hospitals or drugs.[21] Such an interpretation of biomedicine differs significantly from the more egalitarian social history of pandemics that Catherine Arnold and others have written.

To trace the history of Western medicine in India is, David Arnold suggests, to scrutinise the colonial system. It is also to duly recognise the influence of local circumstances and Indian medical traditions. In what has become a common theme in the historiography of colonial medicine, Arnold highlights how disease outbreaks enabled the British to categorise their subjects as inferior races. Colonial doctors held that Indians were more vulnerable to disease and blamed this on their undesirable cultural practices.[22] Such 'Othering' of locals also occurred in colonial Singapore, a majority Chinese city though more ethnically diverse than in India. In our previous book, we found that the British viewed tuberculosis in Singapore as a disease of the Chinese, who allegedly built their houses horizontally with disregard for sanitation and created ideal conditions for the spread of tuberculosis.[23]

In this book, we find colonial officials and doctors in Singapore making repeated references to the unlawful and uncivil actions of Asiatics, including the Chinese, Mohammedans (Malays), Chettiars, Hindoos and Klings (Indians). The island's pandemics reinforced the British policy to simplify a polyglot society into a small number of races with unmodern social characteristics. To racial difference was added the divide between the social elite and the coolie class, as in the case of tuberculosis. Race and class were major factors that influenced the building of a new infectious diseases hospital in Singapore in 1913, with separate wards for different categories of patients.

Another classic work in the 'tools of empire' approach is Lenore Manderson's *Sickness and the State* on the medical history of colonial Malaya and Singapore. Manderson writes, 'Tropical medicine was a cultural construct, the scientific stepchild of colonial domination and control'.[24] As with David Arnold in India, she maps a medical pluralism in colonial Malaya. Biomedicine was only one of several medical systems there, having to contend with the healing traditions of various Asian groups. A similar medical pluralism operated among the people of colonial Africa.[25] Medical pluralism is a useful concept in the history of medicine in colonial societies. Despite what the imperial rulers believed, the 'native races' did not have fixed attitudes to biomedicine. People in Singapore began to accept biomedical therapies and vaccines for a range of infectious diseases after the war.

It is crucial to recognise that the various causes of pandemics – the colonial factor, long-term demographic trends and ecological change – are not mutually exclusive: they interacted and affected one another. Recent work on colonial India has shown how British concerns over infectious diseases was shaped by international perspectives and debates as much as local developments. Colonial health interventions were not merely tools of empire but multi-faceted outcomes of the interactions between international, colonial and local forces.[26]

Colonial rule in some parts of Asia was brief; Nicholas Tarling deemed it 'a fleeting, passing phase' in Southeast Asia.[27] An exception is the Philippines, where the relatively short period of American colonialism was preceded by over three centuries of Spanish rule. Warwick Anderson has traced a history of racial policy and deferred citizenship during the American period, where Filipinos were marked as a race inferior to the Americans, yet also deemed capable of being civilised and becoming like them. In the perspective of many American hygienists, Filipinos were 'half devil and half child', whose contaminating bodies could be put right by American physicians and the few enlightened Filipino doctors.[28]

Quite different is Ken De Bevoise's study of the origins of the health crisis in the Philippines in the late 19th century during the final years of Spanish rule. De Bevoise is no less critical of power and domination, but he writes instead an ecological account of epidemic disease. Long-term factors have an explanatory force in his work: it was the demographic, economic, social, technological, and political changes over the longue durée that reshaped the relationship between humans, pathogens and the environment in the Philippines.[29]

There are also cases of semi-colonial countries such as modern China in the 19th and 20th centuries. They remind us that colonialism was never complete nor hegemonic. In Ruth Rogaski's nuanced reading, the pursuit of hygiene was a major part of China's difficult struggle for modernity. The biomedicine practised in the treaty ports was not monolithic or all-conquering. It changed over time and it involved collaboration between foreigners and locals.[30] The semi-colonial period in China was also a relatively short interlude as in the Philippines. Mary Augusta Brazelton's survey of vaccination after 1949 shows how, as a form of medical technology, it gave the Maoist state vast control not only over disease but also Chinese bodies and lives. The outcome was not a suppressed population, as David Arnold and others would have argued. In China, there was widespread support for vaccines because they worked, so much so that they came to define the very meaning of Chinese citizenship.[31]

Such findings are pertinent to Singapore, and so is another aspect of the Chinese literature. The study of Maoist China tells us that a history of pandemics needs to traverse into the post-colonial era. Colonial rule gave historians a substantial trove of archival documents that recorded not only the work of health departments and administrators, but also their perspectives, priorities and politics. It is undoubtedly more difficult to gain access to the post-colonial archives. In Singapore, most government records after the British left are still classified, including those of the ministries responsible for health and disease.[32] This is likely true for most Asian countries. Yet, it is paramount that creative efforts be made to locate a range of sources, including local sources and oral history, so that post-colonial histories can be written.

As much as the colonial era ought not to be seen in isolation from the longue durée, it also cannot be divorced from the period that followed it. Colonial medicine may have had an impact on its successor through the international circuits of scientific collaboration and exchange that accompanied the end of colonialism. The question at hand is the balance of historical change and continuity. A post-colonial history of pandemics helps place colonial accounts in perspective, and vice-versa. There are also pandemics that straddled both periods, such as those of influenza, cholera, poliomyelitis, and diphtheria in Singapore. Recent or contemporary pandemics may offer new insights into what happened in the distant past. We can better understand both the past and present by venturing into the post-colonial era.

## Singapore in Pandemic Times

As a tiny island shorn of a hinterland, Singapore is the quintessential city-state. The book charts its modern history in the 19th and 20th centuries as being interwoven with the threat of infectious diseases from all over the world.[33] During the British colonial era, Singapore was an open port city where flows of global capital and labour converged and dispersed. At times, ships and travellers brought with them deadly and rapidly spreading microbes. At the beginning of this history in 1819, Stamford Raffles established a trading post at the southern tip of the island for the British East India Company. This reinvigorated Singapore's long tradition of trade with the region that had begun in the 13th century.[34] For nearly 120 years between 1826 and 1942, Singapore was the jewel of the British colony of the Straits Settlements. It quickly superseded the other two settlements, Malacca and Penang, to become a thriving entrepôt port and distribution centre. Singapore produced no export goods of its own (save briefly for gambier and pepper), but the variety of world staples it handled was a crucial engine of its growth.[35] In one direction, its port transferred tropical produce from the region (later tin and rubber) and exports from China to markets in the West. In the reverse direction, Western manufactured products passed through the island to domestic consumers elsewhere in Asia.[36]

Singapore's growth was due partly to two British decisions: to adopt a policy of free trade and make it a free port. These policies drew ships from all over the world, from European steamers to Chinese junks and Bugis prows.[37] Also crucial to the island's success was its location along the global trade routes in Southeast Asia – the 'lands beneath the winds' with a long history of world trade, as Anthony Reid put it.[38] The opening of the Suez Canal in 1869 consolidated the trade and Singapore's prosperity, prompting Mary Turnbull to describe the city as the 'Clapman Junction of the Eastern Seas'.[39]

British rule has sometimes been hailed as enlightened compared to other European powers in Southeast Asia.[40] On matters of public health, however, the colonial record is mixed. In the first half of the 19th century, the Straits administration and the colonial government in India to which it reported to were reluctant to spend adequately on public services, including healthcare. The notorious opium farm, which resulted in widespread addiction among the Chinese working class, was the main source of colonial and municipal income well into the second half of the century.[41] In 1867, the administration changed when the Straits Settlements were transferred from India to the Colonial Office in Britain. Henceforth, there was more political will and money for infrastructure and social services. An increasingly interventionist colonial health policy began to take shape in the early 20th century. However, the control of infectious diseases evolved very unevenly, limited by competing priorities over resources and manpower, as well as a conservative epidemiology that focused primarily on bubonic plague, cholera and smallpox – the trinity of infectious diseases.

Colonial public health was further complicated by the social factor. Chinese merchants played a key role as middlemen in the island's global trade. They had the requisite connections to producers in the region, both in the early days of gambier and pepper cultivation, and subsequently in entrepôt trade.[42] They were a small but powerful group, some being locally born

Straits Chinese while others had arrived from China and succeeded in business. The merchants served as Legislative Councillors, Municipal Commissioners and Justices of the Peace – appointments that enabled the colonial administration to govern the Chinese population. Among the matters they handled were periodic disease outbreaks, over which they sometimes diverged from the Europeans, representing the interests of the Chinese community.

The Chinese were not only an economic force but also Singapore's majority population from the second half of the 19th century. From the 1920s, they formed three-fourths of the population they do today, mostly Chinese immigrants of peasant background who arrived to work the menial jobs and services that moved the levers of commerce and made the city hum.[43] These migrants were lowly paid, working-class sojourners who had more of a transient and politically distant presence than their mercantile counterparts. Typically, they worked for a few years before returning home with what savings they could muster. They dwelt near two little locales of trade at the southern tip of Singapore: along the Singapore River and at Keppel Harbour to the south, living and working in close quarters. James Warren has aptly described this overcrowded urban zone as a 'coolie town'.[44] This was where most disease outbreaks occurred.

Besides the Chinese, Singapore had smaller numbers of Malays (around 15 per cent of the population from the 1900s) and Indians (8 per cent). Most of them also dwelt in or near the town.[45] Singapore was a typical colonial city in Southeast Asia inhabited largely by foreigners. The Malays were the most settled group and the one that could be considered 'native', though among their numbers were immigrants from the Malay peninsula, Java, Bugis and other parts of the Dutch East Indies, and the Middle East. Similarly, the Indians comprised various groups from different (mostly southern) parts of British India. They had the strongest employment ties with the colonial administration: Indian convicts built Singapore's early public structures and infrastructure, while Malayalees serviced the Naval Base built in 1938 and other British military installations.

Typical of European imperial policy, the British bracketed ethnic groups with similar appearance and social characteristics, disregarding significant differences in culture, language, religion and place of origins. A polyglot population was condensed into three distinct 'races' – Chinese, Malays and Indians. There was a fourth 'race', 'Others', who did not fall into one of the trio, such as Eurasians and Armenians. The racial organisation made colonial Singapore a plural society, where the different groups had economic relations with each other but not the socio-cultural bonds necessary to build an integrated community.[46] Outbreaks of epidemics reinforced the racism embedded into this colonial plural society, for they appeared to distinguish between modern Europeans and irrational Asians. Undeniably, the latter responded to the appearance of infectious diseases in ways that fundamentally differed from colonial health policy. The British viewed such responses through racial lenses, ignoring how their own policies had shaped Asian behaviour.

Asians also viewed infectious diseases in distinct ways. A social and cultural history of pandemics takes us away from colonial narratives to the deeper reasons why Asians often did not cooperate with the British regime when an epidemic occurred. Till the Second World War, colonial and municipal administrators struggled to enforce public health measures and change Asian behaviour. Great numbers of labouring immigrants crowded into congested shophouses, living and sometimes dying in tiny shared cubicles without light, adequate airflow or a proper sewage disposal. To colonial officials, these living conditions were ripe for a devastating epidemic. But they could defray the cost of rent and transport to the places of work.[47] They also allowed coolies to live close to their kin and people from their community, who would support them in a foreign city. The areas where the people could best live were thus also perilous places where the outbreak of tuberculosis or cholera was likely.

In this context, colonial measures to remove people from infected areas during an epidemic and to disinfect (or destroy) unclean shophouses and personal belongings disrupted the Asians' livelihood and social security. It was largely due to these reasons that the plebian classes seemingly wanted to be left alone, refusing to report cases of infectious disease to the authorities. As Brenda Yeoh showed in her incisive work on the Municipal Commission, its efforts to stem the outbreak of disease in the shophouses were frustrated by a game of cat and mouse between the officials and their Asian subjects.[48]

British rule came to a temporary end in 1942 when the supposedly impregnable fortress of Singapore surrendered meekly to the Japanese. But the war, while a difficult time for the people, ushered in a period of momentous change. Much of Singapore's post-war history, including that of public health, is owed to the political and social impact of the Japanese Occupation. Among their many travails, people experienced severe medical shortages and disease outbreaks during the war. This led to a nationalist awakening afterwards, while also reorientating people's political outlook from their home countries towards Malaya and Singapore. Among them were doctors who gained war-time experience in the administration of the healthcare system while European officials were interned by the Japanese. Others were subsequently educated in the College of Medicine and after 1949, the University of Malaya.[49]

The British took a more active role in social policy when they returned to Singapore in 1945. They increased investments in healthcare and other social services that had been planned in the 1930s as part of a newly envisioned colonial trusteeship with the locals. After the war, however, the reforms, including the ten-year Medical Plan of 1948, were for quite different and more expansive purposes: initially to restore confidence in British power and subsequently to prepare Singapore for self-government in an orderly fashion and in the British image.

The post-war years were a time of left-wing political and social activism. To the British, decolonisation was to steer Singapore away from the communist path. From 1948, many local politicians participated in one of the two administrations of the day: the Singapore government (the Straits Settlements was abolished when the island was made a separate colony in 1946) and the Municipal Commission, quickly renamed the City Council when Singapore gained the status of a city of a million people in 1951. Among the issues which would allow these nationalists to win over voters and widen their political base were outbreaks of epidemic disease. The People's Action Party (PAP) came to power in 1959 because it was able to do both. Led by long-time Prime Minister Lee Kuan Yew, it had the majority support of the population. His government retained the colonial bureaucracy but expanded it substantially to build a new nation-state. This mix of continuity and change gave the post-colonial government greater success than its predecessor in dealing with pandemic disease. The PAP had the political commitment, resources, expertise, and technology to implement public health programmes on a national scale.

However, the government still had to contend with the longstanding open economy and urban context of Singapore. The island remained susceptible to periodic outbreaks of infectious disease. The growth of the city beyond a million inhabitants reflected new demographic trends after the war, with large numbers of baby boomers born in the two decades after the war. The sojourning that was prevalent pre-war diminished as the city became more settled; post-war migration comprised people joining their spouses in Singapore or looking to form families. The population was a young one, made up of nuclear families with several children. The population growth rate plateaued in the 1970s due to vigorous family planning measures. But Singaporeans continued to dwell as small families in high-rise flats located in dense housing estates, the fulcrum of the nation's mass public housing programme.[50] Although vastly different in their physical quality and social amenities, the three main housing typologies throughout Singapore history – shophouse, urban kampong and Housing and Development Board (HDB) apartment – all entailed living in close quarters with others.

Other post-war changes and continuities complicated this scenario. Singapore society remained culturally diverse, comprising of the officially demarcated 'races' from the colonial era: Chinese, Malays, Indians and Others. Indeed, the diversity increased when the island became even more open to global visitors, permanent residents and low-wage migrant workers. Much of the openness stemmed from the government's economic policy, as in the colonial era. In 1965, the PAP abandoned the strife-ridden merger with Malaysia to become an independent republic. The government duly embarked on an export-led industrialisation programme to reduce the reliance on the entrepôt trade and provide jobs for the young population.[51] Singapore soon became one of the four flourishing 'Asian Tigers', its remarkable growth based on foreign capital investment to make industrial products for the world market. 'Made in Singapore' manufacturing, together with the development of mass public housing, hospitality facilities and infrastructure, meant that global tourists, European managerial staff and Asian workers continued to arrive and leave the island for short periods of time.

Singaporeans themselves, with excess wages to spend, were also increasingly travelling abroad. The aircraft superseded the ship as the main mode of global transport, rendering the old system of quarantine largely obsolete.

Medical infrastructure that could monitor infectious diseases and survey the population was part of what Lee called Singapore's 'Third World to First' transformation.[52] Western observers have criticised Singapore for its illiberal government in contrast to its openness to foreign capital and labour.[53] But the medico-technocratic achievements in the post-1965 period were remarkable. Central to these was the creation of a national public health system. It had these supporting pillars: epidemiological surveillance, mass vaccination, a tightly knit network of public hospitals and outpatient clinics and a range of public health campaigns. Epidemiological surveillance, which relegated quarantine to a secondary role, was fortified by the willingness of general practitioners to notify cases of dangerous infectious diseases to the government. This was a major change from the colonial era. Another was Singaporeans' increasing acceptance of biomedicine, vaccination and their improved standards of living and nutrition at this time.

Yet, as our book will show, these public health policies were not completely successful. Important continuities from the colonial past persisted: Singaporeans and migrants alike still practiced medical pluralism and possessed differing notions of illness and healing from the state. Medical and state officials also had blind spots and made erroneous judgements on the infections of concern. One major problem is historical: it has been difficult to let go of the colonial fixation with the trinity of quarantinable infectious diseases (plague, cholera and smallpox). Achieving the balance between retaining what had worked and what needed to change has not been easy for Singapore. But change seems necessary in light of the emerging infectious diseases of the 21st century.

Another historical problem is that most pandemics in Singapore were quickly forgotten. History itself was sidelined by the science- and technology-driven approach to pandemic control. Singapore's policymakers and health officials were aware of a few precedent epidemics. But generally a sense of historicity – that the present was somehow connected to the past – was lacking. In the case of influenza, the epidemics of 1918 and 1957 were vaguely remembered though this failed to translate into a policy for the disease. In the present pandemic, the government initially referred to the most recent outbreak (the Severe acute respiratory syndrome or SARS outbreak in 2003) as a template, while using the biggest one (the 1918 influenza pandemic) as proof of why history is not a guide to action. In a sense, the political, institutional and social memories of pandemics are as important as their histories, where modest lessons of history could be drawn from Singapore's experience.

The social memory of pandemics deserves special emphasis. Pandemics are not merely the domain of the policymaker or the medical doctor. To some extent, we find that Singapore society as a whole remembered and documented many significant epidemics better than the professionals. There were many letters to the press and reminiscences from oral history, written and recalled immediately after the event or many years later. A mix of personal experience and reflection, these sources show what and how people select and emphasise as the key events in their lives. Many people remembered the pandemics as important moments. Their social memories are archival documents that reveal the devastating impact of disease as well as the repercussions of official policy, which policymakers and health officials ought to take into account. These memories remind us that informed, socially responsible people have a role to play in pandemic control, in addition to governance and biomedical expertise.

The book focuses on diseases of historical significance in Singapore, namely, the old trinity of plague, cholera and smallpox, as well as influenza and novel coronaviruses. We've had to leave out a number of diseases that deserve study: typhoid (important for its environmental and social dimensions), diphtheria, poliomyelitis and measles (which occasioned parental resistance to biomedicine and vaccination). But to some extent these issues are explored in the diseases we studied while the book also examines the social stigma surrounding HIV/AIDS (the human immunodeficiency virus-acquired immunodeficiency syndrome) in Singapore.

Plague, cholera and smallpox tell us much about the limits of imperial measures to keep Singapore safe from pandemic disease. This is traced through the evolution of the quarantine system during the colonial era and the new paradigm of epidemiological surveillance that superseded it after Singapore became independent. The history of the 'Big 3' is also discussed through the long struggle to build a proper infectious diseases hospital in Singapore, spanning the late 19th century, the aftermath of the Second World War and in the present millennium. Colonial efforts were hampered by the self-interested nature of British rule and developed unevenly, while the post-colonial administration was more committed and successful in its endeavours. Still, there were similarities and continuities across the two periods.

We dwelt at length on the influenza pandemics of 1890, 1918 and 1957 (recent evidence suggests that the first could have been caused by a human coronavirus).[54] Influenza is important because it highlights differences with the Big 3. Historically, it was not regarded as a dangerous disease despite causing a number of severe outbreaks. It was also deemed to be a 'slippery disease'.[55] Because it could mutate into new strains and evade the immunity system, influenza was long thought to be beyond quarantine and vaccines. As a respiratory disease, it also relates to the threat of novel coronaviruses. The 2003 SARS outbreak led the Singapore government to draw up a national response programme for influenza – the first in the island's history. Just as coronaviruses have made us turn to quarantine and vaccines, it is timely to revisit long-standing beliefs that influenza pandemics were impossible to control. While we commonly look to history for insights into contemporary problems, current developments also compel us to revise our interpretations of the past.[56]

The study of influenza not only fills a gap in Singapore's epidemic history. Along with plague, cholera and smallpox, it shows how people have historically lived with endemic diseases. Thus our book is not only concerned with major outbreaks but also the long aftermaths and interludes between them. How historically we co-existed with a range of deadly pathogens – whether as a conscious decision or by default due to inaction – is a pertinent question in the age of COVID-19. We can learn from Singapore's endemic histories through official efforts at quarantine and epidemiological surveillance, but also the social experiences of people for whom living with a dangerous disease was the norm.

Unlike most histories of Singapore, our research extends into the post-colonial years, seeking continuity and change with the colonial past. The post-colonial period is just over half a century long, though we have been hampered by the limited access to the government archives. We were able to obtain the use of some declassified Ministry of Health (MOH) records, but most of the sources we consulted consists of conventional published material, including medical journals, and oral history interviews.

## The Narrative in the Book

The book begins with a historical account of efforts to keep Singapore safe from infectious diseases through quarantine and epidemiological surveillance. We traced Singapore's long struggle to establish an effective quarantine system during the colonial era, before the shift to epidemiology in the 1970s. Both systems focused on the trinity of dangerous infectious diseases, with less emphasis on other diseases like influenza.

Chapter 2 discusses how plague exemplified the fears of Singapore's colonial officials and doctors towards infectious diseases. Even though it rarely caused epidemics, the disease was greatly feared as an 'endemic Sinbad' that had taken root amid the filth of the town. To some extent, this official concern persisted into the post-colonial period. But plague also had an important social history that offers insights into why the immigrant Asian population did not notify cases of the disease or cooperate with the colonial government.

The social history of non-cooperation continues in Chapter 3 on smallpox. To Singapore's Asian working class, Western biomedicine appeared incomprehensible and harmful. The compulsory vaccination of children for smallpox aroused much social resistance and avoidance. Conversely, colonial officials and doctors viewed the disease through racial lenses, blaming the Asian population, especially the Malay minority, for its alleged apathy to official measures. But the real reasons for non-cooperation were practical and political rather than racial. After the Second World War, the mass vaccination efforts of the late colonial state had the support of the majority of the people.

The last of the trinity of dangerous infectious diseases, cholera, is the subject of Chapter 4. As a sickness of environmental sanitation, the control of cholera was instrumental in transforming Singapore over the long haul from an unclean coolie town to an orderly nation-state. At the same time, the history of cholera reveals ethnic and class cleavages: between those who had access to potable water and modern public utilities and others who did not. There was also a parallel divide between the colonial regime and the Asian coolie class, such as rickshaw pullers, whose socio-economic predicaments in the face of cholera the British failed to comprehend. In the post-colonial years, the control of cholera contributed to the making of a garden city, a socially aware citizenry and the close surveillance of hawkers.

Chapter 5 charts the protracted struggle to build a modern infectious diseases hospital in Singapore. We first traced the difficulties that plagued the early Infectious Diseases Hospital-cum-Quarantine Camp at Balestier Road, widely known as a slaughterhouse. This was replaced by a new Moulmein Road Hospital in 1913, renamed the Middleton Hospital in 1920 and the Communicable Disease Centre (CDC) in 1985. In 2019, the CDC made way for the present-day National Centre for Infectious Diseases. The history of these facilities reveals an underlying tension in developing an infectious diseases hospital: it would be expensive to build and maintain, while only demonstrating its value during a pandemic.

The next three chapters are on influenza, which caused historically significant epidemics in Singapore in 1890, 1918 and 1957. The 1890 influenza outbreak was Singapore's first documented flu epidemic. As in subsequent outbreaks, colonial and municipal responses were half-hearted and inadequate in dealing with a disease that surfaced and disappeared equally quickly. Unlike plague, cholera and smallpox, influenza did not seem to be quarantinable. But while the authorities subsequently did not adopt an influenza policy, the 1890 outbreak was not completely forgotten. Educated people in colonial Singapore wrote about it and kept its memory alive, as did chemists who offered purported cures for influenza and colds. Social memory is a useful resource in combating infectious disease outbreaks.

Chapter 7 discusses one of the worst pandemics of the 20th century – the influenza outbreak that devastated much of the world in 1918–1920. In Singapore, a serious outbreak occurred, highlighting the blind spot and inertia of the colonial regime in the early 20th century. The quarantine system's focus on the trinity of infectious diseases had become entrenched and resistant to change, making Singapore unprepared for a mass outbreak of influenza. The epidemic caught the government by surprise despite recent efforts to improve the quarantine service and the state of public health in the town. Influenza was briefly made a notifiable disease during the epidemic, but again, no firm policy on the disease was made in the aftermath.

As the 1918 outbreak revealed the weaknesses of the colonial system, the 'Asian flu' epidemic of 1957 discussed in Chapter 8 showed the limits of British-sanctioned decolonisation in Singapore after the Second World War. At a time when the late colonial state was undertaking a number of crucial medical reforms, the 1957 epidemic was remarkable for how little the Labour Front government attempted to do to stem it. As its leaders dismissed any active response to the epidemic as misguided and unfeasible, the people of Singapore, especially the low-income urban population, suffered greatly from the outbreak. It was rather the improved healthcare system that successfully identified the flu virus and treated a large number of patients, but it still had to be augmented by volunteer doctors and nurses.

Chapter 9 outlines how Singapore's quarantine system was superseded by a national epidemiological system to track cases of influenza and other infectious diseases after independence. As surveillance became increasingly sophisticated and comprehensive, two influenza outbreaks were of note in this period. The first was the swine flu scare in 1976, which led the government to vaccinate its employees. This was a historic move, for previous administrations had deemed influenza outbreaks to occur too quickly for a vaccine to be manufactured in time, though mass vaccination was affected by widespread fears of side effects. The second event was another scare, caused by the outbreak of bird flu in Hong Kong in 1997. Though the disease did not surface in Singapore, official and public concern over the Hong Kong outbreak was a precursor to the SARS pandemic several years later.

The final two chapters dwell on coronavirus pandemics. Chapter 10 discusses why the 2003 SARS outbreak in Singapore was a seminal event. The government's vigorous efforts to contain the outbreak have been hailed as a success story. However, while SARS was a turning point in some ways, the government also made mistakes in managing what was ultimately a mini-epidemic. Among the mistakes was the failure to pay heed to the history of pandemics in Singapore. The SARS experience would also hinder Singapore's initial response to the COVID-19 pandemic. This is a good reason to note that leaning on the most recent outbreak while ignoring earlier historical precedents is likely to lead to error.

The book's last pandemic is the worldwide outbreak of coronavirus disease in 2019. Chapter 11 examines the COVID-19 pandemic in Singapore within the span of the island's history. It underlines the consequences of basing a pandemic response on the SARS experience without considering other epidemics in Singapore history. As with previous outbreaks, the impact of COVID-19 was particularly severe on vulnerable groups such as low-income families, the elderly and migrant workers. The pandemic brought to light longstanding issues that had affected these groups. It also suggests that continuing to ignore Singapore's pandemic history could be a costly error.

The conclusion offers a number of modest lessons, insights and further questions on what and how we can learn from Singapore's history of pandemics to deal with future outbreaks, and whether the island state's experiences have any application for the rest of the world.

## Notes

1 Bill Fawcett, *Doomed to Repeat: The Lessons of History We've Failed to Learn* (New York: William Morrow, 2013).
2 John Tosh, *The Pursuit of History: Aims, Methods and New Directions in the Study of History* (London: Routledge, 2015), 6th edition.

3 Tosh, *The Pursuit of History*.
4 Peter Furtado (ed.), *Plague, Pestilence and Pandemic: Voices from History* (London: Thames & Hudson, 2021).
5 Ernest R. May, *Lessons of the Past: The Use and Misuse of History in American Foreign Policy* (New York: Oxford University Press, 1973).
6 Tosh, *The Pursuit of History*.
7 See for instance Kari Nixon, *Quarantine Life from Cholera to COVID-19* (New York: Tiller Press, 2021); Ishaan Tharoor, 'How Epidemics Have Changed the World', *The Washington Post*, 8 March 2020, www.washingtonpost.com/world/2020/03/06/how-epidemics-have-changed-world/; Elizabeth Kolbert, 'Pandemics and the Shape of Human History', *The New Yorker*, 6 April 2020, www.newyorker.com/magazine/2020/04/06/pandemics-and-the-shape-of-human-history
8 Guillaume Lachenal and Gaëtan Thomas, 'COVID-19: When History Has No Lessons', *The History Workshop*, 30 March 2020, www.historyworkshop.org.uk/COVID-19-when-history-has-no-lessons/
9 Yuval Noah Harari, *21 Lessons for the 21st Century* (London: Jonathan Cape, 2019); Yuval Noah Harari, 'The World after Coronavirus', *Financial Times*, 20 March 2020, www.ft.com/content/19d90308-6858-11ea-a3c9-1fe6fedcca75
10 Darshana Narayanan, 'The Dangerous Populist Science of Yuval Noah Harari', *Current Affairs*, July 2022, www.currentaffairs.org/2022/07/the-dangerous-populist-science-of-yuval-noah-harari
11 Tamara Giles-Vernick and James L.A. Webb Jr. (eds), *Global Health in Africa: Historical Perspectives on Disease Control* (Athens: Ohio University Press, 2013).
12 George Dehner, *Global Flu and You: A History of Influenza* (London: Reaktion Books, 2012).
13 Mark Honigsbaum, *The Pandemic Century: A History of Global Contagion from the Spanish Flu to COVID-19* (London: W.H. Allen, 2020).
14 Niall Johnson, *Britain and the 1918–19 Influenza Pandemic: A Dark Epilogue* (London: Routledge, 2006).
15 Catherine Arnold, *Pandemic 1918: Eyewitness Accounts from the Greatest Medical Holocaust in Modern History* (New York: St Martin's Press, 2018), p. 13.
16 Furtado, *Plague, Pestilence and Pandemic*, p. 12.
17 David Arnold, 'Pandemic India: Coronavirus and the Uses of History', *The Journal of Asian Studies*, Vol. 79, No. 3, August 2020, pp. 569–577.
18 Johnson, *Britain and the 1918–19 Influenza Pandemic*.
19 Furtado, *Plague, Pestilence and Pandemic*, p. 12.
20 Ed Yong, 'How Did This Many Deaths Become Normal?', *The Atlantic*, 8 March 2022, www.theatlantic.com/health/archive/2022/03/COVID-us-death-rate/626972/
21 David Arnold, *Colonising the Body: State Medicine and Epidemic Disease in Nineteenth-Century India* (Berkeley: University of California Press, 1993).
22 Arnold, *Colonising the Body*.
23 Kah Seng Loh and Li Yang Hsu, *Tuberculosis – The Singapore Experience, 1867–2018: Disease, Society and the State* (New York: Routledge, 2020).
24 Lenore Manderson, *Sickness and the State: Health and Illness in Colonial Malaya, 1870–1940* (New York: Cambridge University Press, 1996), p. 10.
25 Giles-Vernick and Webb Jr., *Global Health in Africa*.
26 Sandhya L. Polu, *Infectious Disease in India, 1892–1940: Policy-Making and the Perception of Risk* (New York: Palgrave Macmillan, 2012).
27 Nicholas Tarling, *Imperialism in Southeast Asia: 'A Fleeting, Passing Phase'* (London: Routledge, 2001).
28 Warwick Anderson, *Colonial Pathologies: American Tropical Medicine, Race, and Hygiene in the Philippines* (Durham: Duke University Press, 2006), p. 4.
29 Ken De Bevoise, *Agents of Apocalypse: Epidemic Disease in the Colonial Philippines* (Princeton: Princeton University Press, 1995).

30 Ruth Rogaski, *Hygienic Modernity: Meanings of Health and Disease in Treaty-Port China* (Berkeley: University of California Press, 2004).

31 Mary Augusta Brazelton, *Mass Vaccination: Citizens' Body and State Power in Modern China* (Ithaca: Cornell University Press, 2019).

32 Loh Kah Seng and Liew Kai Khiun (eds.), *The Makers and Keepers of Singapore History* (Singapore: Ethos Books and Singapore Heritage Society, 2010).

33 The colonial past is well-documented and enables us to chart long-term developments in demography, immigration, urban growth, and economic development. Recent scholarship has traced a 500-year history of Singapore prior to the British arrival, but its focus on trade and geopolitics tells us little about outbreaks of disease. See Kwa Chong Guan, Derek Heng, Peter Borschberg and Tan Tai Yong, *Seven Hundred Years: A History of Singapore* (Singapore: National Library Board, Singapore: Marshall Cavendish Editions, 2019).

34 Kwa et al., *Seven Hundred Years: A History of Singapore.*

35 W.G. Huff, *The Economic Growth of Singapore: Trade and Development in the Twentieth Century* (New York: Cambridge University Press, 1994).

36 C.M. Turnbull, *A History of Singapore, 1819–1988* (Singapore: Oxford University Press, 1989), 2nd edition.

37 Stephen Dobbs, *The Singapore River: A Social History 1819–2002* (Singapore: Singapore University Press, 2003).

38 Anthony Reid, *Southeast Asia in the Age of Commerce, 1450–1680* (New Haven: Yale University Press, 1988, 1993), 2 volumes.

39 Turnbull, *A History of Singapore.*

40 Turnbull, *A History of Singapore.*

41 Carl A. Trocki, *Opium and Empire: Chinese Society in Colonial Singapore, 1800–1910* (Ithaca, NY: Cornell University Press, 1990).

42 Trocki, *Opium and Empire.*

43 Saw Swee Hock, *The Population of Singapore* (Singapore: Institute of Southeast Asian Studies, 1999).

44 James Francis Warren, *Rickshaw Coolie: A People's History of Singapore* (Singapore: Singapore University Press, 2003).

45 Saw, *The Population of Singapore.*

46 J.S. Furnivall, *Colonial Policy and Practice: A Comparative Study of Burma and Netherlands India* (Cambridge: Cambridge University Press, 1948).

47 Warren, *Rickshaw Coolie*; Dobbs, *The Singapore River.*

48 Brenda S.A. Yeoh, *Contesting Space in Colonial Singapore: Power Relations and the Urban Built Environment* (Singapore: Singapore University Press, 2003), 2nd edition.

49 Paul H. Kratoska, *The Japanese Occupation of Malaya: A Social and Economic History* (London: C. Hurst, 1998).

50 Saw, *The Population of Singapore.*

51 Garry Rodan, *The Political Economy of Singapore's Industrialization: National State and International Capital* (London: Palgrave Macmillan UK, 1989).

52 Lee Kuan Yew, *From Third World to First: The Singapore Story 1965–2000: Memoirs of Lee Kuan Yew* (Singapore: Singapore Press Holdings: Times Editions, 2000).

53 Rodan, *The Political Economy of Singapore's Industrialization*; Michael D. Barr, *Singapore: A Modern History* (London: I.B. Taurus, 2019); Lily Zubaidah Rahim and Michael D. Barr (eds), *The Limits of Authoritarian Governance in Singapore's Developmental State* (Singapore: Springer Singapore, 2019).

54 H. Brüssow and L. Brüssow, 'Clinical Evidence that the Pandemic from 1889 to 1891 Commonly called the Russian Flu Might Have Been an Earlier Coronavirus Pandemic', *Microbial Biotechnology*, Vol. 14, 2021, pp. 1860–1870.

55 Richard E. Neustadt and Harvey V. Fineberg, *The Swine Flu Affair: Decision-making on a Slippery Disease* (Washington DC: National Academies Press, 1978).

56 E.H. Carr, *What Is History?* (London: Penguin Books, 1987), 2nd edition.

# 1 The Quarantine of the Trinity

The development of a quarantine system in Singapore was long in the making. The need to screen for epidemic disease was clear for an open entrepôt and popular port of call for immigrants. In 1927, Dr Gilbert Brooke, who as the Port Health Officer was responsible for quarantine, highlighted Singapore's susceptibility to deadly infectious diseases: as a world port, it had ships hailing from 349 ocean ports.[1] Despite this, the development of quarantine in colonial Singapore was hampered by an underlying tension between British policies of free trade and open immigration on the one hand and prerogatives of public health on the other.

Advocates of quarantine, like Brooke, faced opposition from the influential mercantile community and their allies in government. Even the colonial and municipal administrations – the two separate layers of Singapore's government – were divided on the matter till the early 20th century. The result was chronic underinvestment in the quarantine system and its confused practice. The development of quarantine was thus a factor of those junctures when epidemics had an impact serious enough to force a change to the open-door policy. Improvements were conceded only when it was clear that a severe outbreak had breached the defences and was wreaking havoc in the town. Quarantine in colonial Singapore was essentially reactionary.

That progress in quarantine was hard won also contributed to its conservative nature. Throughout the colonial era, the British targeted the trinity of plague, cholera and smallpox, as well as afflictions that were uncommon in Singapore, notably yellow fever. These were dangerous infectious diseases, but their more important shared characteristic was that they were greatly feared in the West. Other dangerous infections such as dysentery and influenza received relatively little emphasis. In 1914, a health official urged vainly for dysentery to be made notifiable,

> Measures are taken for the isolation of small-pox, plague and cholera but where these diseases slay their tens it is no exaggeration to state that in Malaya dysentery slays its thousands.[2]

DOI: 10.4324/9781003384014-2

The gradual and uneven development of quarantine, achieved in the face of commercial and political resistance, had a cumulative historical effect. Over time, a strong tradition of quarantine emerged, centred around a trinity of diseases where the likely sick few could be separated from the healthy vast majority. Even after Singapore became independent and epidemiological sur-veillance superseded quarantine in the 1970s, the list of dangerous infectious diseases remained similar to the colonial period. They were typically quar-antinable diseases.

While by the mid-20th century a more effective quarantine system had emerged in Singapore, being quarantined remained a traumatic experience for many people who had to endure it. This was due to the unequal relationship between the colonial rulers and Asian subjects. The quarantine system was beset by the same problems that caused people not to notify infectious disease to the British or seek help at a hospital when they fell ill. For many Asians, quarantine was not an experience of being kept safe from a dangerous dis-ease, but a great hardship imposed for reasons that seemed incomprehensible.

## No Walled City

In 1867, the colony of the Straits Settlements was transferred from the Indian Office to the Colonial Office, establishing an administration directly answerable to London. The Straits government became more interventionist on matters of public health. The following year, it passed the Quarantine Ordinance along-side proposals to deal more effectively with plague, smallpox, beriberi, and venereal disease, as well as to expand institutions for sufferers of leprosy and mental illness.[3] But initially the quarantine law was a paper document. The Straits Settlements Association, representing influential mercantile interests, protested that quarantine measures would hurt the commerce of the entrepôt. This led Governor Harry Ord to announce that he had no intention of imple-menting the ordinance unless circumstances made it necessary to do so.[4]

It took a cholera outbreak in Singapore in 1873, suspected to have been imported by a ship sailing from Bangkok, to nudge the Straits government to build a rudimentary quarantine facility on St. John's Island. This was a small island five miles to the south of Singapore, a mile long and to a maximum of half a mile in breadth – later to be called 'one of the world's greatest beauty spots'.[5] Still, the colonial government received complaints that the stringent measures imposed during the outbreak had seriously affected the trade of Singapore.[6]

The events of 1873 heralded the beginning of an arduous struggle to con-struct an effective containment, surveillance and notification system against pandemic disease. Advocates of free trade viewed quarantine as a costly nui-sance and a farce injurious to personal liberty, while others argued that cho-lera was not contagious.[7] The Quarantine Ordinance consequently had no teeth; for a decade thereafter the quarantine staff did not even inspect ships.[8]

A year after the cholera outbreak, the opponents of quarantine immedi-ately tested the administration's will. Guthrie & Co., a major trading house and shipping agent in Singapore, submitted a claim to the Straits government for damages and expenses accrued when its steamer, the *S.S. Milton* from Swatow, China, was sent into quarantine for having cases of cholera onboard. This included the cost of the company's building temporary sheds on St. John's for crew and passengers, for the island's lazaretto had not yet been completed.[9] The *Straits Times* condemned the government's decision to quarantine the ship when it had no quarantine facility prepared.[10] Guthrie argued that as there was no legal basis to quarantine a vessel that had no case of cholera when it left port, the ship should have been permitted to sail into the harbour.[11] It alleged that sick patients were not separated from those who seemed well.[12]

The government dismissed the claim, stating that quarantine was necessary in the interest of public safety,[13] and chided Guthrie's solicitors for their 'ungracious' language.[14] What was especially noteworthy was the government's claim that the decision to detain the vessel was not its own, but made freely by the company (the alternative was the ship sailing into the open waters beyond Singapore harbour).[15] Clearly, the legal basis of quarantine was lacking.

A review of the quarantine system was undertaken, which urged that quarantine measures be strictly adhered to. Ship officers would be quizzed about the presence of 'cholera, plague or any epidemic infections or contagious disease' on their vessel. Officers who hid the illnesses of passengers from the authorities should be severely punished, as would those attempting to escape from quarantine. Those found to be ill with cholera would be quarantined for 14 days from the death or recovery of the person last affected. For smallpox, the duration was 21 days.[16] These recommendations were a step forward for the quarantine system and were later written into a new law, the Quarantine and Prevention of Disease Ordinance of 1886. The ordinance gave the Governor the power to quarantine vessels arriving from a port where an outbreak of epidemic disease such as cholera or smallpox had occurred.[17]

By the 1880s, a partial quarantine system had emerged, though it was shaped by local circumstances and compromises. The lazaretto on the eastern side of St. John's differed from immigration depots in other parts of the world, such as Ellis Island in the US, where all arrivals were screened. This was deemed impractical in the Straits Settlements due to the large numbers of people passing through and travelling onward to other ports. Those who were allowed to disembark in Singapore would be difficult to trace afterward. Rather, Straits practice was to isolate suspected carriers of infectious disease, disinfect the ships and cargo and detain the remaining crew and passengers on St. John's for a period of observation, after which they were allowed to land in Singapore.[18] This compromise was accepted as economically expedient by the Medical Department, as 'unnecessarily stringent restrictions to trade through a long detention ... would be attended without any corresponding benefit or gain'.[19]

In 1882, Straits health officials again conceded the limits of quarantine when there was an outbreak of cholera in Batavia:

Perfectly effective measures to exclude by means of quarantine, epidemic disease from Singapore as from any other open town would be impossible. This is not a walled city at the gates of which every passer in and out could be inspected, and on the other hand to place a sanitary cordon round the island would be as impracticable as the cost would be enormous.[20]

In 1889, two more wards and accommodation for a police guard were built on St. John's.[21] The outbreak of plague in Hong Kong in 1894 (discussed in the next chapter) was the catalyst for further building: a plague hospital, five additional attap sheds, a disinfecting chamber and a decision to inspect ships from infected ports.[22] These were the first major improvements to the quarantine system. The Hong Kong Chamber of Commerce complained about the stringent measures adopted by the Straits government to ward off the plague as being 'not in the natural order of things'.[23] The government denied that the measures were unnecessarily harsh, claiming that it had the full support of merchants in Singapore and Penang.[24]

The quarantine system relied on regional epidemiological intelligence and locally, the vigilance of inspectors. As Max F. Simon, the Principal Civil Medical Officer of the Straits Settlements noted in 1897, the system was principally based on that of the Port of London:

> [It] may be described by the three words – inspection, isolation, disinfection. At London, if, on inspection, cases of disease or suspected disease are found, these are promptly isolated, the remainder of the passengers are allowed to land, but the destination of each one is ascertained, the ship is then disinfected as may be necessary, and allowed pratique. Communication is made to the Sanitary Authority of the parishes to which passengers are going, so that they may be kept in view. Our practice here consists likewise in isolating any sick, clearing the ship of the rest of the passengers, disinfecting it, and allowing pratique.

But there was, Simon admitted, a local factor that required a significant departure from the London system:

> inasmuch as it would be utterly futile, as any one who has had experience must know, to attempt to ascertain the destination of each one of a batch of perhaps eight or nine hundred Chinese coolies, we are unable to let them land, as they allow passengers to land at home, but we land them on St. John's Island, and keep them there under observation for a reasonable time ... they are then released, provided, of course, that no fresh cases of disease have appeared. If any fresh cases appear, these are promptly isolated, and the period of observation of the remainder is prolonged as may be necessary.[25]

Quarantine officials had to reckon with overcrowding and deception on the ships they were to inspect. Two classes of vessels were a perennial problem.

One was those highlighted by Simon: ships arriving from southern Chinese ports and Hong Kong loaded with poor immigrants of peasant background. From the second half of the 19th century to the early 20th century, great numbers of these migrants fled war, famine and an explosive population growth in southeast China. They either stopped at Singapore or passed through it, and those who disembarked there formed the basis of a growing coolie town. Between 1871 and 1931, the population of Singapore jumped from 96,000 to 558,000, making the Chinese the island's majority ethnic group.

The other difficulty was Muslim pilgrims returning from Mecca through the Arabian port city of Jeddah. Pilgrimage ships in the 1860s were as over-crowded as the Chinese craft and equally able to evade sanitary measures imposed at a British port of departure like Singapore. Overflowing with pas-sengers and luggage well in excess of their tonnage, the ships were alleged to contain 'an extent of mortality and other concomitant evils which is truly appalling'.[26] In 1869, one such vessel, licensed at Singapore to carry 216 passengers, departed with 150. It proceeded to add 23 unauthorised passen-gers at Malacca, 50 at Penang, 154 at the Pedier Coast, 63 at Passangan, 91 at Jonkow, 35 at Pedier and 50 at Arheen, for a total of 616. Ships like this typically shed their excess passengers on the return journey.[27]

Throughout the 1890s, the number of sea passengers from Jeddah and Chi-nese ports continued to rise, exceeding the expanded quarantine facilities on St. John's. Vessels returning from Mecca were more susceptible to a disease out-break than those commencing on the pilgrimage, for passengers could contract an illness in the holy city or be exhausted by the travails of the long journey. A British medical official claimed that 'there are many aged and unhealthy per-sons, not only likely to die on the voyage, but really happy to die on pilgrim-age'.[28] The lack of quarantine and sanitary facilities at Jeddah made the pilgrims even more susceptible to infectious disease.[29] As late as 1920, an esti-mated 10,000 out of 58,000 pilgrims there were unaccounted for, most of whom were thought to have died from heat exhaustion, diarrhoea and dysentery.[30]

Ironically, the mass quarantine of migrants at St. John's was criticised as excessively stringent, departing from the terms of the International Sanitary Convention of 1892. In 1899, the Straits government defended its practice to the Indian government when quarantining ships from Calcutta, where a plague outbreak had occurred. It explained that the surveillance of passengers landing from crowded coolie ships from infected ports in India and China was 'absolutely impossible'. It pointed out that the practice had kept the colony safe from plague.[31] From this time, the administration began to laud the quarantine system to be a success, helping to keep dangerous infectious dis-eases at bay and the number of local cases low.[32]

### A Tale of Two Administrations

The sea was not the only zone of quarantine. There was also surveillance on the main island of Singapore and particularly the town. This required the isolation of infectious disease patients and quarantine of their close contacts. If maritime quarantine had been affected by commercial interests, land surveillance was decidedly haphazard. It was a victim of bureaucratic politics. There were initially two administrations: the colonial government in charge of Singapore as a whole and the municipal administration, mostly appointed and largely funded by the government, which handled the affairs of the town. These administrations were tied to each other but had separate responsibilities and, as we will see, priorities.

Parallel to the two administrations was a pair of ordinances that had a bearing on land surveillance. One dealt with quarantine matters while the other defined the powers of the Municipality. Originally, the colonial government was responsible for both the land and the sea. According to the Quarantine and Prevention of Disease Ordinance of 1886, cases of infectious disease on land should be reported to the police, who would notify the Health Officer, who were all employees of the colonial administration. The officer would visit the patient where he was empowered to seal off and disinfect the patient's room or house. The government could have the patient removed to the General Hospital (GH, intended for Europeans) or Infectious Diseases Hospital (for Asians).[33]

In the 1880s, the colonial government wanted to transfer this responsibility to the Municipal Commission, as most cases of infectious disease in Singapore occurred within town limits. The Municipal Ordinance of 1887 demarcated the boundary of the town and created the post of the Municipal Health Officer who would replace the government Health Officer for controlling infectious diseases in the town. The new office was delayed for several years, forcing the colonial government to continue to carry out 'public health services of a very primitive character' within municipal limits, while the Municipal Commission remained focused on matters such as roads and bridges, water supply and lighting.[34] The commission was less keen on shouldering responsibility for infectious disease.

In 1893, the Municipal Health Officer was finally ready to take charge of public health matters in the town.[35] This meant that the owner of a cowshed dairy or milk seller in the town had to immediately report a case of cholera, smallpox or other infectious disease to the Municipality.[36] Outside the town (that is, in the rural area), however, medical practitioners were to immediately report a known case of an epidemic, endemic or dangerous infectious disease to the colonial government.[37] The duality of administration for public health led the Colonial Secretary to acknowledge 'a certain amount of conflict of duty and authority between the Government and the Municipal Officer'.[38]

The following year, after the scare from the plague outbreak in Hong Kong, the Municipal Commission belatedly agreed to be responsible for the control of epidemic diseases in the town, namely, cholera, smallpox, bubonic plague, fever and any other dangerous contagious or infectious disease. The Quarantine and Prevention of Diseases Ordinance was amended to reflect this change. Municipal, rather than government, health officers, were to inspect, close and disinfect the patient's room, while the President of the commission was authorised to remove the patient to a government hospital.[39]

But these new regulations, the commission admitted, were still 'indistinct and imperfect'. In particular, municipal officers found it difficult to remove unwilling patients from their homes and disinfect the houses.[40] In response, another amendment to the Quarantine and Prevention of Diseases Ordinance stipulated that the Municipal Health Officer could order patients to be treated in their home, instead of being removed to a hospital, with the house sealed off by the police and disinfected if necessary.[41]

This task was virtually impossible to fulfil. Policemen posted to seal off an infected house were not reliable enforcers. They often did not adequately understand the nature of an infectious disease to carry out their duties or lacked language skills, especially in the various Chinese languages, to communicate with the dwellers.[42] It was not uncommon to find a policeman asleep on the job inside the house, and in one damning instance, 'sleeping with his head on a contact's chest'.[43] Not surprisingly, the number of people supposedly under quarantine or isolation inside a house fell as the days passed.[44]

Alex Gentle, the President of the Municipal Commission, conceded that establishments with abundant daily human traffic, such as a carpenter's shop or rickshaw coolie depot, were difficult to effectively quarantine.[45] In 1897, the commission tried to resolve the problem by prosecuting violations, with $5 fines handed out to three persons for not reporting cases of epidemic diseases and another for leaving a house under quarantine.[46] But these numbers were only the tip of the iceberg.

Thus, land surveillance roles were poorly divided between the Municipal Commission and the Straits government. The former took charge of the town where most epidemics occurred, while the government was responsible for the rural area and the sea. This arrangement overlooked the obvious: the likely transmission of infectious disease between the sea and the town, and between the municipal and rural areas. The official borders were porous, and locals soon exploited the loopholes. Equally, neither the commission nor the government were happy with the system.

In 1899, a debate between the colonial and municipal governments surfaced over two issues: quarantine and a new infectious diseases hospital. On the first, J.A. Swettenham, the Colonial Secretary, sided with the Inspector-General of Police E. Pennefather – both government officials – about the heavy demands being placed on the police for quarantine duty.[47] Pennefather pointed out that he had only 21 men available during a recent smallpox outbreak. He was also worried that police constables guarding the houses might have unnecessary contact with smallpox patients, and so contract and transmit the disease to police stations. He even proposed pensioners to be used as house guards.[48]

Gentle replied curtly that the demands on the police were not onerous. Guard duty in the Municipality was routine work, long governed by the provisions of the Quarantine and Prevention of Diseases Ordinance. During the smallpox outbreak, only seven houses were isolated at any one time for a period of between 7 and 10 days. The commission was not required to grant a subvention to the government for the police work, as the costs were not prohibitive. He pointed out that contrary to the Quarantine and Prevention of Diseases Ordinance, the Municipal Ordinance did not authorise the patient's removal to a hospital, only isolation in his or her home.[49] Swettenham wrote back immediately, referring to several ordinances that made the control of infectious diseases a municipal responsibility. He noted that the commissioners' decision to utilise policemen as quarantine enforcers in 1894 was of 'doubtful legality'.[50] Gentle rejoined that the use of policemen was a standard procedure under the Municipal Ordinance and not a 'special measure'.[51]

There were clearly grey areas between the Quarantine and Prevention of Diseases Ordinance and the Municipal Ordinance. The crux of the issue though was the Municipal Commission's reluctance to accept the responsibility that the government was seeking to hoist upon it. But the latter had the political and financial leverage. In 1901, the Municipal Commission finally moved to adopt a new Municipal Ordinance to bring it in line with the Quarantine Ordinance. Some of the key changes owed to William Robert Covin Middleton, the Municipal Health Officer and a Scot, who adapted them from the Public Health Act in Scotland.[52] It took six long years before the new ordinance was passed in 1907.[53]

The Municipal Ordinance XXXVII of 1907 contained key sections from the 1886 Quarantine and Prevention of Disease Ordinance that fortified the Municipal Commission's role for infectious disease.[54] It dealt with the existing issues: the suppression and prevention of dangerous infectious diseases in the town, the segregation of patients and overcrowding and insanitation in the Municipality. Municipal sanitary officers were now empowered to enter, inspect, cleanse and demolish houses and buildings in the town suspected of infectious disease.

The Municipal Health Officer could also remove all persons living in a house infected with a quarantinable disease like bubonic plague to the quarantine station on St. John's.[55] This meant that contacts were no longer to be quarantined at home, relieving the police of a task for which they were ill-equipped. But this would strain the island's quarantine facilities while also sending contacts to an offshore island away from their family. In 1902, over 500 contacts in the Municipality were sent to the quarantine station. At this time, reconstruction works were being carried out on St. John's, while a new Isolation Hospital being planned would also accommodate these contacts within Singapore (discussed in Chapter 5).[56] Nevertheless, the responsibility of the Municipal Commission (and its successor the City Council) for infectious disease in the town endured till Singapore became a self-governing state in 1959. Thereafter, city government was abolished and the control of infectious disease in Singapore was centralised under the Ministry of Health.

Despite the new legislation in 1907, there were still numerous cases of concealment and non-cooperation among the local population. Five years earlier, the Municipal Commission stated, 'The prevention and suppression of outbreaks of Zymotic Disease is always a matter of greater difficulty in countries a large part of whose population consists of Asiatics'.[57] This was a comment on a case where locals had removed a patient from Market Street in the town to Geylang in the rural area so that the former premises would not be placed under quarantine. The commissioners prosecuted the Chinese doctor for making a false report.[58] Two years later, the Municipality was frustrated by another case where the patient and his or her friends provided misleading information as to whether the disease was local or imported and as to how the infection had spread.[59]

Blaming Asians for the transmission of infectious disease was a common response by both colonial and municipal officials that persisted into the mid-20th century. It reflected their failure to understand the social repercussions of notification, quarantine and disinfection. These effects stemmed from the very intent and implementation of the colonial ordinances. It took the work of a major Quarantine Commission in 1912 to unveil the grim social history of isolation and quarantine for patients and contacts.

## The 1912 Quarantine Commission

The work of the Straits Settlements Quarantine Inquiry Commission under Charles James Saunders to investigate existing arrangements in 1911 was a milestone in the history of quarantine and surveillance in Singapore. The commission amassed a wealth of information from the persons it interviewed and proposed a range of reforms. It was concerned with two institutions: the quarantine facility on St. John's Island and the Infectious Diseases Hospital at Balestier Road.[60] This section is concerned with the former, while the latter is the subject of Chapter 5.

The Quarantine Commission endorsed St. John's as a suitable site for the quarantine station. Situated near to the south of the Singapore port and 45 minutes from the town by steamship, it was large enough for sufficient accommodation for 5,000–6,000 persons. The commission deemed the existing quarantine wards to be comfortable, particularly for working-class deck passengers who endured inferior accommodation in their voyage to Singapore. The European ward was especially good and located some distance from other buildings. The commission recommended that the Municipal Commission should build one or more wards of good quality on the island for municipal contacts, and hire one or more attendants for the new ward(s). On the negative side, it found many general-purpose buildings to be old and dilapidated. It urged their replacement without delay and for all buildings to have adequate lighting. In terms of manpower, the commission deemed the Medical Superintendent to be overly burdened with administrative work and proposed that a European administrator be appointed to take charge of the non-medical work.[61]

There was also unhappiness with quarantine practice among Straits merchants and shipping lines – a long-running issue. As Elliot Dunville Hewan, a partner of the shipping agent Boustead & Co., told the commission, steamers were often delayed by the lack of accommodation on St. John's for their crew and passengers to serve their quarantine. This problem was, he said, 'almost chronic now'.[62] He also took issue with the shipowner having to bear the costs of feeding the crew and passengers – much too high at 13.5 cents per head – which he argued should be borne by the government. He proposed employing an additional Port Health Officer to expedite the inspection, and that the quarantine system be less stringent. Lim Peng Siang, the owner of the Ho Hong Steamship Co., agreed that the accommodation was lacking and the quarantine expensive, costing him more than a thousand dollars a day for a large ship. The coolies onboard the ships, who had to wait two to three hours to be ferried from the steamer to St. John's, considered the island 'a prison'.[63] Neither shipping companies discussed the overcrowding and insanitary conditions onboard the ships.

But the most galling revelations were about the grim conditions faced by municipal contacts quarantined on St. John's. Cramped closely together, the contacts, especially the women, children and the elderly, had to endure a two-hour journey from Singapore to St. John's under the hot sun or in rain on an open *tongkang* (a Chinese boat) towed by a steam-launch.[64] On landing, they had to haul their luggage to the shore, before waiting some time for it to be disinfected. Thereafter they were quarantined on the island for two weeks, losing contact with their family and business dealings in Singapore in the process. The Quarantine Commission proposed that the landing site on St. John's be extended and improved to expedite the process, while the capacity of the disinfection equipment should be at least doubled. For all this trouble, it was doubtful if the quarantine had any utility. The contacts generally had only a tenuous connection with the patient and were at little risk of developing smallpox; in the five years leading to 1910, only one contact had developed smallpox out of 4,000-odd municipal contacts isolated on the island. There, they dwelt together in large numbers, which threw into doubt the very aim of isolation.[65]

The travails of quarantine on St. John's were especially grave for certain groups of people: better-off Asians, women, and children. Often, the husband of a married woman had to join her in quarantine (losing his income or business in the process) and screen off a part of the isolation ward for some privacy. But the presence of the man could not compensate for the other facilities St. John's did not have: changing rooms, toilets and baths for women. Many women had to change in the sea or inside a latrine (for the latter, they had to wait in a queue behind men). Javanese women would slip a clean sarong over the one they were wearing.[66]

Complaints abounded that the food was poor or unsuitable (there were rumours that the food catered for Muslims contained pork). Contacts could do their own cooking (or have an accompanying servant do it), but there were no proper equipment or utensils for them to do so, Many people resorted to cooking in tin buckets, earthen basins or even a hole in the ground serving as a makeshift stove.[67] Some coolies from ships under quarantine even had to use chamber pots to cook their food – it was 'miserable' to say the least.[68] Drinking water was insufficient while there was no treated water for washing laundry or cleaning the premises and drains – contacts had to fetch water from the sea for these purposes.[69] The Quarantine Commission proposed that additional tanks be commissioned for collecting rainwater for drinking, while sea water could be pumped to a service reservoir for washing purposes.[70]

These quarantine problems were to discourage Asians, including those of the educated and middle class, from reporting cases of infectious disease. Gilbert Brooke, the Port Health Officer, told the commission that cases were often 'hushed up' until the patient recovered or died, when a burial permit would be sought from the police or worse, when the body was dumped in the street. The behaviour was prompted by fears of ill-treatment: the patient being treated in hospital or the contacts sent away to St. John's. Brooke admitted, 'Possibly their fears are not groundless'.[71] A Justice of the Peace who visited St. John's saw cane marks on contacts, likely inflicted by police constables.[72]

It seemed that compliance with quarantine regulations rarely benefitted Asians, even those of higher social and economic standing. An article in the *Straits Times* noted,

> we have heard from scores of educated natives, who perfectly agree with the principle of isolation, that until the methods of treating Asiatics are radically reformed there will be deliberate, wilful and systematic evasion of the law no matter what fines or other penalties are imposed.[73]

Richard Arthur Campbell, the Second Assistant Municipal Health Officer, identified People's Park (his ward in the centre of town) as a popular site for dumping corpses, for it was also close to a police station. When someone died of cholera, the neighbours would often remove the person's effects and send someone else to report the death at the nearest police station before disappearing.[74]

These issues revealed that the Chinese were not ignorant about infectious diseases, at least at a basic level. They knew cholera to be infectious, for they would place the body alone in the darkest cubicle in the shophouse and wait for it to be disinfected before returning to their rooms. Campbell related that the Chinese would sometimes sleep beside a corpse when death was due to a non-infectious cause, but they never did so when it was an infectious case. Inevitably, all occupants in the house would deny knowing about the death. He revealed that he was seen as an enemy by the Asian public and 'the worst of a very bad bunch [of medical officials]'.[75] These views highlighted the utter failure of notification of infectious disease. J.A.R. Glennie, the Assistant Municipal Health Officer, concurred that 'one is unable to get information from the people, particularly as to the probable cause of the disease'. He added, 'It is really terribly difficult to get any information whatever'.[76]

An equally serious problem was the disinfection and destruction of suspected infected goods. The British believed the compensation they offered to be reasonable, but Asians evidently thought otherwise. The British missed the point: it was not the amount of compensation that mattered, but the manner of the handling. As James Handy, a medical practitioner, told the Quarantine Commission, health officials would roughly take hold of an item to be disinfected and throw it down.[77] Humans were treated with similar disregard. It was not uncommon for people to have disinfecting Izal or Jeyes fluid poured over their heads and walk home soaked with it.[78]

Due to these shared grievances, many Asians shunned the public hospital for their own traditional physicians and healers, believing that 'If we go in we are sure to die'.[79] Dr W.R.C. Middleton, the Municipal Health Officer, was aware of the social range of Chinese who actively avoided public health measures and concealed cases of the sick. Those who went about their daily lives without notifying their illness were not only ignorant coolies but also well-informed, upper-class Straits Chinese lawyers, merchants and bank clerks. It was not just an individual's act of avoidance either but a community's collusion: fines levied upon those found guilty of not notifying the authorities were often paid by contributions from 'friends and kongsis' (Chinese businesses).[80]

Such behaviour reinforced the vicious cycle of concealment and dying in public hospitals. In 1910 for example, the Quarantine Commission learned that 138 deaths were recorded at the Infectious Diseases Hospital out of 483 cases treated. The high mortality rate of 28.6 per cent was due to many cases being admitted at an advanced stage of illness. Furthermore, in that year, the 61 persons who died from cholera and 47 from smallpox were not reported to the government as required by the Quarantine and Prevention of Disease Ordinance; they were discovered only after death had occurred while the smallpox cases were mostly unvaccinated.[81] Campbell revealed that his own servants had refused to go to a hospital or take Western medicine when ill.[82] When an outbreak of plague, cholera or smallpox occurred, it was usually not due to a newly arrived immigrant, as Gilbert Brooke observed, the patients having been in Singapore for some time.[83]

Instead of holding contacts on St. John's, the medical experts proposed alternatives to the Quarantine Commission. Brooke argued that the island was ill-prepared to accommodate a large number of municipal contacts.[84] Smallpox and bubonic plague contacts need not be isolated after they had been vaccinated and disinfection carried out. They could be released on condition that they would present themselves daily to the Health Officer or a qualified doctor for inspection for a period of 15 days. For plague, the best control was the destruction of rats rather than isolation of contacts.[85] Cholera contacts would have to be isolated, though not on St. John's but at the new infectious diseases hospital (provisionally called the Isolation Hospital) being built at Moulmein Road to replace the Balestier Road facility. The isolation, which would be for five days or more, would be more acceptable than being confined on St. John's, while it would also reduce the risk of the disease spreading to non-cholera contacts.[86] The Municipal Commission expressed the hope that the 'properly equipped' new hospital would resolve the problem of concealment.[87]

Finally, the Quarantine Commission found the surveillance of epidemic diseases in the rural areas of Singapore to be wanting. Avoidance and concealment were again sources of frustration. There were instances of patients being smuggled out of the town (where municipal officers had no jurisdiction), and occasionally in the opposite direction. Many cases were also brought from the Federated Malay States into rural Singapore via railways beyond the control of the Municipality.[88] As Campbell said,

> There are lots of them [infectious disease cases] at Siglap and Pasir Panjang [rural areas] … They are never seen by anybody. All anybody has got to do is to go across the municipal border and they can incubate the disease to their heart's content.[89]

The failure of surveillance was partly due to the shortage of staff for the Port Health Officer, who was also responsible for the rural area. This was despite increments to the department's staff in previous years.[90] The Quarantine Commission proposed that the Municipal Commission be given charge of the whole island of Singapore, but this was not accepted. It also recommended that an additional Port Health Officer be appointed, though what seemed more sensible was to appoint a separate rural health officer.[91]

For all the data and expert advice it had, the Quarantine Commission largely failed to address the fundamental problems in quarantine and surveillance. Cholera and smallpox contacts continued to be sent to St. John's, as no quarantine facilities were built at the new Infectious Diseases Hospital established at Moulmein Road in 1913 due to the reduced budget. Cholera contacts, mostly local residents, continued to arrive at St. John's in their hundreds. In 1914, when a cholera outbreak ravaged the town, the Moulmein Road hospital was severely taxed and 440 contacts had to be hived off to the island.[92] This was even though additional land had been bought for the new hospital to accommodate cholera contacts.[93]

In the early 1920s, the contact section of the quarantine facility at St. John's had more than 20 wards for about 250 people. These were now equipped with an attached kitchen and freshwater standpipe, as the Quarantine Commission had recommended. Brooke painted a picturesque image of the wards as being 'situated on the natural slopes, kept wonderfully cool beneath the shade afforded by plentiful trees and palms'.[94] Even the treatment wards that were fenced away from the contacts section were reported to be in beautifully maintained grounds and on green slopes, with 'an abundance of glorious purple bougainvillaea'.[95] The use of St. John's as a quarantine facility for contacts continued right up to the 1960s.

However, within the Municipality the problems of control persisted. Many of the proposed reforms had to be shouldered by a reluctant Municipality instead of the Straits government, including the responsibility for municipal and rural health. The Municipal Commissioners turned a blind eye to key criticisms of the existing system, particularly the underlying Asian distrust of the quarantine regulations. They thought that this could be resolved by providing more information on the laws dealing with infectious diseases and the ways to limit their spread. But information was not the main problem; it was the very practice of isolation and surveillance that swayed people's decisions and behaviour.

The five-member Quarantine Commission had a single Asian: Dr Suat Chuan Yin, a Western-trained doctor, businessman and Municipal Commissioner. He seemed to have agreed with his European colleagues on many of the commission's recommendations. Some of the witnesses called before the commission were discerning enough to realise that Asian responses to public health regulations were in large part influenced by colonial policies. As Handy, who had more than ten years' experience in Singapore, related, Asians placed in quarantine felt they were being treated as criminals.[96]

But there were also undeniably strong views held by European doctors and officials that the Asian view of disease was innate and immutable. Campbell thought Asians to be 'absolutely selfish' in not reporting cases to the government.[97] Glennie's assessment of what he thought to be the quintessential 'native' is revealing:

> The native wants to do as he likes and have his friends about him when he is ill. He does not like such restraint of his actions as would be necessary during hospital treatment. He does not want to have his house upset by cleaning or disinfecting. He does not understand what cleanliness is. It practically comes to this – he does not want to be bothered – he does not want his ordinary routine to be interrupted.[98]

Apart from the blame rhetoric, the quarantine system was little changed up till the Second World War. Middleton had described its central flaw aptly to the Quarantine Commission, 'They [The government] protect the port but the other three sides of the town they leave open for all sorts of disease'.[99] He had warned that the existing healthcare service emphasised treatment rather than prevention, of which there was 'Practically none'.[100] But the reforms proposed by the commission would not transform healthcare into public health. It would remain offensive and injurious to patients and contacts whose need was for kindness and empathy from government officials, rather than be treated as transgressive Asians.

Repeatedly, the Quarantine Commission called for an expansion of staff and facilities. These were genuine problems and in subsequent years, much-needed improvements were made to facilities, infrastructure, staff and patient accommodation on St. John's.[101] By the time a League of Nations team of quarantine officers visited the island in 1930, there were separate bathing blocks for males and females. The island quarantined over 84,000 persons that year, the bulk of whom were immigrants from China, India and Burma. It carried out more than 21,000 smallpox vaccinations or revaccinations.[102]

But by and large, the addition of staff and facilities was not the real solution. It meant increased government expenses, which always triggered resistance, but also a greater need for technical expertise that was not readily found. For example, the commission thought to improve notification and inspection simply by fixing the hours or personnel for locals to report to at the Municipal Health Office or the Moulmein Road hospital. But while it might have been possible to recruit additional staff, they might not be suitably qualified or culturally predisposed to treat the contacts with respect and kindness.[103]

## The Singapore Bureau: Handmaiden of Hygiene

Following the report of the Quarantine Commission, a committee was formed the same year to reconsider the quarantine legislation. This led to the passing of the Quarantine and Prevention of Disease Ordinance of 1915. In some ways, however, the new law was an update rather than a departure. It aimed to simplify quarantine rules and reconcile with commercial interests. Regional epidemiology was key to this. As Gilbert Brooke later related in 1927, it was always difficult to obtain up-to-date information on infections in the region's ports. The returns obtained by the Straits government ranged from periods of 10 days to half a month or even a whole month. The 1915 ordinance attempted to lay down a 'standard of epidemicity' for infectious diseases, based on weekly returns and the number of infected arrivals over a period of ten years. According to Brooke, the returns henceforth became more regular and systematic, enabling a smoother imposition and withdrawal of quarantine measures in the colony.[104]

The 1915 ordinance also gave discretionary powers to the government to detain and treat immigrants with infectious diseases and to repatriate the chronic sick.[105] However, the list of epidemic diseases remained small and bound by tradition, though yellow fever and syphilis were added to the trinity of plague, cholera and smallpox. Under the ordinance, all passengers and crew from China and India had to show proof of vaccination for smallpox within the last five years, as the Quarantine Commission had proposed.[106]

But the ordinance did not substantially improve the surveillance system for the town and rural areas. At the imminent end of World War One in 1918 but prior to the onset of the influenza epidemic in Singapore, quarantine regulations for plague, cholera, smallpox and yellow fever were extended to all dangerous infectious diseases, including cerebrospinal fever, which had caused an earlier outbreak that year.[107] Despite the severity of the pandemic, influenza did not appear on the ordinance until early 1920, when the Port Health Officer was momentarily empowered to quarantine ships arriving from a port affected by an influenza outbreak.[108] Much of the epidemic in Singapore had passed by then. The absence of a health officer for the rural area meant that much surveillance and sanitary work there, such as malaria control, could not be carried out.[109] In 1920, a rural health officer was finally appointed, but the registration of deaths in the rural area remained difficult owing to the lack of qualified medical practitioners.[110]

Throughout the interwar years, only minor amendments were made to the Quarantine Ordinance, pertaining to the duration of quarantine and import of animals, especially cattle and dogs.[111] An exception was in 1926, when it was made compulsory to revaccinate all children for smallpox within six months of them reaching the year of seven. The government would also require the compulsory vaccination of all persons living in a district experiencing an outbreak of smallpox.[112] In 1927, the Government Health Department reported that 'the standard of responsibility, technical ability and departmental enthusiasm continued to be maintained at a satisfactory level'.[113]

As the quarantine system expanded in the interwar years, the incidence of zymotic diseases in Singapore declined. By the early 1920s, the quarantine station on St. John's had become one of the largest in the world, capable of accommodating 6,000 people. It was probably surpassed only by the Ellis Island Station off New York City and the Quarantine Camp at El Tor in Egypt.[114] Its staff had expanded from 9 in 1902 to 385 in 1927, among whom 106 were involved in quarantine work while 240 were responsible for the rural area.[115] Those who died at St. John's were buried at the adjacent Lazarus Island, which was uninhabited. When Brooke led a team of doctors to visit the quarantine station in 1923, it had a temporary lockup, laundry and general store. The police force there consisted of 20-odd Sikhs, who had become nothing less than 'a community in itself'.[116] The water supply had risen to three thousand gallons per day of condensed seawater, 70 thousand gallons from the reservoir and an indeterminate amount of rainwater for washing.

In 1930, passengers arriving at St. John's from an infected port would muster at the quarantine station for medical inspection. They would be vaccinated for cholera if necessary and their baggage brought up by trucks and disinfected. The passengers would be warded in separate parts of the hospital for dangerous diseases, minor infections and general observation. Passengers from different ships would be separated by railed enclosures, but so would the different classes. Contacts from Singapore were examined daily. The buildings, according to the authorities at least, had good construction, ventilation and lighting, with each camp having its own kitchen, bathroom, pail latrine (subsequently replaced by water closets) and incinerator. Three brick-lined wells catered to the religious sensibilities of Sikhs, Javanese and Hindus, while individuals and families were given their own cooking pot, rations and firewood to cook their own meals.[117]

Ng Kar Lee, a Chinese migrant who sailed to Singapore twice in the early 1920s, found the fresh coastal air on St. John's an improvement on the poorly ventilated steamers he had arrived on. The accommodation where he was quarantined was airy, and he found nothing to complain about the housing conditions. Although there were some migrants who tried to run away, this was because they disliked being detained. The inspection of passengers and crew was taken seriously, but entry to Singapore was easy and did not require a permit, as long as one met the health regulations.[118] Twenty-odd years later, another Chinese arrival, Teong Eng Siong, deemed the medical inspections to be normal, since most passengers were healthy. His most memorable time on St. John's was the good food and drinks – he had eggs and milk tea, which he had never drunk before.[119]

But Teo Choon Hong, who arrived in Singapore in 1937, had a quite different experience. Like Ng, he remarked that entry to the island required no permit. This was really a comment on the administrative changes between past and present immigration procedures, with written papers required in post-colonial Singapore. But Teo felt that the British officials subjected him and other arrivals to an inhumane experience on St. John's, shuffling them from one place to another like poultry.[120] It seems that some of the colonisers' behaviour towards their subjects on matters of health and quarantine were still present prior to the outbreak of war.

By this time, the British had acquired a self-confidence towards the quarantine system. Port health officials such as Dr W.D. D'Cruz were experienced hands dealing with ships commandeered by captains of different nationalities. German and Japanese vessels were purportedly well-maintained and provided reliable information, but French captains arriving from Saigon did not seem overly concerned about cases of cholera onboard. Straits officials were most wary of ships from China as before. These were helmed by British captains, who were merely 'paid navigators', and the Chinese owners frequently exceeded the legal quota for their vessels in order to maximise their profit. Excess numbers of poor passengers who paid for steerage were issued a second-class ticket and hidden in some part of the ship such as the forward hold. From there they were retrieved to the second-class saloon for inspection when the ship was directed to St. John's. These passengers were quite likely to carry infectious disease.[121]

Despite real improvements on St. John's, the quarantine system remained fixated on a select few diseases that were no longer as dangerous as they once were.[122] This created a false sense of security. Roland Braddell surmised, 'Week after week the League of Nations Health Bureau in its tabulations of the cities of the Orient marks nil against Singapore in respect of smallpox, plague, and cholera'.[123] While the quarantine work had expanded considerably since the early 20th century, its scope remained decidedly narrow.

Singapore's situation was a mirror of the international epidemiological system. Niall Johnson has suggested that the 1918 flu pandemic might have contributed to the need for an international health organisation to deal with future pandemics. It was really only with the formation of the World Health Organisation after the Second World War that a programme for influenza was implemented.[124] In the interwar years, there were rudimentary efforts towards an epidemiological system in Asia. In 1920, the League of Nations established a health organisation. Three years later, the 5th Congress of the Far Eastern Association of Tropical Medicine, held in Singapore, deemed the quarantine regulations of the International Sanitary Convention of Paris of 1912 as unsuitable for East Asia and proposed a different set of rules for the region.[125] In 1924, Dr F. Norman White, Director of the League of Nations' Bureau of Epidemics, proposed a new sanitary convention to the League's Health

Committee. Governor Laurence Guillemard of the Straits Settlements formed a rival committee in Singapore, strongly represented by local commercial and shipping interests, to reject the proposed convention and pitched its own alternative.[126]

The Straits committee's primary concern was trade and shipping cargo. It alleged that White's draft convention would 'impose intolerable burdens on free commercial intercourse' and was too onerous to implement. Its proposal was superior and more practical, doing away with White's requirements for the regular fumigation of ships or the authority of governments to implement additional measures beyond those stated in the convention. The committee also felt it was unfair that the damage to goods caused by disinfection be borne by the owners. It urged to use a disinfecting gas that would not damage the cargo.[127]

Guillemard nominated Singapore as the headquarters of the League's proposed health bureau.[128] In March 1925, the League of Nations, with funding from the Rockefeller Foundation, established an Eastern Epidemiological Bureau in Singapore.[129] This was, Brooke intimated, the 'last rung' in regional epidemiology in Asia.[130] The bureau reported to the head office in Paris and was advised by a council of member states. Brooke became its first director. The bureau's membership initially encompassed 13 Asian territories: China, Japan, Korea, Formosa, Siam, the Dutch East Indies, French Indochina, Macao, India, Hong Kong, Ceylon, the Federated Malay States, and the Straits Settlements; subsequently, others like Australia and Madagascar were added to the list.[131] The Straits Settlements and the Malay states under British protection were thus part of an Asian epidemiological network decades before they became independent nations.

The workings of an international epidemiological bureau made up of diverse imperial and territorial interests is the subject of a separate study. But what relates to quarantine in Singapore is worth examining. Utilising a two-digit code, the bureau broadcast in code weekly telegraph reports to ports as far as Cairo in the west, Tokyo in the east and the Pacific Islands. Information included the population of the port, the tonnage entering it, the location of the quarantine anchorages and stations. As a clearing-house for epidemiological intelligence in Asia, the bureau was, as Brooke put it, 'an incalculable boon to every maritime Health Officer'.[132] He likened the data to a handmaiden of hygiene, indispensable in a war against pandemic disease.[133] The *Straits Times* cheered the Singapore bureau as a truly international venture that 'scorns all racial and political distinctions'.[134] In 1930, the League carried out a study of quarantine stations in East Asia, including St. John's.[135] Discussions about what constituted 'the East' and whether to admit territories such as Australia and the Pacific Islands showed that public health and epidemiology helped shape the idea of Asia in the interwar years.[136]

However, the bureau was also tied to epidemiological tradition, being similarly fixated on plague, cholera and smallpox. It lauded itself for much of the 'steady annual diminution' of these diseases in the region during the 1920s.[137] The epidemiological work did not simply involve the collection and distribution of information; the bureau was also creating an intelligence archive and database that would shape public health in the region. But its reports, though considered valuable, were not sent regularly enough to the member states.[138] This perennial problem improved within the next few years, but it remained difficult to speedily collect information from more far-flung ports.[139] While the League's health bulletins covered 98 per cent of the population of Europe and 87 per cent for Australasia, the coverage for Asia and Africa was only 54 per cent and 64 per cent respectively.[140]

The pan-Asian network attempted to include medical research, but its scope was predictably narrow. The coordination of epidemiological research among so many different countries proved difficult, as the bureau admitted in 1928.[141] That year, the bureau decided to concentrate on a plague research programme, with the Penang-born physician Wu Lien Teh as a leading proponent.[142] There was subsequent interest in other infections such as pneumonia, yellow fever and malaria, and in oral vaccines.[143] The concern with yellow fever, a greatly feared disease in the West, was soon embraced by administrators in Asia, including Singapore, though it never became a public health hazard of the first order in the region.[144] The plague research produced the best results among the diseases surveyed.[145] The bureau also deserved credit for significantly reducing cholera outbreaks in the region in the interwar years.[146] But while influenza cases onboard ships were documented, the illness was not on the priority list of epidemic diseases in the brief span of time the bureau was active. White admitted in 1926 that it was extremely difficult to obtain information on influenza, measles and whooping cough.[147]

In 1930s Singapore, a new Quarantine and Prevention of Disease Ordinance (Chapter 186 of 1938) stipulated detailed terms of quarantine for epidemic diseases such as plague, cholera, smallpox, yellow fever and typhus.[148] It permitted the detention of immigrants for a period not exceeding seven days for a thorough medical examination for leprosy.[149] It reiterated the need for medical practitioners or occupants of a house to notify cases to the police, Health Officer or (for the Malay community) the penghulu (Malay village headman).[150] Despite the new ruling for Malays, there was no new legislation to tackle longstanding problems in municipal and rural health. Prior to the outbreak of war in the Pacific, Singapore's medical officers had become accustomed to declaring in the Eastern Bureau's weekly bulletins that the island was free of dangerous infections.[151] It seemed the quarantine system was working.

## Home Defences to the Fore

British quarantine measures were reinstituted in Singapore after the Second World War. According to epidemiologist Goh Kee Tai, they were successful, especially in detecting cases of smallpox.[152] The central issue in this time was how far quarantine measures should be pursued in the context of the growing internationalisation of trade and movement of people after the war. Newly formed global organisations such as the United Nations sought to replace the ruinous competition between nation-states in the 1930s and early 1940s, giving rise to international networks of collaborative relations in the realms of commerce, economic development, scientific and technical cooperation.[153] For Singapore, the practice of quarantine was once again questioned, as many of the traditional diseases were no longer the menace they used to be. In 1952, the Medical Department declared that the city-state had not experienced outbreaks of quarantinable diseases despite its proximity to countries where they were endemic, namely, smallpox, cholera, plague, typhus and yellow fever.[154] Influenza was still not on the list, having been deemed a disease that could not be controlled by quarantine.

With the advent of mass air travel in the interwar years and after the war, another question that arose was the quarantine of aircraft. This had been stressed by the Eastern Bureau as early as 1929, particularly for the control of cholera and yellow fever.[155] In Singapore, quarantine measures had first been introduced at Seletar Airport in 1934 and then at Kallang Airport five years later. The 1938 Quarantine and Prevention of Disease Ordinance included provisions for the quarantine of persons arriving in the colony by aircraft.[156] At this time, the risk of the spread of infectious diseases by air travel was deemed to be low.[157] After the war, quarantine measures were extended to the new Paya Lebar Airport two years after it opened, in 1958.[158]

In the 1950s, Singapore remained steadfast about its quarantine policy. In 1956, M. Doraisingham, the Acting Permanent Secretary of the MOH, criticised the WHO for relaxing quarantine controls in favour of facilitating the movement of global air and sea traffic. He deemed such a shift as premature and risky: it favoured developed countries with strong healthcare systems and responsible citizens, both of which were lacking in Southeast Asia and the Western Pacific. It was not enough for passengers to present vaccination certificates; contacts of a dangerous infectious disease and travellers from infected areas should be quarantined. He counted cholera, smallpox and yellow fever as the continuing threats.[159] Doraisingham's comments were characteristically nationalist and anti-colonial. Interestingly, he would, as discussed in Chapter 8, allow the influenza epidemic to 'burn itself out' in Singapore the following year.

After Singapore attained self-government in 1959, the new People's Action Party government decided not to sign the WHO's International Sanitary Regulations of 1951 and the International Health Regulations that replaced them in 1969. Singapore was one of the few countries in the world not to do so. Its government insisted on its flexibility to implement additional quarantine measures if it deemed them necessary. This reflected the weight of a national tradition of quarantine against international norms. The Quarantine and Prevention of Disease Ordinance of 1938 had conveyed to the government greater powers than those stipulated in the WHO's regulations.[160] As Doraisingham argued, Singapore's position was that priority should be given to public health controls rather than facilitation of international travel, as diseases like plague, cholera and smallpox were still endemic in the region.[161]

The Singapore government had five reservations towards the international regulations: that the concept of 'infected area' was too broad and general;

that isolation expenses should be borne by carriers; that it was necessary to take additional quarantine measures against passengers who pose a high risk of transmitting dangerous infectious diseases that were endemic in Southeast Asia; that the certification of sanitary ports and airports by external agencies constrained the authority of the national health administration; and that the period of infectivity for yellow fever ought to be nine days.[162] In not signing the WHO's regulations of 1951 and 1969, Singapore departed from its involvement in the League of Nations' regional epidemiological network before the war.

In 1962, the government reorganised the Public Health Division of the MOH and formed a Quarantine and Epidemiology Branch within the division. The branch comprised two units: an Epidemiological Unit for plague prevention, epidemiological investigation into infectious diseases and mosquito control, and a Quarantine Service for port and airport health, the quarantine station on St. John's and vaccination. The MOH still spoke about maintaining an 'effective barrier' against epidemic diseases for the open city-state.[163] But with rising volumes of maritime and air traffic and in the absence of major outbreaks, traditional quarantine began to take a secondary role to epidemiology.

By the 1970s, quarantine had lost its high place in infectious diseases control after Singapore became a nation-state in 1965. Writing at the end of the decade, Goh deemed it to be based on an 'obsolete and time-consuming approach' to public health.[164] As the colonial regime had done, the post-colonial government recognised that quarantine controls were especially ineffective against cholera. It was rather improvements in epidemiological surveillance, personal hygiene and environmental sanitation, pertaining to water supply, human waste and refuse disposal and sewage treatment, that had been decisive in curtailing the disease.[165] Globally, the threat of pandemic disease seemed to have significantly receded; in 1972, famed virologist Sir Macfarlane Burnet believed that the future of infectious diseases would be a 'very dull' one.

Singapore's achievements were decisive in moving the government to reconsider its previous objections to the International Health Regulations. As early as 1970, a WHO expert Dr B. Velimiroric had noted of Singapore,

[T]he existence of a well developed health services and the availability of conscientious and highly qualified personnel warrant total acceptance of the I.H.R. Protective measures ... acceptance of the I.H.R. by the Government will not limit its freedom of action if a case of quarantinable disease is imported.[166]

Likewise, in his study of quarantine services in Singapore at the time, Dr Parry Quah agreed that the government's objections were no longer valid. Plague and smallpox were no longer health threats while quarantine was ineffective against cholera. He added that the morale of Port Health Officers – which had been prestigious appointments 50 years ago – was often low as they were usually posted to the job against their choice. The assignment was seen to consist of routine paperwork, be it signing health documents or checking international health certificates.[167]

Belatedly, in 1980, the Singapore government agreed that its reservations to the regulations were no longer valid due to these reasons. It noted that smallpox had just been eradicated as a disease, Singapore's quarantine measures for yellow fever had been reviewed and modified, the standard of environmental sanitation in the country had improved, and its epidemiological surveillance had proven to be effective.[168] The following year, the republic finally signed the International Health Regulations.

Air travel had a further impact as Singapore turned away from its long-standing role as a global entrepôt towards manufacturing, tourism and hospitality in the 1970s. In the decade, the vast majority of arrivals came through the airport rather than the maritime port.[169] As the island became a global air hub, it was no longer feasible to quarantine the air crew and passengers as it had been for the ships.[170] In 1970, air passengers to Singapore were no longer required to present vaccination certificates, a move extended to sea arrivals four years later. In 1978, a major change occurred with vaccination certificates for smallpox no longer being required from arrivals except if they came from infected countries. Plague remained a concern in the clearance of ships arriving at the port. In 1980, vessels no longer had to be boarded except if they came from a port infected with plague or had cases of sickness or death.[171]

The ascendancy of epidemiological surveillance also led to the formation of the Quarantine and Epidemiology Department in the Ministry of the Environment and the Joint Co-ordinating Committee on Epidemic Diseases in the early 1970s (discussed further in Chapter 9). By then, epidemiological surveillance had replaced quarantine as the main instrument of defence. Gradually, the quarantine camps on St. John's Island closed or were converted into an opium treatment centre. In 1973, the venerable lazaretto ceased a century's work of inspecting ships and quarantining arrivals. The historic quarantine station was closed three years later. The government did not want an entire island devoted to the treatment of ageing opium addicts either.[172] The quarantine station had, as Parry Quah noted, become a costly white elephant by that time, with no epidemiological rationale to support the quarantine of healthy deck passengers. Most of these passengers were not the sojourners of the colonial period, but Singaporean citizens returning from overseas trips with valid health certificates endorsed in the republic.[173] The Middleton Hospital was preferred as a quarantine facility. St. John's was thus designated as a holiday resort for locals – a very different political and economic milieu from a century ago.[174]

These changes typified post-colonial policy towards the threat of pandemic disease. The Infectious Diseases Act of 1976, which replaced the 1938 Quarantine and Prevention of Disease Ordinance, emphasised notification by medical practitioners and epidemiological surveillance.[175] Practitioners had been required to notify the government of cases of dangerous infectious diseases since the colonial era. But the policy was now effectively pursued by a strong post-colonial government that viewed the control of infectious disease as underpinning national and especially economic development. As discussed in Chapter 9, notifications for influenza grew in the 1970s even though it was not a notifiable disease.

In his book, *Epidemiological Surveillance of Communicable Diseases in Singapore* (1983), Goh noted the growing belief that epidemic diseases, while not fully eradicated, did not require the institution of quarantine:

> The best safeguard to prevent the introduction of infectious diseases is to strengthen the home defences through improvement in environmental sanitation, vaccination of population and developing a comprehensive system of epidemiological surveillance, rather than erecting barriers against their introduction from outside.[176]

Goh expressed the confidence of the early 1980s in 'home defences' as the new paradigm against what was seen to be an archaic system of quarantine. The end of his book discussed the panic over epidemics of viral haemorrhagic fevers in Africa, which had led to the imposition of strict quarantine measures. In the end, however, the outbreaks were found to be 'not that terrifying at all'.[177] Goh's optimism was a product of his times, differing from the views of his colonial predecessors. In 1919, Gilbert Brooke had favourably depicted quarantine as a sieve rather than a dam, a sophisticated system that would avoid the wholesale destruction of goods and calamitous financial loss.[178] But this had frequently not been the experience of Asians during the colonial period.

As Alex Chase-Levenson notes of the Mediterranean between the late 18th and mid-19th centuries, quarantines are systems of control, applied universally to the passage of people and goods in the absence of an epidemic.[179] In this sense, a quarantine system is not a pre-modern oddity but an integral part of the modern world. Quarantine shaped the history of Singapore, raising difficult questions and experiences about its role as an open port city and destination for immigrants and foreign visitors. It also reinforced the unequal and fraught relationship between the British and Asian society. In Singapore and much of the world during the COVID-19 pandemic, quarantine has shown itself to be relevant in the 21st century, contrary to what Goh had predicted.

If quarantine is here to stay, two observations may be made from its history. One, Singapore's quarantine system was both difficult to establish and slow to change. Since the colonial period, it had largely followed tradition and eschewed diseases like influenza that not only were more prevalent, but had also caused severe epidemics in Singapore. Two, quarantine was shaped by its socio-political context as much as by prevailing public health concerns. The ways the British segregated Chinese immigrants arriving in infected ships or contacts of sick patients from the town grew out of the view that Asians were insanitary and backward. The effective quarantine system of the new millennia will not only need to keep out dangerous diseases, but also find ways to persuade people that they are being kept safe.

# Notes

1   CO 275/119 *Straits Settlements Medical Report* (thereafter SSMR) 1927, p. 723.
2   CO 275/94 SSMR 1914, 532.
3   Kah Seng Loh and Li Yang Hsu, *Tuberculosis – The Singapore Experience, 1867–2018: Disease, Society and the State* (New York: Routledge, 2020).
4   CO 273/22 Governor's Despatch to the Colonial Office, 4 December 1868.
5   'Historical Synopsis of Preventive Medicine in Singapore', *The Malayan Medical Journal*, 1930, pp. 97–102; League of Nations Health Organisation Eastern Bureau, *Report on Study Tour of Quarantine Officers in Eastern Ports* (26 June–8 August 1930) (Singapore: 1930).
6   CO 273/71 Governor's Despatch to the Colonial Office, 25 November 1873.
7   *Straits Times*, 11 November 1876, p. 4.
8   CO 275/119 SSMR 1927.
9   CO 273/79 Letter from Guthrie & Co., 13 November 1874.
10  *Straits Times*, 19 November 1874.
11  CO 273/79 Letter from Guthrie & Co., 1 February 1875.
12  CO 273/79 Letter from Guthrie & Co., 14 November 1874; CO 273/79 Letter from Guthrie & Co., 17 November 1874.
13  CO 273/79 Letter from the Colonial Secretary to Guthrie & Co., 14 November 1874.
14  CO 273/79 Letter from the Colonial Secretary to Guthrie & Co., 19 November 1874.
15  CO 273/79 Memo from the Principal Civil Medical Officer, 10 March 1875.
16  CO 275/18 Joint report on the Subject of Quarantine and Emigration Arrangements, 7 October 1875.
17  CO 275/34 The Quarantine and Prevention of Disease Ordinance, 1886, 7 July 1887.
18  'Historical Synopsis of Preventive Medicine in Singapore'.
19  CO 275/25 AMRCHSS 1880, p. 59.
20  CO 275/28 AMRCHSS 1882, p. 247.
21  CO 275/36 AMRCHSS 1889.
22  CO 275/53 AMRCHSS 1896; League of Nations, *Report on Study Tour of Quarantine Officers in Eastern Ports*.
23  CO 273/202 Extract from a letter from the Hong Kong Chamber of Commerce 10 December 1894.
24  CO 273/202 Memo from the Acting Colonial Secretary, Straits Settlements, to the Acting Colonial Secretary, Hongkong, 9 January, 1895.
25  CO 275/55 *Annual Medical Report of the Civil Hospitals in the Straits Settlements for the Year* (thereafter AMRCHSS) 1897, p. 406.
26  CO 273/30 Memo by Chief Secretary R.S. Ellis, 17 May 1869.
27  CO 273/30 Memo from Chief Secretary R.S. Ellis, 17 May 1869.
28  CO 273/244 Memo by Brigade-Surgeon Lieut.-Col. Edward Nicholson, c.1898.
29  CO 273/505 Report on the Future Sanitary Control of the Pilgrimage.
30  CO 273/505 Report by Major W.E. Marshall, ILA on the Pilgrimage, 1920.
31  CO 273/246 Memo from C. Mitchell to Secretary of State for the Colonies, 16 March 1899.
32  CO 275/57 SSMR 1898.
33  CO 275/34 The Quarantine and Prevention of Disease Ordinance, 1886, 7 July 1887.
34  J.W. Scharff, 'The Growth of Public Health Services in Singapore in Relation to Preventive Medicine in War Time', *Journal of the Malayan Branch of the British Medical Association*, Vol. 3 No. 3, December 1939, p. 345.
35  CO 275/60 Extract from letter from Acting Colonial Secretary to President, Municipal Commissioners, Singapore, 30 September 1893.
36  CO 275/39 The Quarantine and Prevention of Disease Ordinance 1886, 20 March 1890.

37   CO 275/41 The Quarantine and Prevention of Disease Ordinance 1886, 9 April 1891.

38   CO 275/60 Extract from letter from Acting Colonial Secretary to President, Municipal Commissioners, Singapore, 30 September 1893.

39   CO 275/48 The Quarantine and Prevention of Disease Ordinance 1886, 19 July 1894.

40   Singapore Municipality, *Administration Report* (thereafter SMAR) 1894, p. 9.

41   CO 275/51 The Quarantine and Prevention of Disease Ordinance 1886, 2 September 1895.

42   SMAR 1893, Memo from Alex Gentle to the Acting Colonial Secretary, S.S., 30 October 1893.

43   Evidence by Thomas Oswald Mayhew, Straits Settlements Quarantine Inquiry Commission, *Proceedings of the Commission Appointed to Inquire into the Working of the Quarantine and Prevention of Diseases Ordinance in the Settlement of Singapore, in the Colony of the Straits Settlements* (Singapore: Government Printing Office, 1912), Vol. 2, p. 17.

44   Written statement by Dr Glennie, Straits Settlements Quarantine Inquiry Commission, *Proceedings of the Commission*, Vol. 2, Appendix A, p. 14.

45   SMAR 1893, Memo from Alex Gentle to the Acting Colonial Secretary, S.S., 30 October 1893.

46   SMAR 1897.

47   SMAR 1899, Memo from J.A. Swettenham, Colonial Secretary S.S. to the President of the Municipal Commissioners, 17 March 1899.

48   SMAR 1899, Memo from E. Pennefather, Inspector-General of Police, to Colonial Secretary, S.S., 17 February 1899.

49   SMAR 1899, Memo from A. Gentle to the Hon'ble Colonial Secretary S.S., 29 March 1899.

50   SMAR 1899, Memo from J.A. Swettenham, Colonial Secretary S.S. to the President of the Municipal Commissioners, 30 March 1899.

51   SMAR 1899, Memo from Alex Gentle to the Hon'ble Colonial Secretary S.S., 21 April 1899.

52   SMAR 1901.

53   SMAR 1907.

54   SMAR 1901.

55   SMAR 1901, Appendix K: Regulations to Check the Spread of Infectious Disease.

56   G.E. Brooke, 'Excursion to the Quarantine Station at St. John's Island', *Journal of the Malayan Branch of the British Medical Association*, No. XI, 1922–23, pp. 37–38.

57   SMAR 1902, p. 124.

58   SMAR 1903.

59   SMAR 1904.

60   Straits Settlements Quarantine Inquiry Commission, *Proceedings of the Commission*. The other members of the commission were William Wallace Cook, Thomas Murray Robertson, Dr Suat Chuan Yin, and Alexander William Still.

61   Straits Settlements Quarantine Inquiry Commission, *Proceedings of the Commission*, Vol. 1.

62   Evidence by Elliot Dunville Hewan, Straits Settlements Quarantine Inquiry Commission, *Proceedings of the Commission*, Vol. 2, p. 84.

63   Evidence by Lim Peng Siang, Straits Settlements Quarantine Inquiry Commission, *Proceedings of the Commission*, Vol. 2, p. 92.

64   Straits Settlements Quarantine Inquiry Commission, *Proceedings of the Commission*, Vol. 1.

65   Straits Settlements Quarantine Inquiry Commission, *Proceedings of the Commission*, Vol. 1.

66   Evidence by Dr Henry Wallace Furnivall, Straits Settlements Quarantine Inquiry Commission, *Proceedings of the Commission*, Vol. 2.
67   Evidence by Dr George Alexander Finlayson, Straits Settlements Quarantine Inquiry Commission, *Proceedings of the Commission*, Vol. 2.
68   Evidence by Lim Peng Siang, Straits Settlements Quarantine Inquiry Commission, *Proceedings of the Commission*, Vol. 2, p. 92.
69   Evidence by Mohamed Syed Daghastani, Straits Settlements Quarantine Inquiry Commission, *Proceedings of the Commission*, Vol. 2.
70   Straits Settlements Quarantine Inquiry Commission, *Proceedings of the Commission*, Vol. 1.
71   Written statement by Gilbert E. Brooke, Straits Settlements Quarantine Inquiry Commission, *Proceedings of the Commission*, Vol. 2, Appendix A, p. 2.
72   Evidence by Leong Man Sau, Straits Settlements Quarantine Inquiry Commission, *Proceedings of the Commission*, Vol. 2.
73   *Straits Times*, 27 July 1911, p. 7.
74   Written statement by Dr Campbell, Straits Settlements Quarantine Inquiry Commission, *Proceedings of the Commission*, Vol. 2, Appendix A.
75   Evidence by Dr Richard Arthur Campbell, Straits Settlements Quarantine Inquiry Commission, *Proceedings of the Commission*, Vol. 2, p. 31.
76   Evidence by Dr John Arthur Rinder Glennie, Straits Settlements Quarantine Inquiry Commission, *Proceedings of the Commission*, Vol. 2, p. 24.
77   Evidence by Dr James Handy, Straits Settlements Quarantine Inquiry Commission, *Proceedings of the Commission*, Vol. 2.
78   Evidence by Thomas Oswald Mayhew and Dr Richard Arthur Campbell, Straits Settlements Quarantine Inquiry Commission, *Proceedings of the Commission*, Vol. 2.
79   Evidence by Thomas Oswald Mayhew, Straits Settlements Quarantine Inquiry Commission, *Proceedings of the Commission*, Vol. 2, p. 15.
80   Written statement by Dr Middleton, Straits Settlements Quarantine Inquiry Commission, *Proceedings of the Commission*, Vol. 2, Appendix A, p. 18.
81   Straits Settlements Quarantine Inquiry Commission, *Proceedings of the Commission*, Vol. 1.
82   Evidence by Dr Richard Arthur Campbell, Straits Settlements Quarantine Inquiry Commission, *Proceedings of the Commission*, Vol. 2.
83   Evidence by Dr Gilbert Edward Brooke, Straits Settlements Quarantine Inquiry Commission, *Proceedings of the Commission*, Vol. 2.
84   Evidence by Dr Gilbert Edward Brooke, Straits Settlements Quarantine Inquiry Commission, *Proceedings of the Commission*, Vol. 2.
85   Evidence by Dr George Alexander Finlayson, Straits Settlements Quarantine Inquiry Commission, *Proceedings of the Commission*, Vol. 2.
86   Straits Settlements Quarantine Inquiry Commission, *Proceedings of the Commission*, Vol. 1.
87   SMAR 1913, p. 13.
88   Evidence by Dr Gilbert Edward Brooke, Straits Settlements Quarantine Inquiry Commission, *Proceedings of the Commission*, Vol. 2.
89   Evidence by Dr Richard Arthur Campbell, Straits Settlements Quarantine Inquiry Commission, *Proceedings of the Commission*, Vol. 2, p. 29.
90   CO 273/396 Report to a Committee Appointed for the Purpose of Enquiring into the Medical Service and Hospitals of the Straits Settlements, 12 June 1913.
91   Straits Settlements Quarantine Inquiry Commission, *Proceedings of the Commission*, Vol. 1.
92   SMAR 1914.
93   SMAR 1912.
94   Brooke, 'Excursion to the Quarantine Station at St. John's Island', p. 38.

95    Brooke, 'Excursion to the Quarantine Station at St. John's Island', p. 38.

96    Evidence by Dr James Handy, Straits Settlements Quarantine Inquiry Commission, *Proceedings of the Commission*, Vol. 2.

97    Written statement by Dr Campbell, Straits Settlements Quarantine Inquiry Commission, *Proceedings of the Commission*, Vol. 2, Appendix A, p. 8.

98    Written statement by Dr Glennie, Straits Settlements Quarantine Inquiry Commission, *Proceedings of the Commission*, Vol. 2, Appendix A, p. 14.

99    Evidence by Dr William Robert Colvin Middleton, Straits Settlements Quarantine Inquiry Commission, *Proceedings of the Commission*, Vol. 2, p. 75.

100   Evidence by Dr William Robert Colvin Middleton, Straits Settlements Quarantine Inquiry Commission, *Proceedings of the Commission*, Vol. 2, p. 75.

101   CO 275/70 SSMR 1904.

102   League of Nations, *Report on Study Tour of Quarantine Officers in Eastern Ports.*

103   Straits Settlements Quarantine Inquiry Commission, *Proceedings of the Commission*, Vol. 1.

104   CO 275/119 SSMR 1927.

105   CO 275/96 SSMR 1915.

106   CO 275/97 The Quarantine and Prevention of Disease Ordinance, 1915, 31 March 1916.

107   CO 275/99 The Quarantine and Prevention of Disease Ordinance, 1915, 27 May 1918.

108   CO275/102 The Quarantine and Prevention of Disease Ordinance, 1915, 8 March 1920.

109   CO 275/103 SSMR 1919.

110   CO 275/107 SSMR 1922.

111   See for instance CO 275/128 Committee Representative of the Government and of the Municipality Regarding the Quarantine Camp and New Abattoirs, 3 March 1931.

112   CO 275/117 SSMR 1926.

113   CO 275/119 SSMR 1927, p. 722.

114   *Singapore Free Press*, 4 April 1923, p. 221.

115   Brooke, 'Excursion to the Quarantine Station at St. John's Island'.

116   Brooke, 'Excursion to the Quarantine Station at St. John's Island', p. 37.

117   'Historical Synopsis of Preventive Medicine in Singapore'.

118   Oral History Centre, National Archives of Singapore, Interview with Ng Lee Kar, Reel 1, 16 March 1982.

119   Oral History Centre, National Archives of Singapore, Interview with Teong Eng Siong, Reel 1, 1 February 2002.

120   Oral History Centre, National Archives of Singapore, Interview with Teo Choon Hong, Reel 2, 16 September 1983.

121   J.H. Strahan, 'Reflections on the Course of Preventive Medicine in Malaya', *The Medical Journal of Malaya*, Vol. 2 No. 4, June 1948.

122   CO 275/144 The Quarantine and Prevention of Disease Ordinance (Chapter 186).

123   Roland St. John Braddell, *The Lights of Singapore* (London: Methuen, 1947), p. 19.

124   Niall Johnson, *Britain and the 1918–19 Influenza Pandemic: A Dark Epilogue* (London: Routledge, 2006).

125   CO 275/110 SSMR 1923.

126   CO 273/526 Memo from L. Guillemard, 7 October 1924.

127   CO 273/526 Memo to Sir Laurence Nunns Guillemard, 7 October 1924, p. 1.

128   CO 273/526 Memo from L. Guillemard, 7 October 1924.

129   'Epidemiological Bureau at Singapore', *British Medical Journal*, 20 June 1925.

130   CO 275/119 SSMR 1927, p. 723.

131   CO 275/119 SSMR 1927.

132 CO 275/119 SSMR 1927, p. 723.
133 G.E. Brooke, 'A System of Intelligence as a Handmaiden of Hygiene', *The Malayan Medical Journal*, 1926.
134 *Straits Times*, 5 February 1925, p. 8.
135 League of Nations, *Report on Study Tour of Quarantine Officers in Eastern Ports.*
136 A separate centre was later established in Australia for the Pacific zone, overlapping with the Asian one.
137 CO 275/119 SSMR 1927, p. 724.
138 CO 273/535/10 Minutes of Proceedings of the International Pacific Health Conference, 15–22 December 1926.
139 CO 273/555/10 League of Nations, Health Organisation, Eastern Bureau, *Annual Report for 1928 and Minutes of the Fourth Session of the Advisory Council.*
140 Brooke, 'A System of Intelligence as a Handmaiden of Hygiene'.
141 CO 275/119 SSMR 1927, p. 723.
142 CO 275/121 SSMR 1928.
143 CO 273/574/12 Memo from A.L. Hoops, 28 March 1931.
144 Tan Joo Lin, *A Review of the Singapore Quarantine Services*, unpublished Master of Science dissertation, University of Singapore, 1979.
145 CO 273/566/7 Memo by A.L. Hoops on the Fifth Session of the Advisory Council of the League of Nations Health Bureau, 7 May 1930.
146 Stefan Hell, 'The Singapore Bureau: Lessons from Asia's First Early Warning System for Epidemic Diseases', *New Mandala*, 6 May 2020, www.newmandala.org/singapore-bureau/
147 CO 273/535/10 Minutes of Proceedings of the International Pacific Health Conference, 15–22 December 1926.
148 CO 275/144 The Quarantine and Prevention of Disease Ordinance (Chapter 186), 14 February 1938.
149 CO 275/150 SSMR 1938.
150 CO 275/153 Appendix: Quarantine and Prevention of Disease Ordinance (Chapter 186).
151 Scharff, 'The Growth of Public Health Services in Singapore'.
152 Goh K.T., *Epidemiological Surveillance of Communicable Diseases in Singapore* (Tokyo: Southeast Asian Medical Information Centre, 1983).
153 Akira Iriye, *Global Community: The Role of International Organisations in the Making of the Contemporary World* (Berkeley: University of California Press, 2002).
154 Singapore Health Department, *Annual Report* (thereafter SHDAR) 1952.
155 CO 275/124 SSMR 1929.
156 CO175/144 The Quarantine and Prevention of Disease Ordinance (Chapter 186), 15 February 1938.
157 CO 275/148 SSMR 1937.
158 Goh, *Epidemiological Surveillance of Communicable Diseases in Singapore.*
159 M. Doraisingham, 'Preventive Measures with Special Reference to Quarantine', *The Medical Journal of Malaya,* Vol. 11 No. 1, September 1956, pp. 76–80.
160 Quah Parry, *A Study of Quarantine Services in Singapore Today*, unpublished dissertation for the Diploma in Public Health, University of Singapore, 1971.
161 Goh, *Epidemiological Surveillance of Communicable Diseases in Singapore.*
162 MOH 024/58/01–000 Vol. 06 Letter from Dr K. Kanagaratnam to the Director-General, World Health Organisation, 12 Sep 1969.
163 SHDAR 1962, p. 28.
164 Goh, *Epidemiological Surveillance of Communicable Diseases in Singapore*, p. 279.
165 Goh, *Epidemiological Surveillance of Communicable Diseases in Singapore.*
166 Quah, *A Study of Quarantine Services in Singapore Today*, p. 15.
167 Quah, *A Study of Quarantine Services in Singapore Today.*

168　MOH 024/58/01–000 Vol. 06 Minutes of the 60th Meeting of the Joint Co-ordinating Committee of Epidemic Diseases, 31 Jan 1980.

169　Tan, *A Review of the Singapore Quarantine Services.*

170　W.G. Huff, *The Economic Growth of Singapore: Trade and Development in the Twentieth Century* (Cambridge; New York: Cambridge University Press, 1994).

171　Goh, *Epidemiological Surveillance of Communicable Diseases in Singapore.*

172　Oral History Centre, National Archives of Singapore, Interview with Dr Sathiamoorthy Ramalingam Sayampanathan, Reel 7, 26 August 1999.

173　Quah, *A Study of Quarantine Services in Singapore Today.*

174　Quah, *A Study of Quarantine Services in Singapore Today.*

175　Goh, *Epidemiological Surveillance of Communicable Diseases in Singapore.*

176　Goh, *Epidemiological Surveillance of Communicable Diseases in Singapore*, p. 279.

177　Goh, *Epidemiological Surveillance of Communicable Diseases in Singapore*, p. 281.

178　*Straits Times*, 21 April 1919, p. 11.

179　Alex Chase-Levenson, *The Yellow Flag: Quarantine and the British Mediterranean World, 1780–1860* (Cambridge: Cambridge University Press, 2020).

# 2 Plague

## An Endemic Sinbad

In 1927, the Medical Department called plague 'one of the endemic "Sinbads" which simmers without flaring up, and is kept alive by a bi-focal epizootic'.[1] This was a revealing statement at a time when the disease was becoming rare in Singapore. To the officials, plague was a border-crossing pandemic disease that had become endemic in the town. It illustrates the high place the disease had in the colonial mind across the 19th and early 20th centuries, regardless of the actual number of cases. Bubonic plague, along with cholera and smallpox (the other Sinbads), formed the trinity of infectious diseases that the British government deemed to be dangerous. It was a severe illness, often fatal, and the threat of an explosive outbreak seemed real in a town characterised by overcrowding and insanitation.

Fears of this universally feared zoonotic disease have a long history. Bubonic plague killed over 25 million people across Europe, Asia and North Africa in the 14th century to earn the epithet, the 'Black Death'. Plague is caused by the bacterium *Yersinia pestis*, which spreads from rodents to humans via the bites of infected fleas. The bubonic form – the form prevalent in Singapore as elsewhere – develops between two to eight days after an infected rodent bites a human. Illness is characterised by fever, weakness and swollen painful lymph nodes called buboes, giving the disease its name. Untreated, the bacteria may spread into the bloodstream (causing septicemic plague) and lungs (pneumonic plague). Even today when plague can be treated with antibiotics, the mortality rate remains high if treatment is started late.

In colonial Singapore, however, plague was arguably not one of the 'Big 3'. The 1930 issue of the *Malayan Medical Journal* noted that local epidemics had been rare.[2] Plague was not really an endemic disease either, with fluctuating numbers (between 5 and 35 cases yearly in the town) in the early 20th century, and there were none after 1933. Tuberculosis and influenza were far more numerous. As a medical doctor noted in 1934, 'In spite of its high mortality plague has had no appreciable effect on the death rate of the town'.[3]

That plague was among the notifiable diseases reflected British anxiety about the vulnerability of an entrepôt port to the transmission of disease along the maritime trade routes. It fixated colonial officials and doctors far beyond its actual incidence. Various theories were propounded to explain its

DOI: 10.4324/9781003384014-3

perceived endemicity, as efforts were made to deal with it. In 1898, the Acting Colonial Secretary C.W.S Kynnersley warned that 'nothing could be more detrimental to British shipping and trade' if a single case of plague occurred 'in this over-crowded community'.[4] It was due to such heightened fears that plague scares became as historically important as outbreaks in Singapore. Some of the most significant developments in plague control took place when no epidemic occurred.

If the British placed a heavy emphasis on plague, the local population related to it in a quite different way. The town where the majority of Asians dwelt was the source of their business, livelihood, residence, and social support. Prior to the scientific breakthroughs in plague research, many Chinese viewed plague as punishment by the gods. Official efforts to track cases and outbreaks often disrupted people's lives and sensibilities. The crude application of quarantine and surveillance aroused widespread social resistance. Not surprisingly, the municipal reports were filled with anguish at the Asians' refusal to inform and cooperate with the authorities. This reinforced the colonial image of the ignorant, recalcitrant native, in effect racialising the disease. Plague was universal, but its history in Singapore was marked by local factors that stemmed from British rule of the Asians.

Despite longstanding non-cooperation, the efforts of the Straits government and Municipal Commission to control the plague succeeded to a large extent. But this was to create a different problem in the long run. The way plague was controlled through the instruments of quarantine and surveillance, with emphasis on its environmental and 'racial' causes, would have a major impact on epidemiological policy in Singapore.

### The 1894 Plague Scare: Disease or Disaster?

Though it was a scare that did not materialise in Singapore, the 1894 plague pandemic in Hong Kong was historically significant. Globally, it was the outbreak that led to the discovery of the bacillus *Yersinia pestis* by Alexandre Yersin. This was followed in 1905 by Dr W.G. Liston's flea theory for the transmission of bubonic plague. Nearly another decade later, researchers established how fleas transmitted the disease – in 1914.[5]

In Singapore, the 1894 outbreak spurred the development of quarantine facilities on St. John's Island.[6] When news of the pandemic reached Singapore in April/May, the Straits government applied the usual practices of the Port of London: inspection, isolation and disinfection. These had been used routinely for prior cases of cholera and smallpox. But on this occasion, the imposition of quarantine was deemed necessary. Ships arriving from Hong Kong were quarantined at St. John's for nine days, one more than the maximum eight days thought to be the incubation period for the bacillus.[7]

During the quarantine, among the 600 odd passengers onboard the *S.S. Pakshan* from the Chinese ports of Swatow and Amoy, a fireman had shown symptoms of bubonic plague several days after boarding the vessel. He was isolated and treated on St. John's, where he recovered after some difficulty. None of the other firemen on the ship who were his close contacts contracted the disease. This led to the view that since the disease did not seem to be contagious outside its endemic area, strict measures could prevent an outbreak onboard a ship. As news that the Hong Kong outbreak was worsening reached the Straits Settlements, the Legislative Council acknowledged the threat posed by Chinese ships carrying large numbers of coolies.[8] The government decided to cease Chinese immigration to the colony altogether on 18 June till 28 September, when the pandemic was declared to be over.[9]

In early July, the Hong Kong Chamber of Commerce petitioned the Straits government on the economic hardship caused by the quarantine. Governor Charles Mitchell replied: 'Regret to say that I cannot under our Quarantine Regulations relax existing arrangements, but they shall not be kept up longer than I can help'.[10] By the time Chinese immigration resumed, the cessation had caused shortages of Chinese labour at the Tanjong Pagar wharves in Singapore and in the tin mines northward in the Malay states of Perak and Selangor.[11] The inspection of all Chinese arrivals to the colony continued till the year's end. The *Singapore Free Press* praised the stringent measures that had averted an even lengthier period of quarantine from the mercantile world should Singapore be declared an infected port.[12]

Such fears of a dangerous Sinbad arriving at the port coincided with concerns about the insanitary state of the town. The latter had long been bemoaned as an entry point for pandemic disease. As early as 1845, a letter to the *Singapore Free Press* wondered 'how we have escaped the plague' given the longstanding failure of the East India Company to invest in municipal improvements.[13] In response to the 1894 plague outbreak, as discussed in the previous chapter, the Municipal Commission introduced new bylaws for cases of dangerous infectious diseases to be reported to the police and for these to be removed to the hospital. Its officers were authorised to inspect, disinfect or close insanitary buildings.[14]

Perceived as the root of the problem at this time were three classes of houses that reportedly could facilitate the spread of plague. The first was the 'very dirty and very filthy' houses such as rickshaw depots for large numbers of single men, which had to be thoroughly cleansed. There were then the large numbers of buildings (presumably shophouses) subdivided into 'lofts and little cells', which besides disinfection required the partitions to be taken down. Finally, there were informal buildings such as cattle sheds and godowns that were in similarly neglected states.[15] A temporary campsite near Mt. Faber near the port was put up for plague cases should the disease enter Singapore.[16] None eventually did. Rumours spread of 'a case or two of plague' in the town, but the commission found them to be groundless.[17]

Writing much later in 1934, Dr C.C.B. Gilmour's doubted if the Municipality's drastic and unnecessary measures in 1894 'prevented a single case of the disease, or hindered an infected rat, or flea from entering the colony'.[18] Singapore remained in constant contact with various infected ports in the next five years yet did not experience any outbreak. In passing the bylaws that year, the Municipal Commission believed that the Hong Kong epidemic had convinced the Chinese community about the peril of a plague outbreak in their midst, especially their customary practice of subdividing shophouse cubicles into smaller cells 'where light never penetrates, and from which the filth is never removed'.[19]

This was a premature conclusion. Municipal efforts to pull down the shophouse partitions were repeatedly frustrated, for the owners would simply put them back up.[20] In 1895, the *Mid-day Herald* reported that most of the preventive measures taken against the plague the previous year had been discontinued.[21] The town's insanitary houses remained, 'each a plague in itself'.[22] But the measures did signal the commission's expanding intervention in the affairs of the town and the lives of its denizens into the 20th century.

These colonial measures were ineffectual largely because the views of the Chinese community towards the plague of 1894 were quite different. The discovery of the plague germ and the flea's role still lay in the future. On 16 May, the local Chinese newspaper *Lat Pau* brought news that disease was ravaging the city of Canton (before spreading to Hong Kong). It distinguished two types of plague and listed herbal remedies for each.[23] But to most Chinese, the solution was to be found beyond the realm of medicine. The following month, the paper urged people to be kind and do good deeds in normal times, not only when there was a plague outbreak. This was apparently the message conveyed from a spirit medium in China, which should be taken to heart as an 'evening drum and morning bell' – a wake-up call for those living immoral lives.[24]

An article in *Lat Pau* argued that plague was not so much a disease as a disaster that required spiritual intervention:

> Western people are realistic. They clean houses or isolate patients; they do what they can do to eliminate disaster. However, the Chinese believe in Gods ... They rely on the power of Gods to eliminate disaster ... the disaster that comes from Heaven cannot be solved by people's efforts. Maybe it is because people do not show enough kindness ... Everyone could do good deeds, such as filial piety to parents, respect the elderly, remove falsehoods and punish evil, be loyal and fair, not to be double-faced, not to harm others for own benefit and so on. In my opinion, these are the most important values that help to eliminate disaster.[25]

Medical interventions, such as setting up more hospitals or providing free medical services and medicine, could only treat the symptoms. It was only by doing good deeds that plague could be cured. But such spiritual injunctions could also be exploited or misused. The *Lat Pau* found itself having to dispel widespread rumours that another outbreak of plague had been divinely foretold.[26]

Singapore's relative freedom from plague at the end of the 19th century was remarkable given the large numbers of immigrants arriving yearly from ports in China, India, Southeast Asia, the Middle East, and Australia. Chinese coolies in particular posed a perennial problem. Those infected with plague were often able to evade detection at the port of departure, while upon landing in Singapore, there were so many of their number in excess of the passenger list that they could easily be smuggled away.[27]

In 1895, among the 325 ships from Amoy, Swatow, Hong Kong, and Haihow inspected, cases of cholera were found but none of plague. Immigration from Chinese ports was again halted in May due to a plague outbreak in Canton and Macao.[28] Another epidemic in Hong Kong in February 1896 saw the London rules of inspection, isolation and disinfection reapplied to vessels from the colony. One case was detected – a Chinese coolie onboard the *S.S. Wingsang* from Hong Kong, who died the following day. Some 175,000 Chinese immigrants were quarantined but the plague did not appear in Singapore's town.[29]

The inspection of Chinese deck passengers for bubonic plague was described in detail in 1899, when the Chinese made allegations of outrage of modesty during the procedure. The work was time-consuming and difficult to perform well due to the sheer number of passengers:

> All saloon passengers are examined in the saloon. Women and children are, as you know, inspected by a woman. The examination of male deck passengers is conducted as follows – The passengers are collected at one part of the deck, the Deputy Health Officer and the Boarding Officer ... station themselves in a narrow part of the ship, generally by the side of the companion, and the passengers pass one by one. Chinese coolies, as you know, are not heavily clad – As a rule each one is dressed in a pair of short cotton Chinese trousers only – Each one also has a jacket, which he sometimes puts on. They do not take off their trousers ... As each one comes up the Deputy Health Officer takes a note of his general appearance, feels his arm or body to ascertain if there is any indication of fever, and feels under his arms in search of swollen glands. The coolie loosens his trousers and lets them down to permit examination of his groins for swollen glands, and then passes on, tying up his trousers as he goes. At the time of exposure he has his back to the rest of the passengers to follow. Any passenger showing any (the least) suspicious signs at this inspection is put on one side for more careful examination afterwards.[30]

Besides the Chinese immigrants, the global eye of the British watch for plague was trained on Muslim pilgrims travelling to or returning from Jeddah on the way to Mecca. This was very much the 'Sinbad' the Medical Department referred to, in its view the greatest source of danger. At the end of the 19th century, the Straits government closely followed news of plague in Jeddah, seemingly prepared to take action to prevent local Malays and Indian Muslims from embarking on the *Haj*. But officials admitted any such move to be impracticable. They had to wait for the Turkish authorities to act and prevent pilgrims from landing if there was an outbreak of plague in Jeddah.[31]

In 1897, after screening over 120,000 passengers from infected Chinese, Indian, and Middle Eastern ports, the quarantine staff found a 'somewhat doubtful' imported case of plague.[32] Several suspected cases resembling bubonic plague were also reported in the town.[33] These instances of 'aborted plague'[34] excited much public comment, especially when they appeared to be linked to cases of sudden death involving persons of means, such as Chettiars.[35] Chinese refrain from reporting cases added to colonial and public anxiety about the likelihood of a devastating outbreak in an unclean town.[36]

In the absence of any confirmed case, the perceived danger turned from imported plague, but local circumstances and habits – the endemic Sinbad of Singapore. Plague figured strongly in the minds of colonial officials and the educated public as a 'filth disease', conflated with deeply rooted issues of urban insanitation and bad housing.[37] In the same year, Governor Mitchell bemoaned the low-lying site of the Tan Tock Seng Hospital (TTSH):

> It seems to me extremely pitiable that such a condition of affairs should be allowed to exist, and I imagine that, if it had been a disease such as cholera or plague that continually broke out amongst the patients, prompt action will have been taken though the death rate in neither of these disease would have been so high., nor the helpless condition of those who did not die so complete as in beri-beri.[38]

March 1898 brought new reports of bubonic plague in Hong Kong, again leading the Straits administration to declare it an infected port and impose another nine-day quarantine on its arrivals to the colony. As the outbreak subsided, the British in Hong Kong asked for the quarantine to be lifted, to which the Straits government replied via telegram,

> Governor much regrets inability to comply your suggestion[,] crowded population here and constant immigration of lowest class Chinese render extreme caution imperative. Quarantine will be worked with every consideration and removed directly you have been clear for prescribed time.[39]

The Hong Kong Chamber of Commerce also protested the quarantine to its Singapore counterpart, which said it could do nothing as the measures were 'fully justified'.[40] The London rules seemed to work. After screening over 500 vessels that year, three cases were found onboard ships from China and quarantined on St. John's. The sick died quickly but did not infect their fellow passengers, who were all inspected for feverish symptoms.[41] The Municipal Commission gave a nil return on plague that year.[42]

In 1899, Singapore was again declared free of plague even as the disease was spreading in China, India and the Straits Settlement of Penang. Ten cases were found on ships bound for Singapore, of whom eight died, but all were detected at St. John's and isolated.[43] The Captain of the *Marqis Bacquehem*, with over 600 Chinese passengers onboard, was convicted of violating the quarantine regulations. He had failed to report a case of plague on his vessel, delegating the inspection work to a number of 'assistant cooks', while the ship doctor conducted no checks of his own unless cases were brought to him by the assistants. In his defence, the captain protested that it was impossible to examine so many coolies onboard his ship.[44]

In the same year, the Straits government laid down the three possible courses of action for the mercantile community should an outbreak of plague occur in the town: the prohibited export of goods, disinfection of goods prior to export or inaction, which could spur a major reaction from the government.[45] The Chamber of Commerce reluctantly took the second option as the least of the evils.[46] The Municipal Commission deemed it prudent to count the number of dead rats in the streets in case the disease found its way into Singapore.[47] By the end of the 19th century, plague had established itself as a quarantinable and notifiable disease in Singapore.

## Recurrent Disease of Filth

The early 20th century saw a turn in the history of plague. The seaward surveillance continued and the London measures continued to prevent the entry of plague.[48] A trend became discernible: a small number of cases were discovered and duly quarantined on St. John's Island. But the situation in the town was changing. There were now actual cases and outbreaks, comprising isolated cases distributed across different months of the year. It was difficult to establish connections between the cases because the patients and contacts usually did not provide accurate information. There was no clear link between the quarantine system and the town's cases. Whether the municipal cases were imported due to gaps in the surveillance net, or endemic, spread by rats amid the filth of the town, was a question that puzzled British officials.

There remained a gulf between colonial and local responses. In late 19th-century India, as David Arnold notes, the British viewed plague as the most serious disease, but Indians did not see it the same way. Because efforts to prevent the spread of plague there were imposed from above, they were often more disruptive to the population than the outbreaks themselves. Driven by biomedical expertise and international sanitary regulations, these efforts ignored local opinion and social institutions such as caste and religion. Indians came to view measures such as physical examination and isolation as an assault on their bodies by the colonial power. This aroused resistance and rumours about the true intentions of the policies.[49] India's experience has resonance with Singapore, where the vast majority of cases were Chinese. The British could not obtain reliable information on plague while rumours of suspected cases circulated among the population. Both the Chinese middle and working classes actively resisted the official controls.

The crux of the problem lay in the official measures. A letter to the press in 1905 bemoaned how sanitary bylaws undermined local cooperation:

> Take it that an ordinarily well-to-do Chinaman reports a case of plague at his house. The person suffering from the disease will be removed to St. John's, the bedding, clothing or other articles likely to retain infection will be destroyed, he and the other members of his family will be segregated for some time, his business will suffer in his absence and his house will be disinfected and locked up for at least a fortnight.[50]

The year 1900 saw the first confirmed case of plague in Singapore. In the early months of the year, the colonial regime monitored outbreaks in a number of regional ports. In June, following two months of indecision after another outbreak in Hong Kong, the Straits government decided to halt Chinese coolie immigration.[51] Colonial officials passed the Plague Ordinance and were happy to announce the absence of the disease in the colony.[52]

But on Christmas Day two deaths from bubonic plague were discovered, both immigrants from China. One case was detected at St. John's onboard the *S.S. Hong Wan I* in quarantine carrying over 900 passengers from Amoy and Swatow; he died on the island.[53] But the other patient, a 32-year-old coolie, managed to escape to Singapore, making his way to Ellenborough Market in the densely populated Chinese section of the town. He was found and removed to St. John's the same day, dying there shortly. This was possible only because a fortune-teller had the wit to predict great wealth for a rick-shaw puller if he conveyed the man to a hospital. After bringing the patient to TTSH's gates, the puller left and remained at large. The port health unit was absolved of culpability for both slips.[54] Subsequently, the Municipality attempted to exterminate rats in the town, offering three cents for every rat killed.[55] Such efforts, common in many countries, likely backfired, forcing fleas to seek human hosts when the rat population declined.[56] As the President of the Municipal Commission warned, high rewards also encouraged the breeding of rats.[57]

Singapore was to rue the slips. The events of December contributed to a significant epidemic the following February and March. Two fatal cases were found on St. John's, but more serious were 14 others, mostly fatal, discovered in the town. All of the dead save one were males, comprising nine Chinese, six Indians and one Japanese. Ominously, six cases were discovered after death – proof that the community had not notified the government. The *Straits Times* urged that the houses of the cases be burnt.[58] The dead were buried in a special cemetery in Yio Chu Kang, a rural area far from the town. More than 60 cases were admitted to the hospital on suspicion of infection, but most were eventually cleared.[59] Singapore was declared an infected port by the governments of the Dutch East Indies and British Burma, while immigration from Hong Kong was halted till early August.

The outbreak spanned different districts of the town, though this was not useful information as many cases were likely moved from their dwellings. It was especially severe in the southern part of Chinatown where Straits Chinese of a better economic class dwelt. The Municipality moved to disinfect or demolish the affected houses, inoculate a large number of contacts, using Haffkine's serum, and isolate them at St. John's. But many other contacts had already fled their houses. The Municipal Commission continued to attack the rat population, with over 140,000 rats destroyed, and remove cows from the infected districts to a newly erected cattle shed. The commissioners believed they had stemmed the epidemic.[60] Governor James Alexander Swettenham, who reported to the Colonial Office in late March that the outbreak had been swiftly suppressed by the Medical Department's 'indefatigable exertions', assured that its recrudescence was unlikely.[61]

But the epidemic was not yet contained, for four fatal cases surfaced in the town the following year. The epidemiological evidence was troubling. Among the quartet of cases, one was a Chettiar from Market Street, occupied by the well-off Indian moneylending community and the scene of cases the previous year. Some Chettiars tried to prevent the closure of shops along the street by removing the body to a hut in Geylang on the eastern side of the town. The Chinese doctor who held back his report from the government till the body was relocated was fined $100 for his part in this 'most deliberate attempt' to mislead the authorities.[62] The Municipality ordered 'extensive alterations' to poorly ventilated houses along Market Street, straining relations with the community.[63] Despite the attempt at deceit by upper-class residents, Gilmour felt assured that the Municipality would not have missed other cases of plague.[64]

On the outbreak in his area of responsibility, the Municipal Health Officer W.R.C. Middleton alluded to fundamental cultural differences:

> The prevention and suppression of outbreaks of Zymotic Disease is always a matter of greater difficulty in countries a large population of whose population consists than in countries where the knowledge of the dangers of infectious disease is more general, where qualified medical aid is more largely available and more readily sought, where concealment is less common and where early information of the existence of cases is consequently more generally forthcoming. While therefore it would have been more pleasing to have had to record a reduction at least in the number of cases of Zymotic Diseases for the year, it is still a matter for congratulation that the returns for the City should compare favourably with those supplied from surrounding places in which the constitution of the population and other conditions are more or less comparable with those obtaining here.[65]

Middleton's assessment absolved the administration while fixing the blame on social ignorance. As we have seen, it was the adverse consequences of complying with the notification system that discouraged people's cooperation with the authorities. The end result was continuing outbreaks of plague in the town in the next few years.

1903 saw 'a rather severe' epidemic on at St. John's, with 136 cases detected as plague raged in Hong Kong and Amoy.[66] Some coolies under quarantine tried to swim away from the island before they were caught.[67] But 25 deaths were reported in Singapore that year, with three occurring in the town. The Municipal Commission admitted it could not establish the origins of the trio of cases, which were found in different areas.[68] They were not recent arrivals, all having been in Singapore for over a year. The commission disinfected the store where one of the cases, a Chinese girl, was found and burned its contents publicly in the street.[69] The authorities took the outbreak as evidence that the quarantine system was sound. The Medical Department lauded the quarantine staff for 'their vigilance and care in carrying on their arduous and responsible work'.[70]

But belying the positive narrative were the recurring cases in the town. In 1904, St. John's dealt with six ships infected with plague and eight imported (and fatal) cases.[71] But the situation was more serious in the Municipality. As in the previous year, the commission could not trace the source of infection among the 20 deaths from bubonic plague, comprising 17 Chinese and three Indians of the coolie class. But it was a big increase from the previous year and one case was a nine-year-old Chinese female, again from Market Street.[72] Four of the cases were traders, while eight were discovered only after death. Sick individuals had again been removed from their premises to avoid implicating the neighbourhood, so cases were pinned to different parts of the town. Ten Chinese tailors and shopkeepers were charged with failure to notify one case at Pekin Street.[73] The Municipality reported that the patients and their friends lied about whether their illness was local or imported, and how they might have contracted it. The Protector of Chinese – a colonial official who oversaw Chinese affairs – was also unable to trace the infections.[74] Ten Chinese escaped from a coolie house before they could be sent to St. John's for observation.[75] Singapore was again declared an infected port.

In 1905, there were 19 municipal cases, spread across all months of the year except November. The Municipal Commission again did not know the source of infection, continuing to bemoan the unreliable information from patients and contacts. It was thought unlikely that rats were the cause as no sick or dead specimens had been found on the premises.[76] Such thinking was flawed as the bodies could have been moved. The following year, the number of fatalities in the town fell to 10, none of whom were new arrivals, while 105 contacts were isolated at St. John's.[77] Examination of several hundred rats failed to reveal any evidence of infection. In 1907, a proposal to form a special department to catch rats was rejected, as only three specimens out of 1,035 were shown to have chronic plague that year.[78]

Among the 12 cases of plague in 1908 were Dr C.T. Raikes, the Resident Medical Officer on St. John's, and the Assistant Surgeon Dr N.A. Wray; both men contracted the disease while performing a post-mortem at St. John's and died.[79] Three years later, a big jump from five to 33 cases saw Singapore declared an infected port for plague once more by the Dutch East Indies government. The Municipal Commission documented particularly serious outbreaks in the months of November and December, which caused 'some anxiety'. Again, some rats were found to be infected with plague, but the commission remained unsure if the disease was endemic in the town.[80] It welcomed the government's decision to build a new infectious diseases hospital which would have a section for plague.

Plague cases remained high at 37 (with 33 fatalities) in 1912. The commission decided that year that peons would no longer accompany sanitary inspectors on their rounds. The inspectors had made 136,000 checks, leading to 8,350 convictions for insanitary issues that year. But residents had become unhappy at the culturally invasive work:

> the more energetic an officer in interfering with the insanitary habits of centuries the more unpopular with, and therefore liable to be falsely accused by, those whose customs he upsets, he is bound to be.[81]

There was also an economic dimension to the issue. The peons served as middlemen in the locals' attempts to bribe the inspectors, so their removal helped reduce allegations of corruption.[82] The bribery cast doubt on the effectiveness of municipal surveillance.

The new Infectious Diseases Hospital at Moulmein Road was completed in 1913. One of its three sections was reserved for plague but its capacity was more modest than originally planned. The government did not anticipate plague cases to be as numerous as smallpox, the only fully built section. The following year, the hospital treated five plague patients (three of whom died) during two outbreaks of the disease, one of them occurring in TTSH. There were a total of 15 cases in Singapore, again distributed in different parts of the town. Whether they were local or imported could not be ascertained, though Hong Kong had been declared an infected port in February.[83] The outbreak continued into mid-1915, causing 34 cases and a great deal of anxiety.[84] In 1917, when 45 cases (39 fatalities) surfaced, the Municipal Commission complained that 'the usual difficulty was experienced in getting information in connection with the cases'.[85]

In 1918, before the first wave of the influenza pandemic swept into Singapore, there was a large outbreak of plague in the town in the first two months of the year. It was initially thought that the outbreak had some unstipulated effect on the influenza, which the commission eventually dismissed. A record 176 cases and 160 fatalities of plague were reported, mostly of the Chinese: 73 were discovered only after death. Infected rats and fleas were found in stores and shops selling food, though 1.39% of the rats examined were found to be infected with plague.

While the Straits government claimed that 'The outbreak of plague did not assume alarming proportions', it was a serious epidemic, proof of non-cooperation on a big scale.[86] This was despite information on the disease being translated into Chinese and circulated to the community.[87] The epidemic spread widely, aided by the lack of cooperation from residents and doctors. The first patient admitted to the TTSH merely said he was from 10th Mile Thomson Road, which the Municipal Commission recognised as a 'favourite form of false address', because it was far from the town and would not implicate the locals.[88] In some cases, patients had been taken out of their accommodation or evicted, as they were found wandering on the streets: 17 dead bodies were dumped in the streets and other public spaces, while one case was found in Ulu Pandan beyond municipal limits.[89] As the *Singapore Free Press* observed, 'Concealment is common, and also the removal of patients from one place to another to "avoid trouble" in the house'.[90]

The commissioners believed that the outbreak began at the Tanjong Pagar Docks before moving northward to the rice godowns of the Singapore River, where it lingered and spread. Both areas were densely populated arrival points for immigrants and goods. Whereas in past outbreaks, patients had absconded from the old Infectious Diseases Hospital at Balestier Road, this crisis was so serious that one patient had climbed the fence surrounding the new hospital at Moulmein Road to get in. The hospital admitted a record 66 cases of plague (50 died), the commission inoculated 2,621 contacts, while government buildings were disinfected.[91]

By this time, Chinese public opinion on plague had drawn closer to biomedicine. How fleas transmitted the sickness to humans had been discovered four years earlier. The *Lat Pau*, having criticised Western medicine as superficial in 1894, published the Chinese Chamber of Commerce's translation of the official statement on the 1918 outbreak. The statement urged the Chinese to support government measures such as cleansing houses and not storing food inside to avoid attracting mice. Mice should be trapped and handed over to the Municipality, which should also be notified of people with fever and swollen lymph nodes. It is wrong, the statement emphasised, for people living close to the infected person to run away from the dwelling.[92] This was the beginning of the transformation of Chinese understanding of plague in the 20th century.

## A Mystery of Rat Fleas and the Climate

Still, the flea theory could not answer all questions on the incidence of plague in Singapore. In 1923, the new Municipal Health Officer P.S. Hunter noted 'several disquieting features' among the 52 cases of plague that year.[93] The majority had no clear connection to one another, as in previous years. Hunter thought that while plague was believed to be imported, it was more likely to be endemic in the town. He proffered a new explanation that would replace the theory of filth. In 1914, scientists established the role of fleas in the transmission of bubonic plague. Hunter pointed to the *Xenopsylla cheopis* flea (the Oriental rat flea) that was common in the town. As to why human outbreaks were not more frequent or serious, he ventured:

> There must be some protective mechanism of which, as yet, we know nothing, and one day that protection may break down. It is essential therefore that we should have all the information it is possible to get, of our rat population and its flea infestation.[94]

Accordingly, Hunter launched a small campaign to trap rats in October. Initially, there was little response from the public, but this soon improved. His office started studying fleas, which by 1933 showed that the number of fleas per rat in the town was small, ranging from 3.7 to 1.0. The studies suggested that the fleas were established in certain parts of the town and specifically in some houses. One such place was reportedly the plague ward in the Middleton Hospital, where C.C.B. Gilmour saw 'hordes of fleas jumping on the floor'! He traced the fleas to musang cats (the Asian palm civet) living on the roof of the ward.[95]

In 1924, the Municipal Health Office began to burn attap houses suspected of rat infestation and plague in Serangoon Road as the rat campaign expanded. The action had been taken as it was deemed impossible to disinfect the houses, although, as the office admitted, there was no clear connection between the cases in different houses. This was based on residents' testimony that 'many dead rats had been found a little time previously in the district'. The houses were 'mere hovels with mud floors', fenced up to prevent the rats from escaping and then incinerated.[96] No further cases of plague occurred in the area. However, the office deemed the rat extermination campaign to be ineffective as there was abundant food enabling the rat population to quickly recover.

Like Middleton before him, Hunter felt that the root of the problem was ignorance and apathy, which made addressing it

> anything but easy in Singapore with its back-to-back, internal drained houses which inter-communicate in such a way that rat plague can spread with impunity over a whole block where many of the ground floors of domestic dwellings are full to overflowing with goods of same description, often food supplies, so that the work of disinfection and disinfestation is well nigh impossible, where food is allowed to be prepared in any insanitary coolie house and hawked about the streets without let or hindrance, where the conditions of overcrowding are so terrible that the wonder is not that we have so few cases of plague, but rather that so many escape it, and where most efforts directed at improving conditions generally are met with apathy if not opposition.[97]

But the rat trapping campaign had to continue, Hunter explained, because rat plague had taken root in many parts of the town and the unknown protection might dissipate at some point. Over 1,200 rats were examined that year, none showing any signs of plague. But the bacteriologist thought it unlikely that many infected rats would be alive to be trapped. Most of the rat fleas were found to be of the *X. cheopis* species, apparently the 'chief and most effective transmitter of plague in this part of the world'.[98]

An increase to 59 human cases (53 deaths) in the first half of 1925 appeared to bring further proof that plague was being spread by local rats, rather than by ships. Most of the cases were found in one district, the South Division, where 11 out of the 12 plague rats had been caught. None were imported. P.S. Hunter considered it 'bewildering' that despite favourable circumstances in the town, no epidemic had occurred. He speculated that the number of fleas on the rats was kept small by the tropical climate and possibly also because some of the rats had developed immunity to the disease. The danger lay in 'a long continued spell of cool weather'.[99] He assured the Municipal Commission that 'though they [the plague cases] are causing him a little anxiety there is no cause for serious alarm'.[100]

Hunter's theory was not new. In 1911, the Government Pathologist Dr George Finlayson had told the Straits Quarantine Commission,

> Personally I do not think plague in Singapore is a thing of very high important on account of the fact that the rat-flea does not breed well in this particular climate. It has been found that in a mean temperature of 80 to 85 degrees the rat-flea breeds very badly.[101]

The source of such thinking would have been the British experience in India, where the incidence of bubonic plague since the 1890s was found to be lower than in Manchuria and attributed to higher temperatures.[102] But the hypothesis was by no means universally held. Writing on the Straits Settlements in 1905, Dr C.W. Daniels had argued,

> As regards diseases introduced affecting human beings, the most severe, plague and cholera have never been wide-spread, through introduced over and over again. The cause of this we cannot explain. Neither the elaborate precautions taken nor the temperature will explain it.[103]

In 1934, Dr Gilmour proposed a multi-factorial explanation, noting that the *X. cheopis* flea did not breed well among *Mus decumanus* (*Rattus norvegicus* or the common brown rat), the rat species prevalent in the town. This was possibly because ants might have destroyed the eggs or larvae or competed for their food. He concluded, 'The flea population varies considerably in different parts of the town and unknown local conditions may account for this'.[104] The flea-climate theory became the government's accepted opinion in the inter-war years.

When the number of human cases fell to seven in 1926, this was 'doubtless due to the unusual heat'.[105] The following year, the number of fatalities dropped further to three, prompting the Straits government to describe plague an endemic Sinbad.[106] It noted that the disease passed by Singapore in 1894 and only once became an epidemic, in 1900 (ignoring the 1918 epidemic). The morbidity of plague remained low till the outbreak of war in Malaya in 1941. 'We are to be congratulated on our luck', Hunter declared in 1930, when the Municipality enjoyed a record year free of plague, cholera and smallpox.[107] The town population's immunity seemed to rest on the relatively small number of fleas – 60 fleas to 100 rats.[108] One fatality surfaced in 1933, the year oft-cited as the last case of plague in Singapore. Nevertheless, a Plague

Prevention Unit was formed that year.[109] On the eve of the Pacific War, the Chief Health Officer J.W. Scharff held that the disease 'has done little here to deserve association with its companion diseases, small-pox and cholera'.[110]

At the time it was diminishing in the town, plague was receiving international attention from the experts. This was possibly linked to broader interest at the League of Nations' Eastern Epidemiological Bureau. In its inaugural meeting in Singapore, the Advisory Council proposed that expert committees be formed to draw up programmes of study for the epidemiology of plague and other serious diseases in the region.[111] Citing difficulties in coordinating such programmes, the council decided to form only one priority committee on bubonic and pneumonic plague, noting the need for accurate information on infected rats. In its first meeting in 1927, the committee laid out its research on the roles of rats, fleas and ship fauna in the transmission of plague, their control and therapeutics and vaccines for the disease.[112] The bureau declared two years later that plague research was 'being continued steadily in several countries', especially India and Japan.[113] It is unclear if the research corroborated the climate theory for the lack of cases in Singapore.

## Unceasing Vigilance After the War

The end of the Pacific War saw the continuation of such epidemiological thinking. 'The right rat here is here, the flea is here', Dr J.H. Strahan wrote in 1948, though fortunately the local rat population was small and the temperature and humidity high.[114] As official and public attention turned to other diseases, plague did not resurface in post-war Singapore. But the illness retained its place as a quarantinable disease in the Quarantine and Prevention of Disease Ordinance, ahead of 'minor' infectious infections such as tuberculosis, poliomyelitis, diphtheria and malaria. It remained a dangerous infectious disease in the 1976 Infectious Diseases Act that replaced the ordinance, and remains so at the time of writing.[115]

In the early 1980s, Dr Goh Kee Tai, Head of the Quarantine and Epidemiology Department at the Ministry of the Environment, still viewed plague as a menace that could find its way into Singapore through infected ships. This was even though quarantine procedures were no longer the chief way to protect the republic from imported infections. In 1980, although port clearance for ships was simplified by radio pratique, those arriving from infected ports still had to be boarded and cleared. In mid-1975, the Joint Co-ordinating Committee on Epidemic Diseases, responsible for the control of communicable diseases in Singapore, had strongly objected to the Ministry of Defence (Mindef)'s supposedly 'relaxed' attitude in allowing boats carrying Vietnamese refugees to berth at the wharves without prior fumigation.[116] The committee was similarly unhappy with the Mindef and Ministry of Home Affairs' response to another group of Vietnamese refugees who crash-landed on the island four years later.[117]

Goh knew the history of plague in colonial Singapore. In his mind, three issues stood out: the Hong Kong scare of 1894, the difficulty of preventing plague's entry into Singapore and the high mortality rate in the early 20th century. In the region, plague was still endemic in Burma, Vietnam, China and Democratic Kampuchea in the early 1980s; hence, 'In view of the proximity of Singapore to the plague endemic countries, special precautionary measures have to be taken to prevent the introduction of the disease into the country'.[118] Another study echoed this position: though last seen in 1933, plague could sporadically recur due to Singapore's openness to maritime and air traffic.[119]

If the past is an account of plague's peril and the present proof of its persistent threat, then to advocates like Goh, history offers the appropriate response. The solution was not quarantine, which had been the main colonial response but deemed outmoded in the 1970s. Rather, epidemiological surveillance was a superior form of disease prevention and control that would build an effective home defence, as discussed in the previous chapter. Goh emphasised 'The system of plague surveillance in Singapore has proved effective in preventing the introduction of the disease into the country since 1933'.[120] There would be continuing vigilance towards the entry of rats and fleas from infected ports; suspected cases of plague; the surveillance, control and dissection of rodents and fleas; and ship sanitation.[121]

But despite the new epidemiology, continuities in disease control were evident, adapted to post-colonial circumstances and technologies. Ships had to be inspected and fumigated if rodent infestation was detected onboard. Vietnamese refugees were a special case that had to be screened for plague before being allowed to disembark, while when a suspected case was found, all passengers and crew had to be quarantined. Conversely, the flea index at four port and coastal stations at the Singapore River, Singapore International Airport, Beach Road and Jalan Besar were systematically monitored.[122] The 8th Malaysia-Singapore Border Health Conference in November 1979 discussed plague as one of the major infections, alongside malaria, dengue, tuberculosis, typhoid and the problem of air pollution.[123]

In 1993, the *Epidemiological News Bulletin* named plague among imported infectious diseases that had been effectively controlled, with the last case reported 60 years ago when the Plague Prevention Unit was formed. This success was attributed to Singapore's robust home defences, built around a basket of measures: high standards of environmental sanitation, vector control and food hygiene, continued vigilance through nation-wide notification and epidemiological surveillance, public education on travel-related infections and the screening of migrant workers.[124]

When an outbreak of plague occurred in India the following year, the Singapore Ministry of Health responded strongly. A Plague Task Force was formed to prevent and control possible outbreaks on the island, while a health alert notice was issued to passengers and crew arriving from India. Medical practitioners in Singapore were reminded to notify suspected cases to the Ministry of the Environment, while wards at the Communicable Disease Centre were identified for plague patients should an outbreak occur. The public was advised not to travel to the infected areas.[125] The CDC received calls from a hundred-odd worried people who had recently travelled to India or intended to do so.[126] The official response was as assured as it was vigorous – plague was dangerous but Singapore knew what to do.

The historical significance of plague in Singapore far exceeded the number of deaths or outbreaks. To colonial administrators and doctors, it was an endemic Sinbad, a deadly disease that took advantage of the island's openness to the world. They made continual efforts to inspect infected ships, quarantine passengers, survey the streets and houses of the town, and punish locals who failed to cooperate. In parallel, the officials tried to explain what seemed contradictory: there were some cases occurring in some parts of the town but an absence of major epidemics. They deployed theories to explain this which dwelt on environmental factors like overcrowding and climate, but which also emphasised Asian apathy.

The history of plague cases, outbreaks, scares, rumours, theories, and responses belies a longstanding colonial concern with the trinity of infectious diseases. This concern was reinforced by people's reluctance to notify cases to the authorities, which only changed after Singapore's independence. In the post-colonial years, plague remained a notifiable disease, with updated methods of control adapted to the new system of epidemiological surveillance. As with cholera and smallpox, plague helped forge a strong epidemiological tradition in Singapore. It seemingly provided precedent and clarity for how Singapore should deal with the threat of pandemic disease – which infectious diseases merited close scrutiny and what might be done to keep the city-state safe from them. In the age of COVID-19, it may be timely to relook the principles upon which such considerations are made. There is a need to adapt epidemiological policy and make it more agile to deal with the emerging diseases of our times. In this, the history of notifiable diseases like plague is a useful guide.

## Notes

1  CO 275/119 SSMR 1927, p. 732.
2  'Historical Synopsis of Preventive Medicine in Singapore', *The Malayan Medical Journal*, Vol. V, 1930, pp. 97–102.
3  C.C.B. Gilmour, 'Bubonic Plague, Rats and Fleas in Singapore', *The Malayan Medical Journal*, Vol. IX, 1934, pp. 177–181.
4  CO 273/235 Memo from C.W.S Kynnersley, Acting Colonial Secretary, to the Colonial Secretary, Hong Kong, 22 March 1898.
5  Gilmour, 'Bubonic Plague, Rats and Fleas in Singapore', p. 178.
6  Quah Parry, *A Study of Quarantine Services in Singapore Today*, unpublished dissertation for the Diploma in Public Health, University of Singapore, 1971.
7  CO 275/49 AMRCHSS 1894.
8  *Singapore Free Press*, 26 June 1894, p. 390.
9  CO 275/49 AMRCHSS 1894.

10  *Straits Times*, 10 July 1894, p. 3.
11  *Singapore Free Press*, 25 September 1894, p. 329.
12  *Singapore Free Press*, 26 June 1894, p. 381.
13  *Singapore Free Press*, 20 November 1845, p. 2.
14  SMAR 1894, Appendix F.
15  *Singapore Free Press*, 26 June 1894, p. 386.
16  *Singapore Free Press*, 19 June 1894, p. 371.
17  *Singapore Free Press*, 10 July 1894, p. 11.
18  Gilmour, 'Bubonic Plague, Rats and Fleas in Singapore', p. 177.
19  SMAR 1894, p. 10.
20  Brenda S.A. Yeoh, *Contesting Space in Colonial Singapore: Power Relations and the Urban Built Environment* (Singapore: Singapore University Press, 2003), 2nd edition.
21  *Mid-day Herald*, 16 September 1895, p. 2.
22  *Mid-day Herald*, 8 May 1895, p. 2.
23  *Lat Pau*, 16 May 1894, p. 5.
24  *Lat Pau*, 20 June 1894, p. 5; 21 June 1894, p. 2.
25  *Lat Pau*, 26 June 1894, p. 1.
26  *Lat Pau*, 27 June 1894, p. 2.
27  CO 273/248 Memo to Joseph Chamberlain, Colonial Office, 4 August 1899.
28  CO 275/50 AMRCHSS 1895.
29  CO 275/53 AMRCHSS 1896.
30  CO 273/247 Memo from Max. F. Simon to Sir James Swettenham, 27 April 1899.
31  CO 273/232 Memo by W. Macnaghten, 17 June 1897; Memo by E.W., 17 June 1897.
32  CO 275/55 AMRCHSS 1897, p. 451.
33  CO 275/55 AMRCHSS 1897.
34  *Straits Times*, 21 December 1897, p. 2.
35  *Singapore Free Press*, 19 January 1897, p. 13. The Chettiars were well-known as a moneylending class.
36  *Singapore Free Press*, 2 March 1897, p. 6.
37  *Straits Times*, 21 January 1897, p. 2.
38  CO 275/55 AMRCHSS 1897, p. 416.
39  CO 275/56 Colonial Secretary, S.S. to Colonial Secretary, Hong Kong, 12 March 1898, p. C-40.
40  CO 275/56 Chamber of Commerce, Singapore, to Chamber of Commerce, Hongkong, 14 March 1896.
41  CO 275/57 SSMR 1898.
42  SMAR 1898.
43  CO 275/59 SSMR 1899.
44  *Singapore Free Press*, 25 May 1899, p. 2.
45  CO 275/58 Colonial Secretary, S.S. to Secretary, Chamber of Commerce, Singapore, 19 September 1899.
46  CO 275/58 Secretary, Chamber of Commerce, Singapore, to Colonial Secretary, S.S., 10 October 1899.
47  SMAR 1899.
48  'Historical Synopsis of Preventive Medicine in Singapore'.
49  David Arnold, *Colonising the Body: State Medicine and Epidemic Disease in Nineteenth-Century India* (Berkeley: University of California Press, 1993).
50  *Singapore Free Press*, 19 January 1905, p. 40.
51  CO 275/62 Minutes of Proceedings of the Executive Council, 6 June 1900.
52  *Straits Times*, 11 July 1900, p. 3.
53  CO 275/61 SSMR 1900; *Straits Times*, 29 December 1900, p. 3.

54  CO 273/268 Memo from W. Egerton, Acting Colonial Secretary, to Sir F.A. Swettenham, 26 December 1900; *Straits Times*, 29 December 1900, p. 3.
55  SMAR 1900.
56  Bollet, *Plagues & Poxes.*
57  *Singapore Free Press*, 22 March 1900, p. 21.
58  *Straits Times*, 25 February 1901, p. 2.
59  CO 275/64 SSMR 1901.
60  SMAR 1901.
61  CO 273/493 Memo from F.A. Swettenham to Joseph Chamberlain, Colonial Office, 23 March 1901.
62  SMAR 1902, p. 23; *Singapore Free Press*, 18 September 1900, p. 178.
63  SMAR 1902, p. 23.
64  Gilmour, 'Bubonic Plague, Rats and Fleas in Singapore'.
65  SMAR 1902, p. 124.
66  CO 275/68 SSMR 1903, p. 733.
67  *Straits Times*, 15 July 1903, p. 5.
68  SMAR 1903.
69  *Straits Times*, 7 May 1903, p. 4.
70  CO 275/68 SSMR 1903, p. 682.
71  CO 275/70 SSMR 1904.
72  *Straits Times*, 3 December 1904, p. 5.
73  *Singapore Free Press*, 19 October 1904, p. 244.
74  SMAR 1904.
75  *Straits Times*, 3 December 1904, p. 5.
76  SMAR 1905.
77  CO 275/74 SSMR 1906, p. 395.
78  SMAR 1907.
79  CO 275/79 SSMR 1908; J.W. Scharff, 'The Growth of Public Health Services in Singapore in Relation to Preventive Medicine in War Time', *Journal of the Malayan Branch of the British Medical Association*, Vol. 3. No. 3, December 1939.
80  SMAR 1907, p. 13.
81  SMAR 1912, p. 14.
82  SMAR 1912.
83  CO 275/94 SSMR 1914.
84  SMAR 1915.
85  SMAR 1917, p. 4.
86  CO 275/101 SSMR 1918, p. 516.
87  *Singapore Free Press*, 28 February 1918, p. 136.
88  SMAR 1918, p. 8.
89  CO 275/101 SSMR 1918.
90  *Singapore Free Press*, 14 February 1918, p. 104.
91  SMAR 1918.
92  *Lat Pau*, 16 February 1918, p. 3; 18 February 1918, p. 3; 19 February 1918, p. 3.
93  SMAR 1923, p. 3-D.
94  SMAR 1923, p. 3-D.
95  Gilmour, 'Bubonic Plague, Rats and Fleas in Singapore', p. 181.
96  SMAR 1924, p. 3-D.
97  SMAR 1924, p. 3-D.
98  SMAR 1924, p. 62-D.
99  SMAR 1925, p. 4–5-D; CO 275/114 SSMR 1925.
100 Singapore Municipality, Minutes of Committee No. 2 Meeting, 7 April 1925.
101 Evidence by Dr George Alexander Finlayson, Government Pathologist, *Proceedings of the Commission Appointed to Inquire into the Working of the Quarantine and Prevention of Diseases Ordinance in the Settlement of Singapore, in the*

*Colony of the Straits Settlements*, 2 volumes (Singapore: Government Printing Office, 1912), Vol. 2, p. 51.

102   Mark Honigsbaum, *The Pandemic Century: A History of Global Contagion from the Spanish Flu to COVID-19* (London: W.H. Allen, 2020).

103   C.W. Daniels, 'The Diffusion of Disease', *Journal of the Malayan Branch of the British Medical Association*, December 1905, p. 26.

104   Gilmour, 'Bubonic Plague, Rats and Fleas in Singapore', p. 181.

105   CO 275/117 SSMR 1926, p. 375.

106   CO 275/119 SSMR 1927, p. 732.

107   SMAR 1930, p. 3-D.

108   SMAR 1932.

109   SMAR 1933.

110   Scharff, 'The Growth of Public Health Services in Singapore', p. 344.

111   CO 275/117 SSMR 1926.

112   CO 275/121 SSMR 1928; R. Gautier, 'The Eastern Bureau of the League of Nations' Health Organisation; Its Aims and Achievements', *The Malayan Medical Journal*, Vol. V, 1930, pp. 81–85.

113   CO 275/124 SSMR 1929, p. 660.

114   J.H. Strahan, 'Reflections on the Course of Preventive Medicine in Malaya', *The Medical Journal of Malaya*, Vol. 2 No. 4, June 1948.

115   Singapore Statutes Online, *Infectious Diseases Act 1976*, https://sso.agc.gov.sg/Act/IDA1976

116   Goh K.T., *Epidemiological Surveillance of Communicable Diseases in Singapore* (Tokyo: Southeast Asian Medical Information Centre, 1983), p. 5.

117   Goh, *Epidemiological Surveillance of Communicable Diseases in Singapore.*

118   Goh, *Epidemiological Surveillance of Communicable Diseases in Singapore.*

119   Quah, *A Study of Quarantine Services in Singapore Today*; Tan Joo Lin, *A Review of the Singapore Quarantine Services*, unpublished Master of Science dissertation, University of Singapore, 1979.

120   MOH 024/58/01–000 Vol. 06 'Prevention of Introduction of Plague into Singapore', undated, p. 3.

121   Goh, *Epidemiological Surveillance of Communicable Diseases in Singapore*, p. 155.

122   Goh, *Epidemiological Surveillance of Communicable Diseases in Singapore; Epidemiological News Bulletin* (thereafter *ENB*), Vol. 6 No. 23, March 1980.

123   Ministry of the Environment, *Annual Report* (thereafter ENVAR) 1972.

124   *ENB* Vol. 19 No. 1, January 1993.

125   *ENB* Vol. 20 No. 9, September 1994.

126   *Straits Times*, 29 September 1994.

# 3 Smallpox

## Racialising the Epidemic

Smallpox was the second of the trio of what were considered to be dangerous infectious diseases in colonial Singapore. The disease is caused by the variola virus, a member of the Orthopoxvirus genus which also contains cowpox and monkeypox. Like plague, smallpox was an ancient and much feared affliction. It had existed for at least 3,000 years, causing periodic epidemics that killed millions of people before finally declared eradicated in 1980. The disease had an incubation period of approximately two weeks, presenting initially as high fever and body aches before the appearance of characteristic pustular rash. Over 10 per cent of infected individuals would die within two weeks of the onset of smallpox.

For much of colonial Singapore, smallpox was more prevalent than plague, causing an epidemic every ten years or so. Nevertheless, British concerns about smallpox were also arguably greater than the number of cases and deaths. Like plague, it had an impact on colonial health policy out of proportion to its actual threat. Smallpox reflected similar fears about Singapore's openness to a severe infectious disease that travelled along the routes of commerce and immigration. In making smallpox a notifiable disease, the British made strenuous efforts to quarantine ships, survey people and prevent outbreaks in the Municipality.

Another issue was important in the history of smallpox in Singapore: vaccination and its attendant racial politics. The term 'vaccination' itself was coined by Dr Edward Jenner after using the cowpox virus *variolae vaccinae* to protect people against smallpox. The British made the vaccination of Asian infants and children compulsory in Singapore, but this provoked widespread social resistance and evasion. The ire of the colonial regime fell especially on the Malay minority, giving rise to what they called the 'Mohammedan problem'. As in other colonial contexts, Asians looked upon vaccination programmes as dangerous and invasive procedures, where not only their bodies but also their beliefs were being dominated by a foreign power.[1] Throughout the colonial period, the British could not persuade most Asians to accept the two pillars of biomedicine for smallpox: hospital treatment and vaccination.

Nevertheless, social attitudes were not etched in stone. As in the case of communist China,[2] most people in Singapore embraced hospital treatment

DOI: 10.4324/9781003384014-4

and vaccination for smallpox after the Second World War. This was to produce generations of vaccinated persons during the years of decolonisation and nation-building. Contrary to colonial beliefs, how Asians looked upon biomedicine was not innate to their 'race', but shaped by historical circumstances. The resistance was not so much a Malay problem as one of colonial rule.

## Early Smallpox: Ravaging, Prevalent and Elusive

Little is known about smallpox in Singapore before the transfer of the Straits Settlements to the Colonial Office in 1867, but outbreaks were apparently not uncommon. As early as 1825, the Superintending Surgeon in Penang noted that smallpox was being introduced into the colony from neighbouring countries, though this failed to move the East India Company to improve the quarantine system.[3] There were 'bad epidemic years' in 1838, 1842, 1849–1850, and 1859–1860, with the government criticised for failing to stem what appeared to be raging outbreaks that were killing numerous locals.[4] In the last outbreak, the administration reported: 'Smallpox has been very prevalent in Singapore during the past three months, no less than 14 cases having been treated in the Convicts Hospital'.[5] Four years later, a similar prognosis declared that 'small pox raged for a long time epidemically, all over the Island'.[6]

For these epidemics, the British blamed the locals, especially the Malays – for 'so apathetic are they, that it is not until smallpox is epidemic, or at their very doors, that they will stir themselves in the matter'.[7] Many patients did flee and go into hiding to avoid being sent to the Smallpox Hospital at Balestier Road which, as we will see in Chapter 5, was a wholly inadequate facility.[8] A writer to the press bemoaned in 1877 that the 'mania' of building numerous shophouses by the Chinese and Arabs without any regard for sanitary measures would create breeding grounds for cholera and smallpox in the town.[9]

Up to the 1890s, the colonial government attempted to detect smallpox on ships arriving at Singapore from destinations as varied as China, India and Mecca. Efforts were also made to vaccinate the crew and passengers of infected ships or those unable to provide proof of vaccination. With a long incubation period of 14 days, a passenger who appeared healthy at the start of the voyage could develop the illness later. Smallpox was an elusive disease that was not easy to screen for. Frequently, little native boats carrying patients from neighbouring islands simply slipped into the waters near Kampong Glam, an area populated by Malays.[10]

Another problem was the rudimentary early quarantine system prior to the 1894 Hong Kong plague outbreak. In 1880, several ships were disinfected and granted pratique to Singapore after isolated cases of smallpox found onboard were quarantined.[11] The Hong Kong scare did improve the quarantine system. In 1908, the captain of the *S.S. Van Riemsdijk* enroute from Amboina in the Dutch East Indies to Singapore was convicted of 'gross carelessness' for failing to detect two cases of smallpox onboard his vessel.[12]

As with plague, Muslim pilgrims returning from Mecca were deemed the most likely way for smallpox to be brought into Singapore.[13] Many ships, such as the steamer *S.S. Dahlia* in 1876 found to have smallpox cases onboard, conveyed many more passengers than their tonnage allowance.[14] There were calls much later in 1928 to revaccinate the passengers as many of them, having developed smallpox on their way to Mecca, had not been properly vaccinated prior to the journey.[15] The British complained that 'Javanese and Malays live for months in Mecca in the filthiest conditions, and numbers, unable to resist owing to physical unfitness or old age, do not live to perform the pilgrimage'. They added,

> Sanitary conditions at Mecca left much to be desired. Latrines were lacking and the streets were foul with animal and human excreta. Houses were dirty and sanitary arrangements therein defective. Though most of the blame for this state of affairs naturally falls on the Hejaz Sanitary Administration, not a little attaches to the pilgrims themselves, who, however near a latrine may be, relieve nature when and where nature calls.[16]

In 1886, of the 14 smallpox cases that year, only three contracted the disease in Singapore, the others, among them six Europeans, having developed it in another country or onboard a vessel bound for the island. The Straits administration took this to mean that the isolation of cases and disinfection of the ship were effective in preventing an outbreak, though it also underlined the need to improve sanitation in the town.[17] Two years later, however, the system fell apart. The *S.S. Electra* landed a passenger with smallpox without reporting him to the government before departing for China, while *S.S. Bisagno*, with a case of smallpox onboard, was put into quarantine only after its Singapore-bound passengers had disembarked. In the same year, a Chinese prahu (junk) landed another smallpox patient, who took a hackney carriage into town before dying two hours later, by which time both the prahu and carriage had vanished.[18] In 1891, the quarantine service was 'rather severely taxed' at one point when large numbers of people had to be isolated for smallpox.[19] It took the post-1894 improvements to the quarantine system to address many of these failings.

But the British remained fearful of smallpox slipping through the surveillance net to cause outbreaks in the Straits Settlements. In 1886, there was a call for a properly equipped smallpox hospital to be built in Penang, for

> small-pox is no respecter of persons, and a curse amongst the families of wealthy natives, and spreads almost as rapidly in streets inhabited by well-to-do or poor classes.[20]

Such fears were not baseless, for the colonial and municipal administrations struggled to control smallpox in the town. In 1874, there was even an outbreak inside the family barracks of the Singapore police force, initially affecting seven people. Despite moving the patients to another building, the disease managed to infect another three persons, and one of the ten cases eventually died.[21] This mini-outbreak reflected a persistent problem for the colonial administration: the lack of information on the true incidence of smallpox in the community or the connections between what appeared to be isolated cases. For example, the 91 cases reported in 1888 had the characteristic features of smallpox in Singapore: they were 'not in great numbers, nor occurring markedly in any particular months of the year or in any particular quarters of the Town'.[22]

The 1872 Medical Report blamed the sporadic nature of smallpox cases on various factors, such as people reusing infected clothing and other belongings of the patient. The remedy proposed was to acquire a steam disinfector.[23] But the underlying cause was the fundamental difference of views between Western officials and the Asian populace. As with plague, smallpox cases in the town were frequently removed from their original premises. The government saw such non-cooperation from their vantage point:

> the opposition met with in removing them [the patients] to the Small-pox Hospital combined with the apathy of the natives in regard to this disease, helped considerably to disseminate the infection.[24]

In 1889, out of 76 cases, 23 were reported after death while the occupants of 16 houses were charged and fined for failing to notify them to the authorities.[25] Two years later, the government claimed that non-cooperation was diminishing, but this proved premature, as numerous people continued to be prosecuted for failure to notify in subsequent years.[26]

Evasion was linked to the lack of a proper hospital for smallpox, so the Asian ill did not view existing colonial facilities as places of treatment and healing. Part of the reason was also cultural, for some Chinese did not subscribe to the theory of infection, fearing that the spirits of the dead would remain in the hospital where they died.[27] But there was also a practical deterrent. In 1872, the Smallpox Hospital admitted 36 smallpox patients, of whom 25 were discharged upon recovery while 10 (or 27.8 per cent) died. This was the very same Infectious Diseases Hospital-cum-Quarantine Camp at Balestier Road for Asian patients we encountered in the previous chapters. This did not stop the government from moving smallpox patients from smallpox and infectious diseases wards at the General Hospital to the Smallpox Hospital in 1883. Two reasons were proffered for the move: that the GH staff were heavily loaded by their own work, and there was a danger of apothecaries and dressers attending to infectious disease patients spreading the sickness to other patients. The move was also prompted by the fairly large number of smallpox cases (62) that year, among which only 24 were treated at the Smallpox Hospital.[28]

The Balestier Road facility was woefully inadequate. In 1887, the British conceded that the Smallpox Hospital would be overwhelmed should a smallpox epidemic occur.[29] Six years on, 63 cases were treated there, prompting the Principal Civil Medical Officer T.S. Kerr to propose its transfer to the Municipal Commission, as most of the cases occurred within town limits and it was not right for him (as an employee of the colonial government) or the TTSH (as a community hospital) to attend to them without 'a suitable allowance'.[30] The following year, after three smallpox patients escaped from the hospital, Kerr again highlighted the lack of a reliable water supply there and the need for a new hospital managed by the commission.[31] In 1895, the government decided that the commission would be responsible for patient fees in normal circumstances, though it could apply for a government loan in the event of an epidemic.[32] But the problem was only addressed in 1913 when a new infectious diseases hospital was built at Moulmein Road under the charge of the Municipality. Compared to Asians, Europeans received superior treatment in their own ward within the GH. After 1893, a smallpox ward for Europeans was built within the compounds of the hospital.

## Vaccination and 'Native Apathy'

The earliest attempts at vaccinating locals in Singapore against smallpox up to the 1850s utilised the method of inoculation. As this involved inserting scabs containing the smallpox virus into the skin to trigger an infection, it posed a risk to the individual and their close contacts. Parents frequently refused to bring their children to be inoculated, while the East India Company was unwilling to bear the costs. These failings were a contributing factor to severe outbreaks in 1838 and 1859–1860. In the latter case, the Governor stressed the 'apathy and indifference of the natives' and the need for compulsory vaccination.[33] By this time, the procedure was likely to use the cowpox virus, which was considerably safer. Nevertheless, local response to vaccination remained lukewarm.

In 1868, another outbreak purportedly imported by Javanese pilgrims killed 'several hundred people' in Singapore, mostly Malays.[34] Yet, when a bill for compulsory vaccination was mooted that year, based on the English Vaccination Act,[35] the Attorney-General T. Braddell opposed it on ethno-religious grounds:

I fear we are not yet prepared for this measure. The Commissioner of Police reports that the Mahomedans consider vaccination to be an impious attempt to interfere with the decrees of Providence, and if as I believe such a feeling does exist among a large class of our population, however irrational it may be, it would be a strong measure to force them to act in opposition to it without attempting before hand to remove the prejudice.

The Chinese are said fully to appreciate the advantages of vaccination, and it is to be hoped that if proper means are taken for making known to all classes of natives and uses of the system that any prejudice now existing against it will in a short time disappear.[36]

There was a further impediment to vaccination: the government was unable to track the number of births among the population, which also depended on local cooperation. It was better, Braddell suggested, to first implement a voluntary system to demonstrate the efficacy of vaccination before making it mandatory.[37] But he was overridden by (interestingly) the Commissioner of Police Thos Dunman himself and the Colonial Surgeon H.L. Randell, who argued that opposition to vaccination among 'Chinese, Islams and Hindoos' was not insurmountable and would be reduced with the cooperation of their community leaders.[38]

The following year, the Vaccination Ordinance was passed. It authorised the compulsory vaccination of infants within three months of their birth, along with an amendment to the Ordinance for the Registration of Births and Deaths to reliably track the births.[39] When it commenced, the vaccination campaign was hailed a success in Singapore – 'the demand ... so very great', with 2,300 individuals vaccinated – and Malacca, compared to resistance in Penang and Province Wellesley.[40] But Singapore's numbers fell off subsequently. In 1873, the Principal Civil Medical Officer related that 'the working of the Act [Vaccination Ordinance] was far from satisfactory', with only 900 persons vaccinated, compared to 2,524 the previous year and out of which only slightly more than half were successful.[41] In addition, the failure rate was high, which increased the costs of vaccination per person. In 1882, Governor Frederick Weld admitted that the percentage of successful vaccinations in the Straits Settlements and the Malay States under British protection was very low.[42]

Understanding Asian responses to vaccination takes us down the rabbit hole of the colonial archives. The documentary record reveals difficulties common to the Straits Settlements, British India and Spanish Philippines. The unifying thread across these countries was the colonial experience. The difficulties seemed varied: they were practical (the logistics of vaccine delivery, or sufficient manpower), medico-technical (the quality or safety of the vaccine) and financial (the costs of vaccination, taking into account failed vaccinations).[43] But the key to an explanation is to see Asian evasion as a form of 'weapons of the weak', by which subordinate groups (we include here upper-class Asians) could passively contest official policies with maximal effect and at the least cost (in their view) to themselves.[44]

Why did passive resistance occur? Until 1886, there was only one public vaccinator for all of Singapore,[45] while there were numerous complaints about the quality of calf lymph imported from Savory and Moore, London, that contributed to the low success rate in the early years.[46] In 1892, the Medical Department tried to manufacture the vaccine locally but this was shelved as being costly, with the vaccine imported from Saigon and Hong Kong instead.[47] These practical difficulties cut across ethno-religious lines.

Another problem was the confusion of diseases with similar symptoms, namely, smallpox, chickenpox and measles. In 1898, the *Singapore Free Press* reported a case where local Malays disagreed with the clinical diagnosis of smallpox in the community, deeming the illness to be *jaluntong* (chickenpox), a supposedly milder disease.[48] During the 1935 outbreak (discussed below), two Western doctors initially diagnosed a Malay woman to be suffering from measles. But she was later found to have died from smallpox, and her father was charged and convicted with failing to report the illness to the Municipality.[49]

Colonial officials, keen to attribute blame, understood little of these difficulties. It was simpler to racialise the behaviour of the locals, especially the Malays. Racial politics was at work during the colonial period, ultimately cleaving a gulf between the British regime and its Asian subjects. This gap was in part cultural, as it pertained to differences in values or worldviews. It was also political, because the differences were exacerbated by the unequal relationship between the two sides. But this means that practical, cultural and political difficulties were not innate to a social group but historical. They could be resolved when the cultural gap was closed and the colonial system removed.

Part of the cultural difference was Asian religious beliefs about smallpox. In colonial India, vaccination was known to have been hindered by Hindu beliefs associating smallpox with the goddess Shitala, and it was only at the end of the 19th century before it became acceptable to Indians. Interestingly, inoculation efforts fared better in India as the British were mindful to involve Brahmin priests and Hindu rituals to invoke the power of the deity in a way that a vaccine derived from the cow (a holy animal in Hinduism) could not.[50] In the Straits Settlements, the Hindu minority responded to a smallpox outbreak in 1896 by making offerings to the goddess and using cooling treatments; they did not notify the authorities or seek medical help.[51] The Chinese also did not look upon biomedical treatment and vaccination for smallpox favourably. Leong Man Sau, a Chinese community leader, told the 1912 Quarantine Commission that they did not regard smallpox to be a serious disease.[52]

The community most targeted for ignorant behaviour was the Malays. At the alleged root of the problem were their superstitions, as shown in a newspaper report on an outbreak in a kampong in Johore in 1899. Many Malays fled from their homes, while

> A rope of rattan is stretched entirely round the fence of the Campong ... and a rope of lalang leaves and white thread with queer slip-knots of coconut fronds depending from it is stretched across the top of the gate. In the gateway are buried, cross-wise, two stems of the 'Bedara Pahit' [a type of plant], which is supposed, owing to its bitterness, to scare away the small-pox spirits. The road from Biserat to Jalor is similarly defended against the spirits, the object being to stop them from pursuing travellers on the road![53]

The colonial archives did not highlight as a problem something that would be obvious to us today: vaccination's association with the police. For four decades after compulsory vaccination commenced, it was the police who gathered unvaccinated children in police stations, schools and (for adults) gaols and brothels.[54] The role of the police made Malay parents fearful about their children being forcibly taken away from them to the hospital.[55] The Quarantine and Prevention of Disease Ordinance authorised policemen to forcibly enter dwellings suspected of harbouring cases of smallpox and other notifiable diseases. In 1895, an editorial in the *Mid-Day Herald* complained about the vast authority of the police and potential for abuse, as when 'a constable who knows as much about a case of smallpox as does a mule, chooses to raise trouble on a matter of which he is super-latively ignorant'.[56]

Public vaccinators were likewise feared and hated. The British recognised that many parents who refused vaccination for their infants viewed it as a 'painful operation'.[57] In this context, some degree of coercion was likely used during vaccination, as suggested by a 1882 medical report:

> The Vaccinator here appears to have some difficulty in combating the native prejudice against vaccination, and it is only by patience and per-severance on his part that this can be overcome.[58]

That year, the vaccination programme was considered a success owing to a higher percentage (73 per cent) of successful cases and the lowered cost (20 cents per successful case). The ethnic breakdown of vaccinations is interest-ing. In 1883, Indians, who often worked for the colonial and municipal administrations, were over-represented, comprising two-fifths of the vaccina-tions though only 9 per cent of the total population. The Chinese were underrepresented (about half the vaccinations compared to 63 per cent of the population). Malays constituted 8.5 per cent of the vaccinations, far below their forming a quarter of the population.[59] This underlines the difficulty of convincing the Chinese and particularly the Malays about the benefits of vaccination.

In 1873, a number of Malays in Province Wellesley submitted a petition to the Straits government, protesting that the vaccinators were

> not men of character and respectability, were not fitted to vaccinate chil-dren and were persons to whom the lowest and meanest European in the Settlement would not have entrusted the vaccination of his children.[60]

The vaccination, the petition claimed, had killed many children. It had also driven a thousand people into neighbouring territories in order to avoid being arrested, fined and otherwise punished for not reporting cases of smallpox or for not having the children vaccinated. The Malay protest was practical in nature. The petition emphasised that it was not against vaccination per se but that the procedure be carried out by 'a respectable professional vaccinator' using a 'proper virus'.[61] As early as 1863, the Temenggong of Singapore, a top Malay official, was reportedly willing to support the vaccination of Malays under his charge.[62]

But while Malay unhappiness was largely due to practical reasons, it was circumscribed by the colonial factor. There were basic differences between the perspectives of the Europeans and Malays over the efficacy and risks of vaccination, but only one side had the power to rule whose viewpoints and whose difficulties were legitimate. A report in the *Straits Observer* in 1875 made the accusation that 'The Pinang Malays are still stupidly opposed to the practice'.[63] The cultural divide would hinder the vaccination programme for many decades, as would the power wielded by the police and public vaccinators.

In 1898, the Principal Civil Medical Officer Max F. Simon surmised the benefits of vaccination, 'the bulk of the population [in the Straits Settlements] may be considered to be fairly well-protected against small-pox'.[64] This missed important ethnic variations: only 22.9 per cent of the Malay smallpox cases in the town were vaccinated that year, compared to 37.5 per cent and 17.6 per cent among the Chinese and Indians respectively. The Malays formed the largest proportion of the cases (41.6 per cent) and had the highest mortality rate (65.7 per cent), which pointed to a lower vaccination rate. There were no deaths among the three European smallpox cases.[65]

In reality, colonial vaccination reached only a fraction of the population. The number of individuals vaccinated by private practitioners was unknown but this was probably small, limited to the upper echelons of society. Struggles over vaccination undermined the control of smallpox in the town, for unvaccinated persons were more likely to die from the sickness. In 1889, 57 of the 76 smallpox cases were unvaccinated or partially vaccinated, contributing to a mortality rate of 66.7 per cent, compared to 5.2 per cent among the vaccinated group.[66] The Municipal Commission noted two unsatisfactory characteristics of the outbreak: that the mortality rate among the vaccinated was still more than twice in Britain, and the proportion of unprotected persons was too high.[67]

The troubles of the vaccination programme were investigated by the 1912 Straits Quarantine Commission. Many parents were able to elude the vaccination net. The commission assessed the Public Vaccinator Charles Pang as 'a very earnest official' but lacking the medical expertise or even 'general intelligence' for the task.[68] Dr Richard Arthur Campbell, the Second Assistant Municipal Health Officer, was scathing about Pang's methods: in full view of the public (for the vaccination of adults), he used a knife to 'gore' the arm and did not clean the wound.[69] Such rough handling frequently produced ulcers and eczema on the person and caused a 'hue and cry' among onlookers and parents of children.[70] By his own admission, Pang was not a certified vaccinator, calling himself 'only a simple vaccinator'. He was also unable to locate many newborn infants for vaccination, alluding to continuing difficulties in tracking births in the colony.[71]

For all his faults, Pang was hampered by systemic issues: he was the only government vaccinator for the whole of Singapore, having to divide his time between the town and rural areas. Parents often withheld information such as the birth or true age of their child from the authorities. As Pang admitted,

'There is a great deal of confusion in vaccination', making it difficult to compel people to be vaccinated.[72] The Municipal Health Officer, W.R.C. Middleton, proposed that the vaccination of children be made the responsibility of the Municipal Health Department and carried out by qualified medical men.[73] This finally removed vaccination's long association with the police, though not other difficulties. The commission also mandated that adults be vaccinated or revaccinated free of charge, and that immigrants show proof of effective vaccination, without which they should be revaccinated.[74] In 1915, the age of infants for vaccination was raised from three to six months to widen the vaccination net.[75] By then, the social costs of non-vaccination had become manifest.

### Turn of the Century Epidemic

A slew of smallpox cases in 1899 turned into a major epidemic in the Municipality the following year.[76] A total of 316 cases were reported, a big jump from 84 the previous year. Nearly a third died. The Municipal Commission downplayed the crisis, denying it was an epidemic and deeming the death rate to be not higher than in other towns.[77] But it admitted that the outbreak was serious enough to have 'caused a good deal of trouble to the Sanitary Staff'.[78]

The ethnic dimensions of the outbreak are telling. The Malays, with 96 cases, edged the Chinese (92) and Indians (86) as the group disproportionately affected. But there were also similarities across the communities. The mortality rate was highest among Malays (41.7 per cent), followed closely by the Chinese (37 per cent) and somewhat less so the Indians (29 per cent). The unprotected ratio was uniformly high: 59.4 per cent of Malay cases, 63 per cent of the Chinese and 62.8 per cent of the Indians. The Municipality was frustrated by Asian non-cooperation in reporting cases, noting 'when fined the cheerfulness with which they pay the fine'.[79] In addition, the *Straits Times* reported, 'The Malays are beginning to resist being removed to the hospital when suffering from small-pox'.[80]

As related in Chapter 1, the epidemic intensified the debate between the Straits government and the Municipality on their respective roles in the control of infectious diseases in the town. This was resolved only with the passing of a new Municipal Ordinance in 1907. During the epidemic, the Principal Civil Medical Officer and Colonial Engineer inspected the Balestier Road hospital. They reported that the patients, including the Malay families, were satisfied with their accommodation and treatment.[81] This convinced the government that no new hospital was needed.

The 1899 outbreak continued to prevail in the town. The following year, there were 220 cases, among them many unvaccinated Indians. The Smallpox Hospital, which treated half the cases, reported a death rate of 27.5 per cent, mostly among the unvaccinated. This belied the higher overall rate in the town (38.1 per cent), because a third of the cases were found after death. The police caught a man with smallpox symptoms walking along Serangoon Road in the early morning.[82] Straits officials continued to insist that the population had good protection from the vaccine and were confident that the outbreak was tapering off in the second half of the year.[83] The number of cases dropped to 62 in 1901. Middleton wrote a long article to the *Straits Times* detailing the Municipality's efforts to track down cases and disinfect homes and personal effects.[84]

But the number jumped to 159 in 1902, though this failed to excite comment from the Governor of the Straits Settlements, probably because a larger outbreak had occurred in Penang while Singapore was also struck by a severe cholera epidemic.[85] Fifty-nine patients died of smallpox (a 37.1 per cent mortality rate), all of whom save six were unvaccinated. The Municipality did admit that the outbreak spanned different parts of the town, though many cases were concentrated near the Tanjong Pagar docks where many Indians worked and the Telok Ayer district where upper-class Chinese dwelt. Eleven patients of a higher class refused to go to the Smallpox Hospital and were treated in their homes. The Municipality combed premises house by house, disinfecting and in some cases demolishing infected dwellings.[86] Still, a hack gharry used to ferry two patients to another area was used for a full day by other passengers before it was found and impounded.[87]

Asian non-cooperation was a constant source of frustration, as 'The existence of a large number of cases was concealed from the authorities and it was only by a systematic search that a great many cases were found'.[88] Many residents sought to avoid disinfection and vaccination, while patients ferried to hospital by gharries and rickshaws did not willingly provide their real addresses. The Municipality was unable to establish the residence of 25 cases. It was unequivocal that 'The hostility of the natives to taking the ordinary precautions, required by law in the case of the infectious diseases, was probably the main cause of this spread of the disease'.[89] But from the locals' perspective, taking these precautions, which entailed likely damage to their housing and harm to their bodies, was anything but logical. The number of cases fell to 109 in 1903, largely in the same districts as before, as did a lower mortality rate of 26.6 per cent. Heavy fines were imposed on people who failed to report cases.[90]

This marked the end of the turn of the century epidemic. Smaller numbers of smallpox continued to surface, but more serious was the inability to obtain accurate information from the patients and contacts. In 1909, several groups of cases were traced to Tamil coolie houses at Craig Road and Telok Ayer Street. One group in fact consisted of medical students who, by changing their address and removing infected items, were able to avoid being revaccinated. The occupier of a house was sentenced to jail for harbouring smallpox cases, but the conviction was overturned upon appeal due to a technicality.[91]

## The Largest Smallpox Epidemic, 1910–1911

The simmering smallpox was a prelude to the largest smallpox epidemic in Singapore in 1910–1911, as part of a wave of outbreaks throughout the Straits

Settlements. The epidemic saw 414 cases and 152 deaths (a 36.7 per cent mortality rate) in 1910 and 241 cases and 98 deaths (40.7 per cent) the following year. Again, there were disproportionately large numbers of Malay (25.1 per cent) and Indian (36.4 per cent) cases, with the Chinese forming just over a third of the total. The Municipal Health Officer believed that the outbreak was imported into Singapore at the incubation stage in the early part of the year, before spreading rapidly from the northern part of the town to the south.[92] In 1910, 26 ships were deemed to be infected with smallpox, including six returning from Jeddah; this rose to 40 the following year.[93]

In 1910, the death rate among roughly half of the patients who were vaccinated was 16 per cent, compared to 46.9 per cent for the unvaccinated. But even vaccinated persons were likely to have been vaccinated once in infancy without revaccination. A medical doctor's study of a sample of cases that year showed that the true death rate was lower – 11.5 per cent for the vaccinated and above 36 per cent for the unvaccinated. More than four-fifths of the children under five had not been vaccinated at all.[94] The Medical Department deemed it necessary to amend the Vaccination Ordinance to raise the vaccination rate in the colony. In Malacca, school teachers were instructed to carry out vaccination, which persuaded more locals to come forward.[95] Following the epidemic, the government decided to enforce an old rule: all children had to produce a vaccination certificate before being admitted into primary school.

The Municipal Health Office continued to receive little public cooperation during the epidemic: 47 and 18 cases were found after death in 1910 and 1911 respectively, with five of the latter figure dumped in the street. The commission was disappointed that even educated people sought to conceal smallpox by moving the sick to other areas and allowing contacts to move freely and spread the disease. A tenth of the cases were in fact moved to rural areas. On a single day in 1910, 12 concealed cases were unearthed after the office conducted house-to-house inspections in the town.[96] Over 1,300 contacts were sent to St. John's for observation, but in many instances these were the wrong persons.[97]

The Municipal Health Office blamed the continuation of the epidemic into 1911 on concealment.[98] As before, its response was punitive, charging and fining individuals and households for failing to report cases or absconding from quarantine.[99] Along with six other Javanese, a Javanese imam (Islamic leader) who resided at the local residence of the Sultan of Johore was fined for failing to report a case to the Municipality.[100] These prosecutions further strained the tenuous relationship between the government and the community.

Once again, the passive resistance was practical in nature with political undertones. Take the experience of Lim Hong Quee of Neil Road in the town, a Chinese of reasonable means. His wife, young nephew and niece contracted smallpox and were admitted to hospital; the two youngsters had not been vaccinated. Lim and eight other members of his family were sent to St. John's as contacts. He had not reported the outbreak for a week because he claimed he did not know it was smallpox. It was detected only after Thomas Mayhew, the Chief Sanitary Inspector, inspected his house. Under isolation, Lim complained that he was 'mixed up with coolies, Chinese and Kling' in a rough shed. It was an open space with no partition for privacy; the women were uncomfortable with so many male coolies in close proximity. Drinking water was scarce and the food 'not very good' (white rice with pork and salted fish on alternate days). When it rained at night, the water came in through holes in the roofs and rudely awakened them from their sleep.[101]

Another socially prominent group, the Chettiars, were also unhappy with their treatment. One of them sent to the Smallpox Hospital said that he had to refuse the food cooked by Chinese for caste reasons, as a result of which he was given only a coconut, two bananas and two slices of bread daily.[102] Such reports elicited public sympathy for the Chettiars and other persons of means.[103] The following years witnessed measures that helped allay these grievances. As related in Chapter 5, the Municipality completed a new infectious diseases hospital in 1913, with a fully built section for smallpox and separate wards for upper- and working-class Asians. Improvements were also made to the isolation facility on St. John's following the recommendations of the Quarantine Commission. But non-cooperation persisted.

## Mohammedans and Bomors, 1921–1922

The disease flared up again at the start of the 1920s. Ten years after the previous outbreak, there were 407 cases with 102 deaths (a death rate of 39.2 per cent) in 1921–1922. This epidemic was notable for the Municipality's pointed criticism of the Malay population. It charged that 'Concealment is rife especially among Mohamedans', who had the most number of cases.[104] The commission claimed that Malay 'hospital-phobia' would likely not be resolved soon. Some 100,000 vaccinations were carried out, which the commission deemed to have helped stem the outbreak. It proposed that 'powers should be obtained to enforce compulsory vaccination or revaccination by house-to-house visitation'.[105] These measures were implemented the following year.

In reality, part of the problem lay with conditions prevailing at the Middleton Hospital. Certain ward attendants were dismissed for 'disciplinary reasons' during the epidemic, though the reasons were not specified.[106] But the hospital, while fairly new, was still not wholly welcoming to Asian patients. As a letter to the press noted, there was no Hindu cook at the hospital, which discouraged Hindus who did not want to consume food cooked by the Chinese or Malays from seeking treatment.[107]

In tracing the outbreak, the commission claimed that 'The epidemic began very quietly'. It was not due to pilgrims returning from Mecca, but started locally with a Tamil couple residing at Albert Street in the northern part of the town, before spreading to a Chinese at Queen Street, who promptly relocated to Geylang Lorong 16 east of the municipal limits. The commission could not establish any connection between the two cases, as 'it was most difficult – in fact practically impossible – to obtain information from patients or their relatives'.[108] Then a dead six-month-old Chinese infant was found in another *lorong* ('street') in Geylang. Thereafter the outbreak grew in the two locales – the northeastern section of the town and the Geylang *lorongs* adjacent to it – while spreading to other parts of the Municipality. The Middleton Hospital admitted rural patients, who were mostly Malays. The commission found that 'Malays suffered from the disease more than any other nationality both actually and proportionately'.[109] In 1922, less than three-fifths of the 418 cases were certified as vaccinated, who had a mortality rate of just over 10 per cent, against 37.6 per cent among the unvaccinated.

Concealment again hindered the efforts to contain the epidemic despite the sanitary inspectors conducting house-to-house checks and the newspapers warning the public about the dangers of smallpox and highlighting the need for vaccination. Twenty-six of the year's cases were found after death, including seven dumped in open areas and five discovered after they had recovered. The Municipality offered a reward of $10 for each case of smallpox reported, but there was only one claim for it. A total of 179,620 vaccinations were made in 1922, including children in both government and non-government schools, though this was notable for 'the lethargic way they [the people] came forward to be vaccinated'.[110]

On the reasons for the spread of the outbreak, the commission was certain that 'although all Asiatic races were offenders in this respect, the Malay were the worst'. In 1922, 94 Malay patients were found after their first week of illness, compared to 54 Chinese and 32 Indians. On the whole, 118 out of 171 prosecutions were convicted of concealment, and the scale of the problem led the commission to impose the full fine of $100, which appeared to work.[111] In the minds of the commissioners, it was concealment that prolonged the epidemic, rather than anything to do with the hospital conditions or vaccination.

Still, some officials were aware that the epidemic was experienced very differently by the people, as the Municipal Health Officer Dr Dawson observed,

> I think this must be put down chiefly to segregation and treatment in Hospital. Asiatics in general and Mohammedans in particular object to the control which they have to submit to when in Hospital. In addition Mohammedans put great faith in their 'Bomors' [traditional healers], persons supposed to be skilled in treatment of Small Pox. A few Chinese believe in the 'Bomor' also.[112]

The commission blamed the bomors for failing to disinfect their equipment or using treatments that had no effect on smallpox. It lauded its own efforts in ending the epidemic: the extensive vaccination campaign, cleansing of the town and hefty fines. It also enlisted the Chinese Chamber of Commerce, Mohammedan and Hindu Advisory Boards to persuade the major ethnic groups, though this had little effect. In its reckoning, the epidemic was not particularly severe but 'most annoying in its incidence and [which] prevented as much attention being given to other matters as desired'.[113]

The commissioners could not understand why the Malays viewed the hospital as 'a death trap'.[114] During and after the epidemic, they met with the Mohammedan Advisory Board to discuss the possible reasons. They learned about a rumour that female patients were placed under the charge of male attendants, something serious enough for a Malay petition to be submitted to the commission. The concern was real as the Malay population was settled and had more females than immigrant Chinese and Indians. To encourage Asians to go to the Middleton Hospital, the commission was willing to have community leaders visit the hospital and allow Asian patients their traditional treatments for smallpox.[115] Desperate, it even considered setting up a smallpox ward for Malays within the hospital. But the plan collapsed when the Health Department, though willing to admit bomors as regular ward attendants, refused to give them control over Malay patients.[116]

No compromise with the Malays was achieved. The Municipality's response to the epidemic was to carry out vaccination immediately rather than wait for people to request it. The existing Quarantine and Prevention of Disease Ordinance empowered Health Officers to vaccinate persons at risk from smallpox and remove those who refused to be vaccinated to a quarantine station or fine them up to $25. After the epidemic, 'special measures' were considered, such as immediate vaccination and raising the fine up to $100.[117] But vaccination remained unpopular; in 1924, it was estimated that a third of infants were still unvaccinated. The fact it remained policemen who rounded up people to be vaccinated had much to do with the problem, making the procedure seem criminal rather than medical.[118]

In 1926, the Quarantine and Prevention of Disease Ordinance was finally amended for the compulsory revaccination of all children within six months after they turned seven and of all residents in an area where a smallpox epidemic had broken out.[119] Other than these legal measures, the government had only a vague sense of public education as a solution to the perspectives of the populace:

> the key to the situation lies in the school-room from which alone can spring that intelligent personal appreciation and whole-hearted public co-operation without which we shall never be able to efface the all-pervading and disgraceful blot on the page of our much vaunted modern civilisation.[120]

In the 1930s, along with plague, smallpox petered out in the town. But the underlying problems persisted. In one instance, sanitary inspectors on their rounds at Sago Street – a lane with Chinese death houses – found a man who had died of smallpox propped up at a table with a pair of chopsticks in his hands.[121] In a small outbreak among Malays in 1932, a number of people were prosecuted and fined for concealment, among them a police constable. Most of the patients insisted that they had just arrived from the Malay states or refused to reveal their movement history. Nevertheless, the Municipality deemed the vaccination of infants to be satisfactory.[122]

This lull was disrupted by a smallpox outbreak of 65 cases and 21 deaths in 1935 – the most serious in 15 years. Thought to be imported by a ship from a Chinese port, the outbreak affected the major ethnic groups, including Malays residing in the area east of the town. The Municipality again conducted individual house inspections, burned four unsanitary huts, stepped up vaccinations, and hived 364 contacts off to St. John's. It was satisfied that the outbreak was a small one with no cause for alarm.[123] Concealment remained prevalent with only a few voluntary notifications.[124] Six Malays were fined for failing to report smallpox to the Municipality that year.[125] The commission charged,

> As was to be expected the Malays, with their abhorrence of isolation and hospital treatment, gave us little or no assistance and, indeed, did everything in their power to conceal the disease and to spread it beyond its original boundaries by secretly removing cases elsewhere. This without doubt is the explanation of the small localised outbreaks outside the Municipal limits in Bedok and Johore.[126]

There was a simple social explanation for this behaviour. Malays living in the kampongs were usually related to one another and thus reluctant to report a smallpox patient living in their midst.[127] This compounded other practical objections among the Malays: the distance to travel to the town for help, the fear of Malay women being cared for by male attendants in the hospital or being served food with pork. The only solution, the Municipal Health Officer P.S. Hunter urged, was to imprison the offenders as a deterrent.[128]

Hence, Hunter was puzzled to find out that news of the outbreak had caused 'a minor panic ... [and] a mild stampede for vaccination'; 155,880 vaccinations were carried out in 1935. He thought this was partly due to the previous absence of smallpox in Singapore and partly to 'one or two somewhat alarmist articles in the press'. He thought 'it was rather a surprise to find how readily even Malays accepted vaccination when it was brought to their doors so to speak'.[129] Just as he had ignored the practical and social reasons for Malay non-cooperation, he now failed to understand their wish to be vaccinated. Clearly, Malay attitudes changed when vaccinators arrived at the kampongs.

Prior to the outbreak of the Second World War, the threat of smallpox had diminished. The Chief Health Officer, J.W. Scharff, attributed this to two measures. One was effective quarantine. Experienced quarantine officials were able to detect smallpox cases hidden on Chinese ships.[130] The other factor was compulsory vaccination, first carried out in infancy and again at primary school age. He noted that most smallpox cases by this time were adults or older children over ten years old.[131]

Writing in 1947, Dr M. Doraisingham declared that few people were able to evade vaccination before the war. Infants and school children were systematically being vaccinated or revaccinated, though numerous children of working-class backgrounds who did not attend school would have been missed. The majority of immigrants onboard infected ships or vessels sailing from infected ports had also been vaccinated, including an unknown number of returning Malay (and Indian Muslim) pilgrims. Doraisingham also noted that at the start of the Japanese Occupation in early 1942, over 600,000 out of a population of 770,000 people (78 per cent) were vaccinated on Japanese orders, using lymph produced by the Institute of Medical Research in Kuala Lumpur. This likely achieved herd immunity in the population, though in the later years of the occupation, the quality of lymph deteriorated, leaving newly born infants vulnerable to a smallpox infection.[132]

## The Vaccinated Generations

The herd immunity helped mitigate an outbreak of smallpox (likely imported) in 1946–1947, causing 152 cases and 52 deaths.[133] The Municipality made a public appeal for infants and young children to be vaccinated for free during the outbreak, but this yielded disappointing results.[134] As Doraisingham warned, many cases were still being found a substantial time after the onset of illness with bodies being deposited at the Chinese death houses. Smallpox remained a threat in the overcrowded slums of the town, the unregulated kampongs at the urban margins and the rural areas where official surveillance was expanding into.[135]

The geographical region that was to dominate official discussions on smallpox after the war was 'the ring of infected countries' around Singapore, especially Indonesia.[136] As with plague, post-1947 Singapore was deemed largely free but not safe from smallpox. In 1947, a case found onboard a ship led to the passengers' quarantine on St. John's. They went on a hunger strike, alleging discrimination in favour of cabin passengers and seven deck passengers who were allowed to land without serving their quarantine.[137] In 1950, a ship with a case onboard managed to slip into Singapore harbour but was detected and sent into quarantine.[138]

So it was in April 1959 – just before Singapore became a self-governing state – that a minor outbreak excited much official and press comment after years without a single case of smallpox. The City Council documented the index case as an Indian boy, aged 11, who contracted the disease in India. Holding a valid vaccination certificate though his childhood vaccination had been ineffective, he arrived in Singapore by train from Penang (a common way of travelling to the city-state). He developed a rash, but was concealed in a wooden house at Kampong Alexandra in the outer city for nearly a month until a Malay woman living nearby was diagnosed with smallpox at a hospital. The City Council and the Ministry of Health conducted a house-to-house search of 860 huts in a half-mile radius around the kampong over ten days and isolated 244 contacts on St. John's for a fortnight. This involved a lengthy search to trace the passengers who had ridden in a taxi driven by the father of an infected month-old infant.[139] The government decided to vaccinate all travellers from Malaya, causing long jams at the Causeway, the Federation's entry point into Singapore.[140] More than a million people on the island were vaccinated within a month, including over 22,000 children.[141]

While the boy's concealment recalled earlier practices, the response to case finding and vaccination was more characteristic of the reinforced medical system and a more cooperative population after the war. The outbreak affected only ten people, of whom two died, including the infant who was too young to be vaccinated (he was also the last case and the only one living outside the kampong).[142] The MOH declared the outbreak to be an 'explosive' one in terms of public response, akin to a mass panic though 72 per cent of the population had been vaccinated.[143] In its view, the comprehensive vaccination exercise had localised the outbreak. The outbreak thus lent justification for Singapore to have its own quarantine legislation independent of the WHO's International Sanitary Regulations. The Indian boy had slipped through the net because Singapore and Malaya formed a single quarantine zone. Because passengers disembarking at Penang did not have to be quarantined as Malaysia was a signatory to the WHO regulations, they could travel overland to Singapore and avoid quarantine on St. John's.[144] On the other hand, the outbreak also highlighted the limitations of quarantine in detecting mild cases of smallpox, especially when the person possessed a vaccination certificate.[145] The 1959 outbreak saw the last cases of smallpox in Singapore.

But the main story of smallpox after the war was undoubtedly mass vaccination. While there had been practical or cultural difficulties in the pre-war period, these had begun to be surmounted in the 1930s. The end of war provided the final push. The efforts of the post-war government were driven by the fear that herd immunity conferred at the start of the Japanese Occupation was waning.[146] The number of vaccinations surged as the programme expanded from the town and became island-wide. Maternal and child clinics, outpatient and mobile dispensaries all carried the vaccination programme to the rural areas.

Public education was a pillar of the vaccination programme. Doctors emphasised that publicity in the press was inadequate as poor people living in the slums were illiterate. It was thus necessary to go directly to them. Information on smallpox and vaccination was broadcasted in the major languages, using loudspeakers installed in public areas.[147] During the 1947 outbreak, a municipal van roved the streets of the town, broadcasting information on smallpox in Chinese and Malay and drawing numerous questions from crowds. This helped allay concerns that the Chinese would avoid being vaccinated as their sores would disrupt the Lunar New Year celebrations.[148] Wariness of vaccination thus transformed into interest, if not outright enthusiasm.

In 1951, the government decided to implement mass vaccination on a voluntary basis, an idea first mooted by T. Braddell in 1868.[149] The following August, voluntary vaccination started on a strong note, involving the government medical services, the armed forces and the City Council. A 'startling' poster of a child covered in a rash was put up in public places.[150] Over 70 per cent of the population would eventually be vaccinated. In the remaining months of 1952 alone, over 280,000 people above three years of age were revaccinated and more than 27,000 infants were vaccinated in the city, comprising 38.9 per cent of the urban population.[151]

The campaign was a major success, especially in contrast to the lack of public enthusiasm for diphtheria vaccination launched at the same time.[152] Together with successful B.C.G. immunisation for tuberculosis, smallpox vaccination heralded the expanded medical reach of the late colonial state. There was also genuine popular support for vaccination, which allowed it to be quickly made compulsory, as Braddell had argued. By 1955, mothers were required to have their newborns vaccinated by the sixth month and were encouraged to do so between three and four months old, while children were revaccinated upon enrolling into primary school.[153] In 1957, the MOH envisioned,

> Routine immunisation against diphtheria, whooping cough and tetanus was done in all clinics for children from 4 weeks old, vaccination against small-pox from about 4 months old – and the new generation of 1957 found itself well able to withstand the 4 dreaded childhood diseases before it was 6 months old.[154]

In December 1959, the new Minister for Health Ahmad Ibrahim urged those who were unvaccinated to get themselves vaccinated immediately.[155] By 1961, nearly 73 per cent of children had been vaccinated against smallpox, compared to 39 per cent for tuberculosis and 31 per cent for diphtheria and poliomyelitis.[156] Acceptance of vaccines was thus not absolute but differed from disease to disease. The number of smallpox vaccinations further increased after Singapore became a self-governing state and eventually an independent nation. In 1980, it achieved high rates of vaccination: 88.9 per cent of newborns and 95.6 per cent of primary school entrants.[157]

By this time, though smallpox remained in the class of dangerous infectious diseases, Singapore's vaccination policy was about to be overtaken by global events. In 1967, the WHO had launched a worldwide campaign to eradicate smallpox. The last known case of the disease was documented a decade later in Somalia in 1977. This achievement was largely based on the strategy of surveillance containment, which built a ring of protected people around an outbreak so that the disease eventually burnt itself out.[158] In 1978, after Malaysia ceased checking vaccination certificates except for passengers arriving from an infected area, Singapore followed suit, while compulsory vaccination for national servicemen was discontinued in July 1979.[159]

Up to the middle of 1979, two key committees, the Joint Co-ordinating Committee on Epidemic Diseases and the Expert Committee on the Immunisation Programme, recognised the greatly diminished threat of smallpox. But they were reluctant to reconsider Singapore's vaccination policy, fearing that the disease could still resurface from residual foci, laboratory leaks, terrorist actions or genetic viral mutation in animals. The expert committee was concerned that if future vaccination had to be carried out on adults, they had a greater risk of complications such as encephalitis, whereas newborns suffered little illness when vaccinated. The committees decided to wait till the WHO's announcement on the worldwide eradication of smallpox.[160] In December 1979, as they anticipated, the WHO did so. The following month, the Singapore government announced that smallpox vaccination for international travel was unnecessary since the risk of complications was higher than that of contracting smallpox.[161]

In May 1980, the expert committee recommended ceasing compulsory vaccination for infants and primary school entrants with immediate effect and stockpiling 200,000 doses of the smallpox vaccine. It noted that countries in the region had terminated their vaccination programmes or made them voluntary, leaving Singapore the only Association of South East Asian Nations (ASEAN) country with a compulsory policy.[162] Only four countries in the world – Chad, Kampuchea, Djibouti, and Madagascar – still required vaccination certificates from travellers. The committee accepted that the risk of smallpox's reintroduction was a theoretical one, as the virus no longer existed. The WHO's declaration had led to pressure from parents, doctors and the press in Singapore to reconsider the compulsory vaccination of children.[163] The joint committee concurred with these proposals, followed by the cabinet. On 6 March 1981, compulsory vaccination for smallpox was discontinued in Singapore.[164]

This decision, based on expert analysis, showed how far Singapore had come in the control of smallpox. The long fight against the disease was a struggle between the colonial state and the diverse Asian population of the port city. It was a contestation between two sets of views and experiences of smallpox and its control. People were unwilling to cooperate with the authorities and accept the vaccines because of the specifics of time and place. Their attitudes were thus capable of changing and being transformed. There were many reasons why this happened: a safe and effective vaccine, a good health administration, capable vaccinators, national publicity and political commitment.

By contrast, smallpox treatment and vaccination during the colonial era were synonymous with problems of a practical, technical or cultural nature. These were historical problems that could be resolved when the strategy changed from coercion to persuasion. What did not help the colonial cause was to racialise the threat of smallpox and blame it on the ethnic groups, especially those that were socially marginal like the Malays. The history of smallpox reminds us that people had legitimate reasons for shunning biomedicine. These reasons need to be understood before they can be resolved – a timely lesson given widespread resistance to the COVID-19 vaccines in the present day.

# Notes

1 David Arnold, *Colonising the Body: State Medicine and Epidemic Disease in Nineteenth-Century India* (Berkeley: University of California Press, 1993).
2 Mary Augusta Brazelton, *Mass Vaccination: Citizens' Body and State Power in Modern China* (Ithaca: Cornell University Press, 2019).
3 CO 275/101 SSMR 1918.
4 'Historical Synopsis of Preventive Medicine in Singapore', *The Malayan Medical Journal*, Vol. V, 1930, p. 98; Lee Y.K., 'Smallpox and Vaccination in Early Singapore (Part I) (1819–1829)', *The Singapore Medical Journal*, Vol. 14 No. 4, December 1973, pp. 525–531; Y.K. Lee, 'Smallpox in Early Singapore (Part II) (1830–1849)', *The Singapore Medical Journal*, Vol. 17 No. 4, December 1976, pp. 202–206; Y.K. Lee, 'Smallpox in Early Singapore (Part III) (1850–1859)', *The Singapore Medical Journal*, Vol. 18 No. 1, March 1977, pp. 16–20; Y.K. Lee, 'Smallpox in Early Singapore (Part IV) (1860–1872)', *The Singapore Medical Journal*, Vol. 18 No. 2, June 1977, pp. 126–135; *Singapore Free Press*, 28 June 1849, p. 2.
5 Robert L. Jarman (ed.), *Annual Report on the Administration of the Straits Settlements, 1858–1859* (Archive Editions, 1998), Vol. 1, p. 160.
6 Jarman, *Annual Report on the Administration of the Straits Settlements, 1863–1864*, p. 40.
7 *Singapore Free Press*, 26 April 1860, p. 3.
8 Lee, 'Smallpox in Early Singapore (Part IV) (1860–1872)'.
9 *Singapore Daily Times*, 7 September 1877, p. 2.
10 *Straits Times Overland Journal*, 13 June 1874, p. 8.
11 CO 275/25 AMRCHSS 1880.
12 *Singapore Free Press*, 17 September 1908, p. 5.
13 SMAR 1922.
14 CO 273/89 Memo by G. Beyts, 31 March 1876.
15 CO 273/557 Memo by Minister for Foreign Affairs, 7 November 1928.
16 CO 273/535 Memo from Consul Stonehewer-Bird to Sir Austen Chamberlain, 24 September 1927.
17 CO 275/32 AMRCHSS 1886.
18 CO 275/35 AMRCHSS 1888.
19 CO 275/42 AMRCHSS 1891, p. 261.
20 CO 275/32 AMRCHSS 1886, p. 38.
21 CO 275/19 AMRCHSS 1874.
22 CO 275/35 AMRCHSS 1888, p. 87.
23 SMAR 1892.
24 CO 275/17 AMRCHSS 1872, p. xxvi.
25 CO 275/36 AMRCHSS 1889.
26 CO 275/42 AMRCHSS 1891.
27 *Straits Times*, 30 November 1892, p. 7.
28 CO 275/29 AMRCHSS 1883.
29 CO 275/33 AMRCHSS 1887.
30 CO 275/47 AMRCHSS 1893, p. 356.
31 CO 275/49 AMRCHSS 1894.
32 SMAR 1895, Appendix U, A.P. Talbot, Acting Colonial Secretary of the S.S. to President of the Municipal Commissioners, 27 March 1895.
33 Lee, 'Smallpox and Vaccination in Early Singapore (Part I) (1819–1829)'; 'Smallpox in Early Singapore (Part II) (1830–1849)'; 'Smallpox in Early Singapore (Part III) (1850–1859)'; 'Smallpox in Early Singapore (Part IV) (1860–1872)'.
34 CO 275/8 Letter from the Commissioner of Police, Straits Settlements, and the Colonial Surgeon on the Subject of Vaccination, 9 October 1868.

35  D.H.S. Gill, *A Study of Small Pox Vaccination of Infants in Singapore*, unpublished dissertation for the Diploma in Public Health, University of Singapore, 1963.

36  CO 275/8 'Bill for Compulsory Vaccination', 2 October 1868; CO 273/113 Memo from George Ord, 1 January 1868.

37  CO 275/8 'Bill for Compulsory Vaccination', 2 October 1868.

38  CO 275/8 Letter from the Commissioner of Police, Straits Settlements, and the Colonial Surgeon on the Subject of Vaccination, 9 October 1868.

39  Lee, 'Smallpox in Early Singapore (Part IV) (1860–1872)'.

40  CO 275/70 Report on the Working of the Vaccination Ordinance No. XIX of 1868, 7 November 1872.

41  CO 275/18 AMRCHSS 1873, p. lxviii.

42  CO 273/113 Memo by Frederick Weld, 7 March 1882.

43  Arnold, *Colonising the Body*; Ken De Bevoise, *Agents of Apocalypse: Epidemic Disease in the Colonial Philippines* (Princeton: Princeton University Press, 1995).

44  James C. Scott, *Weapons of the Weak: Everyday Forms of Peasant Resistance* (New Haven: Yale University Press, 1985).

45  CO 275/25 AMRCHSS 1880.

46  CO 275/27 AMRCHSS 1881.

47  'Historical Synopsis of Preventive Medicine in Singapore'.

48  *Singapore Free Press*, 7 April 1898, p. 12.

49  *Malaya Tribune*, 4 February 1936, p. 9.

50  Arnold, *Colonising the Body*.

51  *Mid-Day Herald and Daily*, 23 July 1896, p. 3.

52  Evidence by Leong Man Sau, Straits Settlements Quarantine Inquiry Commission, *Proceedings of the Commission Appointed to Inquire into the Working of the Quarantine and Prevention of Diseases Ordinance in the Settlement of Singapore, in the Colony of the Straits Settlements* (Singapore: Government Printing Office, 1912), Vol. 2.

53  *Straits Times*, 18 July 1899, p. 2.

54  CO 275/70 Report of the Superintendent of Vaccination, 23 May 1870.

55  *Straits Times*, 14 September 1872, p. 2.

56  *Mid-Day Herald*, 13 February 1895, p. 2.

57  CO 275/70 SSMR 1904, p. 747.

58  CO 275/28 AMRCHSS 1882, p. 216.

59  CO 275/29 AMRCHSS 1883.

60  *Straits Times*, 10 January 1874, p. 2.

61  *Straits Times*, 10 January 1874, p. 2.

62  *Straits Times*, 20 June 1863, p. 2.

63  *Straits Observer*, 2 November 1875, p. 2.

64  CO 275/57 SSMR 1898, p. 622.

65  SMAR 1898.

66  CO 275/36 AMRCHSS 1889.

67  SMAR 1892.

68  Straits Settlements Quarantine Inquiry Commission, *Proceedings of the Commission*, Vol. 1, p. 15.

69  Evidence by Dr Richard Arthur Campbell, Straits Settlements Quarantine Inquiry Commission, *Proceedings of the Commission*, Vol. 2.

70  Evidence by Dr James Handy, Straits Settlements Quarantine Inquiry Commission, *Proceedings of the Commission*, Vol. 2, p. 35.

71  Evidence by Charles Pang, Straits Settlements Quarantine Inquiry Commission, *Proceedings of the Commission*, Vol. 2, p. 47.

72  Evidence by Charles Pang, Straits Settlements Quarantine Inquiry Commission, *Proceedings of the Commission*, Vol. 2, p. 48.

73  Evidence by Dr William Robert Colvin Middleton, Straits Settlements Quarantine Inquiry Commission, *Proceedings of the Commission*, Vol. 2.
74  Straits Settlements Quarantine Inquiry Commission, *Proceedings of the Commission*, Vol. 1.
75  Gill, *A Study of Small Pox Vaccination of Infants in Singapore.*
76  CO 275/59 SSMR 1899.
77  SMAR 1899, p. 35.
78  SMAR 1899, p. 35.
79  SMAR 1899, p. 35.
80  *Straits Times*, 10 April 1899, p. 2.
81  SMAR 1899, Appendix I. Max F. Simon, Principal Civil Medical Officer S.S. and A. Murray, Colonial Engineer and Surveyor-General S.S. to the Hon'ble Colonial Secretary S.S., 15 May 1899.
82  *Singapore Free Press*, 10 February 1900, p. 3.
83  CO 275/61 SSMR 1900; SMAR 1900.
84  *Straits Times*, 8 March 1901, p. 3.
85  CO 275/66 SSMR 1902.
86  SMAR 1902.
87  *Straits Times*, 26 September 1902, p. 5.
88  SMAR 1902, p. 22.
89  SMAR 1902, p. 23.
90  CO 275/68 SSMR 1903; SMAR 1903.
91  SMAR 1909.
92  SMAR 1910.
93  CO 275/84 SSMR 1910.
94  SMAR 1910.
95  CO 275/87 SSMR 1911; CO 275/89 SSMR 1912.
96  SMAR 1910.
97  CO 275/84 SSMR 1910.
98  SMAR 1911.
99  *Straits Times*, 18 May 1910, p. 9; *Singapore Free Press*, 7 September 1910, p. 7.
100  *Straits Times*, 20 October 1911, p. 7.
101  Evidence by Lim Hong Quee, Straits Settlements Quarantine Inquiry Commission, *Proceedings of the Commission*, Vol. 2, p. 37.
102  *Straits Times*, 27 July 1911, p. 7.
103  *Straits Times*, 7 July 1911, p. 7.
104  SMAR 1921, p. 5.
105  SMAR 1921, p. 5.
106  SMAR 1921, p. 54-E.
107  *Singapore Free Press*, 17 November 1921, p. 314.
108  SMAR 1922, p. 3-D.
109  SMAR 1922, p. 4-D.
110  SMAR 1922.
111  SMAR 1922, p. 7-D.
112  SMAR 1922, p. 7-D.
113  SMAR 1922, p. 8-D.
114  *Malaya Tribune*, 16 February 1922, p. 4.
115  *Straits Times*, 29 October 1921, p. 9.
116  SMAR 1922.
117  SMAR 1922, p. 9-D.
118  SMAR 1924.
119  SMAR 1926.
120  CO 275/119 SSMR 1927, p. 732.
121  *Singapore Free Press*, 30 November 1951, p. 5.

122   SMAR 1932.
123   Singapore Municipality, Minutes of Proceedings of the Municipal Commissioners, 26 July 1935.
124   CO 275/139 SSMR 1935.
125   *Malaya Tribune*, 31 August 1935, p. 13.
126   SMAR 1935, p. 4-D.
127   SMAR 1935.
128   SMAR 1935.
129   SMAR 1935, p. 4-D.
130   J.H. Strahan, 'Reflections on the Course of Preventive Medicine in Malaya', *The Medical Journal of Malaya*, Vol. 2 No. 4, June 1948.
131   J.W. Scharff, 'The Growth of Public Health Services in Singapore in Relation to Preventive Medicine in War Time', *Journal of the Malayan Branch of the British Medical Association*, Vol. 3 No. 3, December 1939.
132   M. Doraisingham, 'The Immune Reaction as a Measure of Immunity to Small-Pox', *The Medical Journal of Malaya*, Vol. 1 No. 4, June 1947.
133   Medical Department, *Annual Report* (thereafter MDAR) 1951.
134   *Malaya Tribune*, 28 September 1946, p. 8.
135   Doraisingham, 'The Immune Reaction as a Measure of Immunity to Small-Pox'.
136   MDAR 1951, p. 50.
137   *Straits Times*, 5 November 1947, p. 5.
138   MDAR 1950.
139   *Straits Times*, 8 May 1959, p. 1.
140   *Straits Times*, 17 April 1959, p. 6.
141   City Council, *Annual Report* (thereafter CCAR) 1959; Ministry of Health, *Annual Report* (thereafter MOHAR) 1959.
142   CCAR 1959; MOHAR 1959.
143   MOHAR 1959, p. 90.
144   MOHAR 1959.
145   Quah Parry, *A Study of Quarantine Services in Singapore Today*, unpublished dissertation for the Diploma in Public Health, University of Singapore, 1971.
146   MDAR 1951.
147   *Straits Times*, 4 January 1947, p. 5.
148   *Singapore Free Press*, 13 January 1947, p. 5.
149   MDAR 1951.
150   *Straits Times*, 9 September 1952, p. 5.
151   CCAR 1952.
152   MDAR 1952.
153   MOHAR 1955.
154   MOHAR 1957, p. 57.
155   *Singapore Free Press*, 17 December 1959, p. 3.
156   T.A. Lloyd Davies and Rosemary Mills, 'Survey of Sickness in Singapore, with Notes on Births, Deaths, Handicapped Persons, Puberty, Menopause, Immunisation, Incidence of Cough and Adoption', *Medical Journal of Malaya*, Vol. XV No. 3, March 1961, pp. 117–156.
157   Goh K.T., *Epidemiological Surveillance of Communicable Diseases in Singapore* (Tokyo: Southeast Asian Medical Information Centre, 1983).
158   Alfred Jay Bollet, *Plagues & Poxes: The Impact of Human History on Epidemic Disease* (New York: Demos, 2004).
159   Goh, *Epidemiological Surveillance of Communicable Diseases in Singapore*.
160   MOH 024/58/01–000 Vol. 06 Minutes of the 57th Meeting of the Joint Co-ordinating Committee on Epidemic Disease, 31 July 1979; Goh, *Epidemiological Surveillance of Communicable Diseases in Singapore*.
161   *ENB*, Vol. 6 No. 1, January 1980.

162  MOH 024/58/01–000 Vol. 07 Minutes of the 65th Meeting of the Joint Co-ordinating Committee on Epidemic Disease, 18 November 1980.

163  MOH 024/58/01–000 Vol. 06 Minutes of the Meeting of the Expert Committee on the Immunisation Programme, 29 May 1980.

164  Goh, *Epidemiological Surveillance of Communicable Diseases in Singapore.*

# 4 Cholera and Remaking the City

More than the other two members of the Big 3, cholera in Singapore was a disease of the urban environment. Historically, it was a fast-killing sickness imported from infected ports in the region, particularly China, India, Malaya and the Middle East. Cholera epidemics occurred when the water supply in an area was contaminated by the stool of infected persons. The disease is caused by *Vibrio cholera*, a bacterium that lives in coastal aquatic environments in many parts of the world, including Asia. Illness is characterised by profuse watery diarrhoea, described in the past as 'rice water diarrhoea' because of the pale colour and watery nature of the stool. Death results from the rapid dehydration that occurs, but with early and proper treatment, the fatality rate today has fallen well below 1 per cent.

In colonial Singapore, cholera was more prevalent than plague or smallpox, and death rates of 80–90 per cent were not uncommon at the dawn of the 20th century. In explosive outbreaks in the Municipality, the disease spread quickly through the small and big spaces of the town, crossing rivers, drains, eating places, coolie lines, shophouse cubicles and urban kampongs. Public buildings such as hospitals, asylums and jails were not spared. Singapore's urban experience differed from colonial India where cholera's 'apparent predilection for the poor and undernourished' occurred largely in times of famine and affected the rural poor.[1]

Cholera was also endemic in Singapore – more of an endemic 'Sinbad' than plague ever was. It was a historically important disease because its incidence was tied to the lack of a clean water supply and proper sewerage disposal in the town. The colonial regime failed to provide these basic social amenities for the working class and keep pace with the town's rapid growth in the late 19th and early 20th centuries. By the same token, cholera was increasingly brought under control after the Second World War when Singapore underwent a physical and social transformation, aided by comprehensive urban planning and public health projects. The history of cholera is one of urban change and social struggle, in which the island was remade from a seemingly filthy and unruly coolie town to a clean and organised city-state.

As with smallpox, the colonial power treated cholera as a racial disease. Globally, there is a long tradition of viewing 'Asiatic cholera' as distinct from

DOI: 10.4324/9781003384014-5

and deadlier than milder European types of acute diarrhoeal diseases.[2] The British in Singapore blamed cholera outbreaks on the unsanitary ways of the Asian immigrants, particularly the Chinese coolies. They interpreted Chinese and Indian rituals to drive away the 'cholera demons' as proof of the disorderly native.

But again, like smallpox, the history of cholera shows that Asians were not racially predisposed to ignore biomedicine. Their resistance was conditioned by the colonial context and was to change after the Second World War. As Singapore underwent a remarkable transformation to become a garden city, how people regarded cholera and what they could do to protect themselves similarly changed. Whereas the immigrants of colonial Singapore had utilised tactics of evasion during cholera outbreaks, the citizens of the republic were more willing to accept biomedical treatment, surveillance and vaccination by the state. In fact, some Singaporeans became acutely worried about hawkers who might be silent carriers of the disease.

## Water and Waste, Blunders and Miscalculations

The cholera experience was tied – directly or indirectly – to colonial rule. In India, colonial officials and Christian missionaries condemned the Hindu ritual, practiced by the pilgrims, of bathing in the Ganges and drinking the river's water as a major factor in the transmission of the disease. In contrast, many Indians attributed cholera epidemics to the disruption of the Hindu cosmos or violation of social taboos caused by colonial rule.[3] In Singapore, the British similarly blamed the outbreaks on the unsanitary habits of the Asians, particularly the working class. Yet Asian behaviour was very much shaped by failings over matters for which the British were responsible: housing, water supply, drainage and sewage disposal.

For much of the 19th and early 20th centuries, only the town had a supply of piped water while rural dwellers had to rely on wells. Yet even within municipal limits, piped water had to be paid for and was available chiefly to the upper echelons of society, namely, the Europeans, wealthy Asians and big businesses (a few of the latter had their own reservoirs). It was thought during the 1873 cholera epidemic that people were obtaining water from duck ponds for drinking and cooking.[4] While the Municipal Commission claimed in 1896 that public standpipes would provide sufficient water to the coolies,[5] the vast majority of the municipal population obtained their water from private wells.[6]

The association between cholera and unclean water was obvious to learned contemporaries. In 1851, a severe epidemic was reportedly responsible for 220 fatalities (mostly Malays and Chinese), though the actual death toll was probably higher. This spurred the town's educated residents to form a commission to study the causes of insanitation and call for the drains and sewerage system to be thoroughly cleaned.[7] The Resident Councillor proposed amendments to the Municipal Act to sanction such action.[8] However, he was blocked by the Governor, who cited the lack of funds and suggested that bonfires should be lit when a cholera epidemic occurred to purify the atmosphere and dispel the disease.[9]

Nevertheless, the epidemic was a historic event for Singapore. This was due to the responses of two Asian community leaders – Syed Ali bin Mohammed Al-Junied in 1851 and Tan Kim Seng in 1857 – who made donations to the government to provide clean water for the general population.[10] In particular, Tan's offer to donate $13,000 was pivotal, leading the colonial government to build Singapore's first public reservoir, the Impounding Reservoir (later renamed MacRitchie Reservoir). This was completed only in 1867, 16 years after the epidemic, and it was a further decade before the reservoir had pumps to deliver a consistent supply of water to the town. It was only in 1891 that filters were built at Bukit Timah to clean the reservoir's water before it was delivered to the taps. But even the filters suffered repeatedly from the lack of maintenance.[11] And the water was available only to a fraction of the town population.

In 1872, an article in the *Daily Times* criticised how the transfer of the Straits Settlements to the Colonial Office had little improved the town's water supply:

> The story of these Waterworks is anything but creditable to all concerned – Governors and Engineers – who have had to do with them. They must bear a share of the blame and discredit, from Governors Blundell and Cavenagh, with Col. Collyer and Captain Mayne under the Indian regime, to Sir Harry Ord and Major McNair under the Colonial office. It is the story of a continuous series of blunders and miscalculations.[12]

The link between cholera and the water supply was so obvious that at the start of the 20th century, opportunistic lodging house keepers were known to use the appearance of the disease in their premises to obtain a free supply of water from the Municipality.[13]

The protracted development of MacRitchie Reservoir showed an underlying flaw in municipal water projects. Typically, they were delayed by cost considerations and the lack of political commitment even as the town's population kept growing. Finally completed, the increased water supply would allow the Municipality to keep abreast of population growth for a few years, but not accommodate future increases driven by mass immigration. Thus water projects could never keep up with population increases from the late 19th century. It is with these limitations in mind that we should view the development of new sources of water in the 20th century: the Kallang Reservoir (later renamed Pierce Reservoir, completed in 1910) and the Gunong Pulai Waterworks in Johore (completed in 1931).

If municipal water was scarce, private wells in the town were often little more than cesspools. Shallow and uncovered, they were frequently situated close to latrines and contaminated by sewage matter. In 1899, the Municipality lamented that 'On the 66 wells analysed there were only five in which it could be said that the water was fit for drinking purposes'.[14] Given the inadequate supply of municipal water, the commission treated wells as a necessary evil. It was aware of the health risks but slow to act. Arguing for the closure of wells in 1905, the Municipal Health Officer stressed that 'water borne disease such as Enteric Fever, Dysentery and Diarrhoea will never be much reduced in Singapore till this reform is carried out'.[15] In 1911, the Municipality finally closed 589 wells; five years later, all wells were to be sealed. But the policy was impossible to enforce, and the lack of alternative water sources and periods of drought drove the working class to reopen the wells on numerous occasions.[16]

Like the water supply, the town's drainage was a chronic problem of long standing. As there was no proper system of collection and disposal, people simply threw their rubbish and waste onto the streets, which became open sewers. Before the theory of contagion was accepted in scientific circles, cholera was attributed to filth via the miasma theory and could conveniently be pinned on the habits of the people living in unsanitary areas. In 1849, a writer to the *Singapore Free Press* racialised the threat of cholera as being due to the 'Filth, stench and dirt' in the 'Kling' (Indian) neighbourhood of Kling Street and Market Street.[17]

As they did over the control of infectious diseases, the Straits government and the Municipal Commission deferred responsibility for drainage and sewage disposal to each other. A year before the 1873 cholera epidemic, the Staff Surgeon-Major H.T. Reade had warned,

> Not only are the drains choked with every description of filth, but the ordinary streets and thoroughfares are considered the proper receptacles for all kinds of accumulated impurities, and the atmosphere is filled with unwholesome emanations in the highest degree dangerous to health; indeed the town is a nursery for disease, and is quite prepared to receive the impression of any of the epidemics which are at all times liable to be imported into the Colony.[18]

Perhaps the most damning aspect of waste disposal in colonial Singapore was the removal of human excreta. Here, the matter was rendered a racial rather than an administrative problem. The town's Asian population utilised the nightsoil system (also called the pail system) to remove the waste. This system was organised by private syndicates, whereby human excreta was gathered inside dwellings and collected at night to be sold as manure to commercial farms. But the system was hazardous to health, capable of transmitting infectious diseases like cholera in overcrowded shophouses and coolie lines and causing epidemics. So was the common practice of washing nightsoil buckets at nearby wells.[19] A European resident vividly described this practice:

> let the Municipal Engineers take the different routes into the suburbs between the hours of 11 a.m. and 1 p.m. and if they do not see, they will certainly smell the evil I am about to introduce to notice. Long files of

Chinese carrying buckets of night soil, which are anything but air tight or water tight will be seen wending their way from the town to the country districts at the hottest part of the day, carrying with them – who can tell? disease and death.[20]

The Municipal Commission initially sought to manage the problem by regulating and improving the nightsoil system, as proposed by its engineers James MacRitchie in 1890 and Robert Pierce in 1905. These changes required house owners to use proper pails or jars and ensure that they were placed on solid floors to prevent the waste from seeping into the ground. The Municipality also built more pail latrines to deter people from discarding waste into the drains.[21]

As Brenda Yeoh documented, the superior alternative to nightsoil collection was the water closet, which the sanitary expert W.J. Simpson recommended to the Municipality in 1907. Although his proposal was accepted, the building of water closets and a system of underground sewers was long in the making. It required a substantial outlay but the Municipality had committed its funds, ironically enough, to the extension of waterworks. It was only in 1916 that the first water closets were installed in houses along Cross Street and Chin Chew Street. Another reason for the delay was the deeply held belief that Asians were intrinsically unhygienic and incapable of using the new system. But this was proven wrong when most residents easily accepted the water closets, just as they would do with biomedical drugs, hospitals and vaccines. On the flip side, the new system increased the consumption of water and also served only a fraction of the urban population, so the nightsoil system and water closets continued to coexist in Singapore till the 1980s, especially in rural areas.[22]

The issues of water supply, drainage and sewage disposal were long known to the town's European and educated Asian residents. Numerous critiques of government inaction – and of the town's unwholesome sights and smells – were published in Singapore's English newspapers. The officials were aware that heavy rains, floods or high tides would wash out the organic waste from the houses located along the rivers and contaminate the drinking water.[23] But improvements were gradual and piecemeal. Although the habits of the Asian working class were unsanitary, they were a result of the low priority the colonial and municipal administrations gave to the urban environment. Major reforms had to await the end of the Japanese Occupation and especially after Singapore became a self-governing state in 1959. Prior to this, the town's population lived under the perpetual threat of cholera.

## Disorder in the Coolie Town

Cholera was endemic in Singapore soon after the establishment of East India Company rule in 1819. Dr Lee Yong Kiat, a medical historian, suggested that outbreaks were generally mild in the first half of the 19th century. This was due to the island's relative isolation from epidemics in the Malay peninsula and effective quarantine measures, though the illness became more prevalent subsequently. Both these explanations are unconvincing; we have seen how porous to disease the borders of Singapore and Malaya were and how lacking the quarantine system (both maritime and on land) was. It is more likely that cholera epidemics were not properly documented.

The 1851 cholera outbreak was the first epidemic that received substantial attention. As discussed earlier, it was a catalyst for the expansion of the municipal water supply. But the *Singapore Free Press* noted during the outbreak that many Asian patients refused to be treated in a hospital, this being where the convicts and vagrants were treated.[24] The outbreak caused panic among the populace, particularly the Malays, whose imams led a procession from one mosque to another, pleading for mercy from the epidemic.[25] In the first half-century after the founding of Singapore, the Malays suffered greatly from cholera outbreaks.

In 1858, the Straits government reported that cholera had been 'hovering about this settlement for nearly the whole of the past year', being also prevalent in Penang and Malacca. Then an explosive epidemic occurred in Singapore in March of that year, creating 'the greatest panic'. It was a severe outbreak, killing numerous Chinese living in the sago and other factories and Malays dwelling in the swampy villages on the outskirts of town, as well as 17 prisoners in the island's jails.[26]

Westerners' fear of cholera was intertwined with tropes of the filthy native and disorderly Asian. In 1884, the government urged the Municipality to increase the number of public standpipes in the town, for 'The habits of the native are well known, and how he will drink almost anything rather than have to go any distance to fetch his supply'.[27] In reality, the Asian groups viewed cholera outbreaks within their own cosmology of sickness. During an epidemic in 1862, a *Straits Times* correspondent expressed disgust at the sight of a 'Churruk Pooja' – a Hindu procession to appease the 'Cholera Divinity' (likely the Hindu goddess Kali). This was headed by a man with a pair of knives stuck into his face (one was pierced through his tongue), who was accompanied by another man beating a gong.[28] The Chinese also had their own boisterous processions, burning joss, firing crackers and beating gongs along the streets to drive away the evil spirits of cholera. The Europeans viewed such acts as injurious to public order and safety, though the Commissioner of Police had given the Chinese permission to set off the crackers.[29]

The fear of cholera in the town was rooted in its endemicity in the region. This was true for much of the 19th century when the quarantine system on St. John's Island was not fully developed. But the official anxiety never dissipated, for cholera, should it elude maritime quarantine, could spread rapidly among the allegedly unsanitary classes living in the Municipality. In 1891, a ship captain's failure to fly the quarantine flag led to his landing infected patients in the town and a minor outbreak of cholera.[30] Six years later, another local cholera outbreak, traced to an epidemic in Java, was blamed on the Javanese immigrants' 'dirty habits' and willingness to dismiss initially mild symptoms.[31] In 1912, the prevalence of cholera in the Dutch East Indies and Bombay led to fears of a costly epidemic among the four to five thousand pilgrims passing through the Straits Settlements.[32]

These fears were compounded when the Municipality grew into a coolie town.[33] Between 1871 and 1931, the population of Singapore jumped five times from 96,087 to 557,745. A major component of the growth was the mass immigration of Chinese peasants looking for manual work in the entrepôt, coupled with increased fertility rates in the 1930s. But housing failed to keep pace with the population surge, limited to coolie lines and tiny shop-houses on the sides of the Singapore River. The 1938 Weisberg Committee reported that the urban population had doubled in the previous five years, rendering the shophouses into 'warrens of cubicles' and 'a proved menace to the health of the people'.[34] The Municipal Commission found that the population density in five congested shophouses had somehow managed to increase further in this time.[35]

At the beginning of this period of hyper-urbanisation, a cholera epidemic occurred in Singapore in 1873 that was to have great historical significance. The Acting Principal Civil Medical Officer A.F. Anderson thought that the epidemic might have been imported by a ship sailing from the infected port of Bangkok. He thought that the outbreak was worsened by the long drought and reduced supply of water, poor drainage system and the unsanitary conditions of the town's houses and compounds.[36] The epidemic reached the Lunatic Asylum located alongside a canal that ran into the Kallang River. It also struck nearby Kampong Kapor, a low-lying settlement of 'squalid huts' on the eastern side of the town, inhabited by poor Malays and Indians.[37] Human waste from the kampong's latrines, which were dug beneath the floor, were washed out by the tides, spreading the infection to other parts of the town, including the densely populated Tanjong Pagar district near the Singapore port.

A total of 857 cases of cholera were reported, of which 357 died, giving rise to a relatively low mortality rate of 41.7 per cent. The government responded by clearing the town's drains but bemoaned the 'prejudices of the Natives' who chose not to report the disease or seek medical help before the illness became advanced. From the Asians' vantage point, their actions made sense, as most patients who did go to the TTSH were thrown into an emergency attap shed to die there in four or five hours. The epidemic was also blamed for discouraging parents from bringing their children to be vaccinated for smallpox, although as we have seen in the previous chapter, the reasons were systemic and preceded the outbreak.[38] The epidemic moved the colonial government to build a rudimentary quarantine station on St. John's.[39] This was seen at the time as the solution that would cause the least disruption to Singapore's trade, by having ships quarantined on an offshore island. But the quarantine system was long beset by mercantile criticisms that it was bad for trade.[40]

To the officials, the epidemic provided proof of the disorderly people they governed. A report in the *Straits Times* claimed that as few Europeans were affected, the outbreak was due to 'the filthy manner in which the natives live, and the nature of their diet, which is very conducive to derangements of the system in a poisoned atmosphere'.[41] Just as revealing was a British Legislative Councillor who was also a medical doctor, who expressed what he saw as rowdy Indian behaviour:

> Since the cholera appeared, there has been a liberty and licence to the inhabitants to break out into processions, and they had these processions every night, of Hindoos and Klings, apparently drunk with bhang and spirits, who proceeded through the principal streets, brandishing swords and knives, and torches, screaming and howling to such a degree that the peaceable inhabitants had no comfort.[42]

The British did not consider the next cholera outbreak in 1885 an epidemic, but while the number of cases and deaths were unknown, it almost certainly was one. This outbreak was also significant for the shift in the ethnic preponderance of the cases from Malays to Chinese. Henceforth, the latter bore much of the criticism for the outbreaks. A lengthy colonial report documented how the disease first appeared among Javanese coolies employed at a public brick kiln at Serangoon Road. Government officials disinfected the area where they lived and burned the huts. The infection was traced to organic waste in the Kallang River – known for its pollution – which was carried to the Javanese settlement via a canal. The outbreak ceased when the TTSH supplied clean water to the settlement. But other employees and residents at Serangoon Road soon fell ill with cholera, which spread to other areas as people continued to drink contaminated water. The final infected area encompassed the Sepoy Lines district that contained the General Hospital, where cholera patients were admitted, and Kampong Malacca, a popular destination for *sinkehs*. These newly arrived Chinese immigrants had also contracted the disease and were deemed to have caused the spread of the outbreak.[43]

The government encountered the same passive resistance as they did with plague and smallpox, with 'most of the sufferers refusing, and all being unwilling, to render any account as to who they were, or whence they came'.[44] Advanced and dying patients were brought outside the hospital by rickshaws and dumped there; as we will see, the rickshawmen themselves paid a heavy price for these services. The Protector of Chinese William Pickering and the Principal Civil Health Officer T. Irvine Rowell visited the Chinese immigrant depots in the town. They despatched, under a police guard, 89 patients and contacts, including the innkeepers, to St. John's for quarantine. One of them got away but died in the jungle. Quarantine, Rowell surmised, finally stemmed the outbreak.[45]

In his post-mortem, Rowell viewed the outbreak as a racial event. It was the housing in the immigrant depots that made the outbreak difficult to control, 'being buildings constructed on principles peculiarly Chinese, with little or no heed paid to sanitation'.[46] He was less judgemental about the drought in the early part of the year which had reduced the water supply from the standpipes and forced people to buy contaminated water from the rivers hawked by 'Chinamen'.[47] He did recognise the need to establish an adequate supply of clean water and a proper drainage system in place of existing 'mud drains'.[48]

### 'Illness enters through the mouth'

A pair of severe cholera epidemics struck in 1895–1896, despite efforts to improve the quarantine service on St. John's in the early part of the decade. The Medical Department was uncertain about how cholera had arrived in Singapore in 1895, but it had been pandemic in Bangkok, Saigon, Amoy, Swatow, and Japan. The overall death rate in Singapore that year was high, but the government was reluctant to pin it on cholera (instead attributing it some unestablished cause).[49] As cases appeared in the town, the Municipal Commission asked the Executive Council to impose a short (five-day) quarantine on ships arriving at Singapore from Chinese ports, but the Principal Civil Medical Health Officer declined this, maintaining that it was sufficient to inspect the vessels.[50]

The subsequent outbreak caused 430 cases, 309 deaths and a high mortality rate of 71.9 per cent, with a small number (17) occurring in the rural area (or likely were removed there). Again, hospitals and asylums were not spared: outbreaks in the TTSH and Lunatic Asylum resulted in death rates of 66 per cent and 44.5 per cent respectively.[51] Though the hospital had a supply of drinking water from the Municipality, its bathing water was drawn from wells dug within its compound, where many of the hospital's cases occurred.[52] The Municipality distributed instructions on what to do in Tamil, Malay and Chinese, while a Chinese was jailed for falsely reporting a cholera death as being due to fever. It admitted that there was inadequate sanitary staff to cope with the large number of cases in the town; worse, the colonial government had just carried out a round of retrenchment in the Medical Department.[53] As the police were initially unaware of the rise in cholera deaths, the 1895 epidemic led to the appointment of two qualified medical inspectors to certify causes of death and obtain reliable information from the community.[54]

The Medical Department could not trace the source of the epidemic, though the Principal Civil Medical Officer thought it was not imported, which would have triggered a large outbreak in the coolie depots.[55] The event was instead blamed on 'some unusual meteorological conditions' – periods of heavy rainfall followed by long dry spells. Thus, the department surmised, 'the poison which may have lain dormant in parts of town for an indefinite time became awakened into life'.[56] Interestingly, the Municipality disagreed, deeming the outbreak to have been imported since there were few cases of cholera in previous years while the rainfall was not a likely factor.[57] The Medical Department also thought, rather dubiously, the town fortunate to escape a worse outbreak due to its 'excellent water supply'.[58]

Such thinking was a holdover from the miasma theory and specifically the 1860s notion that cholera was linked to meteorological conditions rather than contagion. It was only in 1884 that Robert Koch discovered the cholera bacillus, though the theory of contagion still had to accommodate the role of contingent factors like the physical environment and sanitation.[59] This allowed for racial discourses on cholera outbreaks even within the theory of contagion. But the latter did lead to renewed efforts to deliver a supply of potable water and prevent food contamination for the poorer classes.[60] Not surprisingly, the bulk of the cases occurred among coolies who lacked access to potable water; by contrast, only one European had died. The government analyst reported that while the municipal water was fit for drinking, 'the well and ground water [had] to be condemned'.[61]

By this time, the educated Chinese community had accepted cholera as an infectious disease. The *Lat Pau* attributed the epidemic to tiny worms too small to be seen with the naked eye. One should therefore take care not come into contact with the faeces of cholera patients. The paper urged the cleansing of drains and toilets, as well as the boiling of water and proper cooking of food. Like the government, it thought that rainfall was a factor in the emergence of cholera, for the rains would wash away the worms while the cooling effect was beneficial for the human body.[62]

Another epidemic followed in 1896: 592 cases, 474 deaths and a higher mortality rate of 80.1 per cent. The vast majority were again male Chinese coolies in their prime, among them many rickshaw pullers. Evasion remained widespread, with numerous cases found only after death. The outbreak appeared to be a new one that, according to the Municipality, originated within the town, as cholera cases and contacts earlier in the year had been quarantined on St. John's.[63] The commission did not acknowledge the likelihood that many contacts were the wrong ones as the patients or bodies might have been moved. The Medical Department, while still claiming that 'the poison is here', wanted the town's private wells closed and the Municipality to install additional standpipes. This time the commission attributed the outbreak to polluted well water and low rainfall.[64]

James Warren's immersive study of rickshawmen revealed the fear of cholera among denizens of the coolie town who had to drink from wells and lived close to one another in cramped quarters. Through the social history of the town, it is clear that susceptibility to cholera stemmed from the prerogatives of colonial rule and the specifics of the rickshaw trade. The wells were usually polluted, lacking a brick or cement lining to shield them from the contents of latrines and drains that were invariably close by. Worse, nightsoil buckets were also washed at the same wells.[65]

As Warren observed, 'Among all water-borne diseases rickshawmen encountered, in lodginghouses and on the streets, cholera was the most terrifying'.[66] Well water was both life and death to them:

> They didn't dare run and just shuffled along with their heads down. Every well became their lucky star. It didn't matter how far they'd gone-when they saw a well they hurried over to it. They'd just take a long drink

at the trough along with the horses … if there wasn't any freshly drawn water. And there those who, coming down with cholera … just went on and on until they collapsed and never stood up again.[67]

Using the coroner's inquests into the deaths of rickshawmen, Warren was able to reconstruct an eyewitness account of the dumping of a puller who had died of cholera during the 1910 epidemic:

Lim Lye, who was resting on a verandah off Queen Street, watched two Chinese dump the corpse of a rickshaw puller, a cholera victim, on the verandah at about 2 a.m. in the morning. They had taken the body from No. 129–4 Queen Street which stood empty as all the pullers had cleared out.[68]

With the peril of death by cholera ever-present, as Brenda Yeoh noted, Chinese coolies treated the disease as being caused by demons – something they could control, unlike the political economy of their work. In 1907, an outbreak of cholera led hundreds of rickshawmen to organise a noisy festival to scare off the cholera spirits. A procession of coolies, armed with spears and other weapons, beat drums and set off fire crackers while a medium conducted a sophisticated exorcism ritual – all of which were reprehensible to municipal officials.[69] Conversely, traditional Chinese treatment proffered the view that cholera was a cold-based disease that required medicines to warm the blood vessels.[70] During the 1895 epidemic, a Chinese contributor to the *Straits Times* maintained that the popular ginger drink was an effective remedy that should be made widely available to the people.[71]

In 1900–1901, another epidemic occurred, this time with a severe mortality rate of 92.1%. It started in the Lunatic Asylum before spreading to the coolie lines at the Tanjong Pagar docks and other parts of the town. Non-notification was rife, with 82 cases discovered after death in 1901.[72] An article in the *Lat Pau* viewed the epidemic as an example of how 'illness enters through the mouth', as the labouring class in Singapore was not inclined to boil the water, preferring to drink it cool. Interestingly, it did not blame the municipal authorities for the inadequate water supply or allowing the filter tanks to fall into disrepair.[73] In a follow-up article, the paper wrote about the consumption of rotting vegetables and fruits as another way for illness to enter through the mouth. But this time it emphasised the need to wash the streets of the entire town instead of only the European commercial area, while warning that the drinking water should be purified and the filter tanks repaired.[74]

The epidemic was followed by a drought and another massive cholera outbreak in 1902, with 842 cases and a death rate of 90.1 per cent. It again afflicted mostly the Chinese working class residing along the Singapore River, though it had first appeared among Malays living at the mouth of the polluted Kallang River. The Municipality hurriedly despatched sanitary inspectors to conduct a house-to-house search among the coolie lines, death houses, opium dens, eating houses and residences, covering 611 houses daily on average.[75] This was an unpleasant experience for many residents. As an account in the *Straits Times* highlighted, some officials smashed crockery instead of disinfecting it, which would have further discouraged the Chinese from reporting cholera to the authorities.[76]

The *Lat Pau* duly drew caution to the outbreak, citing the measures recommended by the US and Japanese consuls to, among other things, refrain from using nightsoil buckets for other purposes, properly boil drinking water and cook the food, and isolate the patient.[77] Throughout the cholera epidemics of 1895, 1900 and 1902 (the years when the paper was in circulation), the *Lat Pau* had made no reference to the exorcism rituals in previous outbreaks, nor any advocacy of traditional Chinese medicine or divine causes as it did for plague and influenza. It seems that following the discovery of the cholera bacillus, learned Chinese opinion in Singapore had accepted cholera to be an infectious disease.

In 1910, there were 157 cholera cases, including a mental patient who contracted the disease and triggered another outbreak in the Lunatic Asylum, killing nine persons. It was thought that the deteriorating conditions of the Municipality's water pipes beneath the asylum contributed to the outbreak, but this was not proven.[78] A further 30 died among the 194 contacts sent to St. John's, a sign of the spread of infection. The outbreak revealed another high-handed measure of the colonial officials: the Chinese contacts had their queues tied together four in a group as they were brought to the island. The editor of the *Straits Times* considered this deplorable but thought that they would still need to be handcuffed, unlike Europeans who understood the law and abided by the sanitary regulations.[79]

The epidemic the following year caused 296 cases and 270 deaths (a high mortality rate of 91.2 per cent), though the government claimed that it was 'in no sense severe'. The town's water supply had been found to be 'offensive and dirty' several days before the outbreak. Again, cholera invaded the Lunatic Asylum, including its ward at the Pasir Panjang coast five miles from the town. A total of 504 contacts were removed to St. John's.[80] The Municipal Commission found 114 concealed cases and 38 cases dumped in various parts of the town and reported, 'Dumping of dead bodies in the streets and concealment of the occurrence of the disease helped to spread it throughout the town and greatly hampered the work of the Health Department in combating it'.[81]

The question of concealment was linked to the facilities for quarantine. On the quarantine of cholera contacts, the 1912 Quarantine Commission had proposed for a camp for them to be built at the proposed infectious diseases hospital at Moulmein Road and additional land to be acquired for this purpose.[82] In a meeting of the Municipal Commissioners that year, Dr Fowlie argued that quarantine had proved to be 'of no use and a failure', and abolishing it would encourage people to report cases of cholera. The Health Officer disagreed, pointing out that cholera had spread when people had tried to care for the patient or touched infected clothing, while it was also difficult to identify which contacts inside a dwelling might have been infected. Dr Yin, who was part of the Quarantine Commission, also thought that cholera contacts should not be allowed to go about at large. He suggested that the fear of quarantine could be overcome by building proper accommodation for hospital treatment and segregation.[83]

The Municipal Commission voted in favour of quarantine and improved accommodation at the new infectious diseases hospital as ways to reduce concealment of the disease.[84] Nevertheless, when the hospital was completed in 1913, financial considerations had caused its cholera section to be reduced. It only had a section for lower-class Asian patients, while Europeans and upper-class Asians would be treated in the observation wards.[85] Cholera contacts continued to be sent to St. John's, rather than the hospital, for quarantine, especially when there were large numbers. In view of the cholera epidemics in previous years, these municipal decisions were downright disappointing.

A reminder of the public cost did not have to wait long. In 1914, there was another cholera epidemic, involving 311 cases and 240 deaths, with a mortality rate of 77.2%. Again, the disease ravaged the rickshaw trade, spreading among the congested lodging houses in which the pullers dwelt. Most of the patients were isolated at the Moulmein Road Hospital, where an emergency ward had to be built to cater to the large number of cases, placing a heavy strain on the staff.[86] This time, the outbreak affected not only the Lunatic Asylum, but also the TTSH – twice. This was attributed to the lack of fencing around the hospital and the unsanitary habits of the patients, who transmitted the illness to patients treated for other ailments.[87]

The outbreak did hasten the building of a new cholera ward in what became the Middleton Hospital, completed eventually in 1921. This ironically seemed unnecessary in hindsight; the 1914 epidemic was the last major outbreak in Singapore before the Second World War. By then, the municipal gaze had shifted to other infectious diseases like typhoid. As early as 1927, the colonial government was confident enough to state, 'Cholera is definitely tending to die out'.[88] Between the 1920s and 1950s, even though it remained quarantinable and endemic in the region, Singapore was virtually free of cholera. This was due to effective quarantine on St. John's following the report of the 1912 Quarantine Commission, as well as improved sanitation of the town, particularly in the provision of clean drinking water and prompt disinfection of contaminated water sources.[89]

## El Tor Cholera in a Time of Nationhood

Much of the problem of insanitation in the town was resolved during the years of decolonisation and early nation-building. A physically and socially transformed Singapore was in the making. The 1948 Medical Plan aimed to expand the healthcare system to meet the needs of a larger population.[90] But more important was the Master Plan of 1955 that guided it, bringing together medical, housing and other reforms under a single rubric for the development of Singapore over 20 years.[91] Thus the control of cholera was linked to the mass public housing programme to replace the coolie lines, shophouses and urban kampongs with modern housing. This was first begun by the Singapore Improvement Trust after the war and substantially expanded by the Housing and Development Board (HDB) formed in 1960.

The HDB built emergency housing estates equipped with piped water, proper drainage and sewage disposal, giving the residents access to potable water and freedom from water-borne diseases such as cholera. The density of the HDB's high-rise flats was still high, but living closely together no longer posed the same sort of risks for cholera as it did before. Accompanying the physical change in housing was an equally important revolution in people's mindsets and behaviour – as part of changing from 'squatters into citizens'.[92] The new housing and social amenities were modern, but also regulated to engineer new citizens of the nation. Thus most HDB dwellers who accepted a more structured way of life and work were also more inclined to embrace state interventions into matters of health and disease. A particular economic group that encountered these new regulations were the hawkers. Largely itinerant and unlicensed in the colonial era, they were now removed to permanent hawker centres and surveyed for food contamination.

In this context, the 1961 island-wide vaccination campaign for cholera and the epidemic that broke out two years later occurred in a very different Singapore that was making this transition from a coolie town to a planned city-state. Both the campaign and the epidemic were linked to the spread of the El Tor cholera pandemic, often called the seventh cholera pandemic that originated in Sulawesi, Indonesia, in 1961. The El Tor biotype was a more benign strain than classic cholera. First discovered in India's Ganges delta in 1937, it had appeared in Singapore during the Japanese Occupation seven years later. Then, villagers in rural Loyang had eaten cabbages dumped into the sea by an infected Japanese ship.[93]

The 1961 vaccination campaign was part of the post-colonial government's move to vaccinate the entire populace against dangerous infectious diseases, which also included tuberculosis and diphtheria. In this push for mass vaccination, it should be noted that the cholera vaccine conferred only partial, short-term immunity to the disease. The context offers some explanation for this vaccine enthusiasm. By this time, Singapore had attained self-government and the spread of El Tor cholera had reached the surrounding territories, namely, Borneo, the Philippines, Hong Kong, and Macau. Singapore's vaccination exercise spanned the nation: the city, rural areas and offshore islands, covering 474,224 people (a third of the population) that year, including school children. The country also increased its vigilance against the introduction of cholera from ships and aircraft, while placing a ban on the import of fresh vegetables, fruits and meat from infected countries like China, Hong Kong and Taiwan between September and November, 1961.[94]

These measures were vindicated when cholera arrived in Singapore two years later in 1963 – the first time in 17 years. It caused two outbreaks in May and November and was presumably imported from Malaya, though no direct cause was established. The government's responses to both outbreaks were immediate and forceful. The index – and only – case in the May outbreak was a Chinese woman who lived in an urban kampong in Potong Pasir. From the investigations of the Environmental Health Branch of the MOH, she could have caught the infection by eating uncooked cockles sold by a public food handler, but this was not proven to be true.[95] She shared her wooden dwelling with her husband, mother-in-law and five children, and four other families. Branch officials cordoned off an area of about 200 yards radius around the house, including the fencing of the Woodleigh water filters, and inspected 639 persons; 476 latrines in this area were sprayed with a solution of Jeyes fluid and 69 wells and four ponds were disinfected with chlorinated lime. The ponds were precariously connected to the latrines and used for a variety of purposes, such as breeding fish, washing laundry, growing vegetables, and bathing cattle.[96]

The November–December outbreak was a bigger event. It was traced to a resident in Kampong Chia Heng. There were 26 cases, mostly Chinese, resulting in two deaths (an elderly woman and an opium addict with severe malnutrition). Half of the cases had contracted the disease after attending a mooncake festival dinner.[97] The majority (19) had not been vaccinated, illustrating how difficult it still was for vaccinators to operate effectively in rural settlements. Disinfection and chlorination of water containers and wells were again carried out. By this time, Singapore had joined the Federation of Malaysia as a constituent state, but its government retained control over the health ministry.[98]

The administration launched emergency immunisation campaigns during the two outbreaks. Nation-wide publicity in the mass media drove the campaigns forward. Totals of 1.2 million and 800,000 people respectively were vaccinated in May and November–December at maternal and child health centres and outpatient dispensaries, as health services penetrated the rural areas. Mobile teams performed vaccinations in outlying villages and offshore islands. The MOH carried out other measures, such as improving the disinfection of aircraft toilet wastes, quarantining contacts on St. John's and at the Middleton Hospital and investigating cockles imported from Johore (the results were negative).

The social response to the outbreaks and vaccinations reflected a new political milieu in Singapore. On the one hand, manpower for the first vaccination exercise was affected by a nurses' strike in June, though this was resolved by calling up over a hundred Singapore Hospital Reserve volunteers. The MOH reported 'a certain degree of public apathy' in the second exercise, though this was understandable given the success of the first and overall the mass vaccination was deemed to be satisfactory.[99] An unnamed doctor, G.A.L., wrote in the *Singapore Medical Journal* that the first exercise would have moved more quickly had general practitioners been involved in the vaccination.[100]

On the other hand, the events of 1963 witnessed an emerging sense of medical citizenship – the belief that being a good citizen entails embracing concepts of cleanliness and hygiene so as to support Singapore's survival.

Letters in the newspapers exhorted the importance of timely government intervention and people's civic responsibility. Much of the national obligation fell onto the shoulders of hawkers, who seemed at odds with the idea of a clean city envisaged by the government. One letter urged that while they had to ply their trade, hawkers should not ignore hygiene and cleanliness, noting that those at Koek Road were dumping leftovers into the drain or five-foot-way.[101] Another letter drew attention to the choked drains at the Dunman and Joo Chiat Roads where hawker food was sold and eaten on the spot.[102] 'Kim', another writer, asked people to replace old habits with modern hygiene standards, so that Singapore's beautiful beaches could attract foreign tourists.[103]

Overall, the government assessed the 1963 epidemic to be a minor one. It was confident about its ability to contain the threat of cholera: although the disease was endemic in Malaysia, its incidence, severity and mortality rate in Singapore would likely remain low. It accepted the El Tor strain to be endemic, transmitted by an unknown group of asymptomatic carriers. In the 1960s and 1970s, oral rehydration therapy became an effective and inexpensive method for quickly replacing fluids lost by patients. It meant cholera was no longer the feared killer it once was. But social responsibility was paramount: as cholera was a bowel disease, good public health was essential, and the importance of personal hygiene in using water and disposing waste, especially in rural areas, could not be replaced by vaccination alone.[104]

Singapore's experiences with El Tor cholera in the early 1960s can be compared with Fang Xiaoping's micro-study of the 1962 cholera pandemic in Wenzhou Prefecture, China. There, the epidemic connected with a massive social restructuring programme to produce what he called an 'emergency disciplinary state', armed with big data and a capacity to command mass quarantine for its subjects.[105] On a smaller scale, Singapore's cholera epidemic had a similar social and political impact, giving an emergent nation-state the means to forge a socially aware citizenry. This became clear in the ensuing years.

After Singapore became independent in 1965, epidemiological surveillance became the chief means of preventing another cholera epidemic through the swift notification and investigation of cases.[106] The idea of ringfencing an outbreak through quarantine was dismissed as 'practically useless'.[107] Sporadic outbreaks of El Tor cholera occurred in the post-colonial period, often imported from the region and affecting working-class Chinese living in high-density HDB flats. The slum and squatter housing of old were being rapidly replaced by modern public housing.[108] The outbreaks also affected male foreign construction workers, in 1982 and 1993, who lived closely together in temporary shelters called 'bangsals'. This was a result of Singapore becoming increasingly reliant on low-wage migrant labour from the 1970s.[109]

The social effect of epidemiological surveillance was to create the ominous figure of the hawker as a potential asymptomatic carrier selling contaminated food to the public.[110] The government held that contaminated food (such as shellfish) sold by infected food handlers was the chief means of spreading cholera.[111] Unlike individuals who would only make themselves and their household members ill, hawkers could infect the wider community. Stringent measures against hawkers were thus needed to safeguard the safety of the garden city.[112] During an outbreak in 1972 (Singapore's worst since independence), thousands of hawkers and food handlers came under scrutiny and were screened for cholera and typhoid.[113] When 'Doctor' wrote in the *New Nation* that unlicenced hawkers were unfairly scapegoated by the government,[114] he received a stern rebuke from the MOH's Public Health Division denying such discrimination.[115]

The social response was just as telling. The public was urged not to purchase food from unhygienic hawkers in order to force them to change their ways. But this led to social judgements on hawkers' physical actions and immediate surroundings, inviting much pressure and censure upon the group.[116] A letter to the press warned that an unclean hawker could be a potential cholera or typhoid carrier.[117] Another drew attention to the manifest practices of unhygienic hawkers who might transmit cholera to others: those who did not properly wash their plates and cutlery, used bare hands to handle food and did not remove the dust and dirt in their proximity.[118] These incriminations recalled the complaints about filthy Chinese coolies that upheld the colonial system and the classification of races and classes. But the historical context was quite different: the problems of water supply, drainage and sewage disposal had mostly been resolved. Instead, the post-colonial government's priorities were to regulate the hawker industry, socialise the people into medical citizens and develop Singapore into a garden city.

The government followed closely the medical science for cholera. It accepted that the disease could not be prevented at the points of entry into Singapore. Following similar changes in the International Health Regulations, Singapore ceased to require cholera vaccination certificates for air arrivals in December 1970 and sea arrivals four years later.[119] At the end of the decade, the government decided that cholera contacts no longer had to be isolated at the Middleton Hospital unless they were handling food or had diarrhoea.

The Joint Coordinating Committee on Epidemic Disease, a high-level interministerial group tasked with monitoring infectious diseases, was initially concerned with cholera. It surveyed the sporadic outbreaks, aided by early notification from general practitioners. Much of its concern stemmed from the possible spread of the illness from Malaysia to Singapore and the resulting impact on trade and travel.[120] In January 1979, the committee decided that Singapore would be declared an infected area only if two or more related cholera cases were reported.[121] By the end of the year, the committee was confident that while cholera would continue to be imported into Singapore, the risk of transmission was negligible due to the high standards of environmental sanitation.[122] There was some apprehension that new strains of antibiotic-resistant cholera could be introduced into Singapore.[123] But generally, the committee was more concerned about other severe diarrhoeal diseases caused by *Vibrio parahaemolyticus, Salmonella* species and other foodborne organisms.[124]

While El Tor cholera had devastating effects on weak and failed states in Africa, its impact on Singapore has been quite different.[125] In the 2000s, the incidence of cholera and other foodborne diseases declined despite Singapore being situated in an endemic region. The government attributed this to high standards of environmental sanitation, food hygiene practices, comprehensive surveillance, licensing and control of food factories and retail outlets, health education, and supervision of public food handlers. Quarantine was not one of the listed factors. There were still ethnic differences in the incidence of cholera: the Chinese were sometimes found to have contracted the disease by eating raw or undercooked food such as cockles and oysters, while foreign workers did so by consuming wild caught shellfish collected from sewage-contaminated areas.[126]

As one of the trinity of infectious diseases in Singapore, cholera was a sickness of the urban environment. Beginning with the construction of MacRitchie Reservoir, cholera outbreaks eventually contributed to far-reaching environmental improvements after the war. Nevertheless, the history of cholera is not simply one of the progress of modern science and engineering. It was marked by political, ethnic and class divides during the colonial era, as well as by historical continuities. British officials and doctors had demarcated Europeans and Asians – the former were educated and sound, while the latter were filthy and unruly. This did not help control outbreaks of cholera but it was germane to the racial hierarchies of colonial domination.

The threat of cholera also differed greatly between the houses and neighbourhoods of the officials and mandarins that had access to potable water and proper sewerage disposal, and the vast majority of the coolie town that did not. Among the port city's labouring classes, rickshaw pullers paid a heavy price for the failings of the Municipality and the colonial government to provide basic social amenities for the people. We can still see social dimensions of cholera control after Singapore became an independent state and such amenities became widely available. Cholera became a marker of citizenship, with hawkers deemed a high-risk group who had to be regularly tested by the state and scrutinised by fellow citizens.

## Notes

1  David Arnold, *Colonising the Body: State Medicine and Epidemic Disease in Nineteenth-Century India* (Berkeley: University of California Press, 1993), p. 166.
2  Myron Echenberg, *Africa in the Time of Cholera: A History of Pandemics from 1815 to the Present* (Cambridge: Cambridge University Press, 2011).
3  Arnold, *Colonising the Body*.
4  *Straits Times*, 19 November 1873, p. 5.
5  *Mid-Day Herald*, 9 May 1896, p. 2.
6  See Kwa Chong Guan and Joey Long, *Water: A Precious Resource for Singapore* (Singapore: Public Utilities Board, Singapore, 2002); Jillian Geno-Oehlers, *The Water Supply of Singapore*, unpublished academic exercise, Department of Geography, University of Singapore, 1966; Balakrishnan Jayakumar, *The Singapore Water Supply, 1819–1945: The Evolution of a Governmental Responsibility*,

unpublished academic exercise, Department of History, Faculty of Arts & Social Sciences, National University of Singapore, 1989; and Joel Teo, 'Singapore Legal History of Water: The Municipal and the Singapore Story – Past, Present and Future', *Singapore Law Review*, Vol. 24, 2004, pp. 22–51.

7   *Singapore Free Press*, 24 January 1851, p. 3.
8   *Singapore Free Press*, 25 April 1851, p. 2.
9   Lee Yong Kiat, *The Medical History of Early Singapore* (Tokyo: Southeast Asian Medical Information Centre, 1978).
10  Teo, 'Singapore Legal History of Water'.
11  *The Singapore Free Press and Mercantile Advertiser*, 3 March 1896, p. 4.
12  Goh Chor Boon, *Technology and Entrepôt Colonialism in Singapore, 1819–1940* (Singapore: Institute of Southeast Asian Studies, 2013), p. 17.
13  SMAR 1901.
14  SMAR 1899, p. 58.
15  SMAR 1905, pp. 29–30.
16  SMAR 1897.
17  *Singapore Free Press*, 18 October 1849, p. 2.
18  CO 275/15 Memo from Staff Surgeon-Major H.T. Reade to the Hon'ble Colonial Secretary, Straits Settlements, 24 July 1872.
19  Brenda S.A. Yeoh, *Contesting Space in Colonial Singapore: Power Relations and the Built Environment* (Singapore: Singapore University Press, 2003).
20  *Straits Observer*, 31 May 1875, p. 3.
21  Yeoh, *Contesting Space in Colonial Singapore*.
22  Centre for Liveable Cities, 'The Sanitation System in Singapore', *Infopedia*, https://eresources.nlb.gov.sg/infopedia/articles/SIP_2020-02-06_113509.html
23  CO 275/30 AMRCHSS 1884.
24  *Singapore Free Press*, 24 January 1851, p. 3.
25  *Singapore Free Press*, 31 January 1851, p. 3.
26  Robert L. Jarman (ed.), *Annual Report on the Administration of the Straits Settlements, 1857–1858* (Archive Editions, 1998), Vol. 1, pp. 135–136.
27  CO 275/30 AMRCHSS 1884, p. C-27.
28  *Straits Times*, 5 April 1862, p. 2.
29  *Singapore Free Press*, 7 April 1862, p. 1; *Straits Times*, 15 March 1862, p. 2.
30  CO 275/42 AMRCHSS 1891.
31  SMAR 1897, p. 69.
32  CO 273/528, Memo from Under-Secretary of State for Foreign Affairs to Under-Secretary of State for the Colonial Office, 22 August 1912.
33  James Francis Warren, *Rickshaw Coolie: A People's History of Singapore, 1880–1940* (Singapore: Singapore University Press, 2003).
34  SIT 70/41 Report of the Committee Appointed to Make Recommendations for the Redevelopment of Certain Crown Lease Land in Singapore.
35  SMAR 1939.
36  CO 275/16 The Acting Principal Civil Medical Officer's Report on the Epidemic of Cholera, 22 July 1873.
37  CO 275/18 AMRCHSS 1873, p. xxxi.
38  CO 275/18 AMRCHSS 1873.
39  CO 275/119 SSMR 1927.
40  *Straits Times Overland Journal*, 9 August 1873, p. 14; *Straits Times Overland Journal*, 4 December 1873, p. 8.
41  *Straits Times Overland Journal*, 9 August 1873, p. 1.
42  *Straits Times Overland Journal*, 6 September 1873, p. 5.
43  CO 275/31 AMRCHSS 1885.
44  CO 275/31 AMRCHSS 1885, p. C-21.
45  CO 275/31 AMRCHSS 1885.

46  CO 275/31 AMRCHSS 1885, p. C-22.
47  CO 275/31 AMRCHSS 1885, p. C-22.
48  CO 275/31 AMRCHSS 1885, p. C-23.
49  CO 275/50 AMRCHSS 1895.
50  CO 275/52 Minutes of Executive Council Meeting, 12 August 1895.
51  CO 275/50 AMRCHSS 1895.
52  CO 273/206 Report by Principal Civil Medical Officer, 5 October 1895.
53  SMAR 1895.
54  W.R.C. Middleton, 'The Working of the Births and Deaths Registration Ordi-
    nance', *The Malaya Medical Journal*, July 1911, pp. 33–50.
55  CO 273/206 Report by Principal Civil Medical Officer, 5 October 1895.
56  CO 275/50 AMRCHSS 1895, p. 561.
57  SMAR 1895.
58  CO 275/50 AMRCHSS 1895, p. 561.
59  Arnold, *Colonising the Body*.
60  Alfred Jay Bollet, *Plagues & Poxes: The Impact of Human History on Epidemic
    Disease* (New York: Demos, 2004).
61  CO 275/50 AMRCHSS 1895, p. 624.
62  *Lat Pau*, 4 July 1895, p. 2.
63  SMAR 1896.
64  CO 275/53 AMRCHSS 1896, p. 542.
65  Warren, *Rickshaw Coolie*.
66  Warren, *Rickshaw Coolie*, p. 266.
67  Warren, *Rickshaw Coolie*, p. 266.
68  Warren, *Rickshaw Coolie*, p. 268.
69  *Singapore Free Press*, 29 August 1907, p. 13.
70  Yeoh, *Contesting Space in Colonial Singapore*.
71  *Straits Times*, 12 August 1895, p. 3.
72  SMAR 1901.
73  *Lat Pau*, 21 December 1900, p. 1.
74  *Lat Pau*, 22 December 1900, p. 1.
75  SMAR 1902.
76  *Straits Times*, 25 July 1902, p. 5.
77  *Lat Pau*, 9 September 1902, p. 2.
78  CO 275/84 SSMR 1910.
79  *Straits Times*, 8 February 1910, p. 8.
80  CO 275/87 SSMR 1911, p. 519.
81  SMAR 1911, p. 11.
82  Straits Settlements Quarantine Inquiry Commission, *Proceedings of the Com-
    mission Appointed to Inquire into the Working of the Quarantine and Prevention
    of Diseases Ordinance in the Settlement of Singapore, in the Colony of the Straits
    Settlements* (Singapore: Government Printing Office, 1912), 2 volumes.
83  Singapore Municipality, Minutes of Special Joint Meeting, 24 September 1912.
84  Singapore Municipality, Minutes of Special Joint Meeting, 27 September 1912.
85  SMAR 1913.
86  SMAR 1914.
87  CO 275/94 SSMR 1914.
88  CO 275/119 SSMR 1927, p. 732.
89  J.W. Scharff, 'The Growth of Public Health Services in Singapore in Relation to
    Preventive Medicine in War Time', *Journal of the Malayan Branch of the British
    Medical Association*, Vol. 3. No. 3, December 1939; J.H. Strahan, 'Reflections on
    the Course of Preventive Medicine in Malaya', *The Medical Journal of Malaya*,
    Vol. 2 No. 4, June 1948.

90   Proceedings of the Legislative Council of Singapore, *The Medical Plan for Singapore*, 18 May 1948.
91   Singapore, *Master Plan* (Singapore: Government Printing Office, 1955–1958).
92   Loh Kah Seng, *Squatters into Citizens: The 1961 Bukit Ho Swee Fire and the Making of Modern Singapore* (NUS Press and Asian Studies of Australia Association Southeast Asia Series, 2013).
93   *ENB*, Vol. 36 No. 2, April–June 2010.
94   MOHAR 1961.
95   MOH 024/58/01–000 Vol. 07 Report titled 'Cholera in Singapore', undated.
96   MOHAR 1963.
97   MOH 024/58/01–000 Vol. 07 Report titled 'Cholera in Singapore', undated.
98   MOHAR 1963.
99   MOHAR 1963, p. 87.
100  'Editorial: Cholera Outbreak', *The Singapore Medical Journal*, Vol. 4 No. 3, June 1963, pp. 52–54.
101  *Straits Times*, 11 December 1963, p. 10.
102  *Straits Times*, 23 November 1963, p. 13.
103  *Straits Times*, 7 November 1964, p. 11.
104  MOHAR 1963.
105  Xiaoping Fang, *China and the Cholera Pandemic* (Pittsburgh: University of Pittsburgh Press, 2021), p. 7.
106  MOH 024/58/01–000 Vol. 07 Report titled 'Cholera in Singapore', undated.
107  K.T. Goh, *Epidemiological Surveillance of Communicable Diseases in Singapore* (Tokyo: Southeast Asian Medical Information Centre, 1983), p. 275.
108  MOH 024/58/01–000 Vol. 07 Report titled 'Cholera in Singapore', undated; *ENB*, Vol. 7 No. 42, February 1981.
109  *ENB*, Vol. 8 No. 12, December 1982; *ENB*, Vol. 19 No. 12, December 1993; MOH 024/58/01–000 Vol. 09 Minutes of the 76th Meeting of the Joint Coordinating Committee on Epidemic Diseases, 16 November 1982.
110  *Straits Times*, 10 June 1972, p. 14.
111  MOH 024/58/01–000 Vol. 07 Report titled 'Cholera in Singapore', undated.
112  *New Nation*, 14 June 1972, p. 8.
113  *New Nation*, 10 August 1972, p. 11.
114  *New Nation*, 20 July 1972, p. 10.
115  *New Nation*, 2 August 1972, p. 8.
116  *Straits Times*, 16 June 1972, p. 20.
117  *Straits Times*, 27 November 1972, p. 16.
118  *Straits Times*, 7 June 1972, p. 29.
119  Goh, *Epidemiological Surveillance of Communicable Diseases in Singapore*.
120  Goh, *Epidemiological Surveillance of Communicable Diseases in Singapore*.
121  MOH 024/58/01–000 Vol. 06 Minutes of the 60th Meeting of the Joint Coordinating Committee on Epidemic Diseases, 31 January 1980.
122  Goh, *Epidemiological Surveillance of Communicable Diseases in Singapore*.
123  MOH 024/58/01–000 Vol. 07 Report titled 'Cholera in Singapore', undated.
124  MOH 024/58/01–000 Vol. 07 Report titled 'Cholera in Singapore', undated.
125  Echenberg, *Africa in the Time of Cholera*.
126  *ENB*, Vol. 36 No. 2, April–June 2010.

# 5 The Infectious Diseases Hospital
## Hanging Fire

The development of a modern infectious diseases hospital in Singapore was long in the making. The first documented hospital was a woefully inadequate facility at Balestier Road in the late 19th century. It had a multitude of names, one of which was the Infectious Diseases Hospital, though its unofficial name, coined by a member of the 1912 Straits Quarantine Commission, was the 'slaughterhouse'. In 1899, Alex Gentle, the President of the Municipal Commission, admitted that upper-class Asians, women and children had a 'fear of injury' if they were warded there.[1] It was only in 1913 that the facility was replaced by a new hospital built close by at Moulmein Road.

Struggles to build a proper infectious diseases hospital in Singapore highlight the imperatives of colonial rule and the difficulties of controlling infectious disease outbreaks. For over two decades, development of the hospital was fought over by the Straits government and the Municipal Commission, which passed the buck back and forth over who should build and run it. But even before the Moulmein Road Hospital was completed, these debates contributed to a slew of legislation on infectious diseases and public health in the town in 1907. It was the Municipality that reluctantly accepted this responsibility.

Yet, the new hospital, renamed the Middleton Hospital in 1920, was not without its shortcomings. The Straits government ordered a scaled-down version of the original scheme to cut costs and so the hospital lagged behind healthcare needs from the outset. It was never really required for the afflictions for which it was built and it was not scaled to cope with those that were infecting and killing large numbers of townsfolk. Designed to deal with the trinity of plague, cholera and smallpox, the Middleton Hospital found itself scrambling to cope with emerging infectious diseases that presented more serious threats. Its wards had to switch their functions as much as they changed their names. When the British implemented the Medical Plan after the Second World War, limited expansions were made to the hospital. The infectious diseases hospital was always a minor medical institution in Singapore.

The Middleton Hospital also has a significant place in the social history of medicine in Singapore. Moulmein Road was its location, but the hospital was built there only because preferred sites elsewhere roused objections from landowners and residents who did not want an infectious diseases hospital in

DOI: 10.4324/9781003384014-6

their neighbourhood. Moreover, discussions of wards and beds in the scheme revealed serious divides over ethnicity and class. European patients would be warded in better rooms and facilities from Asians, but even among the Asians, their accommodation and comfort would depend on their social class. It was largely due to the lobbying from influential Asian merchants that the Moulmein Road institution was built. The municipal planners envisioned a hospital that would treat European, Eurasian and Asian patients equally, but this ideal was never realised.

During the colonial period, the infectious diseases hospital remained marginal to the experience of treating illness and getting well for the vast majority of the population. As we have seen with the trinity of infectious diseases, only the Asian sick who were dead, dying or destitute entered the grounds of the hospital. Most escaped to other parts of the town or the rural area. Sometimes they lived amongst their community, at other times they died alone. Asians commonly treated their sickness with traditional remedies and rituals until it was demonstrated that science was the superior way. It was only after the Second World War that outpatient and mobile clinics would bring the benefits of biomedicine to the Asian population.

After Singapore became independent, the infectious diseases hospital remained a minor institution, with the threat of epidemic disease perceived to be waning. In 1985, the Middleton Hospital was renamed the Communicable Disease Centre, becoming part of the Tan Tock Seng Hospital and losing its status as a hospital. But a few interesting things happened in this period. First, the CDC housed patients of the AIDS pandemic in the mid-1980s and 1990s – socially marginalised patients dying in an old hospital, recalling the liminal status of the hospital in the colonial era. Then in 2003, it was designated to screen suspected cases during the SARS epidemic, though most of the operations soon passed to the better-equipped TTSH, a general hospital. With growing epidemiological concerns over emerging infections, the venerable hospital with sprawling compounds and Nightingale-type wards was showing its age in the new millennia. It had changed little over the course of a century. A new CDC had been proposed since the early 1990s, but was delayed by a succession of events. In 2018, the CDC was finally closed, replaced by the National Centre for Infectious Diseases (NCID), a state-of-the-art hospital built a stone's throw away.

Underneath these struggles for an infectious diseases hospital lies a fundamental policy dilemma. A properly-equipped and -staffed facility would be expensive to build, maintain and upgrade. It would serve its purpose only in the event of a serious pandemic. Its capacity would not be filled most of the time except when it was needed. The management confronted with this dilemma could do one of several things. It could push the responsibility to another department or build a minimum-capacity hospital commensurate with costs. Or it could commit to the least amount of expansion works possible in the present, or infinitely postpone the project. All these decisions were taken at some point in the history of the hospital.

## The Slaughterhouse

The state of infectious disease care at the end of the 19th century was dismal, the need for a proper hospital dire. The best-furnished was the General Hospital (GH, which became the Singapore General Hospital, or SGH, in 1926). Its infectious disease wards were, however, dilapidated and in 1884, the government decided to move patients to an infectious diseases facility at Balestier Road,[2] close to the TTSH, the community-run Pauper Hospital which also had a small ward for infectious diseases. Henceforth, the GH served only European and Eurasian patients with infectious diseases, and a new Smallpox Hospital was built within the hospital in 1893.

Municipal records refer to the Balestier Road facility by a variety of names: the Infectious Diseases Hospital, Isolation Hospital, Quarantine Camp, Smallpox Hospital, and Contagious Diseases Hospital. This multitude of names say one thing: the facility was clearly not a proper hospital. In reality, only the seriously or terminally ill members of the male Asian working class went there. Numerous cases of epidemic diseases were hidden from the official gaze and went unreported. While dangerous diseases such as bubonic plague, cholera and smallpox were notifiable, in practice, sick persons commonly fled from their houses to another part of the town or were evicted by their landlords. Sometimes, the dying ill were removed by rickshaw and dropped off a short distance away from the hospital, while the bodies of the dead were occasionally dumped in the street.[3]

Asian fears of the colonial hospital prompted a vicious cycle: the more often patients died there, the greater the predisposition to avoid it and not to notify the government. Not surprisingly, the Straits government and the Municipal Commission failed to contain many outbreaks of epidemic diseases in the town. Singapore suffered four epidemics of smallpox and five of cholera between 1892 and 1911. Patients frequently died in the hospital, but also in the streets and unknown to others in their own cubicles.

The report of the 1912 Quarantine Commission is the single best source on what we will simply call the Balestier Road hospital. During the commission's proceedings, when Dr Suat Chuan Yin asked Thomas Oswald Mayhew, the Chief Sanitary Inspector to the Singapore Municipality, if the coolie class had 'a great belief that this Isolation Hospital is scarcely anything better than a slaughter-house', the latter replied in the affirmative, adding that people believed that they would die there.[4] The commission's report revealed the facility to be in a dismal state, having been for at least a decade 'unfit to the meet requirements of a large population liable to epidemics of smallpox and cholera and, to a less extent, plague'.[5]

A closer look at the report reveals that the hospital's defects were skewed towards class sentiments rather than its general suitability for patients of all backgrounds:

> there was a deplorable lack of efficient control in the institution; that no adequate medical attendance was assured to the patients; that food was

unsuitable, that it was supplied regardless of social or caste considerations, in a somewhat revolting manner, and that some patients had to be supplied with food by their friends; that the methods of disinfection on discharge were crude and inconsiderate.[6]

In other words, the criticisms became grounds for reform because wealthy or prominent people were making them. The officials of the port city listened to what they deemed to be the 'bitterest and ... most reasonable complaints ... by the better-class Asiatics' who wanted good accommodation and treatment by their standards, instead of those meant for the coolies.[7] The new hospital that would be built would chiefly cater to the upper classes.

Like the quarantine station on St. John's Island, complaints were aplenty about the quality of food, facilities and staff at the hospital – at least for Asians of better means. A newspaper letter by one such patient admitted for smallpox, Low Kway Soo, reveals an upper-class perspective, 'I was given a bare plank bed. There was no curtain, no mat, no mattress nor any pillow. There was only an old and used blanket on the bed'. For him, 'My experience of a night's stay in the native ward was so horrible that it has left an indelible impression on my memory'.[8] He had to bribe an attendant for these items, which turned out to be used ones. He damned the hospital a pigsty and a slaughterhouse, horrific beyond belief in comparison to the GH where he was later moved to.[9] It was galling that Frank Rodrigues, the hospital's Senior Assistant Surgeon, denied the accusation and suggested that Low had rejected the mat.[10] More serious were allegations in Low's letter of physical mistreatment – 'the attendants in one case slapping a Bengali very severely and of poking a Chinaman in the ribs', who was then dragged to his ward and his legs placed in stocks. This was also denied by Rodrigues.[11]

Nevertheless, the hospital was unwelcoming to all patients regardless of class. According to Thomas Mayhew, there was much displeasure with the lack of bathrooms and latrines near the wards, leaving patients to have to crawl out to a tap to wash themselves. The Chinese patient who was poked in the ribs had been punished for crawling out to a latrine 30 feet away.[12] Near the wards, ironically, was the morgue. This was not screened off from the patients' view; in any case, the stench of the bodies there was overpowering. They could see post-mortems being carried out, reaching the conclusion that 'We are not dead yet and there they are cutting people up in our sight'.[13] This compounded fears that the colonial government wanted patients to die in the hospital. The problem with food, as Mayhew pointed out, was that it was brought in from the TTSH. It showed that the Infectious Diseases Hospital was not a standalone facility but an extension of the pauper hospital for the coolie class.[14]

Some of the revelations in the Quarantine Commission's report beggars belief. According to Mayhew, the hospital was in a real sense a clandestine business with little regard for health or hygiene. Its attendants, who were untrained, did little work except to serve tea. They ignored delirious patients who needed attention, and were left to crawl on the floor or lay about in awkward positions. When questioned, the attendants simply uttered, 'What is the use of putting them back? They only crawl out again. We cannot look after them'.[15] One of the attendants reserved his energies for rearing fowl in the grounds of the hospital, which he sold to patients.

Dr James Handy had visited the hospital on several occasions. He described the conditions to the Quarantine Commission,

> the place I am speaking about, the present Balestier Road wards, is not at all suited for the treatment of infectious diseases. I saw in one small room, about 8 feet by 8 feet, five patients huddled together, convalescents, and they had just plank beds, and these men who were in that room were used to greater luxuries than a mere plank bed. There was nothing on the floor and they had attap walls.[16]

Handy recounted the case of a young man admitted for smallpox and was left unattended throughout the night. When he asked a dresser why the patient was not given a blanket, he was told that it was already midnight.[17]

Gan Poo Teong, a Straits Chinese storekeeper employed in a large trading firm, testified to the commission that when he was admitted for smallpox, he was placed into a room with 10 or 11 men and given a plank bed. He found it impossible to sleep surrounded by cries from his room-mates, although the only dresser there was asleep the whole time. The latrines had not been cleaned for a week and were emptied only when full of excreta. He was subsequently transferred to 'the European place' (the GH), which was superior in comfort. Gan was relieved that when discharged, the staff did not pour disinfectant over his clothes as was the common practice. He was adamant that 'If I was sick again I would not report it [his illness] if I had to go into the native ward again'.[18]

## Class and Ethnicity in the Struggle for a New Hospital

A proper infectious diseases hospital would break the vicious circle of avoidance and non-notification. But who would fund and build it? The colonial government consistently demurred, stating that a large part of its budget was devoted to military expenditure. The Municipal Commission gave priority to the water supply and disposal of nightsoil and refuse.[19] Over a period of 20 years, the government and commission passed on the responsibility for the hospital as they did for quarantine. When the 1886 Municipal Ordinance made the isolation of dangerous infectious diseases mandatory, the government wanted the commission to take up this charge. Seven years later, the commission agreed, but not without a host of conditions. It would handle dangerous infectious diseases in the Municipality, provided that government hospitals remained free of charge, the police (as part of the government) continued to enforce people's quarantine or isolation in their homes, and the government continued the quarantine work on St. John's.[20] The commission was able to interpret its role narrowly at the time because while the colonial government was responsible for health matters in Singapore, the Municipal Ordinance did not legislate the commission's responsibility for public health within the town.

This unsatisfactory arrangement persisted while the morbidity of infectious diseases grew. In 1895, the Principal Civil Medical Officer T.S. Kerr urged the government to build an infectious diseases hospital like the one at Province Wellesley, which had helped contain a smallpox outbreak that year. In 1899, the government pressed the matter again, calling for a plan for improved accommodation for Asian patients. Kerr and the colonial engineer duly visited the Infectious Diseases Hospital and Quarantine Camp at Balestier Plain, then occupied by Chinese, Malay and Japanese patients. The visitors surmised the Malays to be 'respectable people', some of whom were living there with their families, and all patients satisfied with their accommodation and treatment.[21] They attributed Asians' reluctance to come forward for treatment not to poor hospital accommodation but 'fear of the unknown'.[22] Governor Charles Mitchell ruled that 'it is not desirable to erect a superior class of hospital for infectious diseases at Balestier Road'.[23]

The sole dissenting voice in the midst of inertia was Dr William Robert Covin Middleton, the knowledgeable Municipal Health Officer. Middleton knew the Balestier hospital well, even how the hospital's walls and floors were 'impregnated with the germs of diseases treated there'.[24] In 1912, he informed the Quarantine Commission that in addition to inadequate beds and poor construction materials, there were refuse pits and patients' excreta near the wards, the drainage was 'primitive', and the mortuary was indeed 'in full view of all'.[25] Seven years earlier, he had advocated for a new hospital. But the Municipal Commissioners were not to be moved until the Municipal Ordinance expressly made them responsible for public health in the town.

Calls for a proper hospital grew within the government. In 1904, W.J. Napier, a member of the Legislative Council, urged the government to build a new facility as the Municipal Commission could not afford the costs. Even the European ward for infectious diseases at the GH was better known, he said, as an 'obstruction to golf', and he reminded the council of the case of a man who died of his illness while the government and commission haggled over responsibility for his hospital fees.[26] The Colonial Secretary C.W.S. Kynnersley disagreed, pointing out that the hospital was invariably the commission's charge, as was the case in Britain. But he assured that preliminary efforts had been made to find a site for the hospital, which would be near the new premises of the TTSH at Moulmein Road, completed in 1909.[27]

The proposal for the hospital contributed to the passing of a new Municipal Ordinance in 1907. This was a milestone, for it expanded the scope of the Municipal Commission in public health in the entire town, including 'to pass By-Laws ... for suppression and prevention of dangerous infectious diseases and segregation of patients suffering from such diseases'.[28] In the drafting of the new ordinance, Middleton, a Scot, had drawn upon the provisions of the Public Health (Scotland) Act. Broadly, the commission would be responsible for detecting overcrowding, demolishing insanitary houses, providing back lanes and open spaces, and rebuilding unhealthy areas. The changes were hailed as 'practically an adaptation of the Home Act for the housing of the working classes'.[29]

But the hospital's location was not yet settled. The government had found a preliminary site, naturally enough, at Moulmein Road close to the TTSH in 1905, and the Legislative Council had voted for a contribution of $31,200 for its construction. The full cost would be jointly borne by the government and the commission. This was the extent of the agreement. The following year, the new Governor John Anderson deemed the hospital plan to be 'too elaborate and the cost excessive'.[30] Some Municipal Commissioners were also fearful about the spread of smallpox to the TTSH and the residential houses nearby. They decided to defer the matter to W.J. Simpson, the sanitary expert from Britain whom Anderson had invited that year to investigate Singapore's high death rates in the town.[31] Simpson felt that the 13-acre Moulmein Road site would be too small to manage an epidemic.

The commissioners turned to alternative sites. One was at Paya Lebar, near the Tramway terminus at Serangoon outside the municipal area. But the government and the commission were quickly inundated by protests from landowners and residents. The editor of the *Singapore Free Press* submitted a litany of reasons why there was 'no greater calamity' than the Paya Lebar site: it was far from town and close to a growing village community and the Recreation Hotel, it would be expensive to acquire the land and would drive down land prices, and infection may be transmitted by mosquitos and flies.[32] A letter to the paper by 'Paya Lebarite', apparently a resident, stressed the resulting unpopularity of the neighbourhood and the need for costly water piping from the 3rd Mile Stone.[33]

Paya Lebar was dropped and other proposals met similar fates. A site at Trafalgar in the northeast of Singapore was judged to be too far from town and also lacking a reliable water supply. The most promising location appeared to be near Hood Eng Estate off Telok Blangah Road at Pasir Panjang, owned by the Tanjong Pagar Dock Company. The Municipal Commission and the company were locked in talks for three months. Although owned by the government, the company submitted various 'contradictory' reasons against the proposal, including the site being earmarked for other purposes (including land reclamation) and the ubiquitous fear of the spread of infection.[34]

Left with no other recourse, the commissioners returned to the Moulmein Road site. Middleton and R. Pierce, the Municipal Engineer, found a solution by adding more land to the site, which nearly doubled to 25 acres. But this still did not bring an end to the matter. In 1910, the Municipality revealed that the original scheme, prepared in 1905, had again been 'condemned as extravagant by the Government and a curtailed scheme proposed instead'.[35]

The 1905 scheme had been fairly elaborate, with a complement of 192 beds and 16 observation wards. There were four sections for plague, cholera, smallpox, and diphtheria. These were divided according to ethnicity, class and gender. Middleton had suggested that the Chinese be separated from the Indians and Malays, believing that they would prefer such an arrangement.[36] The reduced scheme retained these divisions in principle though not always in fact. It simplified and condensed most of the class and ethnic segregation, while removing the diphtheria section altogether (the disease was to be treated at the GH instead). European and Eurasian patients would be treated in the smaller but more comfortable observation and discharge wards. The reduced scheme had only 76 beds, disregarding the 96 emergency beds that did not yet exist but could reportedly be built quickly in the event of an epidemic (but would likely be of inferior quality). The new hospital would have a triple fence, mostly to keep patients from escaping.[37] The Quarantine Commission considered the reductions justified as there had not been a need for a large number of beds in past epidemics.[38]

But this was looking to the past rather than planning for the future. In his view, the Acting Municipal Engineer Benjamin Hall assessed the plague and smallpox sections to be sufficient for their purpose, but not quite so for cholera.[39] Middleton differed, as the original plan was for 250 beds, or one for every thousand persons. He deemed the smallpox section to be the only complete part of the hospital, since European and Eurasian patients would have to use the observation and discharge wards in the event of an outbreak.[40] They would thus have to displace patients meant for these wards.

After nearly a decade, the Municipal Commission lamented in 1910 that the hospital project was 'still hanging fire', like a flintlock musket failing to ignite.[41] On 16 September, the commissioners stood their ground against further proposed cuts to the budget from the government, which finally agreed to contribute half the cost. Finally, there was agreement. This facility acceptable to both parties, it was declared, would overcome social stigma towards the existing hospital and quarantine camp, and it would be welcomed by both sexes and all patients regardless of ethnicity and class. Belatedly, in 1911, construction of the hospital commenced.

In the same year, the well-to-do Chettiar community threw a spanner into the works, submitting a proposal for a hospital of their own to be built at Paya Lebar. The Chettiars, who were upper-caste businessmen and money-lenders, had more than the other groups grown tired of the old hospital and quarantine measures. They had found the food there unacceptable, having to bribe the attendants for their own food to be brought to them.[42] As Dr Handy told the Quarantine Commission, 'there is an idea among the chitties and among some more intelligent people that the authorities would rather these people died in hospital than get cured and infect further'.[43]

The problem was illustrated by the smallpox epidemic of 1911. Thirty-three Chettiars living along Market Street in the town were charged for failing to report cases to the Municipality, while friends of five contacts frantically sought help from lawyers in a vain attempt to block their removal to St. John's for quarantine.[44] The contacts were allegedly 'marched through the town under a Police guard like criminals',[45] though Dr Richard Arthur Campbell, the Second Assistant Municipal Health Officer, claimed that they had refused to take the municipal wagon, deciding to walk to the pier en masse instead.[46]

The Chettiars' plea for their own hospital showed issues of class and ethnicity to be very much alive at the forefront of colonial governance. The Municipal Commission denied the appeal, but only because it did not wish to have separate hospitals. The matter had been duly deliberated by the Quarantine Commission, which agreed that infectious diseases should be dealt with in a single hospital. But it considered the common objections of upper-class Asians to being warded with the coolies to be reasonable, and was not opposed to the building of superior wards for the better-off classes within the new hospital, who could bring their own servants, cooks and nurses.[47] The Quarantine Commission was influenced by the witnesses it called.

To R.A. Campbell, the Assistant Municipal Health Officer, 'the erection of Sectional Infectious Disease Hospitals in Singapore would be a retrogressive step', but he found merit in the idea of communities building their own sections at the new hospital.[48] His colleague John Glennie concurred, for the administration of community hospitals scattered all over Singapore would be complicated. He felt that '"caste" or "custom" has too much stress laid on it'. He did not address the Chettiar community specifically, but instead gave the example of a case where Chinese custom did not impede quarantine.[49] Their boss, Middleton, was more specific in stating, 'Caste and religion have never been brought prominently forward in connection with the Health Department as is the case in India'. He thought it would be difficult to find different sites for sectional hospitals that would fulfil the requisite criteria.[50]

The Municipal Commission accepted these recommendations in principle. On the surface, the reduced scheme for cholera and plague would only have Class B and lower-class wards for working class Asian patients. European and upper-class Asian patients for these diseases could still receive treatment in the superior observation and discharge wards. For smallpox, however, the commission made concessions for a trio of wards – European, Class A and Class B – the last two being for Asians. The hospital's planners looked to accommodate, rather than reform, prevailing class and racial sentiments in colonial Singapore. This had been the thinking behind the new hospital.

### Epidemiological Lag at the Moulmein Road Hospital

On 1 May 1913, the colonial government announced the opening of the new infectious diseases hospital at Moulmein Road.[51] Designed primarily by the Municipal Architect W. Campbell Oman, it was run by the Municipal Commission. It had a complement of 172 beds – though this included the unbuilt emergency beds – divided into sections for each of the main notifiable diseases, plague, cholera and smallpox. The government was apologetic that only the smallpox section had been built to plan, with separate wards for

Europeans, upper- and lower-class Asians. The 'long obsolete' Balestier Road hospital and quarantine camp were closed down and abolished.[52]

The new hospital did not yet have a name and for a number of years was known as the Moulmein Road Hospital. It had cost over $331,000 to build, with the government footing a third of the cost. It had a sprawling layout typical of hospitals of the era, based on the pavilion-ward system that reflected prevailing thinking on sanitation and infectious disease management at the dawn of the 20th century. This system had its roots in the French hospital system in the 18th century before being popularised in Britain by medical practitioners and architects such as John Roberton, George Godwin, Florence Nightingale (hence commonly known as 'Nightingale wards'), and Henry Currey in the mid-19th century.

The premise of the pavilion-ward system was a decentralised layout, with detached or semi-detached wards separated from one another by a considerable distance. This was to isolate the different diseases and prevent the spread of germs to other patients, while allowing for air circulation and exposure to sunlight in the ward. The latter was originally based on the miasma theory (that illness was due to 'bad air'), but later adapted to the germ theory that superseded it in the late 19th century. Nevertheless, despite these metropolitan influences, pavilion hospitals in Singapore, including the Moulmein Road Hospital, were unique in a way. As architectural historian Chang Jiat-Hwee observed, the early iterations of the GH (1882), TTSH (1909) and SGH (1926) were built along the lines of the pavilion hospital. Yet, the designs in Singapore, and earlier in colonial India, were not copied wholesale from Europe, but adapted to tropical conditions, with the use of special verandahs, louvres, roofs, and other equipment to improve cooling.[53]

The pavilion aesthetic at the Moulmein Road Hospital seemed both pleasing and pragmatic at the time. There had indeed been reservations that the original plans for the hospital placed the wards too close to one another, making it more likely for infectious diseases to spread.[54] But the *Straits Times* noted with satisfaction in 1913 that

> the designs are graceful and consistent, with a suggestion of Old English conception about them. From Moulmein Road, the hospital presents a very pleasant pastoral picture to the eye, while the hospital's layout expressed a precautionary forethought that pervades the whole scheme of things.[55]

In 1920, the facility was finally bestowed a formal name as the Middleton Hospital. This fittingly recognised the unceasing work and contributions of W.R.C. Middleton, who had retired from the Municipality (and later passed away) that year. As Municipal Health Officer, he had been a tireless advocate for the hospital and for sanitary improvements in Singapore. The hospital's name would endure for six decades well into the post-colonial era.

The government hailed the facility as a 'great advance' in curbing infectious diseases, being 'properly equipped' and acceptable to the entire community.[56]

Many Asian patients were reportedly brought there by relatives and friends in a new culture of trust, while there were no escapes from the institution in its first year. Subsequent events showed the self-praise to be premature. During the cholera outbreak the following year, the admissions were again mostly males, suggesting that women still distrusted the hospital.[57] Accommodation also quickly became inadequate.

The long gestation period in building the hospital had rendered it nearly outdated by the time it was completed. It became clear that the new hospital was not the complete answer. The shortage of beds was proof that the government had made a major mistake in curtailing the original plan. Even more, the officials had erred in focusing on the three main notifiable diseases. Increasingly, the hospital had to treat other infectious diseases, such as diphtheria (cases of the disease were transferred back from the GH to the Moulmein Road Hospital in 1917), chickenpox and puerperal fever (both made notifiable in 1916), cerebrospinal fever (notifiable in 1917), and tuberculosis (notifiable in 1918). There being no sections or wards for these illnesses (the diphtheria section was a victim of the push for economy), the hospital had to adapt as well as it could.

As will be discussed in Chapter 7, the hospital was little used in the first wave of the global influenza epidemic in 1918, before admitting some cases during the deadlier second wave. Subsequently, a ward for diphtheria was added in 1919 (this was still less than the full section of 20 beds envisaged in the 1905 scheme), followed by a second cholera ward the following year. By then, the hospital premises had expanded substantially and would continue to do so, made possible by the acquisition of small pieces of adjoining land. But the facility was always playing catch up.

Prior to the outbreak of World War Two, plague and smallpox became relatively uncommon in Singapore. This led the Municipal Commission to state in 1933,

> it would seem that the role of the Hospital in the future will become less and less that of an isolation camp for these diseases and more and more than of a Hospital for the treatment of the ordinary infectious diseases of childhood and their sequelae.[58]

Diphtheria, a disease of infants and young children, became the most serious illness treated at the Middleton Hospital after 1917. Numerous cases were admitted in an advanced stage, giving rise to a high mortality rate. Asian distrust of colonial healthcare was continuing regardless of the new hospital. Another major disease of children handled there was poliomyelitis, which was made notifiable in 1941. In the 1930s, the hospital also treated large numbers of typhoid patients. At this time, the Municipal Commission had become alarmed at the frequency of typhoid outbreaks in the town and began cracking down on itinerant hawkers, especially peddlers of contaminated ice-cream and iced drinks.[59]

The hospital came under strain for dealing with a wider range of epidemic diseases than was originally intended. Before the outbreak of the Second World War, the shortage of beds due to an increase in the volume of work had worsened. A major expansion scheme was needed. In 1941, the British made plans to build a 48-bed ward, foundations and services for two 24-bed wards, and three small observation wards.[60] But these plans had to be shelved when the Japanese attacked Malaya and Singapore fell to the invaders the following February.

During the Japanese Occupation, the Middleton Hospital was renamed Densen Byoin ('Infectious Disease Hospital' in Japanese). It was run by Dr Ernest Steven Monteiro, the new Medical Superintendent, and Lang Jun Hua, the Matron. This was a sign of locals taking over the administration during the war from Europeans who had been interned by the Japanese. Information on this period of the hospital's history is sketchy, though officially it had a muster of 200 beds, of which 20 were first class beds, 40 were second class and 140 were third class. What seemed quite remarkable in the context of Japan's ongoing war against the Allies was that a new ward was reportedly built for typhoid and dysentery at this time and that the hospital was allegedly able to continue its pre-war workload.[61] These claims are dubious, given the disruption the war wrought to medical services in Singapore in general.[62]

## Planning and Deadlock

When the Japanese Occupation ended in August 1945, the key issue was to revive the pre-war plans and upgrade the Middleton Hospital. This turned out to be a fraught affair. The British were committed to expand and improve medical services for the population as part of a programme of imperial resuscitation and subsequently orderly decolonisation. The medical report for 1948 alluded to a fresh period of planning and rehabilitation in order to attain the standards of the pre-war medical service, while the following year's report forecast a period of preparation for the future.[63] But could post-war Britain afford to do this and what sort of expansions would be feasible?

As it turned out, the British prioritised improvements to major hospitals such as the Singapore General Hospital, the control of acute diseases and the health of children. Interestingly, when announcing ambitious proposals for a 10-year Medical Plan for Singapore in 1947, they had proposed a second infectious diseases hospital with 50 beds for major diseases outside the Municipality. This was a sound move, for improvements to rural health, as discussed in Chapter 1, had long been overdue. Colonial officials also urged to increase the staff and upgrade the facilities at the Middleton Hospital. However, the finalised Medical Plan of 1948 was a reduced programme with a smaller budget and committed to neither proposal.[64]

The government deferred the matter to a committee that would discuss it together with the Municipal Commission. The committee examined a range of issues pertaining to the shortcomings and requirements of the Middleton Hospital. Some of these owed to the neglect occasioned by the war, but others were long-range issues from the pre-war period, foreseen by the expansion scheme of 1941. In 1950, the committee decided that any expansion works would take place at the Moulmein Road site rather than move the hospital to another location.[65] Dr Ng See Yook, the new Medical Superintendent of the Middleton Hospital, deemed it futile to build a second hospital, preferring to concentrate resources to redevelop the existing hospital.[66] This recalls the outcome of the Chettiars' proposal for a separate hospital 40 years earlier. Subsequently the idea of a second hospital was dropped.

At the heart of the discussions on developing the Middleton Hospital after the war was a long-standing dilemma in Singapore history: that requirements for hospital beds and staff were not large except during an epidemic but this was precisely when they were needed. As M. Hill, the Principal Matron, succinctly put it, 'To keep a large staff for a hospital in which the bedstate was bound to fluctuate widely was uneconomic while in epidemics "demands" would have to be made on Government'.[67]

The question of resources was thus an old one. It can be traced to similar debates at the close of the 19th century while it also foresaw future ones. Given the constraints, Dr Ng See Yook proposed a partial solution, calling for a special Cubicle Ward to be built in the Middleton Hospital,

> the building of cubicle blocks will greatly facilitate the treatment of several infectious diseases simultaneously and also the nursing staff requirement will be reduced. Opinion holds that in a modern hospital 50% of the beds should be in cubicles. A cubicle block is also necessary for cases of doubtful diagnosis, or of double infection and also for those diseases of which few cases are admitted. The present hospital built on a pavilion system where the percentage of patients sent in which a diagnosis subsequently found to be erroneous is high, the need of a cubicle block becomes essential to supplement the present 200 beds accommodation.[68]

Another argument was made by the Deputy Health Officer W.E. Hutchinson, who pressed for increased staff for the hospital:

> It is generally conceded that an Infectious Diseases Hospital requires to carry more staff than a General Hospital owing to the necessary restriction of movement due to the risk of cross infection i.e. the staff of each ward is self contained.

Hutchinson gave two examples to support his position:

> For example, most of the polio cases are children who require a great deal of attention. They must be feed, bathed and clothed; linen has to be changed often and laundered; physiotherapy and hydrotherapy have to be

constantly and patiently applied; splints have to be taken off and re-applied due to frequent 'wetting'. Similarly a diphtheria case, especially if requiring tracheotomy, may monopolise the services of several nurses allowing for duty periods.[69]

In the end, the committee recommended Ng's proposal to build a 20-bed Cubicle Ward with self-contained rooms, with possible air-conditioning for two of the cubicles to be used in lieu of oxygen tents.[70] Much was made of the ward in the English press. Its historic glass partition, the first of its kind in Singapore, allowed nurses to see patients in other rooms.[71] The ward would thus reconcile with the manpower issue without having to greatly expand the staff, which the committee did not recommend. But because the shortage of medical and nursing staff who could work the ward was not resolved, its construction need not commence immediately but would take place over a period of up to five years. The Cubicle Ward was completed only in 1956 – over a decade after the end of war. Architecturally, it stood apart from the early 20th-century pavilion wards in the Middleton Hospital. Quickly, it became a busy part of the hospital.

The committee did propose other expansions: an operating theatre for major surgical emergencies and unit wards for the treatment of bowel diseases, in addition to the acquisition of much-needed medical equipment, such as a portable X-ray and electrocardiograph.[72] In the post-war years, the Middleton Hospital continued to deal with cases of cholera, poliomyelitis, diphtheria, and typhoid, albeit on a smaller scale (see the following section). In the 1960s, it screened employees of ice-cream factories for typhoid, similar to the colonial surveillance of hawkers and vendors for the disease three decades earlier.

Even with the hospital's limited expansion, additional staff housing was needed. Such housing was part of an 'immediate and urgent problem' in the government medical service as a whole.[73] Dr Ng penned a long memorandum on the issue at the Middleton Hospital in 1950:

> The quarters problem for the Staff is acute. There is a definite shortage of quarters for them. The Nurses' quarters are most unsuitable for the existing nurses. Out of the five Staff Nurses, three are married with children and live outside in private residence, and the remaining two each occupy rooms at the back which were considered before as servants' quarters. I feel that the Municipal Commissioners did not consider the suitability of the quarters when they ruled that as free quarters are available for them, they are not eligible for housing allowance. Before the war, the three ambulance drives were not stationed in this Hospital, but now, quarters have to be made available for them, thus introducing a further shortage. I strongly recommend that the present shortage of quarters should be remedied at once and more quarters should be constructed to house all the nurses and the attendants.[74]

Between 1953 and 1955, the City Council built, rented and acquired additional accommodation for its staff, including a hostel with modern amenities at the nearby Moulmein-Rangoon-Norfolk roads junction for nurses. However, with the advent of mass public housing for the general population in the 1960s and 1970s, the colonial practice of providing housing for government employees ceased. In post-colonial Singapore, hospital staff increasingly resided in their own homes.

Another major question surfaced after the war: whose responsibility was it to manage infectious diseases in Singapore – the colonial government or the City Council? In 1951, an Infectious Diseases Committee was formed to consider this question. The issue hearkened to the convoluted debates that preceded the Middleton Hospital's formation in 1913. The committee recommended that the government assume complete responsibility of the hospital, since it administered other public hospitals in Singapore. Responsibility for quarantine would be split as before the war: the government would oversee the port and rural areas, while the City Council would be responsible for the city.[75] In a reversal of history, the City Council objected to the first point, arguing that it could not manage infectious diseases without having control over the Middleton Hospital.[76] The government countered that the council could continue to administer the hospital, but both parties would have 'dual control' over infectious diseases, as before.[77] This led to an impasse that remained unresolved till Singapore became a self-governing state in 1959. The City Council was then abolished by the new government and the Middleton Hospital came under the Ministry of Health.

## New Infections, Adapted Uses

In 1985, the Middleton Hospital was absorbed into the TTSH and renamed the Communicable Disease Centre. It thus lost both its historic name 'Middleton' and the status of a hospital. The Medical Director Dr Edmund Monteiro, the son of E.S. Monteiro, surmised the changes to be due to reasons of 'economy and common sense'.[78] By the early 1980s, the hospital had almost as many staff as patients, so a full-fledged hospital with a large staff did not seem necessary. In 1992, the TTSH was restructured into a corporatised, state-owned hospital under a government holding company, the Health Corporation of Singapore. Three of its departments involved with infectious diseases, the Epidemiology Department, Department of Infectious Diseases and Department of Tuberculosis Control, merged to form the Communicable Disease Centre. The reconstituted centre remained under the purview of the MOH. It was responsible for the monitoring, prevention and control of infectious diseases, including tuberculosis and HIV/AIDS.[79]

On 1 April 1995, the MOH placed the CDC under the direct administration of the TTSH. The ministry stated later that 'The change in administration has enabled the CDC to provide better medical care to patients with infectious diseases with the support of TTSH'.[80] The restructuring of hospitals in Singapore in the late 1980s and early 1990s made them more autonomous in their management and operations, according to principles of commercial accounting, cost awareness and financial discipline. In the CDC's case, the MOH did not want to manage clinical services. According to Medical Director Dr Chew Suok Kai at the time, the change gave the CDC the best of both worlds: the increased operational capacity and manpower from the restructured TTSH and continued funding from the government to support the Epidemiology Department's study of diseases such as HIV.[81] On the flip side, job positions and responsibilities overlapped as a result, whereas the CDC's duties had been more clearly defined prior to the restructuring.[82]

Following Singapore's independence, the CDC continued to repurpose its sections and wards to deal with new infections. Its original (and oldest) three sections for plague, cholera and smallpox had been built in 1913. Subsequently, the plague section, first to be rendered irrelevant, probably became Blocks 873–875 as of the late 2010s.[83] It was used for chickenpox patients, including National Servicemen and migrant workers – groups that lived in close quarters that facilitated the spread of the disease. The smallpox section was renamed and likely became Blocks 877–879. These wards were used for the treatment of patients with chickenpox, poliomyelitis, dysentery, diarrhoea and eventually those with skin diseases from the nearby National Skin Centre. The cholera section, the longest relevant, likely became Blocks 876, 876A and an unnamed ward north of Block 871.

Block 876 was previously known as the E Ward, an open, Nightingale-type ward. In 1950, the Director of Medical Services and the Municipal Commissioners agreed that post-infectious cases of poliomyelitis that required physiotherapy would be warded at the Middleton Hospital. A year later, a post-poliomyelitis unit was developed there due to the increase in cases after the war.[84] E Ward was staffed and equipped for this purpose, including the acquisition of four iron lung respirators. The ward had approximately 40 beds for the treatment of early and advanced cases of poliomyelitis. During the 1958 poliomyelitis outbreak in Singapore, the chickenpox ward at the Middleton Hospital was closed while its dysentery cases were transferred to the SGH to make room for poliomyelitis patients.[85] This offers a sense of how busy Ward E was at a time when poliomyelitis was a major health hazard. As the disease was brought under control in the 1960s through mass vaccination, the ward awaited a new identity from the next epidemic.

This was to be the advent of HIV/AIDS in Singapore in 1985. Ward E was renamed Ward 76 and converted for the care of AIDS inpatients the following year. The refurbished ward had 12 beds to give the patients some privacy, each with a bathroom attached. It admitted its first patient on 8 September. The patients fell into two groups: those who needed intravenous injections several times a day and others at an advanced stage of the disease who were unable to care for themselves.

The ward's sister building, Block 876A, underwent similar changes of functions. In 1917, the hospital began to admit convalescent diphtheria patients from the GH, and what was originally known as L Ward was built for these patients two years later. By the late 1960s, diphtheria, like polio-myelitis, had disappeared from Singapore due to mass immunisation. During the HIV/AIDS pandemic, the increase in the number of patients after 1995 added pressure on Ward 76. L Ward was thus renamed Ward 76A and converted into a palliative ward for terminally ill AIDS patients. It was a 30-bed ward with B2 Class rooms, a small operating theatre for tracheo-tomies and a day infusion clinic for patients. Most patients opted to die at the CDC, not at home, which their families often had difficulty accepting. The centre offered terminal care facilities and grief counselling.[86]

Despite its more recent vintage, the Cubicle Ward was also repeatedly repurposed. In Edmund Monteiro's memory, it was an acute ward. When measles was a major childhood problem in the past, half of its patients were children with measles. By the late 1990s, it treated patients with chickenpox, dengue and occasionally enteric fever. It was then the busiest part of the CDC, treating mostly the low-wage migrant workers admitted for these and the diarrhoeal diseases. Dr David Allen recalled a contingent of Gurkha guards warded there with cholera. It impressed him that these legendary warrior-soldiers were laid low by diarrhoea.[87]

In 1971, as part of the government's hospital modernisation programme, the first air-conditioned ward in the Middleton Hospital was announced. As a response to people's rising expectations for healthcare, the ward was initially named Ward 1. With a modern architectural design that made it stand out in the hospital, the ward would accommodate 28–30 first- and second-class paying patients.[88] The Middleton Hospital had been a free hospital with non-air-conditioned Class C wards – though we should not forget that it had been built due to pressure from colonial Singapore's wealthy and influential Asians. Monteiro thought that a Class A ward (likely an observation or discharge ward) and another ward had been demolished to make way for Ward 1. Subsequently renamed Ward 72 and then Block 872, the ward had 22 rooms, with single beds and attached bathrooms. It offered A Class and B1 Class accommodation, with air-conditioned and non-air-conditioned single rooms respectively. Only the Class A rooms had a telephone and a television set.[89]

But the hospital could never fill these beds, and patients with dermatological conditions, if they wished, could move from a B2 ward (with four patients to a room) to an A1 or B1 room on a case-by-case, first-come-first-served basis.[90] At different times, the ward was used for these dermatological patients and for patients with HIV/AIDS, as well as the isolation of patients with tuberculosis and patients suspected of having the Middle-East Respiratory Syndrome cor-onavirus (MERS-CoV) in the early 2010s. During the 2003 SARS epidemic, the ward was also used for triaging and isolating probable SARS cases.

Among the various adapted uses of the CDC, two stand out as milestones. One was the treatment and care of patients with HIV/AIDS, an initially terminal and much feared disease. Until effective and affordable drugs for the illness appeared in the late 1990s, much of the CDC's early work with AIDS patients was limited to segregation, palliative care and counselling. A 1995 study by Dr Laurence Wai-Teng Leong found that the segregation of patients with the disease in effect made CDC an 'isolation ward' and 'a medical jail where no bail was permitted'.[91]

The government's initial response to the HIV epidemic in Singapore was fraught. A major labour issue quickly emerged: the perceived threat to the well-being of the nursing staff. In April 1985, Dr Kwa Soon Bee, the Permanent Secretary of the MOH and the Director of Medical Services, met with Govindasamy Kandasamy, the General Secretary of the Amalgamated Union of Public Employees, whose members included hospital staff. The discussion centred on the care of AIDS patients. Kandasamy made several proposals: that the patients be quarantined elsewhere as it was an incurable illness, that only volunteers should care for them, and that there be compensation for staff infected by the disease while working there. He criticised the facilities at the CDC as inadequate, with the patients not separated from the nursing station.[92]

Upon discovering that three male prostitutes with AIDS had been warded in the CDC in 1985, some of the medical staff at the CDC and the Middle Road Hospital for sexually-transmitted diseases resigned or asked to be transferred elsewhere. The *Singapore Monitor* called this a 'revolt' of the staff – probably because there were few major industrial stoppages in post-colonial Singapore.[93] As Edmund Monteiro recalled, two of his doctors left the CDC because their families did not want them to work there, while nurses petitioned the government through the union against treating AIDS patients; they 'almost wanted to down tools'.[94]

This was ultimately a 'storm in a teacup', for the staffing issues were mostly resolved and safety measures implemented in the care of AIDS patients at the CDC.[95] The centre was important for another aspect of HIV/AIDS care. In 1995, it opened a Patient Care Centre (PCC) as a meeting place and sanctuary for AIDS patients. This was located at what was originally the doctors' quarters (Block 811). There, the CDC's doctors, nurses and counsellors assisted outpatients with non-medical needs. More importantly, the patients had a place to meet and support one another. The MOH provided seed money to renovate the block. A female patient taught her fellow patients to make artificial roses to be sold to raise funds for the PCC's activities. Subsequently, a nursing officer from the CDC managed the centre, recruiting volunteers to visit the CDC's inpatients in the wards.[96]

There are conflicting patient memories of the history of the AIDS epidemic at the CDC. Paul Toh, a survivor, found the centre to be 'very scary' when he first went there to visit a close friend hospitalised for the disease in 1989. The CDC 'did not even look like a hospital' and the wards were 'dark and gloomy', resembling army barracks. He found his friend in a makeshift intensive care unit without air-conditioning. Taxi drivers often refused to drive inside the compounds, preferring to drop off the patients outside. The facility, smelling strongly of Dettol, was akin to a 'death trap' for AIDS patients and an 'abandoned child', removed from the city of Singapore. But there was a sense of tranquillity and peacefulness when the patients passed away.[97] Another survivor, Tong, called the CDC 'a place of ghosts' ('鬼地方'). AIDS patients wore sunglasses and caps to hide their faces when entering the centre, while making sure no acquaintances of theirs were around. He had been warded in Room 9 in Ward 76. Though he remembered the details, he found little about the CDC worth reminiscing.[98]

The 2013 book, *Inter-views: A Photovoice Collection*, contains recollections of HIV/AIDS patients. It used participatory photography to help people narrate their stories. The editors worked with the TTSH and held an eight-week long photo-interview workshop at the CDC for 16 members of a support group for people with HIV. One of the participants, nicknamed Soul, wrote about the CDC in a chapter titled 'Life':

> I was admitted to CDC ward with high fever and suspected pneumonia. March 2008. My start of taking HIV cocktails of medication ... Life was lonely and depressing with no one to turn to except the medical doctors, the staff in CDC and a very close friend whom I always confide in. I was ashamed of the stigma associated with HIV. I kept the secret from family and friends. I was a walking mannequin ... August 2012 ... One of the peer group activities organised by the CDC medical social workers was an outdoor gathering of HIV positive people at East Coast Beach. It was an opening to socialise and make more friends with people suffering the same illness. It was an awakening. Among the group, there was one. We became friends. We shared our life and supported each other. Life suddenly opened its doors to me. I was not alone anymore.[99]

The second and last major epidemic at the CDC was SARS in 2003. Initially, the centre was designated to screen suspected cases. But the facility struggled. Lacking radiology equipment, sufficient telephones and computers, the doctors evaluated 522 patients and admitted 165 patients over an intense 11-day period until the screening work was moved to the Emergency Department at the TTSH. A number of less serious, probable or recovering cases were warded in Wards 71, 72 and 76 in the CDC at some point.[100] There were insufficient isolation beds at the centre – only 37 of 123 beds in five wards. Probable SARS patients in the early phase of the outbreak had to be warded together to allow suspect cases to be placed in single rooms to prevent cross-infection. Four emergency cabin wards, named Wards 91–94, with a total of 80 single rooms had to be constructed over the course of two months to fulfil the urgent need for isolation facilities.

Most cases were subsequently isolated and treated at the TTSH, which became the main SARS hospital. The CDC had looked upon the outbreak as its 'finest hour'.[101] Again, many taxi drivers and buses refused to stop in front of both the CDC and TTSH.[102] Senior nurse Harbhajan Singh recalled the SARS outbreak as 'the worst period in my life'. It was difficult to deal with the large number of suspected and probable SARS cases, as J Clinic was small and the CDC lacked facilities such as X-ray equipment (though a small X-ray centre was subsequently set up), a clinical laboratory (blood samples had to be sent to the TTSH) and transport (which was provided by TTSH). The work included separating routine admissions from persons with travel advisories who were considered higher priority.[103]

Like AIDS, SARS was a virus that was not well understood in the beginning. As a nursing manager, Singh had to lift the nurses' morale. Some nurses from China and the Philippines wanted to return home during the epidemic, and the CDC had to allow the nurses off days to raise their morale.[104] One of the Singaporean nurses, Akhterun Nisha, found the SARS outbreak 'the most difficult to handle' as some patients did not want to come to the CDC. They doubted if it was really a hospital because of its rundown appearance, asking, 'What place is this?'. They wanted to be treated at the TTSH instead.[105] HIV/AIDS and SARS were reminders that people's acceptance of hospitals is historical, liable to change and not to be taken for granted.

The inadequacies of the CDC during the SARS pandemic further underlined the need for a new hospital. But this was not the first time the idea had been mooted. Increasingly, the dispersed pavilion system of the CDC had become an anachronism. This was not a local issue but a global one. As architectural historian Jeanne Kisacky explained, the considerable distance between pavilion wards – originally intended for the quarantine of diseases – was at odds with the need for patients and hospital staff to traverse often and quickly between the increasingly specialised departments of biomedicine in a modern hospital.[106]

There had been plans to build a new infectious diseases hospital in Singapore in the early 1990s. The 1993 and 1995 annual reports of the MOH announced that the CDC would be rebuilt on a 0.65 ha site north of the new TTSH premises, with the new facility projected to be ready in 1998 or 1999.[107] These plans did not materialise but were never completely rejected. Dr Chew Suok Kai had proposed them when he was Medical Director of the CDC between 1993 and 1995. Since the mid-1990s, there had been several versions of the plans in response to emerging trends, namely, the SARS outbreak, the 2014 Ebola virus infection and the threat of bioterrorism. Government officials undertook extensive discussions, studies and overseas site visits to infectious disease centres such as the Centers for Disease Control and Prevention in the US. The NCID, in Chew's view, was the fruition of these deliberations.[108]

It also appears that the closure of Australia's Fairfield Hospital in 1996 gave impetus to the push for a new hospital, as did the Nipah outbreak in Singapore three years later.[109] Then the SARS epidemic highlighted the lack of isolation beds at the CDC and the TTSH. Two months after the epidemic, the Ren Ci nursing home nearby was converted into Communicable Disease Centre 2 (CDC 2) to provide additional isolation beds should another outbreak occur. But the CDC 2 was not the new CDC. The scheme for a new infectious disease centre was shelved due to the 2008 financial crisis, but revitalised after the Ebola outbreak in 2014. Its advocates saw the new facility as a hospital where patients with highly dangerous and transmissible diseases could be segregated from the rest of the population and healthcare system. They hoped that it would not be used except in the event of a major outbreak.[110]

In December 2018, 105 years since its birth, the CDC closed its gates. The historic Moulmein Road site, a sprawl of terrace wards and pavilions in a zone of greenery, was gazetted for residential development. The authors of this book had in a heritage study urged its repurposing as a heritage site.[111] The following August, the Singapore Land Authority organised several heritage tours of the since vacated site, led by heritage blogger and photographer Jerome Lim. One such tour on the morning of 3 August 2018 was attended by a still hale Edmund Monteiro, several of his former staff and the authors. Monteiro quickly regaled the group with stories of the CDC.

The work of the CDC passed to the new NCID built nearby at Jalan Tan Tock Seng, part of the planning zone of Health City Novena. It officially opened in 2019, a large, 330-bed facility with modern technology and equipment. The establishment of the centre had taken considerable time, debate and deliberation, mirroring those efforts preceding the founding of the Moulmein Road Hospital in 1913 and the development plans for the Middleton Hospital after the Second World War. The issue had always been the commitment of resources to a hospital that would only prove its worth during an epidemic. But the hope for the NCID not to be used was quickly dashed, for it was built just before the COVID-19 pandemic.

## Notes

1  SMAR 1899, p. 104.
2  CO 275/29 AMRCHSS 1883.
3  SMAR 1911.
4  Evidence by Thomas Oswald Mayhew, Chief Sanitary Inspector to the Singapore Municipality, Straits Settlements Quarantine Inquiry Commission, *Proceedings of the Commission Appointed to Inquire into the Working of the Quarantine and Prevention of Diseases Ordinance in the Settlement of Singapore, in the Colony of the Straits Settlements*, (Singapore: Government Printing Office, 1912), Vol. 2, p. 15.
5  Straits Settlements Quarantine Inquiry Commission, *Proceedings of the Commission*, Vol. 1, p. 2.
6  Straits Settlements Quarantine Inquiry Commission, *Proceedings of the Commission*, Vol. 1, p. 2.
7  Straits Settlements Quarantine Inquiry Commission, *Proceedings of the Commission*, Vol. 1.
8  Evidence by Low Kway Soo, Straits Settlements Quarantine Inquiry Commission, *Proceedings of the Commission*, Vol. 2, p. 82.
9  *Straits Times*, 19 July 1911; Evidence by Frank Rodrigues, Senior Assistant Surgeon at Tan Tock Seng's Hospital, Straits Settlements Quarantine Inquiry Commission, *Proceedings of the Commission*, Vol. 2, p. 10; Evidence by Low Kway Soo, Straits Settlements Quarantine Inquiry Commission, *Proceedings of the Commission*, Vol. 2, p. 82.
10  Evidence by Frank Rodrigues, Senior Assistant Surgeon at Tan Tock Seng's Hospital, Straits Settlements Quarantine Inquiry Commission, *Proceedings of the Commission*, Vol. 2, p. 10.

11 Evidence by Frank Rodrigues, Senior Assistant Surgeon at Tan Tock Seng's Hospital, Straits Settlements Quarantine Inquiry Commission, *Proceedings of the Commission*, Vol. 2, p. 10; evidence by Evidence by Low Kway Soo, Straits Settlements Quarantine Inquiry Commission, *Proceedings of the Commission*, Vol. 2.

12 Evidence by Low Kway Soo, Straits Settlements Quarantine Inquiry Commission, *Proceedings of the Commission*, Vol. 2, p. 82.

13 Evidence by Thomas Oswald Mayhew, Chief Sanitary Inspector to the Singapore Municipality, Straits Settlements Quarantine Inquiry Commission, *Proceedings of the Commission*, Vol. 2, p. 38.

14 Evidence by Thomas Oswald Mayhew, Chief Sanitary Inspector to the Singapore Municipality, Straits Settlements Quarantine Inquiry Commission, *Proceedings of the Commission*, Vol. 2.

15 Evidence by Thomas Oswald Mayhew, Chief Sanitary Inspector to the Singapore Municipality, Straits Settlements Quarantine Inquiry Commission, *Proceedings of the Commission*, Vol. 2, p. 39.

16 Evidence by Dr James Handy, Medical Practitioner, Straits Settlements Quarantine Inquiry Commission, *Proceedings of the Commission*, Vol. 2, p. 32.

17 Evidence by Dr James Handy, Medical Practitioner, Straits Settlements Quarantine Inquiry Commission, *Proceedings of the Commission*, Vol. 2.

18 Evidence by Gan Poo Teong, storekeeper, Straits Settlements Quarantine Inquiry Commission, *Proceedings of the Commission*, Vol. 2, p. 36.

19 SMAR 1896.

20 SMAR 1893.

21 SMAR 1899, p. 105.

22 SMAR 1899, p. 105.

23 SMAR 1899, p. 106.

24 SMAR 1899, p. 106.

25 Written statement by Dr Middleton, Straits Settlements Quarantine Inquiry Commission, *Proceedings of the Commission*, Vol. 2, Appendix A, pp. 19–20.

26 *Straits Times*, 12 March 1904.

27 *Singapore Free Press*, 12 March 1904.

28 SMAR 1901, p. 25.

29 SMAR 1907, p. 41.

30 SMAR 1906, p. 9.

31 W.J. Simpson, *Report of the Sanitary Condition of Singapore* (London: Waterlow & Sons, 1907).

32 *Singapore Free Press*, 28 June 1907.

33 *Singapore Free Press*, 4 July 1907.

34 *Singapore Free Press*, 7 November 1907.

35 SMAR 1910, p. 11.

36 Evidence by Dr William Robert Colvin Middleton, Municipal Health Officer, Straits Settlements Quarantine Inquiry Commission, *Proceedings of the Commission*, Vol. 2.

37 Evidence by Benjamin Hall, Acting Municipal Engineer, Straits Settlements Quarantine Inquiry Commission, *Proceedings of the Commission*, Vol. 2.

38 Straits Settlements Quarantine Inquiry Commission, *Proceedings of the Commission*, Vol. 1.

39 Evidence by Benjamin Hall, Acting Municipal Engineer, Straits Settlements Quarantine Inquiry Commission, *Proceedings of the Commission*, Vol. 2.

40 Evidence by Dr William Robert Colvin Middleton, Municipal Health Officer, Straits Settlements Quarantine Inquiry Commission, *Proceedings of the Commission*, Vol. 2.

41 SMAR 1910, p. 8.

42 Evidence by Dr James Handy, Medical Practitioner, Straits Settlements Quarantine Inquiry Commission, *Proceedings of the Commission*, Vol. 2.
43 Evidence by Dr James Handy, Medical Practitioner, Straits Settlements Quarantine Inquiry Commission, *Proceedings of the Commission*, Vol. 2, p. 33.
44 *Straits Times*, 1 July 1911, p. 9; *Straits Times*, 24 July 1911, p. 7.
45 *Straits Times*, 27 July 1911, p. 7.
46 Evidence by Dr Richard Arthur Campbell, Second Assistant Municipal Health Officer, Straits Settlements Quarantine Inquiry Commission, *Proceedings of the Commission*, Vol. 2.
47 Straits Settlements Quarantine Inquiry Commission, *Proceedings of the Commission*, Vol. 1.
48 Written statement by Dr Campbell, Straits Settlements Quarantine Inquiry Commission, *Proceedings of the Commission*, Vol. 2, Appendix A, p. 10.
49 Written statement by Dr Glennie, Straits Settlements Quarantine Inquiry Commission, *Proceedings of the Commission*, Vol. 2, Appendix A.
50 Written statement by Dr Middleton, Straits Settlements Quarantine Inquiry Commission, *Proceedings of the Commission*, Vol. 2, Appendix A, p. 20.
51 CO 275/87 SSMR 1913, p. 494.
52 CO 275/87 SSMR 1913, p. 494.
53 Chang Jiat-Hwee, 'Tropicalising Technologies of Environment and Government: The Singapore General Hospital and the Circulation of the Pavilion Plan Hospital in the British Empire, 1860–1930', in Michael Guggenheim and Ola Söderström (eds), *Re-shaping Cities: How Global Mobility Transforms Architecture and Urban Form* (London: Routledge, 2010), pp. 123–142.
54 *Singapore Free Press*, 31 May 1906, p. 1.
55 *Straits Times*, 29 May 1913.
56 SMAR 1913, p. 13.
57 SMAR 1914.
58 SMAR 1933, p. 84-D.
59 SMAR 1933.
60 HD 113/45 Vol. 1 Memo by Director of Medical Services, 15 August 1948.
61 HD 113/45 Vol. 1 Report, 'Re-management of Middleton Hospital' by Medical Superintendent, 113/45.
62 Paul H. Kratoska, *The Japanese Occupation of Malaya and Singapore, 1941–45: A Social and Economic History* (Singapore: NUS Press, 2018), 2nd edition.
63 MDAR 1948; MDAR 1949.
64 Proceedings of the Legislative Council of Singapore, *The Medical Plan for Singapore*, 18 May 1948.
65 HD 113/45 Vol. 1 Minutes of a Conference to discuss the future status of Middleton Hospital, 29 March 1950.
66 HD 113/45 Vol. 1 Memo from Dr Ng See Yook to the Municipal Health Officer, 27 February 1950.
67 HD 113/45 Vol. 1 Minutes of a Conference to discuss the question of staffing at Middleton Hospital, 25 April 1950.
68 HD 113/45 Vol. 1 Memo from Ng See Yook to the Municipal Health Officer, 27 February 1950.
69 HD 113/45 Vol. 2 Memo by W.E. Hutchinson D.H.O., 20 June 1951.
70 HD 113/45 Vol. 1 Minutes of a Conference to discuss the future status of Middleton Hospital, 29 March 1950.
71 *Singapore Standard*, 9 October 1956.
72 HD 113/45 Vol. 1 Minutes of a Conference to discuss the future status of Middleton Hospital, 29 March 1950.
73 MOHAR 1949, p. 12.

74    HD 113/45 Vol. 1 Memo from Ng See Yook to the Municipal Health Officer, 27 February 1950.
75    HD 113/45 Vol. 2 Report of the Infectious Diseases Committee.
76    HD 113/45 Vol. 2 Memo from T.P.F. McNeice, President of the City Council, to the Chief Secretary, 27 September 1952.
77    HD 113/45 Vol. 1 Memo from D.M.S to D.C.I, 18 April 1953.
78    Oral History Centre, National Archives of Singapore, Interview with Edmund Hugh Monteiro, Reel 12, 11 November 1997.
79    MOHAR 1992.
80    MOHAR 1995, p. 5.
81    Loh Kah Seng, Interview with Chew Suok Kai, 13 December 2018.
82    Loh Kah Seng, Interview with Leo Yee Sin, 10 June 2019.
83    The name changes signified the restructuring of the CDC and the adapted uses of its wards over time. By 1932, the wards were named after letters of the alphabet from A to O. In 1971, the letters were replaced by Roman numerals beginning with '1', as apparently implemented by the Medical Superintendent, Dr Leong Kwok Wah. In 1985, Roman numerals beginning from '71' were used when the hospital merged with the TTSH to become the CDC, as the TTSH's ward numbers ended in the '60's. At an indeterminate recent date, Roman numerals beginning from '800' were used.
84    MOHAR 1951.
85    MOHAR 1958.
86    Oral History Centre, National Archives of Singapore, Interview with Edmund Hugh Monteiro, Reel 7, 24 October 1997.
87    David Allen, email correspondence with Loh Kah Seng, 30 June 2019.
88    *Straits Times*, 6 May 1971.
89    Oral History Centre, National Archives of Singapore, Interview with Edmund Hugh Monteiro, Reel 11, 11 November 1997.
90    Oral History Centre, National Archives of Singapore, Interview with Edmund Hugh Monteiro, Reel 11, 11 November 1997.
91    Laurence Wai-Teng Leong, 'Walking the Tightrope: The Role of Action for AIDS in the Provision of Social Services in Singapore', in Gerard Sullivan and Laurence Wai-Teng Leong (eds.), *Gays and Lesbians in Asia and the Pacific: Social and Human Services* (New York: Haworth Press, 1995).
92    *Singapore Monitor*, 17 April 1985.
93    *Singapore Monitor*, 14 April 1985.
94    Loh Kah Seng, Interview with Edmund Monteiro, 11 December 2018.
95    Loh Kah Seng, Interview with Edmund Monteiro, 11 December 2018.
96    Ho Lai Peng, email correspondence with Loh Kah Seng, 9 September 2019.
97    Loh Kah Seng, Interview with Paul Toh, 4 June 2019.
98    Loh Kah Seng, Interview with Tong, 27 September 2019.
99    Photovoice SG (ed.), *Inter-views: A Photovoice Collection* (Singapore: Photovoice SG, 2013), p. 136.
100   Loh Kah Seng, Interview with Harbhajan Singh, 21 March 2019; Loh Kah Seng and Kymelya Sari, Interview with Hsu Li Yang, 5 August 2019.
101   Dr Lim Poh Lian, 'Emerging Infections and CDC', in Communicable Diseases Centre, *100 Years: A Commemorative Publication for the Communicable Diseases Centre* (Singapore: Tan Tock Seng Hospital, 2007), p. 52.
102   Loh Kah Seng and Kymelya Sari, Interview with Hsu Li Yang, 5 August 2019.
103   Loh Kah Seng, Interview with Harbhajan Singh, 21 March 2019.
104   Loh Kah Seng, Interview with Harbhajan Singh, 21 March 2019.
105   Loh Kah Seng, Interview with Akhterun Nisha, 11 March 2019.
106   Jeanne Kisacky, *Rise of the Modern Hospital: An Architectural History of Health and Healing, 1870–1940* (Pittsburgh, PA: University of Pittsburgh Press, 2017).

107 MOHAR 1993, MOHAR 1995.
108 Chew Suok Kai, email correspondence with Loh Kah Seng, 3 July 2019.
109 Loh Kah Seng, Interview with Leo Yee Sin, 10 June 2019.
110 Loh Kah Seng and Kymelya Sari, Interview with Hsu Li Yang, 5 August 2019.
111 Hsu Li Yang, Loh Kah Seng, Deborah Ng, and Margaret Soon, *Documenting Middleton Hospital, Communicable Disease Centre and the Medical Heritage of Singapore*, Heritage Research Project Final Report for the National Heritage Board, 2019.

# 6 1890 Flu

## Poison at the Wharves

Influenza has made itself for many months past too much at home here, and there are many in Singapore who have experienced or are now experiencing these sensations:

'When your clothes from your hat to your socks
Have tickled and scrubbed you all day;
When your brain is a musical box
With a barrel that turns the wrong way;
When you find you're too big for your coat
And a great deal too small for your vest,
With a pint of warm oil for your throat,
And a pound of tin tacks in your chest;
When you've got a beehive in your head,
And a sewing machine in your ear,
And you feel that you've eaten your bed,
And you've got a bad headache down here;
When your lips are like underdone paste,
And you're highly gamboge in the gill,
And your mouth has a coopery taste,
As if you'd just bitten a pill;

    And wherever you tread,
    From a yawning abyss
    You recoil with a yell,
    You are better in bed,
    For depend upon this,
    You are not at all well.'

*Singapore Free Press*, 5 April 1892, p. 210

The 1890 influenza pandemic – evocatively described above – was ostensibly Singapore's first recorded flu epidemic. Having swept the Western countries in previous months, what was commonly known as the 'Russian flu' reportedly 'prevailed almost everywhere' on the island.[1] Historians of Singapore know virtually nothing about the event, but clearly it was not forgotten by contemporaries. As illustrated in the poem published in the *Singapore Free Press*

DOI: 10.4324/9781003384014-7

two years later, falling ill with influenza was no longer an unknown or uncommon experience. Those who were sick had their world turned upside down for a time, with familiar body parts and everyday objects imbued with new, unpleasant meanings. The pandemic left an imprint on people's memories and the poem served as a warning that it could happen again.

With these social memories in mind, we trace the history of the epidemic in Singapore from its origins and spread to the aftermath till the next great influenza pandemic in 1918. Two narratives emerge along the way. One, in contrast to its emphasis on the trinity of quarantinable diseases, the government lacked a strong response to influenza, both during the outbreak and in the aftermath. The second is the pandemic's social impact, which was universal in a sense, affecting all social classes, but particularly marked for coolies and children.

Influenza is a highly contagious respiratory illness caused by the virus of the same name. There are four types of influenza viruses: A, B, C and D, although only the first three affect humans. Because influenza viruses mutate over time (a process known as antigenic drift), they are able to evade the immune system and cause new infections – neither humans nor animals develop lifelong immunity against flu. Influenza A viruses affect multiple mammal and bird species, some of which – such as avian (bird) and swine flu – are able to sporadically infect humans. Rarely, these animal viruses mutate or recombine with human influenza viruses such that they become highly infectious to humans (antigenic shift), which result in pandemics. Influenza vaccines exist but are unable to provide lifelong immunity, hence the current recommendation for people to take annual flu jabs.

For a long time, the 1890 flu pandemic was believed to have been caused by an influenza virus. In 2021, in the midst of the COVID-19 pandemic, two scholars suggested that it could have been caused by a human coronavirus. Given the lack of strong evidence to corroborate this, we have continued in the tradition of the historical literature to view the 1890 event as an influenza pandemic.[2]

## Arrival at the Wharf

Was colonial Singapore prepared for influenza pandemics? In previous chapters, we have seen the gradual development of its quarantine system in the 19th century, but influenza was to pose a bigger challenge. A summary of the history of quarantine will show that the British East India Company was nudged to act only when the fear of epidemics outweighed the priority given to trade and immigration. Though colonial rule started in 1819, a small step towards quarantine was taken only in 1850, when growing numbers of Chinese migrants were observed landing on the island 'in a dying state'.[3] That year, the India Act XLI of 1850 was passed, with provisions to penalise ship masters carrying sick or destitute passengers on their vessels. But the manpower required to carry out the surveillance was not forthcoming till a quarter of a century later, when the Principal Civil Medical Officer Dr Thomas Irvine Rowell proposed to appoint a

Deputy Health Officer with a boat and crew to inspect vessels, especially over-crowded Chinese junks, for signs of infection. At the time, Rowell was aware of the limits of quarantine given Singapore's status as an open port of call for ships and migrants:

> perfectly effectual measures to exclude epidemic disease from Singapore, by means of quarantine, were naturally impossible, but that the danger of introduction might be reduced by intelligent inspection of ships and iso-lation of sources of infection.[4]

The development of quarantine passed influenza by, so those with visible symptoms of the disease would have been allowed to disembark. Other infectious diseases were deemed more deadly. In 1873, as we have seen, a Siamese ship departing from Bangkok caused a major cholera outbreak in Singapore, resulting in 857 cases and 448 deaths. Subsequently, the Acting Master Attendant Henry Ellis asked the Straits government to build a small hospital for infectious disease patients on St. John's Island. A lazaretto, or quarantine station, 'of a very primitive type' (with an attap roof) was built there the following year. Almost immediately it was called upon to house 1,300 cholera contacts onboard the vessel, *S.S. Milton.* [5] It was the cholera outbreak that spurred a small improvement to the quarantine system.[6]

As the British admitted, the quarantine station on St. John's was little used up to the 1880s. Its superintendent was a dresser and it often took a week to disinfect a ship.[7] The official description of the island in this period showed its shortcomings:

> St. John's Island was about half under jungle. Its accommodation consisted of a few attap sheds with mud floors. Its water supply was from 10 wells, which were frequently infected with Cholera. There was only one latrine for the whole island; and not a single disinfector was in use! There were no facilities for disinfecting ships. The sanitation and water supply of the shipping were not thought of. The hours of duty were theoretically sup-posed to be from sunrise to sunset. No wonder therefore that the first Port Health Officer found the situation to be hopeless and left in two months.[8]

Eventually, in 1883, the government approved the long-proposed post of Deputy Health Officer to inspect ships. The following year, he received a small steam-launch allowing him to board vessels and inspect the crew and passen-gers for signs of infectious disease. The passing of a new Quarantine and Pre-vention of Diseases Ordinance in 1886 finally gave him legal powers to carry out this work. It empowered the Governor to place in quarantine vessels arriving from a port where an epidemic such as cholera, smallpox, fever or 'other contagious or infectious disease of a dangerous nature' had occurred.[9] These were much-needed improvements, but other than the open clause quoted above, there was little concern about quarantining influenza cases.

The 1890 influenza pandemic arrived in Singapore in the third week of February and lasted till the start of April before disappearing quite abruptly – a duration of six to seven weeks. While the quarantine system on St. John's had recently received enhancements, no precautions were taken to thwart the entry of influenza. The bulk of quarantine work during the year took place between September and December, mainly to quarantine sea passengers suffering from cholera and smallpox.[10]

On the causes of the epidemic in Singapore, the Acting Principal Civil Medical Officer wrote in his report to the Colonial Office,

> In Singapore I am of the opinion that the disease was introduced by ships, probably by the wharf coolies being infected by contact with persons on board ships suffering from the disease, or working in the air of ships that had become charged with the Influenza poison.[11]

The report was submitted to the Colonial Office nearly half a year later in August 1890. Illness from the flu is characterised by high fever (up to 40 degrees Celsius), severe headaches, back and muscular pains, and intense bouts of coughing, with some patients describing how their heads were 'splitting open'.[12] Others complained of pain in the joints of their limbs.[13] A newly arrived Chinese immigrant who was suspected to have died from the disease had a fit and became hysterical.[14] It was not a mild illness.

Singapore then became the conduit for the spread of influenza to Penang (where the first case was reported in the first week of March) and Malacca (the first week of April). Unlike in Penang where the outbreak was traced to coolies opening cases of piece goods in the local bazaar, the Acting Principal Civil Medical Officer traced the Singapore outbreak to the wharf workers. It was an unsurprisingly severe outbreak as the coolies 'live together in a large building in a very overcrowded condition'.[15] There was a shortage of workers at the Tanjong Pagar wharf after more than 200 workers fell ill with influenza.[16]

The Straits government did not make influenza a notifiable disease, as it did during the 1918 influenza pandemic. No complete official numbers of cases and deaths were released, though there were statistics on the monthly death rate. Both the government and the Municipal Commission stated that the number of direct deaths from influenza was very small, though the complications that resulted were more serious.[17] The Acting Principal Civil Medical Officer estimated the death rate to be no more than 0.5 per cent, due to the 'attenuated condition' of the imported virus; death was due to pneumonia or the poor general health of debilitated coolies.[18] The Municipal Commission noted that most fatalities were old people or others suffering from 'cardiac or pulmonary affections', adding, 'Although not of itself a fatal disease, yet its influence in increasing the death rate during an epidemic is remarkable'.[19] Unfortunately, we have little information on the complications, other than the figures of 800 admissions and 150 deaths due to respiratory illnesses in the Straits Settlements that year.

We have the Registrar-General's submission that the greatest number of deaths in a month in the year occurred in March. In most years, this was apparently among Singapore's healthiest months, but in 1890, there were 661 deaths at the height of the epidemic. This number was noted as the highest number in Singapore since June 1888, though the interval is less than two years. The corresponding mortality figures for February and April 1890 were 420 and 598 respectively, with a monthly average of 546 for the year.[20] This suggests that conservatively influenza was responsible for about 120 deaths. According to the Health Officer, the weather added to the deaths, as 'Influenza, plus a very rainy month [in March], which always gives us more fever, is doubtless the cause of the present increased death rate'.[21]

## To Hospitals, Schools and Beyond

We know little about the local trajectory of influenza from the colonial records. The medical reports continued to focus on the zymotic illnesses the government had long tracked: plague, cholera and smallpox. An exception was the government hospital records, which were the few official sources of information on an acute disease that broke out and ended suddenly. This does not tell us how or how far influenza was spreading in the community. Moreover, hospital records must be regarded with scepticism, for many Asians did not seek treatment there at the time.

The hospitals evidently did not stem the outbreak. In the General Hospital, two cases of influenza were admitted to the European wards during the year; both subsequently recovered. Four cases were admitted to the Native (Asian) wards, who also recovered. As these were small numbers, we can infer they were the severe cases, whereas most patients suffering from a mild infection did not seek help at the hospital. By contrast, there were 46 cases of mild influenza admitted to the Police ward of the GH. In addition, the hospital noted, 'the bulk of the cases of bronchitis, febricula (a mild fever) and rheumatism were admitted at or about the time of the prevalence of influenza'.[22]

The strongest evidence of uncontrolled spread was the large increase in the number of total admissions to the Prison Hospital from 695 in 1889 to a thousand in 1890, with the first admission made on 8 March. The actual number attributed to influenza was only 136, mostly during this month; among them were six Europeans. Three patients later died from pneumonia caused by influenza, including 'a strong young English soldier'.[23] The admissions to the Prison Hospital were only the tip of the iceberg, with half of the one thousand prison inmates reported to be suffering from influenza that year.[24] The prison authorities reported that 'hundreds of slighter cases were treated among the prisoners in the prison, the patients being put on light work'.[25] In general, the Prison Hospital did not admit sick prisoners unless their illness prevented them from working.

Cases were also reported in the hospital for women's sexually transmitted diseases and in outdoor dispensaries, suggesting the spread of the disease into the surrounding municipal areas. Interestingly, the Tan Tock Seng Hospital, a major hospital originally built for Asian paupers in Singapore, reported a mere four cases of influenza. It claimed to have avoided an outbreak of influenza among its patients, but this seems doubtful.[26] The more likely explanation was that Asians were not going there for influenza treatment.

As the disease was not made notifiable, it was difficult to prevent the spread of infection to the general population. We do not know exactly how the 'poison' spread beyond the wharves, as the colonial and municipal records are patchy on the matter. The Acting Principal Civil Medical Officer felt that women were less affected than their husbands, as they resided in well-ventilated homes most of the time, though this would not apply to women who did not dwell in good homes and those of lesser means.[27] Working-class Asian women in the town typically lived in shophouses, which had poor air circulation, or wooden houses.

But transmission within the Prison Hospital suggests there was little resistance to influenza's penetration into an unprepared general population. On 8 March, the *Straits Times* reported that 'there is scarcely a Chinese house in the district of Teluk Ayer street where one or more is not suffering from the disease', including a Chinese Municipal Commissioner and his family and servants. This charts a path of infection from the wharves to the streets of densely-populated Chinatown within walking distance, where the merchants and coolies lived. Three days later, the newspaper deemed that 'Influenza seems to be getting still more prevalent in Singapore, especially among the Asiatics'.[28]

The paper carried a lengthy report on the same day, criticising the 'woful ignorance [sic]' of even the educated public, as described in the following passage:

> O there is nothing dangerous about it; if we get it and it becomes serious, we can consult a doctor, but in the meantime it is no use bothering about it.[29]

The report surmised that the epidemic was spreading unevenly among the social classes and ethnic groups in the town:

> that it is obtaining a daily increasing hold, particularly among the poorer classes of our Asiatic population, those who have been brought into contact with it in the course of their avocations are fully aware.
>
> So far the malady has made only modest headway among the European or Eurasian population, and is most prevalent among the Chinese, Tamils and some of the poorer classes of Portuguese residents; in the General Hospital there are no cases of influenza on the list of patients being treated in the institution, whereas at Tanjong Pagar [near the busy port area] numbers of the wharf coolies are much affected by it.[30]

The article also found increased absences of pupils in Singapore's leading schools. This provides an insight into influenza's movement across different demographics – among students and also within their households. At the Tamil School at Cross Street, some staff and as many as half the students were absent due to '*bona fide* influenza'. St. Anthony's Mission School seemingly 'has got it bad', reporting a similar proportion of student absentees. By contrast, in the day school of Anglo Chinese School, a fifth of the boys were absent from class, alongside a quarter of the boys at the mission house. At the other extreme, Raffles Girls School, Raffles Boys School and St Joseph's Institution reported no outbreaks, showing the unevenness of experience (or more likely lack of reliable data) across Singapore.[31] But these reports provide evidence that influenza was spreading among the upper echelons of society, as it was the better-educated and higher-income residents who had children and were able to send them to good English schools. The bulk of the immigrant Asian population at the time was single or had no children.

Another report in the *Straits Times* traced the outbreak earlier to late January, with allegedly over 200 influenza cases occurring across all the ethnic groups. It alluded to significant under-reporting, with a large number of patients not seen by Western-trained doctors but by 'the native so-called doctors'.[32] Some patients among the latter group (or those who self-medicated) used a herbal remedy called *Kroma susu* (possibly a drink, as *susu* is milk in Malay). This was allegedly 'a common weed' that was popular for treating influenza and asthma.[33] The proliferation of easily available remedies explains why relatively few people were seeking help at hospitals.

For a sufferer inclined towards Western medicine, a London-based company called F. Comar & Son advertised the product, Aubergier's Syrup and Paste, as a 'world-famed and marvellous medicament' for influenza and other respiratory afflictions.[34] Chamberlain's Cough Remedy was popular then as a treatment for 'coughs, colds, croup, whooping cough and influenza' and remained so into the new century.[35] So was Dr Williams' 'pink pills for pale people', which was sold as a 'cure-all' for a princely sum of eight dollars for half a dozen bottles. It was still being sold in Singapore at the time of the 1918 influenza pandemic and thereafter.[36] Advertisements in a Chinese-language newspaper promoted an anti-flu syrup imported from Germany that had proven effective in Europe.[37] There was a boom in the business of dispensaries during the outbreak, and many doctors profited.[38]

The appearance of these commercial products, often replete with glowing testimonials from 'consumers', takes us into the realm of social history and memory. They showed an awareness of influenza and persistence of fear in the community. During the epidemic, a writer to the *Straits Times*, with the moniker 'A Stitch in Time Saves Nine', was worried that the flu would be followed by a cholera outbreak, which allegedly had happened in previous influenza epidemics.[39] Sustained in part by personal anxieties and in part by commercial motives, a strand of social memory survived the epidemic. This differed from the official stance towards influenza in the years after the outbreak.

Against reports and advertisements in English, there was also a quite different realm of experience altogether among the Chinese in Singapore, who numbered two-thirds of the entrepôt's population by this time. The Chinese-medium newspapers, the *Lat Pau* and *Sing Po*, contained surprisingly detailed descriptions and viewpoints of the epidemic, in some ways more so than the English press or the officials. Immigrant Chinese were interpreting and responding to the outbreak in ways that significantly differed from what was reported in the English newspapers.

Compared to the *Straits Times*, the Chinese press took the epidemic seriously. News of infection and death in the community were reported, perhaps exaggerated in some instances. During the outbreak, the *Sing Po* lamented the seasonal or epidemic diseases that killed impoverished migrants, citing the case of a Chinese male who collapsed at South Bridge Road and was sent to a hospital, where he died.[40] Labourers and rickshaw pullers were most at risk, for they were constantly exposed to the elements, yet when they fell ill, they could only continue to work even as their condition worsened. They suffered a double whammy, for some of them also bought fake medicines.[41] Similarly, the *Lat Pau* wrote about whole families starving because everyone was sick and no one was able to cook.[42] Subsequently its tone tampered somewhat, stating that the illness was not very severe, but beware, it was spreading very widely in the town, infecting all races.[43] A few days later, a barber out on the street suddenly collapsed and died, and his body was sent to the hospital for medical examination.[44]

A lengthy treatise published in the newspaper on 27 February captured the panic coursing through the community. It ventured that the influenza outbreak was unlike anything that traditional Chinese medicine had encountered before. The disease rampaging through Singapore was a mysterious one, being neither flu nor the 'direct attack' of a cold. Whereas those afflictions could be purged from the diaphragm at an early stage with suitable medication, the influenza killed within several hours before treatment could be administered. The course of the disease was likely to befuddle physicians, causing them to switch from medicines prescribed for 'cold' (*yin*) illnesses to those for 'warm' (*yang*); it was really a *yin* and *yang* sickness, whereas influenza was traditionally seen as a *yang* disease. Prevention was better than cure, and could be achieved through moderation: by not overeating or consuming unhealthy food, by restraint in sexual activity and by avoiding extremes in the weather and environment.[45] A report by the same paper on 7 March declared the epidemic to be worsening, with no one knowing when it would end.[46]

### Aftermath: Colonial Inaction, Social Remembrance

As soon as it subsided, the 1890 outbreak was virtually forgotten by the authorities. The medical reports of the Straits Settlements noted sporadic cases of influenza in the ensuing years, but no major plans emerged for dealing with a disease that had become endemic. Once again, our main colonial source of information is the medical establishment. In 1891, two cases of influenza were treated in the GH, while the Municipal Commission reported the death of a Eurasian female from the disease four years later. In 1893, the *Straits Times* stated that 'Whole families have been stricken' by a mild strain of local influenza, though this was something the government failed to report.[47]

This happened again in 1895, with outbreaks also occurring in England and Spain.[48] Singapore's outbreak was purportedly a severe one, affecting the various ethnic groups, and complications were not uncommon.[49] The Straits Registrar-General puzzlingly claimed that there was no outbreak of epidemic disease to explain the year's relatively high death rate.[50] But a letter to the press by 'L.' noted that 'The influenza epidemic is right among us', striking down 'Many heads of department'. The disease, the author said, 'is no respector of persons'.[51]

Finally, in the middle of 1897 between the months of June and September, the colonial administration reported a mild but fairly large outbreak of influenza. This transpired among the police force, with 443 patients seen at its outpatient department and many personnel visiting the department two or three times each. The outbreak was widespread, affecting policemen from all stations but especially from the Orchard Road and Kandang Kerbau stations within the town area. It was also a mild outbreak, with few reports of complications except for slight bronchitis and pain in the limbs for several days. Only four patients had to be sent to a hospital, requiring only 'a few days in barracks' for a full recovery.[52] The quarantine station on St John did not report any influenza that year.

In the following year, another mild outbreak emerged in the Prison Hospital, resulting in 73 cases in March and April. There were then no further official reports of influenza events till 1908, when one and three patients were admitted to the European and Native wards of the GH respectively. The next major flu outbreak was the global pandemic of 1918. There were sporadic deaths from influenza in this period: in 1905, a young Chinese male between 25 and 35; in 1914, a Chinese male above 55; and in 1915, a Malay male.

These local outbreaks tell us much about the non-existent official response to the 1890 pandemic and the travails of living with endemic influenza. The British still thought port quarantine to be a matter of secondary importance.[53] The quarantine system continued to develop, but influenza was not added to the trinity of quarantinable diseases. Throughout the 1890s, the screening of immigrants for the latter improved, precipitated by the outbreak of plague in Hong Kong in 1894. In 1901, a Port Health Officer was finally appointed to take charge of quarantine and surveillance at the port. But he was also made responsible for infectious diseases in the rural areas. He had a small office and an assistant surgeon to help him, but no clerk or telephone. As the government noted wryly in 1918, 'If a case of Cholera occurred at Tanah Merah, the office had to be closed for 4 or 5 hours, and the inspection of any ships abandoned!'[54]

By then, the quarantine staff and facilities had expanded. The quarantine station on St. John's had a Chief Health Officer, two Assistant Port Health Officers, a Rural Health Officer, and a Resident Health Officer. These senior European staff oversaw an engineer, a clerk, four dressers, and 'a large subordinate staff'.[55] They ran a 'fairly commodious and very busy public office, with a telephone exchange and staff of clerks'.[56] The jungle on the island had been cleared, with attap structures replaced by camps built of corrugated iron, capable of quarantining 4,000 persons. The threat of a cholera outbreak had been eased with the construction of a large distilling plant, a high-level service reservoir of 50,000 gallons, and seven disinfectors. The maritime inspection capability consisted of two launches, each equipped with a disinfecting plant to promptly cleanse ships. Between 1902 and 1918, the quarantine staff inspected 22,814 vessels carrying over 6 million crew and passengers. They issued 24,710 bills of health and directed close to half a million crew and passengers to the quarantine station.

Immigration Officer Alec Dixon, who inspected at least three 'coolie ships' a day in the 1920s, provided an insider's view of quarantine work. He wrote drily about how 'Any coolie who was able to crawl down a ship's gangway was allowed to land in the Colony on showing proof of vaccination' [for smallpox].[57] However, it was at least as important to spot communist infiltrators among the Chinese immigrants as it was to detect cases of infection. In his memory, what was most memorable was the stench emanating from the ships:

> When several hundreds of Chinese coolies are herded together between-decks for five or six days the smell of their quarters defies description … when a coolie-ship anchors in a windless tropical harbour its cargo of foul air pours through the hatches, and, mounting as high as the bridge, hangs like a ghastly pall over the crowded decks. In that burning Malayan sunlight the very coolies themselves seemed to ferment, giving off a concentration of that fetor which is peculiar to the Chinese peasantry. Although I affected indifference to Oriental smells there were times when my sorely tried stomach revolted. Even my Chinese detectives were heard to remark on one or two occasions that the smell 'tween decks was *'banyak kuat'* (very strong).[58]

After the Second World War, British publisher and resident Donald Moore similarly described the quarantine station as a place where 'hapless travellers from China are left to get the Kwantung bugs out of their systems'.[59] The British officials were not looking for influenza among the immigrants.

On the main island of Singapore, surveillance and epidemiology efforts similarly continued to emphasise the dangerous infectious diseases that could be quarantined: plague, cholera and smallpox. As discussed earlier, the port quarantine staff had to divide their work with the rural areas of Singapore. The Rural Health Officer and sanitary inspector took charge of sanitary and public health affairs in the rubber plantation estates and outlying villages. In 1918, the Straits administration reported major improvements in estate and village sanitation made by the Rural Health Officer. In reality, most of the rural area was poorly covered, and the main focus of epidemiology was on the control of malaria.

Influenza's lack of concern in Singapore stemmed from a wider neglect. During the interwar years, as we noted previously, the colonial port city became a node within a growing regional quarantine and epidemiology. In the 1900s, it had been difficult for the Port Health Officer to obtain up-to-date information about health and disease in neighbouring ports in Asia.[60] After the First World War, however, the League of Nations and the Straits government began to consider plans to make Singapore the headquarters of a Public Health Information Bureau in the East. This would only be realised after the war in 1925 in the form of an Eastern Epidemiological Bureau. Based in Singapore, it would enable the sharing of medical intelligence between the region's ports on a regular basis.[61]

Most tellingly of all, the 1890 epidemic did not nudge the Straits government or the Municipal Commission to take charge of the control of epidemic disease in the town. In 1894, after a long-running debate with the colonial government, the commission became the main authority responsible for the control of epidemic disease in the Municipality. But this formal change belied persistent problems. One of them, discussed in the first chapter, was the enforcement of the notification system: both the upper and coolie classes were loath to report cases of infectious disease to the authorities. It was thus striking that in 1895, the President of the Commission Alex Gentle argued against reforming the system:

> Singapore has suffered very little from epidemics of recent years, and to establish an elaborate and costly system of espionage in the hope of the early detection of cases of disease, is … uncalled for and might prove mischievous as tending to alienate an Asiatic population from European methods and to confirm them in their habits of secrecy and distrust.[62]

Gentle's statement is doubly remarkable. He unhelpfully depicted notification to be a form of 'espionage' that could strain the relationship between the rulers and the ruled. Worse, in portraying Singapore as free of epidemics, he disregarded the experience of the influenza outbreak just five years earlier. Influenza had not been made a notifiable disease in 1890, allowing it to spread widely among the classes, age and ethnic groups of Singapore. The Municipal Commission's stance on notification would have repercussions for the 1918 influenza pandemic, when the disease was belatedly made notifiable. The significance of the 1890 experience was ignored by those who did not feel their brain spinning inside a musical box.

The 1890 flu was a historically significant event in its own right. As George Dehner observed in the West, it was the first time an influenza pandemic had been tracked as it unfolded. Its epidemiology dealt a final blow to the fading humoral notion of disease and paved the way for the rise of germ theory.[63] In colonial Singapore, however, its impact on policy was minimal. It is rather in social history, excavated from the newspapers and colonial records, where we see how quickly infection spread beyond the wharf coolies to the community.

Hospitals were powerless to stem the spread. Reported strikingly by the English and especially Chinese newspapers, the epidemic affected all social classes, ethnic and age groups – albeit unequally. It was symptomatic of a busy entrepôt port that did not halt its commercial and social activities even with the appearance of a dangerous disease. This reflected the economic priorities of the colonial government and its emphasis on the trade of Singapore.

The 1890 epidemic was quickly forgotten by the Straits government and remained buried in the sands of time even when the next global influenza outbreak hit Singapore in 1918. Influenza had no impact on colonial efforts against epidemic disease; the quarantine status quo prevailed as did the ineffective notification system. Yet, as the poem at the start of this chapter reminds us, there were people in Singapore who did not forget the 'poison in the air' in 1890. The newspapers continued to carry reports, recollections and advertisements on influenza, keeping the disease alive in locals' minds. The lesson here is that social memory is a useful resource, capable of shaping people's attitudes and behaviour towards elusive illnesses like the flu. It can form part of the public health repertoire against influenza and other epidemic diseases.

## Notes

1 CO 275/40 AMRCHSS 1890, p. 469.
2 H. Brüssow and L. Brüssow, 'Clinical Evidence that the Pandemic from 1889 to 1891 Commonly called the Russian Flu Might Have Been an Earlier Coronavirus Pandemic', *Microbial Biotechnology*, Vol. 14, 2021, pp. 186–70.
3 CO 275/101 SSMR 1918, p. 512.
4 CO 275/101 SSMR 1918, p. 513.
5 G.E. Brooke, 'Excursion to the Quarantine Station at St. John's Island', *Journal of the Malayan Branch of the British Medical Association*, No. XI, 1922–23, pp. 37–38.
6 CO 275/18 Joint report on the Subject of Quarantine and Emigration Arrangements, 7 October 1875.
7 CO 275/101 SSMR 1918.
8 CO 275/101 SSMR 1918, p. 513.
9 CO 275/34 The Quarantine and Prevention of Disease Ordinance, 1886, 7 July 1887.
10 CO 275/40 AMRCHSS 1890.
11 CO 273/167 Memorandum by the Acting Principal Civil Medical Officer of the Straits Settlements, 22 August 1890. Interestingly, he noted an influenza outbreak among horses in October 1889 and another in March 1890, coinciding with the spread of the pandemic among people. There was also an outbreak of foot and mouth disease in June 1890.
12 CO 273/167 Memorandum by the Acting Principal Civil Medical Officer of the Straits Settlements, 22 August 1890.
13 *Lat Pau*, 27 February 1890, p. 2; *Sing Po*, 6 March 1890, p. 6.
14 *Lat Pau*, 27 February 1890, p. 2.
15 CO 273/167 Memorandum by the Acting Principal Civil Medical Officer of the Straits Settlements, 22 August 1890.
16 *Sing Po*, 11 March 1890, pp. 1, 5.
17 CO 275/40 AMRCHSS 1890.

18  CO 273/167 Memorandum by the Acting Principal Civil Medical Officer of the Straits Settlements, 22 August 1890.
19  SMAR 1890, p. 13.
20  CO 275/40 *Registration of Births and Deaths in the Straits Settlements* (thereafter RBDSS) 1890.
21  Singapore Municipal Commission, Minutes of the Proceedings of the Municipal Commissioners, 23 April 1890.
22  CO 275/40 AMRCHSS 1890, p. 466.
23  CO 273/167 Memorandum by the Acting Principal Civil Medical Officer of the Straits Settlements, 22 August 1890.
24  CO 273/167 Memorandum by the Acting Principal Civil Medical Officer of the Straits Settlements, 22 August 1890.
25  CO 275/40 AMRCHSS 1890, p. 468.
26  CO 275/40 AMRCHSS 1890.
27  CO 273/167 Memorandum by the Acting Principal Civil Medical Officer of the Straits Settlements, 22 August 1890.
28  *Straits Times*, 11 March 1890, p. 2.
29  *Straits Times*, 11 March 1890, p. 9.
30  *Straits Times*, 11 March 1890, p. 9.
31  *Straits Times*, 11 March 1890, p. 9.
32  *Straits Times*, 25 March 1890, p. 6.
33  *Straits Times*, 29 April 1890, p. 9. *Kroma* could be a variant of *Keremak*, the Malay word for weed.
34  *Singapore Free Press*, 7 June 1892, p. 3.
35  *Singapore Free Press*, 22 September 1898, p. 3; *Straits Times*, 28 August 1903, p. 5.
36  *Straits Times*, 12 December 1903, p. 5.
37  *Sing Po*, 6 March 1890, p. 6.
38  *Sing Po*, 14 March 1890, p. 2.
39  *Straits Times*, 11 March 1890, p. 15.
40  *Sing Po*, 27 February 1890, p. 5.
41  *Sing Po*, 27 February 1890, pp. 1–2.
42  *Lat Pau*, 27 February 1890, p. 2.
43  *Lat Pau*, 1 March 1890, p. 2.
44  *Lat Pau*, 4 March 1890, p. 2.
45  *Lat Pau*, 27 February 1890, p. 1.
46  *Lat Pau*, 7 March 1890, p. 2.
47  *Daily Advertiser*, 14 March 1893, p. 3; *Straits Times*, 27 June 1893, p. 8.
48  *Singapore Free Press*, 5 March 1895, p. 131.
49  *Singapore Free Press*, 25 September 1895, p. 3.
50  CO 275/50 RBDSS 1895, p. 132.
51  *Mid-day Herald*, 11 April 1895, p. 3.
52  CO 275/55 AMRCHSS 1897, p. 412.
53  CO 275/101 SSMR 1918.
54  CO 275/101 SSMR 1918, p. 513.
55  CO 275/101 SSMR 1918, p. 513.
56  CO 275/101 SSMR 1918, p. 514.
57  Alec Dixon, *Singapore Patrol* (London: Harrap, 1935), p. 139.
58  Dixon, *Singapore Patrol*, p. 141.
59  Donald Moore, *Far Eastern Journal* (London: Hodder and Stoughton, 1960), p. 204.
60  CO 275/119 SSMR 1927.
61  CO 275/101 SSMR 1918.
62  SMAR 1895, p. 138.
63  George Dehner, *Global Flu and You: A History of Influenza* (London: Reaktion Books, 2012).

# 7 1918 Flu

## Blind Spot in the Colonial System

It was Singapore's largest influenza outbreak yet there is a lack of research on the flu pandemic of 1918. We fill this gap by charting the outbreak in the context of an open port city under British colonial rule with an Asian immigrant population. We track the onset and trajectory of the outbreak, the colonial and municipal responses, the social history, and the long aftermath of endemic influenza during the interwar years up to the Second World War. What emerges is the blind spot for influenza within the colonial system.

The lack of firm action against influenza in Singapore mirrored similar weak responses in other countries, including Britain, to a massive outbreak that started rapidly and diminished swiftly. This was the common nature of an influenza event. Here, however, we pay attention to the specifics of time and place. The global literature on the 1918 pandemic has generally concentrated on Western experiences. In Singapore, the inertia of the colonial system, more so than the nature of an influenza epidemic, was the decisive factor.

The pandemic, caused by the H1N1 virus, was poorly handled by colonial officials and medical experts in Singapore. They were still conditioned to deal with the quarantinable infectious diseases, long regarding influenza as a secondary threat. In 1918, the Straits government still prioritised economic returns from the entrepôt trade of Singapore ahead of much-needed investments in quarantine, public health and housing. Influenza was belatedly made a notifiable disease when much of the outbreak had passed, but sustained measures to control the epidemic were lacking. The government failed to quarantine infected ships or establish the number of cases and deaths, while efforts to stem the epidemic were half-hearted, perfunctory and ultimately ineffectual. The colonial record for the 1918 influenza pandemic was remarkably similar to that in 1890.

The British response was based on Anglo-centric principles of governance that were neither comprehensible nor practicable to the Asian immigrants at large. Distrustful of colonial rule, the denizens of the town largely ignored the official measures. They turned instead to their preferred treatments and tried to continue to work, causing the epidemic to spread quickly across the town's dense living quarters and offices. Similarly, the administration failed to heed the lessons of the pandemic; the quarantine system remained unchanged with

DOI: 10.4324/9781003384014-8

little interest in influenza. Smaller outbreaks continued to occur throughout the 1920s and 1930s. In this time, the British turned towards the scourge of tuberculosis in the overcrowded coolie town, but influenza, which thrived under similar conditions, remained a blind spot.

## The Two Waves

The 1918 pandemic caught Singapore by surprise, but the Straits government ought to have done better. The outbreak hit the port city at a time when the British had become aware of its public health issues and high death rates. They recognised the need for quarantine – both maritime and in the heavily populated municipal area. After the Quarantine and Prevention of Diseases Ordinance of 1886 mandated the isolation of infectious diseases, the Straits government pushed the Municipal Commission to take charge of the control of the matter within the town in 1894.[1] But responsibility for the control of infectious diseases was still divided between the government and the commission. The government would continue to take charge of maritime quarantine and the isolation of patients in their homes.

In 1906, a study by the British sanitary expert W.J.R. Simpson pinpointed tuberculosis among the Chinese labouring class as the primary cause of the high mortality rates in the municipal area. He urged the colonial government to carry out sanitary and housing reforms to reduce the incidence of tuberculosis in the shophouses.[2] Seven years later, under government pressure, the Municipal Commission constructed a much-needed infectious diseases hospital at Moulmein Road. However, the hospital still focused on the traditional 'Big 3' of zymotic diseases: bubonic plague, cholera and smallpox.[3] In 1918, just before the influenza outbreak, the Singapore Housing Commission pushed for further medical and housing reforms in the town. It urged the Straits government to form a separate health agency from the Health Department, as recommended by Simpson.[4]

But despite these developments, Singapore's quarantine system was unable to prevent influenza from reaching the island in 1918. The government knew that an influenza pandemic had broken out in the West in early spring that year. Official records viewed the outbreak as a relatively minor aberration, a distraction from routine work on the traditional diseases. The government did not shift significant attention and resources from such work to the threat of influenza that surfaced in the middle of the year.

While improved, the port quarantine system was not looking specifically for influenza. Two months before the influenza surfaced in Singapore, the Quarantine and Prevention of Disease Ordinance of 1915 had been amended to broaden the surveillance of dangerous infectious diseases from four (plague, cholera, smallpox, and yellow fever) to all infectious diseases.[5] Local quarantine officials were kept appraised of cases of plague, cholera, smallpox, and cerebrospinal fever in ports in Southeast Asia, India and Japan. Ship masters arriving from ports in these regions were routinely informed about such diseases among their crew and passengers; if they arrived from infected ports, they were to hoist the 'Q' Flag at the foremast before reaching the Straits Settlements.[6] To an extent, the British had the means and intelligence to prevent infectious diseases from reaching Singapore. But influenza was not on their radar.

In 1918, the quarantine service boarded 1,709 ships arriving at Singapore. A small number – 26 – were found to carry infectious diseases. The officers were looking for known zymotic diseases. Twelve of the ships had cases of cholera, ten had smallpox, while there were four vessels with cerebrospinal fever infection onboard. The latter, traced to an outbreak in Hong Kong, drew more concern from the authorities than influenza. Between April and October, deck passengers from Hong Kong were prohibited from landing in Singapore, despite protests from the British authorities there against the ban. Ships carrying what Straits officials called 'wily Cantonese' from Hong Kong and other nearby ports tried to sneak into Singapore but were detected and turned back.[7] The British lauded their success in averting a local outbreak of cerebrospinal fever as 'probably saving an immense loss to the community and to trade both in human life and money'.[8] In April, an amendment was made to the 1915 Quarantine and Prevention of Disease Ordinance with cerebrospinal fever in mind, where any disease could be gazetted by the Governor as a dangerous infectious disease, in addition to plague, cholera, smallpox, and yellow fever.[9]

These efforts contrasted with – and possibly diverted from – the watch for influenza. Two waves of flu breached Singapore's quarantine protocols in 1918, as did subsequent waves in the following years. The first wave arrived in the third week of June before abating at the beginning of August; Lee et al. postulated that it could have started earlier in May but was not initially traced to influenza.[10] This is plausible, looking at the confused reports printed in the English press:

> An epidemic of some kind of feverish cold (which some say is influenza, some call dengue fever, and others assert is a new disease) seems to be sweeping through the establishments in Singapore which employ large numbers of Indians.[11]

This concurs with the global literature, which largely accepts that the first wave started earlier than originally believed.[12]

As the transit point for travellers, Singapore became the conduit for the spread of influenza to the other Straits Settlements and Malaya. Apparently, so ran speculation in local newspapers, the disease had reached the island from either Manila or the Russian port of Vladivostok through Hong Kong (subsequently it was called 'the Siberian flu').[13] The Chinese newspaper *Lat Pau* linked the outbreak to seasonal influenza circulating in the Chinese cities of Beijing, Shanghai, Canton and Hong Kong.[14] This mirrored the global speculation on the origins of the 1918 influenza pandemic, which are still unknown today. The British in Singapore seemed satisfied that all deck passengers amongst whom influenza was found were placed in quarantine, though this did not stem the growing epidemic on the main island.

Reportedly, the first wave spread widely but was otherwise of a mild form. This claim is disputed by the appearance of serious cases of influenza-induced pneumonia at the Tan Tock Seng Hospital (further discussed below). The *Lat Pau* reported that the TTSH, along with the General Hospital and the Kwong Wai Shiu Free Hospital (a Chinese community hospital), were filled with influenza patients, while two other community facilities, the Thong Chai Hospital and Sian Chay Hospital, were dispensing free medical services to numerous Chinese patients.[15]

After the first wave appeared, the Straits government activated the existing regional epidemiological network. It despatched notices to ship masters departing from ports in the region for the colony. They were told to look out for bubo (an enlarged lymph node), diarrhoea or pneumonia, and given entry requirements with respect to infectious diseases such as smallpox and leprosy. Influenza was thus not specified. There was a reference to pneumonia, though this was likely to detect tuberculosis.[16]

The second wave, caused by a new strain of influenza, appeared at the start of October. In the middle of the month, the Straits administration received a letter from the British Governor-General of South Africa, warning about a 'violent outbreak of so-called Spanish Fever with highly pneumonic characteristics' that had killed Europeans there.[17] The Singapore government undertook a 'careful look-out' for influenza onboard ships from South Africa but found no cases.[18] This turned out to be the wrong way to look, for the second wave was later believed to have been conveyed to Singapore by sea passengers from India and Ceylon.[19] In its annual report, the government vaguely stated, 'Influenza arrived by shipping from most districts of the Far East'.[20]

An early case in the second outbreak is illustrative. Between 13 October and 8 November 1918, the Acting Resident Medical Officer reported that four Dutch vessels from the East Indies landed passengers with influenza on St. John's Island. This led to an outbreak among the quarantine staff, including ten persons among the engineer's family and his servants: 57 cases of influenza were admitted into hospital and 18 died – a mortality rate of 32 per cent. The high mortality was partly due to the long sea voyage and lack of medical care for the sick onboard the vessel. The authorities disinfected the quarantine station, sunned the bedding and issued gargle to contacts and its staff.[21]

The second wave peaked in the final week of October, before subsiding at the end of the following month, though cases continued to appear till the close of the year. This wave was allegedly more gradual than the first, with most shops and firms not badly affected at first.[22] It turned out undoubtedly to be far more serious, spreading 'with great intensity for about three weeks', with numerous cases of complications of severe broncho-pneumonia.[23] The *Singapore Free Press* tried to calm its readers, claiming the outbreak was a mild one.[24] But the editor of *Lat Pau* disputed this, deeming the wave to be 'slightly different' from the first one and unlike anything documented in the

Chinese medical texts; it was serious and needed to be treated properly.[25] The *Malaya Tribune*, a newspaper for the English-educated Asian community, concurred. It noted at the end of October that the second outbreak had frightened many people and would take a major joint effort by the government, the Municipality and the public to stem the spread of infection.[26]

At the onset of the second wave, the Straits government gazetted influenza a notifiable disease on 19 October for a year till 3 October 1919. This was the first time that influenza was made notifiable in Singapore history. It was also the first instance where influenza was tracked as a cause of death (though not the number of cases) in the Straits Settlements on a yearly basis. The administration continued to track the number of influenza deaths in subsequent years. In July 1919, the Acting Health Officer J.A.R. Glennie admitted that it was unclear whether reported cases that year, which were relatively mild, were of influenza or the common cold. Nevertheless, he had a notice circulated in the main languages of Singapore, urging that the disease was extremely infectious, people should avoid crowds, and free treatment was available at government hospitals.[27]

There was a belief that Singapore's experience was less severe compared to the rest of the Straits Settlements and British Malaya. The 1918 Straits medical report referred to 'two slight epidemics of Influenza' on the island, with the mid-year outbreak conferring valuable immunity to the population prior to the second one.[28] The report added that the October wave 'fortunately was not of an alarming type, although the percentage of Pneumonia was considerably higher than previously'.[29] The *Malaya Tribune* downplayed Singapore's experience, noting that towns in Malaya and cities such as Bangkok, Colombo and Cape Town were worse hit.[30] Another correspondent, observing the greatly reduced number of Chinese and Malay public funerals at the start of November, felt that the epidemic was abating quickly in Singapore.[31] Drawing from these sources, Liew Kai Khiun's study of the pandemic in Malaya reached a similar conclusion, though it was also one that surprised him:

> It is interesting to note that, in spite of being the busiest, congested and densely populated colonial port city, Singapore was spared the calamity of the epidemic that had ravaged the neighbouring states under British jurisdiction.[32]

Lee et al. found that Singapore's influenza mortality was higher than the global average. Specifically, it was higher than those of developed countries such as the United States and England, though lower than in other Asian and African colonies. They associated the higher mortality with an early phase of the pandemic, lower socio-economic status and educational level of the people.[33] But these are generalisations; we should note there were socio-economic differences within Singapore's populace.

The official reports stated that 367 (or 43 per cent) of the registered deaths from influenza in the Straits Settlements (844) occurred in Singapore. This was roughly the proportion of 45 per cent that Singapore formed of the colony's total population. Penang, with less than half of Singapore's population, was worse hit, with close to the same number (318) of registered influenza deaths. The Municipal Commission of Singapore concurred that the pandemic hit Penang and the Federated Malay States harder.[34] The month of October witnessed Singapore's largest number of deaths at 2,056, compared to the monthly average of 1,281 for the year, yet this was slightly better than for the Straits Settlements as a whole. The week ending 26 October 1918 was the deadliest in Singapore that year, with a death rate of 97.57 per mile.

Official mortality statistics were generally unreliable. Many deaths did not occur in a hospital or were certified by a medical practitioner. Instead, a large number of certifications were made after death by a qualified registering officer based on an inspection of the body, or by a junior police officer who 'guessed' the cause from the dead person's relations.[35] In the 1920s, only an estimated one-third of dying persons in the Straits Settlements were seen by a qualified medical practitioner.[36] As a result, many causes of death were officially stated as complications or conditions such as convulsions or undetermined fever, rather than the causal agent itself.

For influenza, the Straits government admitted that 'this figure [844, for the Straits Settlements] bears little relation to the actual number of deaths which resulted directly or indirectly from that disease'.[37] It estimated the true number to be about 3,500 (or four times higher), by including deaths registered under complications arising from pneumonia, bronchitis, tuberculosis, and unspecified fever. All of these were major causes of deaths in the colony. In 1918, there were 2,285 registered deaths for pneumonia, 840 for bronchitis, 3,675 for tuberculosis, and 6,988 for unspecified fever, giving a total of 13,788 such deaths in the colony.[38] The estimate of 3,500 influenza deaths makes influenza responsible for a quarter of those deaths, or 9.6 per cent of all deaths, in the Straits Settlements that year. Yet, this figure is still likely a low estimate, based on registered cases.

Difficulties in counting influenza deaths in the Straits Settlements added to general difficulties experienced in the West. Historically, influenza had always been classified as a single disease, but as Niall Johnson observed, 'disease diagnoses are a perennial problem'. It was often self-diagnosed, based on the severity of symptoms, and thus likely misdiagnosed.[39] In Malaya and Singapore, it was not till 1930 that Dr K. Kanagarayer differentiated influenza from tropical typhus, leptospiral and dengue fevers.[40] The unreliability of data in the Straits Settlements in 1918 was worsened by the social distrust of colonial officials among the Asian population.

By including deaths from the group of complications in 1918, there were 1,517 registered deaths for pneumonia, 438 for bronchitis, 2,184 for tuberculosis, and 922 for unspecified fever – a total of 5,061 deaths. Assuming Singapore's influenza deaths also formed a quarter of those deaths as for the Straits Settlements, its true figure for the influenza epidemic was likely closer to 1,200 deaths – three and a half times the registered number and comprising

8.2 per cent of all its deaths in that year. This suggests that Singapore was badly hit by the pandemic, if not as severely as Penang. In subsequent years, as we will see below, the trend reversed.

Lee et al. attempted to establish the true number of deaths caused by the influenza epidemic through the number of excess deaths. They found a much higher figure of 6,656 deaths and a high excess mortality rate of 1.8 per cent in Singapore between 1918 and 1920.[41] This corroborates the severity of the 1918 epidemic in the port city. Excess deaths, which had been used by the British Registrar-General in Britain,[42] are useful for estimating the number of deaths due to elusive diseases such as influenza and its complications.[43] One weakness in the method though is assuming excess deaths to be due to a single cause over a multi-year period. As we will see later, while influenza was still prevailing in Singapore in 1919 and 1920, the first year was likely the worst. Excess deaths are also dependent on shaky colonial statistics.

The 1918 pandemic is well-known for killing a disproportionately large number of young people in their prime worldwide. This seems to have occurred in Singapore too. The number of total deaths for the youngest age groups actually fell from 1,623 in 1917 to 1,374 in 1918 for infants under three months and from 1,313 to 1,175 for those from three months to under a year old. But there were substantial increases among the older age groups: from 762 to 982 for the 1–5 age group (an increase of 29 per cent), 288 to 391 for the 5–10 group (+36 per cent), 461 to 661 for the 10–20 group (+43 per cent), 865 to 1,069 for the 20–25 group (+24 per cent), from 2,407 to 3,266 for the 25–35 group (+36 per cent), 2,032 to 2,791 for the 35–45 group (+37 per cent). By contrast, there were increases smaller increases for older people: 1,460 to 1,808 for the 45–55 group (+24 per cent), and 1,584 to 1,808 for the 55 and over group (+14 per cent). Though the impact on the 20–25 age group actually appeared lower than the other age groups, it seems that the epidemic more severely affected the population between 1 and 55 years of age. These statistics need to be viewed in context: Singapore's immigrant population was a young one, with a large proportion of working age males and a much smaller group of elderly people.

## Flu in a Hen Coop

What were people's experiences of influenza? Municipal Commissioner Roland Braddell surmised that the high death rate in the first wave of the 'Siberian influenza' was hardly surprising, given the shortage of staff in the Medical Department. He claimed there were only two doctors in Singapore for a population of 385,000 people, while chastising the Medical School as 'a disgrace to the Settlement', producing poorly trained doctors.[44] The *Straits Echo* agreed, adding sardonically that the death rate fell instantly when the Senior Municipal Medical Officer went on leave, but rose once more when he returned.[45]

The 1918 influenza pandemic has been attributed to the mobilisation, movement and concentration of large numbers of people in military and urban settings, particularly in the context of the First World War.[46] In Singapore, the epidemic spread quickly to places where people were concentrated, initially hospitals. As the island's biggest hospital, the General Hospital admitted 314 cases of influenza in 1918. The first arrived in the hospital's Native Wards for Asian patients on 1 July, followed by admission to the European Wards the next day. In July, there were 32 admissions for influenza at the GH, which dropped to seven in August, before the October outbreak saw a bigger surge of 229 cases that month and 46 cases in November. For the year, there were 71 influenza admissions to the European Wards and 243 admissions to the Native Wards. As in previous years, the Asian figures were probably a fraction of the actual numbers in the Asian communities, reflecting their distrust of hospitals as places of dying.

Many Asian admissions to the GH were 'in the last stages of Pneumonia and little could be done for them'.[47] This led the government to conclude: 'The death-rate was exceptionally heavy among the native patients being 23.6%', compared to 2.81 per cent (two fatalities) in the European Wards.[48] Consequently, the 1918 Straits medical report was able to trace in detail the course of the disease among European admissions to GH, but not for Asians.[49] The report also noted the 'great aversion' of even Malay police constables to their treatment at a hospital: 'many of them, apparently to avoid being sent there, take themselves off to remote parts of the Island to which they are with difficulty traced'.[50] This tendency of ill Malays to retreat to the imagined safety of their kampongs shows how difficult it was to control the epidemic among the Asian populace.

There was no effective prevention, treatment or vaccine for influenza in Singapore, as was the case all over the world. In November 1918, the Municipal Commission published the Royal College of Physicians, London's statement that the virus was not well understood and there was no drug to combat it.[51] At this time, the aetiology of influenza was erroneous, with the disease thought to be caused by a bacterium; it was not till 1933 that the 'filter-passing' flu virus was identified.[52] But the situation in Singapore was compounded by the lack of government action. Two weeks into the second wave, on 18 October, the Health Officer informed the commission that 'he does not think there is any necessity at present for the distribution of a free supply of medicine and considers that without proper nursing medicine is of little use'. The best course of action, he said, was for patients to 'immediately go to bed and stay there till well again'.[53]

The Municipal Commission published notices asking influenza patients to isolate themselves. The Singapore Chinese Chamber of Commerce aided this, helping to translate the notices into Chinese. But though the medium was familiar to the Chinese, the biomedical content – such as staying away from crowded places and using disinfectant – was not.[54] The weekly death rate in the town reached 69.11 per mile on the 25th – the highest since the previous

July, with 107 deaths from pneumonia.[55] A week later, the figure peaked at 101 per mile, before appearing to move downward.[56] Still, large crowds – likely European – ignored health warnings to gather and celebrate news of the armistice in the First World War on 11 November.[57]

Gauze masks were the 'icon of the epidemic', as Catherine Arnold put it. It was a symbol of many countries' response to the 1918 pandemic, though also frequently contested or unevenly implemented.[58] Throughout the epidemic, people in Singapore were not required to wear masks, unlike Australia and some cities in the US. They could still leave the island and travel abroad. But upon arriving at a destination like San Francisco, they were surprised to learn that 'everybody had to wear masks or find themselves heavily fined and/or imprisoned'.[59]

In its single most effective move, the colonial government closed schools in Singapore for a week from 21 October 1918. In a letter to the *Straits Times* two days before the closure, contributor 'Cosandrew's' had asked for schools to be shut down immediately, for fear of the spread of infection from within the classroom to the students' homes.[60] At this time, four teachers and four pupil teachers at Outram School were found to be ill from influenza.[61] These were the reported cases. Cosandrew's plea found support from another writer, Chew Cheng Yong, whose letter reflected the fears of a parent driven to act on their own account given the lack of government guidance:

> One of my children is down with this dreadful disease, and I propose to detain my other children at home before they too catch it from others, and also to prevent them from passing it on to their school mates. This is taking the law into one's hands, but common sense and self-protection force it.[62]

The benefit of closing schools was not so much to protect the students, for they were generally less affected by influenza than adults. It did have a benefit in reducing the spread of influenza to adults. But students in colonial Singapore were only a small section of the immigrant population, which was largely made up of young adults. Moreover, adults could still catch the illness in other places.

The other official responses were tokenistic, confined to additional watering of streets and cleansing government buildings. The target was some 'germ-producing dust', as a self-professed influenza patient put it, adding that the roads at River Valley and Oxley were covered with dust 'several inches deep'.[63] For this reason, Municipal Health Officers hoped for rains to alleviate the outbreak.[64] At the end of October, the President of the Municipal Commission W. Peel declared that he had done everything possible to stem the outbreak; with a change in weather and rainfall, the epidemic would hopefully abate.[65]

The Straits government also mandated that all offices be swept on Saturday afternoons. A 'dust-laying disinfectant', composed of cleaning fluid, kerosene and crude oil, was applied to the floors and furniture the following mornings.[66] According to the Rural Health Officer who oversaw this work and disinfected some government quarters himself, 'It can hardly be doubted that this oiling had a considerable effect'.[67] The practice of disinfection spread widely to include rickshaw depots and other public places, and private homes affected by influenza.[68] The Straits Legislative Council approved a special vote of $10,000 to meet these expenses for controlling the epidemic. They had at best a minor effect on reducing the spread of influenza.

Rather than tending to the sick, Singapore's hospitals quickly fell prey to the epidemic. As the Municipal Health Office acknowledged, the hospitals were ill-prepared to cope with 'outbreaks which arise suddenly and quickly assume serious proportions'.[69] The crux of the problem was a long-standing lack of investment in hospitals, with a deleterious effect on bed space. The GH attempted to contain the disease within its grounds by isolating influenza patients from others and making gargling compulsory. These measures were reportedly effective until much larger numbers admitted in October exceeded the accommodation. The colonial medical report stated: 'the disease swept through the whole hospital and there were few patients who escaped', leading to deaths from resulting complications.[70]

The GH's nurses were reduced to half-strength at one point, forcing the hospital to employ former nurses. To cope with the bed shortage, vacant cinemas, which had been closed, were used as makeshift hospitals.[71] A dozen of the GH's 19 nurses were recovering at Labrador Villa during the second wave.[72] For relief, the hospital administered to influenza patients a potassium chlorate gargle, a 'stimulating expectorant mixture' for bronchitis and bronchopneumonia, acelyl salicylic acid for body pains and headache, and quinine in a few cases. But these treatments, aimed at symptoms and complications, were generally ineffective.[73] Globally, the various serums and vaccines produced to combat the influenza also had little benefit.[74]

Nearly half of the cases in the Municipality were treated at the TTSH, used largely by the Chinese population. In the third week of June, the hospital was hit by 'numerous cases of Pneumonia of a particularly violent type', forcing the hospital to recruit six temporary dressers to cope with the workload.[75] The hospital further engaged a temporary assistant surgeon and opened a large temporary ward for influenza patients when the second wave arrived in the third week of September and persisted through October to the first week of November. The wave witnessed 547 admissions, of whom 444 had pneumonia and nearly half – 210 – died. The number of deaths at the TTSH thus accounted for 57 per cent of all registered influenza deaths in Singapore. As the original 'Pauper's Hospital', the spread of the disease across its wards provides a good sense of the outbreak among the Asian population. Even so, as with the GH, many of the Asian sick likely did not seek help at the hospital till in an advanced stage of the disease.

The Moulmein Road Hospital for infectious diseases declared that it had a 'phenomenal' year, admitting the greatest number of patients – 209 – since its opening in 1913.[76] But it was not built for influenza. A mere 70 were influenza patients, out of the 1,259 registered influenza cases in the Municipality. Most of them were from the Kallang Reservoir area to the east of the town. Many patients arrived at the hospital with complications but all were discharged except for two who died from pneumonia and a third who absconded. Equipped with modern wards for plague, cholera and smallpox, the Moulmein Road Hospital lacked the staff and accommodation to deal with the epidemic.[77] During the first wave, it was made available only to municipal employees, but was compelled to isolate cases from congested areas of the town during the October outbreak in its 'G' and 'L' wards for smallpox and cholera respectively.[78]

Elsewhere, 33 cases of influenza were treated at the Kandang Kerbau Hospital for women, four of whom died. At Pearl's Hill Prison 53 inmates were also infected, with four dying from pneumonia. The outbreak in the mental asylum was supposedly 'of a mild type', though it led to several deaths from complications among patients with advanced tuberculosis.[79] Influenza was held to have contributed to the 30 deaths from tuberculosis and 11 from pneumonia in the asylum. The 29 cases in the beriberi hospital at Pasir Panjang were mild ones, and all of them recovered.

The outbreak quickly spread beyond the hospitals to other government institutions and business offices. Here the political economy of the entrepôt port city was at work. A contributor to the *Straits Times* wrote sardonically about the offices of the Municipality, including those of the Health Department, as 'practically a regular hen coop', with clerks huddled close together at work and several of them 'holding coughing competitions'.[80] The government reported over 500 medical certificates issued for influenza to civil servants alone. The outbreak also hit the police force: 131 persons, mostly Sikhs and Malays (who made up the vast majority of the force) were treated for influenza. But this number was likely under-reported, as there were 950 cases treated for unspecified fever and 296 for bronchitis.

The first wave caused a serious absence of junior staff employed in government offices and mercantile firms. The government printing office was unable to print an extraordinary gazette due to more than half of the staff being taken ill, while the Post Office also had to cut down its deliveries across the island. Manpower shortages were worsened by the assertion, made by a doctor, that there was a concurrent dengue epidemic. He claimed to have seen whole families caught in the grip of dengue or influenza, suffering from severe headaches, high fever and diarrhoea in the case of the flu.[81]

Predictably, influenza spread easily to the wider community. It was in the densely built municipal area at the southern tip of Singapore, a mere 20 square miles in size, where the pandemic hit hardest. This was where W.J.R. Simpson had warned about the peril of tuberculosis in the shophouses over a decade ago. The shophouses creatively combined the functions of petty commerce on the ground floor and cheap accommodation on the upper levels. But standing on small land lots, they were built deep and back-to-back with one another. Alongside coolie lines and tenements, they formed the cheap housing of what James Warren has described as a coolie town.[82] An entire population of male Chinese labourers shared myriad tiny shophouse cubicles and partitions to defray the costs of rent and transport to their workplace. The 1918 Housing Commission concluded that the deathly scenario reported by Simpson had not changed a decade on.[83] In the 20 years since 1891, the housing in the municipal area had increased by only 15 per cent, compared to 24 per cent for the population.[84]

During the influenza pandemic, the Royal College of Physicians, London urged people to avoid 'overcrowding and thronging', both in public places and in shared accommodation such as 'dwelling rooms and dormitories', while they should also minimise the likelihood of developing complications by having good air ventilation in private spaces, and nourishing food.[85] As the *Straits Echo* warned, influenza was highly infectious and could spread among large numbers of people through coughs and spitting in enclosed and crowded spaces.[86]

But in the political economy of colonial Singapore, these recommendations fell on deaf ears – both for the merchants of the entrepôt who ran the commerce and the working class who had to continue to work. The latter was unable to afford suitable housing or good food to ward off influenza and its complications. The British colonial government itself had little incentive to reform the shophouse system, for coolie labour moved the entrepôt trade along the Singapore River and Keppel Harbour, both areas within the Municipality.

In 1918, the town reported 1,259 registered influenza cases and 209 deaths, a mortality rate of 0.17. This accounted for 57 per cent of the influenza deaths in Singapore that year; the real figure was probably higher with cases moved outside the Municipality. The number of notifications for infectious disease jumped from 396 in 1917 to 1,994 in 1918 – largely due to influenza and tuberculosis being made notifiable that year. Even so, a mere nine out of the 60-odd private medical practitioners in the Municipality reported 297 of the cases, showing the extent of non-notification or misdiagnosis of the disease.[87] An indeterminate but relatively large number of influenza cases were registered as deaths arising from tuberculosis and especially pneumonia, which rose from 5.4 to 6.6 per thousand and 2.1 to 5.2 per thousand respectively from the previous year.

The Municipal Health Office admitted about its figures: 'the present returns are far from complete and there is little use in making a detailed analysis of them'.[88] There was some initial confusion that the outbreak was linked to plague, though this was denied by the Municipality.[89] Its annual report was more interesting for its statement on the spread of influenza:

> The disease was general over the town. All nationalities and all age periods were attacked and numbers who neglected or were unable to remain in bed until recovery was complete fell victim to complications especially Pneumonia.[90]

For instance, the outdoor dispensary at North Canal Road in the town treated 325 influenza patients in 1918, and a similar number for bronchitis. Most of these patients were dwellers in the municipal area and had spread the illness to their neighbours and social contacts. The dispensary was at least able to provide free medicine to its patients, as prices for medicines such as eucalyptus had become 'exorbitant' during the epidemic.[91]

Nevertheless, though the true number of influenza deaths in the town was underestimated, the demographic breakdown yields interesting social insights: 130 of the 209 municipal deaths, or more than three-fifths, were males. This gender ratio of 1.6 was higher than the 2.5 renumerated for the population of Singapore as a whole in the 1911 census, showing that influenza killed pro-portionally more females than males; among the females were seven pregnant women or women who had just given birth. Most of the municipal deaths due to influenza were of older adolescents and adults from the age of 15 to over 55, accounting for 167 or 80 per cent of the mortality. The largest number of deaths in a sub-age group was 65 in the 25–30 years category. There were no deaths among infants under three months.

Ethnically, the death rate due to influenza was highest among Indians, fol-lowed by Malays and Chinese; European deaths were far less common. There were 123 Chinese deaths (59 per cent of the municipal deaths), 32 Malays (15 per cent), 35 Indians (17 per cent), 3 Europeans (1.4 per cent), 3 Eurasians (1.4 per cent) and 13 Others (6 per cent). Compared to the 1911 census, the ethnic breakdown showed the Chinese (72 per cent of the population) to be underrepresented, while the Others (4.7 per cent, including Europeans and Eurasians) and Indians (9 per cent) were over-represented. This was likely due to non-notification of Chinese deaths, though it is interesting that the Malays, who typically avoided Western medical treatment, were proportionally represented.

Beyond the Municipality, the rubber estates in rural Singapore purportedly 'suffered very little'.[92] The greatest impact was deemed to have occurred along Chua Chu Kang Road to the north of the town but some estates reported no cases at all. This was attributed to management's efforts to improve ventilation in the estates, which were hitherto poorly ventilated. These efforts did not pre-vent 'a few deaths from Influenza and an aftermath of several from Pneumo-nia'.[93] The Rural Health Officer in charge was perplexed as to why the Chua Chu Kang Road area was more affected although it was located further from the town area. It is likely that influenza was under-reported in the estates and rural villages, where there was little data forthcoming.

But while the Straits and municipal administrations were hapless against the epidemic, the colonial system was not inert. The pandemic had a significant impact on racial governance in Singapore. As with other disease outbreaks, influenza provided an opportunity for the Straits government and the Western-educated elite (including Asians) to enjoin in a racialised discourse on the diverse population. The *Malaya Tribune*, whose readers comprised the English-educated elite, ventured this view of the outbreak:

Certain races are more susceptible or more resistant to certain diseases. The Chinese of Singapore seldom suffer from pneumonia, at any rate not until this present influenza epidemic. The South Indian is especially susceptible to pneumonia. The latter seldom if ever suffers from enteric fever. The European and Chinese do. It is evident that the South African negro is especially susceptible to influenza, and it was well known that he used to acquire pneumonia on the slightest provocation.[94]

Public commentary like this not only raised questions about the pandemic (or were just factually wrong). They reinforced the prevailing belief in unequal races. An influenza outbreak might destabilise the colonial order for a time, but the discourses that sought to make sense of it also strengthened the underlying racial ideology. Medicine and disease were two planks of what was widely believed to be a 'scientific' ideology of human society. The *Malaya Tribune* commentary was Eurocentric, its interest in the high death rate among Europeans in South Africa compared to their counterparts in Malaya. It proffered an explanation to its own question: after influenza had passed through an unprotected race, it would have a severe impact on Europeans who usually had greater resistance to it.[95]

The racial view of influenza reflected a Social Darwinist logic at work in the European imperial mind in the early 20th century, as Liew Kai Khiun terms it. Expedient yet predatory, it excused the colonial regime from its failings in handling the epidemic by shifting the blame to alleged racial weaknesses while further justifying imperial rule.[96] The discourse was not dissimilar from mid-14th century Europe, where the Black Death had exacerbated anti-Semitic sentiments among Christian populations, or the casting of Haitians as carriers of HIV during the AIDS pandemic in the 1980s.[97] In all three cases, a disease crisis brings to light the underlying racism in a society, while blame is externalised and transferred to marginal groups.

Just as interestingly, the social history of the 1918 epidemic was distinct from the official narrative. Brenda Yeoh has shown that the worldviews and responses of Singapore's immigrant population on sanitary and health matters largely diverged from those of Western-educated municipal officials.[98] As long-time Municipal Commissioner Roland Braddell claimed, the Malays attributed illnesses such as influenza and dengue to southerly winds blowing towards Java. They allegedly called these winds *angin jehat*, the 'evil winds', which were particularly harmful to health in the months of May and June.[99] Such beliefs were reported in the *Straits Echo*, which attributed the influenza epidemic to 'some evil spirit through the agency of the wind'.[100] Nor were these views limited to those lacking knowledge in modern medicine, for a journalist in Singapore purportedly blamed the epidemic on excessive eating of fruit by the Asians, especially durians.[101] While these reports were Orientalist, they pointed to radically different perspectives of influenza among the Asian populace.

Until biomedicine was able to demonstrate its efficacy and dispel their wariness, most Asians in the early 20th century relied on traditional physicians, healers and herbal treatments commonly utilised by their community.[102] But as Lenore Manderson pointed out, even when biomedicine became more acceptable, healing in colonial Malaya and Singapore was always a pluralistic practice. Modern biomedicine was regarded simply as another option, usable in combination with customary treatments.[103]

Given the lack of a cure for influenza in 1918, the frightened public of Singapore and Malaya turned desperate in their search for a remedy. Whether a medication was Western or traditional mattered less. It clearly benefited the businesses, quacks and profiteers behind it. The *Singapore Free Press* reported the circulation of unspecified 'dark and ugly rumours' following the release of mortality figures for the first wave, indicating big increases in influenza-related deaths from tuberculosis, pneumonia, malarial fever, and unspecified fever.[104] In March 1919, drawing from his experience, a self-professed doctor proffered a preparation called Kola (apparently meaning, 'red oil') as an effective treatment for pneumonia, which 'is used externally, quickly reduces the temperature and cuts short the attack'.[105] Published in the *Singapore Free Press*, his letter excited many readers to the extent that a local chemist ostensibly ordered a supply of Kola. The doctor apologised for not having made the remedy known during the outbreak the previous year.[106]

Among the Chinese population, a popular treatment for the disease was a mixture of boiled pumpkin, potato and coriander leaves. This was allegedly marketed by profiteers in Penang, which drove up the price of potatoes nearly tenfold.[107] An article in the *Lat Pau* warned that the disease could worsen if it was treated erroneously as a *yang* disease with 'acrid', 'warm' medicines. It dismissed as fanciful the claim of Western doctors that influenza was caused by a 'long-shaped microorganism'. Instead, there were simple remedies such as eating cooling vegetables like fresh wax gourd, water chestnut or Chinese parsley; predictably, this also caused their prices to surge.[108] The buyers of these products did not question why cures for influenza were easily obtainable in the marketplace.

At the start of the second wave, the *Lat Pau* even carried advertisements for miraculous pills that could bring the influenza dead back to life.[109] A month later, one for Zhu Zhong Xing's Syrup Medicine appeared – it was a cure for all ills, including the flu, and the proprietor insisted he was no profiteer.[110] The newspaper also published less fanciful prescriptions – one on 25 October contained very precise quantities of various herbs and roots, to be strictly adhered to with half the dosage for children under 10.[111] Around this time, the *Lat Pau* advised influenza patients against consuming rice, all foods and drinks made from rice, and pork.[112]

All of these treatments were profit-driven. At a sporting meet in October 1918, bottles of champagne were reportedly sold on the suggestion that they had a beneficial effect on influenza.[113] For the English-educated population, newspapers in Singapore carried advertisements for 'Dr Williams' pink pills for pale people', which had been in circulation since the 1890 influenza epidemic. The company Dr Williams' Medicine Company had a branch in

Singapore and sold the pills for $2.25 per bottle. They purportedly treated colds and influenza by increasing the blood supply to the body.[114] The resort to alliteration, aimed at the European reader, was blatant enough, but in 1925, the *Straits Times* even printed the story of a woman in Canada whose recovery from influenza was aided by the pink pills.[115] By the mid-1920s, the price had dropped to $1.50 per bottle, but the pills were still selling.[116] In the 1920s, Peps lozenges were also lauded as a cure-all for a range of respiratory ailments from asthma to influenza.[117] Elsewhere in the English-speaking world, newspapers were also carrying advertisements for similar medicines and vaccines.[118]

## The Long Aftermath

The lessons of the 1918 pandemic went unlearnt. The British tracked the course of the second wave for a month between 23 October and 23 November 1918, compiling the returns from 25 departments. It did not continue beyond the latter date, having deemed the disease to be on the decline. However, influenza was still being detected well into 1919 (usually called the third wave of the pandemic in the global literature), with a resurgence in the middle of the year. Belatedly, in November, the Straits government agreed to a request from the Colonial Office to submit information on outbreaks of epidemic disease in the colony, including influenza.[119] In the Straits Settlements, the number of deaths registered under influenza fell to 343 or by three-fifths, and in Singapore, to 127 or by two-thirds. The colony's death rate also fell by a quarter from the previous year to 33.04 per mile, beginning to approximate the rate in the years preceding 1918. Though statistically suspect, these numbers offer an idea of continuity and change in the aftermath.

As the Straits government noted in 1919, there were still influenza deaths registered under complications such as pneumonia, bronchitis, tuberculosis, and unspecified fever.[120] In the GH, 'Occasional cases of Influenza are still being admitted but there has been no resemblance to an epidemic'; most of them were mild, with a death rate of 1.5 per cent.[121] It was similar at the prison hospital, which reported 13 mild cases, and the beriberi hospital, which had five, while surprisingly none were reported at TTSH at all. The quarantine report that year made no mention of influenza. But the government increased the watering of streets while attending to people's requests to disinfect their premises.[122]

In March 1919, the Municipal Commission assured that influenza was no longer present in Singapore and a second epidemic would not happen soon.[123] Upon stating this, three influenza deaths were reported in the Municipality. The *Singapore Free Press* cautioned that 'influenza is no longer a sickness to be laughed at', with recurring outbreaks more severe than the first.[124] In the town, the number of reported influenza cases fell by more than half to 543 in 1919, with nearly half occurring in July. The Moulmein Road Hospital admitted only 23 cases, of which one died of broncho-pneumonia.

The number of registered deaths from influenza was halved to 107 that year. In the distribution by gender and age, the figures approximated those of the previous year, while influenza also reportedly affected all the ethnic groups.[125] People remained anxious about the disease, writing to the newspapers for Outram and Desker Roads to be watered.[126] But the narrative seemed to be of a diminishing public health crisis.

This view turned out to be premature. In 1920, with the disease no longer notifiable, the government acknowledged that 'The aftermath of the influenza pandemic is still heightening the death-rate' in the Straits Settlements, though the rate had fallen from 43.85 per mile in 1918 to 33.2.[127] The number of influenza deaths fell in the other settlements (Penang's to 188), lowering the overall death rate. On the other hand, the number of pneumonia deaths had nearly doubled in the colony since 1917. Although the administration denied there was an influenza epidemic in Singapore, the island was an outlier in 1920. It registered 365 influenza deaths, nearly three times the previous year and just two under the 1918 figure. Most of them (319) occurred in the town, though rather surprisingly the Municipal Commission failed to comment on the high figure. Roughly 150 of the 225 deaths from pneumonia at the GH were attributed to influenza, while there was a lone death at the Middleton Hospital among 14 admissions. Two ships arriving at St. John's in March-April 1920 were found to have influenza cases, though this was prior to the peak of the influenza wave in mid-year.

The *Singapore Free Press* reported on the 1920 wave in Singapore at the beginning of the year, surmising it to be less virulent than the original influenza strain. The paper was uncertain if the vaccine being distributed in England would be made available locally, but highlighted preventive measures to reduce the spread, again to avoid crowds and cough or sneeze into a handkerchief.[128] The *Malaya Tribune* asked that employers send their flu-stricken workers home at once, as they were a danger to themselves and others.[129] In October, the *Straits Times* noted the reduced number of influenza deaths in 1920 as part of a general improvement in public health.[130] By contrast, a writer to the newspaper warned of an endemic influenza being a major cause of death, alongside tuberculosis and malaria.[131]

Influenza became endemic after 1920. In subsequent years, the number of registered influenza deaths in Singapore fell and then stabilised, to 214 in 1921 and 194 the following year. The island accounted for most of the mortality due to influenza in the Straits Settlements in the 1920s. For most of the decade, the disease accounted for less than 150 deaths per year. Considering the 1918 registered figure of 367, these numbers were still quite high, especially after including deaths due to complications. In 1922, the British noted, 'Many deaths due to Influenza are doubtless registered as fever not specified'.[132] The following year, there were 206 admissions for influenza and five deaths in Singapore's hospitals. In 1924, there were 35 cases of influenza treated at the outdoor dispensary at Bukit Timah, suggesting that the disease was circulating in the rural area. In 1926, there were a total of 1,040 admissions for influenza in the Straits Settlements' hospitals, resulting in 43 deaths (a mortality rate of 0.41), and in the following year, 1,304 admissions and 56 deaths (0.43) respectively.

That Singapore reported relatively high figures was unsurprising, for in its densely populated municipal area influenza spread easily. Despite this, the Medical Department's attentiveness to influenza waned. It returned to illnesses that had preoccupied it before 1918, especially malaria. Its annual reports continued to count influenza as a cause of death, but it made few comments on the disease. While in 1920 the government belatedly included influenza among the list of epidemic diseases in the Quarantine and Prevention of Disease Ordinance, subsequent quarantine and epidemiological reports contained little of note on the affliction.[133] Other infectious diseases such as malaria and tuberculosis had come to the fore in the official frame of mind.

In 1926, when there were 139 influenza deaths in Singapore, the department described the year as the unhealthiest since the 1918 pandemic. This was attributed to the increased incidence and mortality of malaria and pneumonia. But the latter failed to provoke further discussion on influenza, being attributed instead to 'heat and overcrowding'.[134] This was a reference to tuberculosis in the shophouses, which was also endemic and had become a major public health concern in the town. In 1927, when the Straits government established the Singapore Improvement Trust, they looked to control insanitation and tuberculosis there. This was the health agency that W.J.R. Simpson had called for, which belatedly began to carry out improvement works such as clearing backlanes and demolishing insanitary houses. Soon though in the early 1930s, the Trust began to build low-cost public housing to disperse the shophouse population and reduce overcrowding.

Amid these reforms, the 1918 influenza pandemic became a minor frame of reference for the administration, a footnote in Singapore's medical history.[135] But it should not have been so, for influenza was endemic in the Municipality under similar conditions as tuberculosis. It soon became clear that deprioritising influenza was a mistake. The number of registered deaths began to rise again – to 170 in 1929 and 255 the following year (one of whom was an infant who died from 'Convulsions'). These figures provoked no official comment either, other than the Municipal Health Department musing about the high number in 1930:

> This is rather a mystery and is difficult to account for as there was no sign of a real epidemic throughout the year. I imagine it includes many real mal-diagnoses which might well be placed elsewhere.[136]

There was an increase in the municipal death rate that year, which the department attributed to the effects of the Great Depression and low rainfall.

Then, between March and May 1931, a supposedly 'mild epidemic of influenza' occurred in Singapore, leading to 318 deaths – not much fewer than the 1918 figure.[137] The outbreak occurred in the trough of the global slump which lasted into the mid-1930s. The economic crisis brought the price of rubber to an all-time low and the entrepôt trade of Singapore to a standstill. Large numbers of Indian labourers and destitute Chinese were repatriated from the island the following year, while the immigration of men, though not women, was heavily curtailed.[138]

Managing the influenza outbreak was the work of an under-resourced colonial administration in these circumstances. Revealingly, unlike the earlier pandemic, this outbreak was concentrated in Singapore, with only 31 reported deaths in the other Straits Settlements. The GH admitted 412 mostly mild cases of influenza, compared to 40 in 1930. The government admitted that while the epidemic was not severe, it contributed to an increase in pneumonia deaths in the colony, though these deaths in Singapore actually fell from 1,801 in 1930 to 1,595. There were 1,506 admissions for influenza in the hospitals of the colony, mostly in Singapore, with 13 deaths and a mortality rate of 0.86. Patients reported 'high fever, sore throat and bronchitis' and many were infants and school children.[139] The epidemic was held responsible for the increase in infant mortality in the Straits Settlements from 193.9 per thousand in 1930 to 259.74.[140] The *Malaya Tribune* published a letter beseeching boys to wear their sweaters after sporting activity to stay warm and avoid catching the disease.[141] Surprisingly, the Municipal Commission did not mention influenza in its annual report, focusing instead on the spread of tuberculosis in the inner-city slums.[142]

Then, the number of registered influenza deaths fell again, though never as low as in the 1920s. It dropped to 174 in 1932, including a minor outbreak in the Singapore prison at the end of the year, which had 140 reported cases, though 'few complications and no deaths'.[143] The figure climbed back to 230 two years later before surging to 344 in 1935 (with 339 deaths in the municipal area). In the latter year, the *Straits Times* reported a cluster of five victims in a single office as 'An influenza epidemic, sudden and severe, has descended upon Singapore'.[144] The mortality rate for influenza was high (1.1), while the number of pneumonia deaths also rose in 1935. Influenza mortality fell back to under 150 in the next two years.

However, in 1936, the authorities surmised that 'Many children suffered from colds and influenza when these were prevalent chiefly during May, November and December'. It was satisfied no influenza epidemic had broken out in the schools of the Straits Settlements.[145] The *Straits Times*, while agreeing that the outbreak was a mild one, reported patients suffering from 'extremely high temperatures' in May.[146] Two months later, the Swimming Club was still largely deserted. There were brisk sales of cures and soaps for colds and cough at chemist shops, while many European employees stayed away from their workplace. The fear of influenza among locals was heightened by the Health Department's reports of more than eight deaths from pneumonia in Singapore daily.[147] The outbreak was blamed on an especially severe heat wave brought about by the delayed arrival of the southwest monsoon in Singapore and Malaya, though an unnamed doctor also attributed it to the lowered resistance of the population.[148]

In January 1937, local doctors reported the spread of an influenza epidemic from Europe, resulting in some mild local cases.[149] An advertisement in the newspapers the following month lauded the wondrous benefits of Clotabs – vitamins containing an extract of halibut cod liver that apparently fortified the body against the flu.[150] Another mild outbreak, again depleting office staff, occurred in the middle of the year, which was attributed to abrupt weather changes.[151]

In 1938, when the last Straits medical report was published before the advent of the Second World War in Malaya in 1941, 227 influenza deaths were registered in Singapore. Among the 1,387 admissions for influenza to the hospitals of the Straits Settlements were 12 prisoners and two staff of the new Changi Prison in Singapore, completed in 1936. In the 1930s, increasing numbers of subordinate municipal staff were treated for the illness; by 1939, this number had risen to 13,886, more than one-third of total cases, as an outbreak in February again depleted many office staff.[152] Clotabs vitamins were still selling behind claims of bringing 'half-dead' men to life.[153]

By the time war broke out in Southeast Asia, the British colonial administration in Singapore remained largely disinterested in influenza. They were content with the narrative of a relatively low incidence of infectious disease in the city.[154] Tuberculosis had become a hot topic in the government and newspapers, though concrete efforts to tackle it had to await the end of the war.[155] But in social and environmental terms, influenza was a similar sort of disease. Issues of overcrowding and insanitation in the shophouses that underpinned the tuberculosis discourse were applicable to influenza. Few doctors in Malaya and Singapore showed an interest in influenza. In 1937, P.N. Bardhan published a medical article on the aetiology and diagnosis of the disease, but this merely summarised findings in the West without research on local conditions.[156]

In a rare exception, the wider implications of influenza were highlighted by Dr N.K. Menon, a doctor and Legislative Councillor from Penang, in a journal article on the eve of war. Malaya, he urged, should not only be geared for warfare, but also food security issues and epidemics of infectious diseases. A 'close watch' ought to be kept on the incidence of influenza, as the 1918 pandemic had killed more people globally than the Great War itself. The onus should be on influenza patients to avoid crowds and stay home, or to go to a hospital if they were severely sick. But Menon, who also supported the use of 'medicated lozenges, gargles, and throat sprays', had little impact on Straits policy towards influenza.[157]

Interestingly, the lack of an influenza policy stimulated ambivalent and varied attitudes among educated members of the public. Writing in the *Malaya Tribune* in 1930, 'Looker-on' showed his long memory of the 1918 epidemic:

> It is a curious thing that in the twelve years since the world war this war-time epidemic, described as influenza for want of a better name, has not been properly defined or controlled! If asked for a method of prevention, doctors are nonplussed, and the only 'cure' they know is that of treating

the symptoms with drugs. Of course, everybody knows that it is wise to avoid crowded places, and to breathe through the nose, use disinfectants and all that sort of thing, but I caught the 'flu' in the last epidemic in spite of following those instructions.[158]

A column by G.S. Hammonds titled 'The Troubles and Trials of the Influenza Victim' was published in the *Sunday Tribune* in 1936. It captured the marginal place of influenza in interwar Malaya and the consequent social stigma for its sufferers. Like the poor and like mumps, Hammonds noted, influenza is ever-present in the country but unable to elicit general sympathy. This caused the patient to try to hide an illness that was not easily hidden. As a result, the patient was shunned by their social contacts, likely to fall into depression. 'The offices of Malaya, Hammonds adds, 'are infested during epidemic periods with people who ought to be kept in strict isolation'.[159] Hammonds' letter illustrates the failure to learn the lessons of 1918 on both levels – governance and society.

In the same year, another column of quite a different kind appeared in the *Straits Times*. Anak Singapura ('son of Singapore' in Malay) wrote in amusement about the two monsoon seasons in Singapore when one could best schedule their local leave: between September and November, and in April and May. The latter was when minor ailments such as influenza, colds and sore throat were more prevalent. In Anak Singapura's worldview, influenza was one of the minor illnesses, similar to the other two, and part of people's lives.[160]

In May 1937, in response to the influenza outbreak earlier in the year, Anak Singapura wrote again to the *Straits Times* about 'repressed flu', being 'influenza which refuses to get out of your system', leading to repeated attacks on the person.[161] In the *Sunday Tribune*, another writer 'H.L. Horkin' surmised his newfound respect for influenza, which he had dismissed as merely exposing 'the tenderness of the younger generation' to illness, after he caught the bug himself and had a difficult time.[162] Clearly, educated locals were coming to grips with a disease long deemed to be mild and unimportant.

In part, the history of the 1918 influenza pandemic in Singapore shows the difficulty of controlling a disease outbreak that occurred suddenly, spread quickly and became endemic just as abruptly. Even when statistics indicated otherwise, the colonial and municipal authorities in Singapore failed to divert part of their attention from known diseases to the new threat. In the 1920s and 1930s, they began to turn towards the problem of tuberculosis in the shophouses, but not to influenza that was endemic under similar conditions. Regional epidemiology showed a similar blind spot, even after Singapore became the base of the Eastern Epidemiological Bureau.

The colonial government's response to the 1918 epidemic was belated, misguided and ineffectual. With limited resources for public health, the Straits government and Municipal Commission tried to muster measures against the epidemic. But influenza spread quickly and unravelled the shortcomings of colonial rule. The lack of staff and beds turned public hospitals into conduits of spread, worsening fears of hospitals as places of dying among the Asian population. The recently built Moulmein Road Hospital played hardly any role during the epidemic. Watering the streets and cleansing government buildings were 'spectacles' to mask the inertia of an administration rendered hapless by the outbreak, as illustrated by the parent who decided to take the law into his own hands and keep his children home.

The closure of schools and cinemas had some benefit. But less so were measures that required or affected people's understanding, support and behaviour – calls to wear masks, avoid crowds and congested places, and have nourishing food. For the coolie population in the town, these admonishments would have sounded alien and impracticable. The economy of the colonial entrepôt meant that the epidemic experiences of the European and Asian upper classes were very different from the plebian groups. One was frequently mentioned in the official documents, the other rarely so. Lacking adequate guidance and help from the government and doctors, the low-income population were frightened into seeking cures from other sources. They favoured treatments in their medical traditions as well as new cures hawked by profiteers. There was little else that ordinary people could do. They were unable to afford masks, avoid crowds where they lived and worked, obtain better accommodation, or pay for good food.

In the longer term, the Straits administration failed to heed the lessons of the 1918 pandemic. This was part of a global phenomenon: there was no public commemoration of the event and little mention of it in the standard historical accounts.[163] In Singapore, the event was not totally forgotten, becoming a marker of Singapore's medical history. But it had no impact on medical policy up to the next major influenza outbreak in 1957. The British also did not look to guide local thinking on influenza in the aftermath, creating a harmful effect on social psychology and behaviour in colonial Singapore.

In an immigrant society with few settlers, where sojourners typically returned home after a few years, it was unlikely that even a killing epidemic would remain long in social memory. Some settled residents like Anak Singapura and others remembered the events of 1918, as did the makers of alleged medicines and vitamins for flu. But they ascribed varying meanings to the pandemic. The vast majority of the population had to continue living haphazardly with the influenza virus – often in ignorance, sometimes in social stigma. This led to further outbreaks in the 1920s and 1930s, but none of these altered the government's policy on the flu.

The 1918 pandemic exposed the colonial failure to recognise the threat posed by an infectious disease like influenza. Singapore's experiences with the SARS and COVID-19 outbreaks offer good reason why the history of influenza pandemics should not be written from the colonial perspective. The British in Singapore, as elsewhere, believed that neither the quarantine system nor containment measures could stop influenza. They had been focused on the trinity of dangerous diseases and would continue to do so. Besides urging people to refrain from congregating in public places and closing schools, the colonial government made no real attempt to stem the outbreak in the community. As late as 1957, in a decade of decolonisation, Singapore again did not adopt a more active response to the influenza pandemic that year.

The social history of the 1918 pandemic shows that influenza was not a mild illness or the outbreak would quickly pass. In Singapore, the gap between the colonial regime and immigrant society was largely responsible for the severity of the pandemic. Due to their pressing socio-economic circumstances, Singapore's Asian immigrants largely rejected or ignored the official injunctions, preventing a unified response to the epidemic. They had to co-exist with endemic influenza in the crowded spaces of the town till the outbreak of war. In seeking to learn from the event, the study of immigrant society, its economic characteristics, social classes and cultural views of illness are all matters deserving of study.

Despite its scale and severity, the other lesson of 1918 is that no single pandemic should overshadow others in history. The lessons of the past are not to be drawn from the most obvious precedent. The year 1918 tells us much about the failings of the colonial state in controlling pandemic influenza in an immigrant society like Singapore. But other historical outbreaks – of influenza and other infectious diseases, as well as in different times and of varying severity – would be needed to corroborate and deepen these insights. With this in mind, we turn to the next flu pandemic in 1957.

## Notes

1  SMAR 1893, 1894; CO 275/48 The Quarantine and Prevention of Disease Ordinance, 1886. On the composition and work of the Municipal Commission, comprising a group of European and Asian elites who ran the affairs of the town, see Brenda S.A. Yeoh, *Contesting Space in Colonial Singapore: Power Relations and the Urban Built Environment* (Singapore: Singapore University Press, 2003), 2nd edition.
2  Loh Kah Seng and Hsu Li Yang, *Tuberculosis – The Singapore Experience, 1867–2018: Disease, Society and the State* (London: Routledge, 2020); W.J. Simpson, *Report of the Sanitary Condition of Singapore* (London: Waterlow & Sons, 1907).
3  Loh Kah Seng and Hsu Li Yang, 'The Origins of Singapore's Communicable Disease Centre: Hanging Fire', *Kyoto Review of Southeast Asia*, Issue 26, November 2019, https://kyotoreview.org/issue-26/the-origins-of-singapores-comm unicable-disease-centre-hanging-fire/
4  Singapore, *Proceedings and Report of the Commission Appointed to Inquire into the Cause of the Present Housing Difficulties in Singapore, and the Steps Which Should be Taken to Remedy Such Difficulties*, Vol. I (Singapore: Government Printing Office, 1918); CO 275/101 SSMR 1918. This agency became the Singapore Improvement Trust, formed in 1927.
5  CO 275/99 The Quarantine and Prevention of Disease Ordinance, 1915.
6  CO 275/101 SSMR 1918.
7  CO 275/101 SSMR 1918, p. 515.
8  CO 275/101 SSMR 1918, p. 515.
9  CO 273/468 Report on an Ordinance to amend the Quarantine and Prevention of Disease Ordinance, 1915, dated 11 April 1918.

10 Vernon Lee et al., 'Influenza Pandemics in Singapore, a Tropical, Globally Connected City', *Emerging Infectious Diseases* 13 (7) July 2007, pp. 1052–1057.

11 *Malaya Tribune*, 2 July 1918, p. 4. Official reports did not indicate a dengue outbreak during the year.

12 Niall Johnson, *Britain and the 1918–19 Influenza Pandemic: A Dark Epilogue* (London: Routledge, 2006).

13 *Malaya Tribune*, 26 October 1918, p. 4; *Straits Echo*, 15 July 1918, p. 6.

14 *Lat Pau*, 16 July 1918, p. 3.

15 *Lat Pau*, 4 July 1918, pp. 3, 6.

16 CO 275/101 SSMR 1918.

17 *Singapore Free Press*, 15 October 1918, p. 12.

18 CO 275/101 SSMR 1918, p. 515.

19 *Malaya Tribune*, 26 October 1918, p. 4.

20 CO 275/101 SSMR 1918, p. 517.

21 CO 275/101 SSMR 1918.

22 *Straits Times*, 22 October 1918, p. 7.

23 CO 275/101 SSMR 1918, p. 435.

24 *Singapore Free Press*, 17 October 1918, p. 244.

25 *Lat Pau*, 23 October 1918, p. 2.

26 *Malaya Tribune*, 28 October 1918, p. 4.

27 *Straits Times*, 26 July 1919, p. 12.

28 CO 275/101 SSMR 1918, p. 516.

29 CO 275/101 SSMR 1918, p. 517.

30 *Malaya Tribune*, 26 October 1918, p. 4.

31 *Straits Echo*, 1 November 1918, p. 3.

32 Liew Kai Khiun, 'Terribly Severe Though Mercifully Short: The Episode of the 1918 Influenza in British Malaya', *Modern Asian Studies*, Vol. 41, No. 2 March 2007, p. 231.

33 Lee et al., 'Influenza Pandemics in Singapore, a Tropical, Globally Connected City'.

34 Report of the Municipal Health Office, SMAR 1918.

35 CO 275/124 SSMR 1929, p. 651.

36 CO 275/117 SSMR 1926.

37 CO 275/101 SSMR 1918, p. 435.

38 CO 275/103 RBDSS 1920.

39 Johnson, *Britain and the 1918–19 Influenza Pandemic*.

40 K. Kanagarayer, 'Some Observations on Differential Diagnosis in the Tropics', *Malayan Medical Journal*, V, 1930, pp. 36–38.

41 Lee et al., 'Influenza Pandemics in Singapore, a Tropical, Globally Connected City'.

42 Johnson, *Britain and the 1918–19 Influenza Pandemic*.

43 George Dehner, *Global Flu and You: A History of Influenza* (London: Reaktion Books, 2012).

44 *Malaya Tribune*, 27 July 1918, p. 5.

45 *Straits Echo*, 30 July 1918, p. 4.

46 Alfred Jay Bollet, *Plagues & Poxes: The Impact of Human History on Epidemic Disease* (New York: Demos, 2004); Dehner, *Global Flu and You*; Johnson, *Britain and the 1918–19 Influenza Pandemic*.

47 CO 275/101 SSMR 1918, p. 440.

48 CO 275/101 SSMR 1918, p. 440.

49 CO 275/101 SSMR 1918, p. 440.

50 CO 275/101 SSMR 1918, p. 471.

51 Report of the Municipal Health Office, SMAR 1918, p. 3.

52 Mark Honigsbaum, *The Pandemic Century: A History of Global Contagion from the Spanish Flu to COVID-19* (London: W.H. Allen, 2020).

53 Singapore Municipal Commission, *Minutes of the Proceedings of the Municipal Commissioners* (thereafter MPMC), 18 October 1918.
54 *Lat Pau*, 16 October 1918, p. 3.
55 MPMC, 25 October 1918.
56 MPMC, 1 November 1918.
57 Liew, 'Terribly Severe Though Mercifully Short'.
58 Catherine Arnold, *Pandemic 1918: Eyewitness Accounts from the Greatest Medical Holocaust in Modern History* (New York: St Martin's Press, 2018), p. 12; Johnson, *Britain and the 1918–19 Influenza Pandemic*.
59 *Straits Times*, 19 February 1919, p. 10.
60 *Straits Times*, 19 October 1918, p. 10.
61 *Singapore Free Press*, 17 October 1918, p. 244.
62 *Straits Times*, 19 October 1918, p. 10.
63 Straits Times, 24 October 1918, p. 8.
64 *Singapore Free Press*, 31 October 1918, p. 279.
65 *Singapore Free Press*, 31 October 1918, p. 279.
66 CO 275/101 SSMR 1918, p. 516.
67 CO 275/101 SSMR 1918, p. 522.
68 *Straits Echo*, 21 October 1918, p. 8.
69 Report of the Municipal Health Office, SMAR 1918.
70 CO 275/101 SSMR 1918, p. 441.
71 Lenore Manderson, *Sickness and the State: Health and Illness in Colonial Malaya, 1870–1940* (New York: Cambridge University Press, 1996).
72 *Straits Echo*, 30 October 1918, p. 5.
73 CO 275/101 SSMR 1918, p. 441.
74 Dehner, *Global Flu and You*; Johnson, *Britain and the 1918–19 Influenza Pandemic*.
75 CO 275/101 SSMR 1918, p. 452.
76 Report of the Municipal Health Office, SMAR 1918, p. 14.
77 *Singapore Free Press*, 31 October 1918, p. 279.
78 Report of the Municipal Health Office, SMAR 1918; MCMP, 25 October 1918; *Malaya Tribune*, 26 October 1918, p. 5.
79 CO 275/101 SSMR 1918, p. 456.
80 *Straits Times*, 21 October 1918, p. 12.
81 *Straits Times*, 3 July 1918, p. 7.
82 James Francis Warren, *Rickshaw Coolie: A People's History* (Singapore: Singapore University Press, 2003).
83 Singapore, *Proceedings and Report of the Commission Appointed to Inquire into the Cause of the Present Housing Difficulties in Singapore*, Vol. I.
84 Singapore, *Proceedings and Report of the Commission Appointed to Inquire into the Cause of the Present Housing Difficulties in Singapore*, Vol. I, p. A67.
85 Report of the Municipal Health Office, SMAR 1918, p. 3.
86 *Straits Echo*, 17 October 1918, p. 5.
87 Report of the Municipal Health Office, SMAR 1918.
88 Report of the Municipal Health Office, SMAR 1918, p. 2.
89 Report of the Municipal Health Office, SMAR 1918.
90 Report of the Municipal Health Office, SMAR 1918.
91 *Straits Echo*, 28 October 1918, p. 5.
92 CO 275/101 SSMR 1918, p. 520.
93 CO 275/101 SSMR 1918, p. 520.
94 *Malaya Tribune*, 26 October 1918, p. 4.
95 *Malaya Tribune*, 26 October 1918, p. 4.
96 Liew, 'Terribly Severe Though Mercifully Short'.
97 Johnson, *Britain and the 1918–19 Influenza Pandemic*.

98    Yeoh, *Contesting Space in Colonial Singapore.*
99    Roland St. John Braddell, *The Lights of Singapore* (London: Methuen, 1947), p. 17.
100   *Straits Echo*, 17 October 1918, p. 5.
101   *Straits Echo*, 6 July 1918, p. 6.
102   Loh Kah Seng, *Making and Unmaking the Asylum: Leprosy and Modernity in Singapore and Malaysia* (Petaling Jaya: SIRD, 2009).
103   Manderson, *Sickness and the State.*
104   *Singapore Free Press*, 20 July 1918, p. 6.
105   *Singapore Free Press*, 10 March 1919, p. 10.
106   *Straits Times*, 1 April 1919, p. 8.
107   *Straits Echo*, 17 October 1918, p. 5.
108   *Lat Pau*, 16 July 1918, p. 3.
109   *Lat Pau*, 2 October 1918, p. 30.
110   *Lat Pau*, 1 November 1918, p. 20.
111   *Lat Pau*, 25 October 1918, p. 9.
112   *Lat Pau*, 24 October 1918, p. 2.
113   *Straits Echo*, 30 October 1918, p. 8.
114   *Singapore Free Press*, 29 March 1920, p. 4; *Singapore Free Press*, 11 April 1919, p. 7.
115   *Straits Times*, 4 May 1925, p. 3.
116   *Malaya Tribune*, 27 September 1926, p. 2.
117   *Malaya Tribune*, 16 December 1922, p. 3.
118   Johnson, *Britain and the 1918–19 Influenza Pandemic.*
119   CO 273/485 Despatch 'Outbreak of Infectious Disease' from the Straits Settlements to the Colonial Office, 15 November 1919.
120   CO 275/101 RBDSS 1919, p. 144.
121   CO 275/103 SSMR 1919, p. 404.
122   *Singapore Free Press*, 14 March 1919, p. 4.
123   *Malaya Tribune*, 1 March 1919, p. 5.
124   *Singapore Free Press*, 6 March 1919, p. 146.
125   SMAR 1919.
126   *Straits Times*, 19 March 1919, p. 10; *Malaya Tribune*, 21 March 1919, p. 5.
127   CO 275/103 RBDSS 1920, p. 302.
128   *Singapore Free Press*, 4 February 1920, p. 6.
129   *Malaya Tribune*, 9 March 1922, p. 4.
130   *Straits Times*, 31 October 1921, p. 9.
131   *Straits Times*, 16 December 1920, p. 8.
132   CO 275/107 SSMR 1922, p. 515.
133   CO 275/102 The Quarantine and Prevention of Disease Ordinance, 1915.
134   Loh and Hsu, *Tuberculosis – The Singapore Experience.*
135   CO 275/117 SSMR 1926, p. 374.
136   SMAR 1930, p. 56-D.
137   CO 275/129 SSMR 1931, p. 1067.
138   W.G. Huff, 'Entitlements, Destitution, and Emigration in the 1930s Singapore Great Depression', *The Economic History Review* Vol. 54, No. 2, 2001, pp. 290–323.
139   CO 275/129 SSMR 1931, p. 1086.
140   *Singapore Free Press*, 29 September 1931, p. 7.
141   *Malaya Tribune*, 7 May 1931, p. 3.
142   SMAR 1931.
143   CO 275/131 SSMR 1932, p. 975.
144   *Straits Times*, 5 May 1935, p. 1.
145   CO 275/142 SSMR 1936, p. 937.
146   *Straits Times*, 17 May 1936, p. 1.
147   *Straits Times*, 10 July 1936, p. 12; *Straits Times*, 7 June 1936, p. 15.

148  *Singapore Free Press*, 8 June 1936, p. 6.
149  *Malaya Tribune*, 27 January 1937, p. 13.
150  *Sunday Tribune*, 14 February 1937, p. 22.
151  *Straits Times*, 12 July 1937, p. 12.
152  *Singapore Free Press*, 16 February 1939, p. 3.
153  *Singapore Free Press*, 1 August 1939, p. 10.
154  CO 275/139 SSMR 1935.
155  Loh and Hsu, *Tuberculosis – The Singapore Experience*.
156  P.N. Bardhan, 'Notes on Etiology and Diagnosis of Influenza', *Malayan Medical Journal*, October 1937, pp. 114–115.
157  N.K. Menon, 'Some Medical Aspects of Local Defence', *Journal of the Malayan Branch of the British Medical Association*, Vol. 5. No. 1, June 1941, p. 23.
158  *Malaya Tribune*, 26 June 1930, p. 8.
159  *Sunday Tribune*, 16 February 1936, p. 14.
160  *Straits Times*, 26 September 1936, p. 10.
161  *Straits Times*, 24 May 1937, p. 10.
162  *Sunday Tribune*, 6 June 1937, p. 9.
163  Dehner, *Global Flu and You*; Johnson, *Britain and the 1918–19 Influenza Pandemic*.

# 8 1957 Flu

## The Limits of Decolonisation

Singapore's influenza epidemic in 1957 was in many respects a repeat of 1918. But what is significant is it should not have been. The historical context was vastly different. By this time, Singapore was at an advanced stage of decolonisation after the Second World War. While the British still controlled security and foreign affairs and the franchise was limited, the island had an elected government led by the Labour Front (LF). There was a Chief Minister, Lim Yew Hock, and a Minister for Health, Armand Joseph Braga. The City Council, which replaced the Municipal Commission in 1951, also had an elected government for the city area, headed by a mayor.[1] Two years after the influenza epidemic, Singapore became a self-governing state will control over its domestic affairs. It then joined a newly-formed Federation of Malaysia in 1963, bringing an end to nearly 150 years of British colonial rule before becoming a sovereign state in 1965. The political history suggests a different outlook and policy against the threat of influenza.

Yet, when the pandemic reached Singapore in May 1957, the LF government's response was to 'let it burn out' – a description which would have been apt in 1918. At a time of socio-political activism on the island, this seemed puzzling. It also received muted criticism from the opposition in the Legislative Assembly. This is not to say that decolonisation completely passed by the influenza outbreak. The healthcare system showed much vigour and range in its response, benefitting from a decade of expansion under the 1948 Medical Plan. Virologists from the University of Malaya, established in 1949, were able to isolate the 'Singapore flu' virus, while volunteers battled to provide medicine and welfare to the low-income population. But these efforts only accentuated the government's passive response to the epidemic. In the aftermath, no influenza policy emerged and once again Singapore found itself co-existing with an endemic disease.

Equally significant was the social history of the outbreak. If we take decolonisation to mean a broad programme to prepare the people for self-rule, the outbreak revealed a major gap between them and the state, as in the colonial era. Despite its expansion, many people still distrusted the healthcare system and preferred their own remedies for influenza. This contrasted with case-finding and vaccination for other infectious diseases such as tuberculosis and

DOI: 10.4324/9781003384014-9

smallpox that were gaining acceptance in the 1950s. Influenza was a disease where social and official perspectives still differed, no doubt affected by the government's limited measures. There were widespread rumours that the pandemic was caused by nuclear tests, reflecting people's keen sense of the dangers of the Cold War. For these reasons, the 1918 and 1957 epidemics are both historically important events, telling us how well Singapore dealt with the mass outbreak of influenza.

## Decolonisation and Expansion of the State

The Second World War was a milestone for Singapore. Between February 1942 and September 1945, the island was occupied by Japanese forces and renamed *Syonan-to* ('Light of the South' in Japanese). In healthcare, the Japanese Occupation is usually seen as a time of deprivation and want due to the ongoing war and cessation of entrepôt trade.[2] The Japanese requisitioned medical supplies for their own use, while European officials and doctors were interned and replaced by locals. At the Middleton Hospital for infectious diseases, a Eurasian, Dr Ernest Steven Monteiro, became the Medical Superintendent.

What we know of influenza during the occupation is fragmentary, but there is evidence that it, like other serious illnesses, was prevalent. Though the Japanese kept records, medical statistics under wartime conditions must be viewed with some scepticism. There was an apparent rise in deaths from bronchitis, pneumonia and pulmonary tuberculosis from 3,696 in 1941 to 5,641 the following year, peaking at 8,635 in 1944. Deaths from acute rheumatism due to influenza (a new category) jumped from 279 in 1941 to 643 the following year, with the subsequent years of the occupation remaining higher than the pre-war period.[3] These were figures from the hospitals, not the community. The new Japanese daily, the *Syonan Simbun*, warned of the likely spread of diseases such as influenza and tuberculosis in the insanitary housing of the town.[4] This was similar to the British discourse before the war, but likely made worse by the conditions of occupation.

When the British returned to Singapore, the official discourse henceforth was one of improving conditions due to the reimposition of colonial rule. The number of deaths due to acute rheumatism from influenza, and from bronchitis, pneumonia and pulmonary tuberculosis was lower than the pre-war figures. The 1948 Medical Department report highlighted a 'marked reduction' in deaths from diseases such as influenza and malaria.[5] From a high of 228 in 1949, the number of hospital admissions for influenza fell to under a hundred between 1952 and 1956, with very occasional deaths. The number of deaths from the disease, islandwide, also dropped from 166 in 1947 to less than 40 in 1951 and thereafter.

Nevertheless, as peacetime conditions returned, no influenza policy was forthcoming. The Medical Department (renamed the Ministry of Health in 1957) resumed its antebellum work of tracking influenza cases and deaths. In 1948, the English press reported more cases of colds and influenza in the month of January, which were attributed to the wet weather.[6] An influenza wave hit Singapore in August 1949, affecting mostly children, though this was not thought to be a serious outbreak.[7] In 1954, a flu outbreak occurred in the Pearl's Hill Prison, and entire blocks in its premises had to be used to isolate influenza patients from healthy inmates.

Compared to the pre-war period, there was a rise in medical interest in the illness. In Malaya, medical officers C.E. Gordon Smith and W.G. Thomson documented three outbreaks and five strains of influenza in the mid-1950s, including one at a residential boys' school. The disease was, they noted, 'not a diagnostic dustbin'.[8] But it was still seen to be a minor affliction. Writing on viruses, Smith surmised that 'Influenza is probably endemic in Malaya mainly as sporadic mild respiratory illnesses'. He added that air travel had made it easier for the virus to spread across borders, while pessimistic that 'About influenza little can be done except to grin and bear it, remembering that at least we are better off than those who live in cold climates'.[9]

There was no sign that medical interest would nudge the colonial government towards an influenza policy. The British seemed to have retained their pre-war blind spot, ignoring how the disease was linked to overcrowding and insanitation in the town. This was despite a 1947 *Malaya Tribune* article that listed influenza among the diseases that were rife in overcrowded shophouses.[10] Urban congestion was in fact worsening due to the rapid population boom in Singapore after the war, rising to 4.5 per cent per annum in the 1950s. Shophouse cubicles meant for single men were unsuitable for large families with several young children. These families began to move to kampongs in the urban area, thus relocating congestion, insanitation and infectious diseases to these informal settlements.[11]

Another immediate post-war problem – also an old one – was that many influenza patients still did not seek help at government hospitals. This was partly because the illness was often mild but going to a hospital remained unpopular with a large segment of the population. It would take several more years before the psychological impact of new antibiotics such as sulphone and streptomycin would make people gradually more receptive to biomedicine. In 1946, when health conditions in Singapore were still dire, there were only 119 hospital admissions for influenza, of whom one died. By comparison, there were 38 influenza admissions at the prison hospital alone.[12] For influenza patients who did not seek medical treatment, it was also likely that many did not isolate themselves from others, thus contributing to the spread of infection.

Despite shortcomings in influenza control, the war was a major catalyst both in a political sense and for the healthcare system. The Straits Settlements were abolished in 1946 and Singapore was made a separate crown colony from the Malay peninsula, which became the Federation of Malaya in 1948.[13] Though politically and financially battered at home, Britain sought to rejuvenate its imperial image in the colonies and chart an orderly path towards their self-rule. Singapore's future, the British envisioned, lay in a multicultural and anti-communist state. These political aims led to the creation of an expansive colonial state on the island and public health became a key element of the decolonisation programme. The British rulers and the elected local representatives made big strides in expanding the healthcare system. Public health and the control of infectious diseases was one way by which a common citizenship would be conferred to what hitherto had been a population of sojourners from varied lands.

Compared to the earlier period, post-war Singapore was a welfare state based on the model of Fabian socialism prevailing in Britain. Across various policy fronts, its symbol was the ambitiously interventionist yet expensive multi-year action plans, unafraid to make major changes in people's lives and prepare them for Singapore's new future. Immediately after the war, a Social Welfare Department was formed to address pressing social issues facing the low-income population and augment the work of other government departments in areas of housing, sanitation, poverty alleviation, and youth welfare.[14] A ten-year educational programme, adopted in 1947, sought to mould the minds of the large and growing population of children for a self-governing Singapore. Numerous English-medium primary schools were built in the 1950s while the government asserted greater control over privately-run vernacular schools that taught in Chinese and Tamil, some of which harboured communist or radical elements.[15] The education reforms benefited tertiary medical education. In 1949, the College of Medicine and Raffles College merged to form the first university in Malaya and Singapore, the University of Malaya.

The most visually arresting accomplishments of the post-war state were the new blocks of concrete housing built by the Singapore Improvement Trust for the low-income population. The Trust had been formed in 1927 but was now given the mandate to decant the town population into modern, sanitary housing at the urban periphery.[16] Health concerns, a legacy of W.J.R. Simpson's venerable 1907 sanitary study, continued to provide justification for these public housing programmes. But they were now guided by a new system of urban planning. Guiding all the individual policy plans was the 1958 Master Plan for the whole of Singapore, linking the town, rural areas and offshore islands. The plan utilised the principles of physical planning and zoned land-use commonplace at the time and aimed to coordinate the organised transformation of Singapore over a 20-year period.[17]

The field of public health witnessed equally impressive achievements. In 1948, the colonial government launched the ten-year Medical Plan. The British officials who crafted it spoke grandiosely of compensating for decades of colonial neglect and investment in the health of the people. First among the reforms, the hospital system was to be overhauled and expanded.[18] The plan was modified and scaled back in the next few years, but its achievements were real. Under pressure from local nationalists, bed space in the hospitals was greatly increased. The biggest hospital, the Singapore General Hospital, was designated for acute diseases, including infectious diseases, together with the Middleton Hospital.

The most notable strides were made in the war on tuberculosis, long seen as an unmanageable chronic disease. Local doctors helped change this view after the war and a tuberculosis policy was adopted within the Medical Plan. The policy precipitated a chain of major public health interventions by the state, including the conversion of the Tan Tock Seng Hospital to a sanatorium. In what became a defining feature of post-war public health, anti-tuberculosis efforts also moved beyond the hospital to the community: mass X-ray screening, home-based recovery, outpatient treatment, contact tracing in the community, tests and screening in schools, and the widespread use of the Bacille Calmette-Guérin (BCG) vaccine. The culmination of these efforts was the establishment of the Tuberculosis Control Unit to track the disease at the national level in 1957, months after the influenza epidemic that year ended.[19]

### 'Let it burn out'

All these policy accomplishments point to an active colonial state run on modern scientific principles of administration. They make the LF government's weak response to the 1957 pandemic seem puzzling. 'Some months' before it reached Singapore, the World Health Organization had warned of the possible spread of influenza from Japan in its bulletin updates to countries in Southeast Asia.[20] But the organisation could hardly claim credit for preparing its member states for the outbreak, for it had failed to detect the emergence of the new H3N2 flu strain responsible in the first place.[21] As we will see, Singapore's lacklustre response was similar to other countries. But it owed more to local circumstances.

There were earlier newspaper reports of major outbreaks in China, Hong Kong and Taiwan before the pandemic reached Singapore.[22] But influenza, as the MOH admitted in 1957, 'was not a disease that called for quarantine measures against International traffic'.[23] Consequently no quarantine measures for influenza were adopted, though some Indian passengers leaving Singapore for India were later screened for influenza.[24] During the outbreak, medical experts in the colony doubted that early warnings would have helped prevent a fast-spreading event.[25]

The influenza pandemic broke out in Singapore at the start of May and peaked for about two weeks between the 6th and 20th. It petered out towards the end of May, though there were still 613 cases and 4,594 attendances for the disease at government hospitals and clinics on the 31st. The government believed the outbreak had likely spread from Japan to Hong Kong, Taiwan and Southeast Asia.[26] But there were also claims that it had originated in China,[27] or more dubiously that Gurkha troops from Hong Kong had brought it to Johor.[28] Once in Singapore, the virus spread northward to the cities of Johor Bahru, Penang and Kuala Lumpur in the Federation of Malaya, as in the 1918 pandemic.[29]

On May Day, the government reported the unusual phenomenon of its daily-rated labourers reporting sick with influenza symptoms, for medical leave was not normally sought on a public holiday. It seemed that these employees had been infected while working onboard ships at the harbour, recalling the 1890 outbreak at the Singapore wharf.[30] Over the next few days, many City Council staff were suddenly taken ill with influenza.[31] On 5 May, the government admitted that the outbreak had 'definitely reached epidemic proportions'.[32] Once again, the damp weather was held responsible for the rapid spread of influenza.[33]

At the same time, 30 cases were reported in a kampong on Pulau Brani, a tiny offshore island south of the port of Singapore. Many of the Malays living there were employees of the Marine Department and had seemingly caught 'an unknown fever' whilst working on boats delivering cargo from the larger ships anchored beyond the harbour.[34] Likely, influenza had entered Singapore by way of ships as in previous outbreaks, and as in previous outbreaks, the quarantine system was not on watch for the disease. The government noted that May was the fasting month of Ramadan for Muslims, and the Malays on Pulau Brani were fasting (and by implication physically weak) when the outbreak occurred.[35]

On 6 May, the *Singapore Free Press* reiterated that 'Influenza has reached epidemic proportions in Singapore'.[36] Long queues of patients were seen at public dispensaries, while some 500 people, including children, arrived at the SGH's outpatient department. The lines lengthened the following day, with mothers breaking queue and scrambling to the dispensary counter to obtain medicine for their children, while men stood on one another's shoulders to do the same.[37] At some queues, hooligans blocked hospital entrances with stones and demanded that patients pay a 'queue tax' before they could enter or risk a beating.[38]

On 7 May, some 12,000 students were reportedly absent from the 160 English primary schools across Singapore. Among the secondary schools, 110 out of the 890 boys at Raffles Institution missed school, as did over a hundred boys from each of St. Andrew's, St. Michael's School and St. Anthony's Boys School. 85 girls and a teacher at Raffles Girls School were also absent.[39] In total, the Ministry of Education estimated 25,000 children had been struck down by influenza, or nearly one in ten students in Singapore. The worst affected schools were those located in Tanjong Pagar and Tiong Bahru, both dense housing areas.[40] In one school, Keppel School (near Keppel Harbour), over a quarter of the students were sick.[41] Absentees were reportedly higher in the Malay schools compared to the English and Chinese schools; if so, Malay families were keeping their children at home.[42] Many parents brought their sick children to the Kandang Kerbau maternity and children's hospital.[43]

Compared to school students, university students continued their studies. 'Scores' of University of Malaya undergraduates were also taken ill with influenza, unhappy that they had to take their mid-year examinations in the middle of May.[44] The examiners handed out aspirin to coughing students, some of whom were worried about catching the disease twice at the examination venue.[45] The Chinese-medium Nanyang University briefly suspended its classes, although it did not seem many of its students were ill.[46] It was only in 1965 that a clinical study of an influenza outbreak in Singapore in 1963–1964 ascertained that undergraduates in prolonged contact with one another were more susceptible to infection.[47]

In early May, the two clinics of the Singapore Harbour Board close to the port of Singapore treated over 300 influenza patients. At the War Department, 200 staff fell ill with influenza, as did a similar number of employees of the Singapore Traction Company, which prevented five buses from running. Employees of major private firms such as Fraser and Neave and Cold Storage also reported sick.[48] The following day, many businesses in Chinatown had to close as apparently 'seven out of eight workers' fell ill.[49] Making things worse for business was 'leadswinging' by staff who were fit.[50]

Amid these signs of a worsening outbreak, the LF government's response was strikingly minimalist. Influenza was not made a notifiable disease – a major step back from the colonial government's decision to do so in 1918. The MOH was resigned to the inevitable spread of infection throughout the island, citing the dense population residing along the Singapore River.[51] Minister Braga explained to the Legislative Assembly:

> The extreme conditions of overcrowding, particularly in the town, must certainly have favoured the spread. It must also be realised from the epidemiological point of view that the entire island of Singapore is one composite urban unit with denser aggregations north and south of the Singapore River. In consequence, an island-wide spread was inevitable and indeed the spread to the Federation of Malaya was inevitable.[52]

The government overlayed this claim with the insistence that the epidemic was a mild one.[53]

It praised the 'untiring and unselfish efforts of doctors, nurses and dispensers' in coping with the outbreak.[54]

Official statements suggest that biomedical science argued against – not for – a robust response. Government officials and many medical officers were of the opinion that nothing could be done to stem the epidemic. Braga acknowledged its economic repercussions but emphasised that 'the hazards and distress posed could be likened to a common cold of equal incidence'.[55] Cinema operators tried to allay public fears by running newspaper advertisements that they would spray antiseptic in the theatres after every show. Braga dismissed the measure, saying, 'It won't do a bit of good' – a contrast to the colonial government's vigorous dust elimination efforts during the 1918 pandemic.[56] The advertisements disappeared.

Braga also dismissed more effective measures:

> If there was a preventive like issuing masks and so forth, we would have done it willingly to factory workers and others but I said that there is no known preventive.[57]

Instead, he urged people to refrain from going to crowded places, adding that the situation was well under control.[58]

These views were echoed by the Director of Medical Services, Dr Muthiah Doraisingham, who assured the people that 'There is nothing alarming'.[59] He described the government's response starkly, 'Let it burn out. We can do nothing about it'. Like Braga, Doraisingham dismissed the use of sterilised masks as a preventive measure, saying, 'I don't want to give false hopes to anyone by asking them to wear them'.[60] The official discourse was that of a quickly passing event that posed little danger to the population at large. It seemed to be based on scientific evidence but was really a justification for the government's relative inaction.

Interestingly, officials in Singapore recalled the 1918 pandemic. A spokesperson for the MOH assured on 6 May that 'There is nothing to worry about. It is not anything like the epidemic of the 1918–19 period'.[61] The WHO itself had helped sustain the memory of that pandemic as the rationale for its influenza control programme after the war.[62] But the 1918 event turned out to be a double-edged sword. It raised public and media concerns about a second and more deadly wave of influenza, thus undercutting official assurances. Early in the outbreak, doctors tried to persuade the public that there was as yet no need to worry about a second wave when the current outbreak had not run its course.[63] But the *Straits Times* was more pessimistic in its commentary on 11 May:

> Australia intends to quarantine suspects from Singapore, but if quarantine is successful it will be for the first time in the history of influenza.
>
> Nothing stopped the great pandemic of 1918–19. No country escaped it. Twenty million people died, and fifty times as many went down with the disease – over a third of the world's population.[64]

The government's main preventive move was to urge people, including children, to stay away from crowded places, especially if they were sick. Attempts were made to prevent or discourage people from going to these places.[65] The first measure relied on suasion and transferred responsibility for controlling the outbreak to the population, while the second was applicable only to certain public places and had a limited effect. Cinemas were closed (as in 1918) and their business suffered throughout the month of May. But attempts to sway people's behaviour and movement were ineffective or impracticable as in past influenza outbreaks. The peaks of attendances for influenza at government and City Council hospitals and clinics were on Mondays, and before and after Vesak Day, a Buddhist holiday. Clearly, people had been out on the weekends and public holidays.[66] The MOH admitted that 'as many [patients] were not ill enough to be confined to bed, they moved freely in the community and spread infection around'.[67]

Perhaps with the 1918 outbreak in mind, Minister Braga and his Education counterpart Chew Swee Kee conferred and decided to close Singapore's 670 schools at an early point in the epidemic, on 8 May. This sent home over a quarter of a million children and harkened to action taken during the 1918 influenza pandemic in Singapore. Explaining the closure, Braga listed three reasons: the high risk of children being infected while travelling to and from schools, their transmitting the illness to family members and the difficulty of holding classes with many teachers struck down by influenza.[68] Chew added, 'It is unfortunate but the epidemic spread so rapidly and there was nothing else we could do.'[69] He again urged parents to keep their children at home and away from crowded places.

In mid-May, Braga was confident enough to publicly urge the Australian government to send medical observers to learn from Singapore's efforts.[70] On 16 May, however, the *Straits Times* criticised the closure of schools as a mistake; the decision should have been left to headmasters, as the Federation government had done.[71] Interestingly, the Chinese-medium *Nanyang Siang Pau* supported the move in preventing the epidemic from worsening.[72] Singapore's schools remained closed for 12 days, reopening when the outbreak was deemed to be diminishing (but still severe in the Federation).[73] On 20 May, the day the schools reopened, the MOH assured that the epidemic was 'decreasing rapidly' and 'within a short time it will disappear'.[74] Students gradually returned to their classrooms, though there were still absentees for a time.[75]

Safeguarding the health of children was a mark of the 1957 outbreak, in contrast to the relative lack of focus on another vulnerable group, the elderly. This reflected in part the priorities of a government presiding over the fast-growing population with a high fertility rate in post-war Singapore. The City Council observed that year that 'The population of Singapore has an abnormally high proportion of young people'.[76] On 13 May, there was a 'near-panic among mothers in crowded areas' at the death of an eight-month-old baby, even though the cause of death had not yet been established.[77] It was later thought that the baby had died of meningitis.[78] Similarly there was concern whether four Chinese children at St. Andrew's Hospital had recently died of influenza.[79]

## The Healthcare System and the Singapore Flu

While the government did little in terms of prevention and containment, the healthcare system emerged from the outbreak with more credit. It was part of the late-colonial civil service, operating separately from the elected administration. It had also undergone considerable Malayanisation to promote locals to senior positions within the framework of decolonisation. The healthcare system made nation-wide efforts to provide treatment and relief for patients, and to determine the number of cases. This reflected its growing capacity under the aegis of the Medical Plan.

Across urban and rural Singapore, various demographic groups of patients were treated at the hospitals, maternal and child welfare clinics and school health centres. In the seven maternal and infant clinics it ran, the City Council reported that 'crowds continued to throng daily, seeking consultation on management problems'.[80] There, 10,500 of the 25,870 attendances in the month of May were for influenza, among them babies, toddlers and mothers.[81] The clinics also saw adult patients, as they did not turn away whole families who arrived for treatment. This openness was, the council rationalised, 'to win the confidence of the mothers sufficiently for them to accept our Health Education teaching'.[82] It was a milestone in Singapore history that illustrated the growing ability of public health institutions to win the hearts and minds of the people as the island transitioned towards self-rule.

Mobile dispensaries were also formed to deliver services to people living in rural areas and supplement the work of outpatient dispensaries. Eighteen people from rural areas (a miniscule number) were admitted into a hospital or clinic for influenza, all of whom were subsequently discharged. There was public criticism that rural residents had to travel far from outlying areas such as Changi, Katong and Tampines to the SGH for treatment.[83] On the other hand, a 'floating dispensary' (a boat) brought twice-weekly services and medicines to the offshore islands.[84] The Medical Department was thus able to extend its influence into areas where this had been lacking before the war. It also provided drugs, equipment and facilities to voluntary clinics that were set up during the epidemic. Though the government may be taken to task for lacking a coherent influenza policy, the healthcare system's work was testament to its growing capabilities in the British-organised programme of decolonisation.

These were mixed attempts, not without predictable difficulties of manpower, logistics and technical expertise, to handle a sudden infectious disease outbreak. As Minister Braga noted, some of the healthcare staff worked 'fifteen hours a day on their feet'.[85] Elective surgeries in the hospitals had to be minimised to free up staff to deal with influenza cases. The spread of influenza deterred mothers from bringing their children for diphtheria immunisation at clinics that were treating large numbers of flu patients.[86] At each of the three City Council's outdoor dispensaries, there were 750 daily attendances, thrice the usual number; more than two-thirds were seen for influenza. But the higher volume of cases also caused 'great congestion' that worsened the rising contagion. Many staff fell sick but continued to work long hours.[87]

It was through the efforts of Singapore's growing corps of medical doctors and virologists that the outbreak ended up placing the island on the world pandemic map. Post-war Singapore was a node in the rejuvenated system of international health helmed by the WHO, which sought to transfer biomedical expertise from the metropole to Asian nationalists in the colonies.[88] At the onset of the outbreak, virologists at the University of Malaya led by Dr Lim Kok Ann began the work of isolating the influenza virus from samples taken from infected residents on Pulau Brani. He did so within three days. Suspecting that it was a virus though he could not identify it, he had the samples packed in iced thermos flasks and sent to the WHO Influenza Centre in London.[89] Other samples were sent to the Commonwealth Serum Laboratories, the Walter Reed Medical Centre in the US and to a medical facility in Melbourne.[90] Lim made newspaper headlines for discovering a new virus, which angered his head of department Professor James Henry Hale, as the head of department was usually given some credit in such cases. Lim clarified that despite the newspaper reports, the discovery of the virus was a team effort.[91]

It was through the work of Lim and his team that the virus was identified as a new strain of influenza called Influenza A Singapore 1/57, a H3N2 virus. In layman terms, it became known as the 'Singapore flu', though its more common name was the 'Asian flu'.[92] Due to the Singaporeans' efforts, the clinical course and features of the illness were described in detail – more so than in previous pandemics. In addition, there were at least two local studies of the outbreak – at the Singapore Naval Base (discussed in the next section) and a closed group study of over 1,800 cases in the Police Force, yielding information on relapses and complications. These studies and virological research at the university again pointed to a fast-developing healthcare system in Singapore. The *Straits Times* hailed the locals' role in alerting the world to a new flu strain, though it submitted a 'mild protest' at the naming of the outbreak after the city-state.[93] Lim subsequently became Director of the WHO Influenza Centre in Singapore.

The litmus test for the healthcare system was the ability to gauge the scope and severity of the outbreak. This had been problematic in 1890 and 1918. In the month of May, the government recorded 77,211 cases and 162,093 attendances for influenza at its hospitals and clinics. The MOH noted that Singapore's 300-odd private clinics were also kept busy during the month.[94] It found the epidemic to have penetrated deeply into the community, affecting males and females equally, as well as infants and young children. It was deemed to be 'markedly present' in Asians, with few infections among Europeans.[95] New infected inmates brought the outbreak to the Pearl's Hill Prison, leading to 35 hospital admissions and over a hundred outpatient cases. At the Naval Base, 800 Asian employers – a tenth of the total workforce – were infected, with a fifth of the cases severe enough to be hospitalised.[96]

But the key figure was the number of cases at the national level. The total official number of 77,211 cases was a large one, comprising 5.5 per cent of Singapore's population of 1.4 million at the time. However, the real figure could not be known with any certainty. The number excluded cases not seen at government institutions and those that occurred after May, as influenza statistics were documented only during that month. Still, the large figure reflected a fairly comprehensive epidemiology at work. On 7 May, the *Singapore Free Press* had estimated nearly 150,000 people to have been infected by the virus in the past four days, adding that the actual number would have been higher.[97] The official number places in perspective what the likely figures were in previous influenza outbreaks. During the 1918 pandemic, the General Hospital had admitted only 314 cases – the serious ones. In 1957, an experienced doctor declared that he had never encountered such an influenza epidemic in the 30 years he had worked in Singapore – he had clearly left out the 1918 predecessor.[98]

At the same time, in the absence of notification, the statistics for the 1957 outbreak were really estimates, as before the war. As the *Straits Times* observed, many Asians still did not seek treatment for influenza at government hospitals and clinics.[99] The MOH conceded that 'it is not possible even to make a guess at its [influenza's] real incidence'.[100] When asked about a vaccine for influenza, Professor Hale said that it was unnecessary as the disease had infected most people in Singapore and Malaya.[101] A large proportion of the population still lay beyond the biomedical system. The extent of social avoidance was revealed in a case of 302 hawkers charged with illegal hawking. Arriving at the court, a fifth of them (66 persons) were suspected of having influenza and sent home.[102] But the case also suggests that the post-war state was more vigilant about detecting carriers of infection.

What of the death rate? The official reports do not offer a figure. Again, we have an answer from Lee et al., who tabulated 680 excess deaths or an excess death rate of 0.47 per cent in the 1957 pandemic, including those who died from complications. This was much lower than the rate of 1.8 per cent they estimated for the pandemic years of 1918–1920. The difference was likely due in part to the general improvement in socioeconomic and health conditions in Singapore in the intervening decades.[103] Regardless, Lee's numbers are much higher than official figures for the 1957 event. The MOH reported only 87 influenza deaths in the hospitals, despite this being more than double the 20- to -30odd deaths from 1951. Among these were 28 deaths at the SGH, where none had occurred in the past two years. The number of deaths from pneumonia at the hospital was 55 more than the previous year.[104] In his report to the Legislative Assembly on 22 May, Minister Braga stated that four people had died of influenza, but even this impossibly small number had not been clinically confirmed. He added vaguely that there were 'a few other fatal cases in which findings suggest influenza but these showed signs of complications such as broncho-pneumonia, heart disease and nervous manifestations'.[105]

Despite the government's claims about a mild outbreak, there is evidence that the 1957 pandemic was a serious one when complications and age groups are taken into account. Of the 77,211 cases seen in May, 326 (or 0.4%) were serious enough to be admitted to hospital, compared to 35 the previous year and 30 in 1955. Three-fifths of these admissions were children. The MOH stated that although most cases were mild, about 13 per cent of the patients had at least one relapse within a fortnight, while half that number (1,103 cases or 1.4 per cent of all cases) developed complications such as bronchitis and tracheitis. There were 22 deaths due to complications from broncho-pneumonia and six from myocarditis or heart failure. Pneumonia could be deadly, especially among infants and older people. Among the 28 registered deaths at the SGH, 21 were infants and young children.[106] In the urban area, the City Council reported 73 certified influenza deaths, a large rise compared to 24 the year before. But more significant was the total of 1,222 deaths and a death rate of 15.6 reported by the City Council in the month of May, nearly double the monthly average of 653 deaths and an 8.52 death rate for the year. The epidemic was likely responsible for much of the excess mortality in May 1957.[107]

## Decolonising Public Health in the Nuclear Age

More broadly, the pandemic was a significant episode in Singapore's path to statehood. It reflected a period of heightened political and social activism, driven by a critical attitude towards the colonial system.[108] British-led decolonisation and action plans were not the only forces that impinged on sickness and health in post-war Singapore. There was also socio-medical activism that arose (semi-)independently of the state. In 1947, a group of European and Asian doctors, professionals and businessmen came together to form a non-governmental organisation called the Singapore Anti-Tuberculosis Association. Critical of the colonial government's initial refusal to mount a tuberculosis policy, the association shouldered a tremendous amount of anti-tuberculosis work in the 1950s, especially X-ray screening, outpatient treatment and care for the chronically ill.[109]

In addition, the decolonisation process struggled to accommodate new political forces and alliances. The British had preferred a gradual pace of constitutional evolution led by a moderate party. Throughout the 1950s, however, Singapore politics shifted to the left and the mass base broadened to include the working class. Political parties, trade unions and other interest groups joined forces to articulate their respective visions of an independent and unified Malaya including Singapore. The most progressive of these coalitions was led by the People's Action Party (PAP), which fronted an alliance of left-wing labour unions, student unions and rural associations. In the second half of the decade, the PAP and its allies adopted radical socialist ideologies and methods, which the colonial and LF governments deemed to be perpetrated by the communist underground.[110] Despite its name, the LF was neither a popular government elected on a universal franchise nor a party of the working class. It was a minority coalition government, increasingly perceived as a pro-colonial government by the majority of the Chinese-speaking and labouring population. The proof of this was when the LF was decisively defeated by the PAP in the general elections of 1959.

Socially, Singapore's population became more politically aware at the same time they were further integrated into the expanding structures of the post-war state – in healthcare, housing, welfare, education, and the economy. Nationalist mobilisation and state integration were two sides of the same coin. While they might criticise the colonial healthcare system as inadequate for the people, nationalists looked to transform people's outlook and behaviour over matters of health and disease. This was part of forging a social compact for the nation-state. Nationalists supported greater use of the healthcare system, public health campaigns and medical surveillance. Post-war healthcare in Singapore was thus a maker of citizenship: it was the state's obligation to provide healthcare for the people while it was the people's duty to support these measures.

It was in such a context that the left-wing National Union of General Workers, formed only in March 1957, wrote to the LF government in mid-May, alleging, 'The Health Ministry has failed to control the epidemic and has not taken adequate steps to stop its spread'.[111] It demanded an inquiry to be held into the causes of the epidemic, the reasons for its spread and the efforts of the government to control it. The union wanted the inquiry to be conducted by an independent tribunal of doctors and members of the public.[112] Dr Doraisingham dismissed it, maintaining that the causes of the epidemic were the same as those in Japan and elsewhere and thus impossible to resolve.[113] The *Straits Times*, a pro-colonial, anti-communist daily, decried the unionists as 'victims of the oldest trick on the Communist trouble-spreaders' bag'.[114] In other words, the union was labelled a communist front organisation. Members of the union had been detained without trial for allegedly subversive activities.[115] This was the first and only real criticism of the government's handling of the epidemic.

Surprisingly, though the 1957 outbreak was the first influenza epidemic in Singapore history to be the object of political controversy, the issue was a minor one. The controversy centred on Minister Braga's two-week trip to Japan in early April, where he had visited medical institutions and teaching hospitals. He then delayed making a report on the influenza outbreak in Singapore to the Legislative Assembly, finally doing so in a session of the assembly on 22 May, when the event was subsiding. After hearing Braga's report, John Ebe of the Liberal-Socialist Party, the biggest opposition group, pressed Braga on the causes of the outbreak, as the National Union of General Workers had done. However, the Liberal-Socialists were not a left-wing party, favouring gradualist political evolution. Ebe also wanted to know if Braga's visit to Japan benefited Singapore's efforts to manage the epidemic, particularly as Braga went on the trip himself instead of sending MOH officials.[116]

The minister replied that his trip was a goodwill mission rather than a purely medical study, as he had also met with the Japanese Prime Minister, helping to cement relations between Japan and Singapore.[117] On the question of confining the outbreak, he offered a telling explanation,

> The only other course – which was unthinkable – was to close the port of Singapore and all ports of the Federation and the Siamese border against the entry of any craft whatsoever, and impose martial law to keep people in their homes until the disease had spent itself on a world-wide career.[118]

The leader of the Liberal-Socialists, Lim Choon Mong, made the preposterous allegation that 'the Minister's goodwill visit to Japan probably has brought back this virus'.[119] This caused Braga to leap to his feet and shout across the floor that the outbreak could not have been prevented.

Having seemed to have done little to control the epidemic, Braga was further pressed to justify his trip. Assemblyman Ahmad Ibrahim, an Independent who later joined the PAP during the 1959 elections, asked if the trip had been worth its cost 'in terms of dollars and cents', while R. Jumabhoy, another Independent, wanted to know the amount of public money spent. Braga's response was more subdued this time. After conferring with the Financial Secretary, he replied, 'I must have notice of this question', and asked for time to find out the answer.[120]

Overall, the decolonisation of public health during the influenza epidemic did not go very far in the Legislative Assembly. Only two opposition members from a right-of-centre party and two Independents raised questions of a relatively limited nature. It seemed the rest of the opposition, particularly the left, accepted the essence of the government's response. The LF administration could have been taken to task for not making influenza notifiable, for not mandating the use of masks or for failing to provide essential medical services for the low-income group (see below on the voluntary efforts). There were no more debates on the outbreak in the assembly after 22 May.

Greater was the social gulf between the colonial government and the low-income Asian population. Being a disease that affected all, influenza epidemics are often perceived to be classless and egalitarian events.[121] However, there is anecdotal evidence that the epidemic's impact varied by social class. In the underdeveloped rural area of Singapore, residents often had larger families with more children. They were doubly handicapped by influenza: the sheer distance from the city, where most medical facilities were located, added to their reduced incomes and wages. Unlike during the 1918 pandemic, the 1957 outbreak hit the rural area hard. As the *Nanyang Siang Pau* reported, many of the rural poor could not even afford medicines. It called for charitable organisations to purchase and distribute cooling products such as herbal tea to these villages, and for companies to do the same for their employees.[122]

In the city itself, the *Singapore Free Press* reported midway through the outbreak that the low-income families of casual hawkers and peddlers in Chinatown were suffering greatly. Social workers related that influenza had struck down the sole breadwinner or able-bodied person in many families, or in the worst of cases, both parents. A social worker said: 'In some instances whole families lie side by side praying for the infection to disappear.' Doctors warned that those patients who were too poor or too ill to seek treatment were at the greatest risk of the disease. Many of them, relying on herbs and the promises of 'quacks' while continuing to work, were further spreading the virus in Chinatown.[123] These included daily-rated workers on meagre pay who had to choose between losing their incomes by staying home or continuing to work while infectious.[124] In an unresolved tragedy, a 64-year-old man hanged himself several days after recovering from influenza. His son, a labourer, could not understand why his father decided to commit suicide when he appeared to be well.[125]

Attempting to mediate between the state and the people were two forms of social responses: the new anti-colonial, nation-centred activism and the more traditional, community-driven self-help networks based on kinship and ethnicity that had long existed before the war. Both responses were in evidence during the outbreak and interacted with each other – a sign of a country in transition. Thus, influenza's impact was mitigated to some extent by these efforts. The Malay Welfare Council sent rice and other foodstuffs to the Malay residents of Pulau Sudong upon hearing of its outbreak of influenza.[126] Hundreds of church attendees in Singapore prayed for a quick end to the epidemic.[127] But it ought to be remembered that these spontaneous community efforts did not avert all hardship for the low-income population.

Moved by the *Singapore Free Press* report of 14 May, Richard Lim Chuan Hoe of the LF and Deputy Speaker of the Legislative Assembly mooted the idea of a free emergency clinic for the sick in Chinatown. The clinic was set up at Pearl's Hill and run by volunteer doctors, nurses and members of the public. Operating daily from 6 pm to 9 pm, it treated 130 patients on its first evening, mostly children.[128] Government doctors and nurses volunteered their services after work. Among the female volunteers was W.W. Yung, a qualified nurse and wife of the Singapore director of the WHO. The LF government supported the project while the MOH agreed to supply medicines and equipment to the clinic.[129] A second free clinic mooted by Lim was later opened at Rangoon Road.[130]

But pandemic disease could also be divisive. As in the 1918 pandemic, the 1957 outbreak fractured the community. Among those who complied with the government's advice were adults and schoolchildren who voluntarily absented themselves from work and school. Attendances at public swimming pools fell in the month of May.[131] On the other hand, a physician from the University of Malaya decried influenza patients who were still moving about in the community as 'criminals'.[132] There was public anger at 'foolish parents' who ignored the official injunctions and brought their children to amusement places, particularly on the Vesak public holiday on 14 May. They were accused of sabotaging the government's efforts to control the outbreak.[133] 'D. Soon', writing to the *Straits Times*, asked for the government to withdraw 'dirty notes' (infected currency) from circulation and have them destroyed.[134]

As in previous influenza outbreaks, the densely populated places of Singapore were rife not only with disease but also rumours on the origins of the epidemic on the one hand and miraculous tales of treatment on the other. While the government wanted to avoid giving people false hope, its failure to control the epidemic aroused great fear among them. This in turn fuelled speculation and rumours as alternatives to science. Deaths that seemed mysterious fanned those sentiments, which were spread by word of mouth. Dr Doraisingham had to dismiss rumours about two children dying from influenza at the SGH.[135] On 16 May, doctors at the hospital had to ask the police to conduct inquests into the deaths of four people who died shortly after their admission, including a two-year-old child.[136]

This epidemic of panic and rumourmongering could be seen on the offshore island of Pulau Sudong. There, the newspapers reported, the entire population of 455 was 'gripped by fear' when three residents were believed to have died from influenza; some 300 locals were even thought to have been taken ill with the disease at one point.[137] The government stepped in to clarify that the figures were 'grossly exaggerated'.[138] The actual number of cases was only 21 (11 children and 10 adults) and the trio of deaths was due to other ailments.[139] A hastily organised investigation by the MOH found two further (mild) cases of influenza and six convalescents.[140]

But the most interesting of the rumours stemmed from the Cold War and had adherents among medical scientists. Norman Wingate Pirie and Professor Sydney Cross Harland had seemingly supported the theory that the influenza virus had mutated due to increased radiation from atomic bomb tests in Siberia and the Pacific.[141] What was interesting in Singapore was how such theorising filtered downwards and outwards to other social groups and societies in the context of a public health emergency. The coffee shops and five-footways (verandahs) of Chinatown and Queenstown New Town (a satellite town of low-cost housing built by the Singapore Improvement Trust) were soon rife with speculation that the flu was due to fallout from Soviet hydrogen bomb tests in the first half of the decade.[142]

The University of Malaya dismissed these rumours as 'utter nonsense'.[143] But educated people were not easily deterred. A writer to the *Straits Times* asked,

> I have heard it said that the present influenza epidemic which has struck the people of Asia from Japan to Malaya is not influenza at all, but some mysterious after-effect of atomic explosions – presumably those carried out in Siberia. Is there any truth in this?[144]

Another writer pondered, 'Is the present outbreak of influenza the result of recent pyrotechnic displays of atom bombs?'[145] The newspaper replied sardonically,

> This present outbreak of influenza has no more to do with atom bombs than the outbreak in Europe after World War I had to do with the Angel of Mons. It has also no connections with flying saucers![146]

These conspiracy theories were not versions of the proverbial 'old wives' tale'.[147] They were testament to the politics of the Cold War, having to live under the fear of mutual assured destruction in the nuclear age. Misguided and baseless they might be, these rumours reflected the adapted globalism of the masses in Singapore, as understood by the working class in Chinatown.

The government might claim the virus to be unavoidable, but locals were willing to undertake their own interventions to keep themselves well. This highlights the limits of decolonisation, failing to convince the people on matters of health and disease. Though large numbers turned up at government dispensaries, others turned to traditional remedies. Among the Chinese, their long-trusted treatments were based on the received notion of 'heatiness', which was in turn part of the Chinese cosmological paradigm of *yin* and *yang*. Heatiness was held to be due to an imbalance of *yin* and *yang* inside the body, which would be corrected by curative agents that restored the balance. In 1957, forerunners of what is known as Traditional Chinese Medicine today offered treatments that claimed to do this.

An example was the 'Three Legs' brand of 'fever powder', popular for relieving headaches and fever. The product was manufactured by a local company, which stepped up its production during the epidemic.[148] Other makers of Chinese medicinal products did the same. Within a week of the outbreak, Chinese medical halls had run out of Guan Jilin tea and other cooling products believed to be effective against the flu.[149] Among them was the 'Axe' brand of medicated oil, which provided relief for headaches and body aches, while helping to keep infection at bay.[150] One patient claimed that the oil could prevent the spread of the virus in public (which did the containment policy no favours).[151] Many low-income Chinese subscribed to the concept of heatiness and trusted such remedies. But their beliefs were also circumscribed by the political geography of state healthcare in post-war Singapore. For rural patients, travelling to a government clinic and waiting in a line for up to three hours for medicine made little sense, whereas self-medication did.[152]

On 6 June, when the worst of the outbreak had passed, the Chairman of the National Association of Chinese Medicine Practitioners, Zheng Mantian, made a public speech on how Traditional Chinese Medicine had helped combat the epidemic. Because illnesses such as influenza were attributed to the convergence of the north and south winds, causing fever, traditional Chinese remedies sought to detangle the winds and remove heatiness from the body. Sang Ju Yin (a cooling drink) and Yin Qiao San (granules with a cooling effect) were two out of 130 ways of treating flu and colds in Chinese medicine, which also included acupuncture. Zheng argued that Traditional Chinese Medicine was superior to Western medicine.[153]

There was still a distinction between this school of Chinese medicine and the miracle cures that were widely sought and claimed during the epidemic. As Western-trained doctors erred on the side of the caution in the public discourse, the working class was also 'relying on "quacks" who dispense a brew made from herbs, roots and carrots', as the *Singapore Free Press* reported on 13 May.[154] The *Nanyang Siang Pau* observed that Chinese fortune tellers and scammers were swindling the ignorant, especially in rural areas where people were less educated and modern medicine was lacking.[155] The *Sin Chew Jit Poh*, another Chinese daily, attributed influenza to sharp weather fluctuations that upset the bodily balance; it also advised people who were ill against self-medicating but to consult a doctor, whether one of modern or traditional medicine.[156]

In the absence of effective state measures or medicine, business opportunism followed closely on the heels of the epidemic. Advised by *sinseh* (traditional Chinese physicians), hundreds of Chinese women believed that carrots and green Chinese olives, when boiled into a juice, could cure influenza, as did watermelon. The *Nanyang Siang Pau* spoke to a man who consumed raw olives and grapes soaked in water as a medical hall counselled; he claimed the remedy to be beneficial.[157] Hawkers happily raised the prices of carrots from 60 cents to $2 per kati (approximately 604 grams), watermelon from 40 cents to $1 each, and olives from 10 to 25 cents for seven.[158] A fruit seller reportedly bought an olive tree for $10 and made ten times the amount.[159] The price of a kati of grapes more than doubled or even tripled in some cases.[160] During the 1918 influenza pandemic, potatoes had been the curative agent of choice.

One continuity of the colonial system was the failure of decolonisation to eradicate the theory of innate racial differences. The old racialist influences lingered, if less strongly. In a report on the epidemic on 9 May, the *Straits Times* noted that the 17,000 Europeans in Singapore had 'almost all escaped it'. By contrast, many doctors held that the Malays were the worst hit due to their lowered biological resistance during the Ramadan. Most postal workers struck down by influenza were Malays, while nearly all the 46 flu patients living in a small urban kampong of 450 people near Rangoon Road were children of Malay and Indian ethnicity.[161] An experienced European doctor told the *Straits Times*, 'I know that many Asians are having a bad time. I've had reports of them fainting at work'.[162] These claims derived from the old belief in the varying biological immunity and resistance of 'unequal races'. It was still influential in 1957, as it had done four decades earlier in the previous influenza pandemic.

The racial discourse was mixed with other familiar factors such as the environment and lifestyle. The Deputy City Health Officer, Dr J. Cameron, disputed the claim that Malays were worst affected, as they 'lead a more open-air life than other races'. Another doctor, Ronald Heywood Bland, formerly the Director of Medical Services and an adviser to the MOH, concurred, as it was the low-income people residing in congested housing who were worst affected by the outbreak.[163] Another *Straits Times* article wondered if 'a different diet, and different eating habits' of Europeans and Asians were also factors, as the latter dined at hawker and street stalls that frequently transmitted the virus.[164] When a reader in Malaya noted that Europeans largely escaped the epidemic because they were more health-conscious about their diet than Asians, the *Straits Times* returned to the racial immunity thesis:

> You could also put it down to the fact that most Europeans had been exposed to coughs, colds and influenza since childhood and have therefore built up a stronger resistance to it.[165]

The diverse explanations showed that the racial vantage point persisted in a time of decolonisation, if no longer as absolute as before. The idea that Europeans were biologically superior to Asians was at odds with the transfer of political and economic power from the former to the latter. On why Europeans appeared little affected by influenza, the MOH offered a combination of racial, class and environmental explanations:

> Whether this was an immuniological [*sic*] or sociological phenomenon it is difficult to state. It is perhaps a combination of both because European children were certainly susceptible given adequate contact whereas in European adults a few cases occurring even in barrack room conditions are not followed by marked spread. Upper class Asians were not affected but this again may be combination of both factors, better living conditions but also they are frequently well travelled.[166]

At the Naval Base, Professor Hale from the University of Malaya and Dr Alwin Smith, a visiting scholar from the WHO, conducted a sample survey of 18,391 persons over 38 days during the epidemic. They found that 19 per cent of Asians and 6.98 per cent of Europeans had contracted the flu.[167] So some Europeans had fallen ill. And rather than racial immunity alone, the differences between Asians and Europeans were also attributed to contingent factors such as living conditions and diet.[168] But the racial perspective was still there and would continue into the post-colonial period.

### In Lieu of an Influenza Policy

The memory of the 1918 pandemic stoked fears of a second deadly wave. These anxieties had surfaced at the start of the 1957 outbreak but grew when it subsided. In mid-July, Dr Doraisingham had to address these concerns, stating that an attack by a new strain of influenza was really a new attack, not a second wave. As this was not much of an assurance, he added that the population had gained immunity from the May outbreak so another major severe epidemic was unlikely. He also said that a vaccine that was developed for the May outbreak might not be effective for the new strain.[169] Dr Lim Kok Ann concurred that, with the epidemic over and a second outbreak unlikely, it was unnecessary to import vaccines for influenza.[170] Nevertheless, in January 1958, a vaccine for the 'Asian flu' was imported into Singapore from Britain by Glaxo Laboratories, purportedly 90 per cent effective.[171] This was followed by an American vaccine developed by the Lederle Laboratories in March.[172]

Thus Singapore denied the likelihood of a second wave while continuing to prepare for a new influenza outbreak. A number of measures were implemented that did not quite amount to a full policy. Exactly a year later after the epidemic, the SGH declared that it had been maintaining a chart of all influenza cases treated at government clinics so that it would not be caught off-guard again by another outbreak.[173] In May 1959, the PAP came to power as Singapore became a fully self-governing state.[174] But no influenza policy was forthcoming from the new administration either. In August, Lee Kooi Jong, a Singapore audiologist, called for a survey on whether the epidemic had caused congenital deafness among babies born during the outbreak, as two cases had occurred in England.[175] An ear, nose and throat specialist and a private practitioner in Singapore thought that this was possible.[176] But the new Minister for Health Ahmad Ibrahim rejected the proposed survey as a waste of the government's limited resources.[177]

In 1960, a *Singapore Free Press* commentary vowed that though most people in Singapore had gained immunity during the previous outbreak, the island would be ready if the influenza returned in a mutated form.[178] That year, Lim Kok Ann, as Director of the WHO Influenza Centre in Singapore, stated that he was researching the 'Japanese B' influenza virus, though admittedly progress was slow.[179] Information on influenza in Singapore in the late 1950s and 1960s is generally sketchy. In 1965, Dora S.K. Tan referred to influenza as a 'diagnostic dump for any respiratory disease of obscure origin' in Malaysia. This was attributed mostly to the actions of untrained rural and estate hospital assistants, but also to medical practitioners.[180]

Influenza was endemic after 1957. In 1958–1960, the Department of Social Medicine and Public Health of the University of Malaya carried out a survey of illness at three sites: a large rural village, a densely populated site in the city and an upper-class residential area. The survey found that influenza (together with tuberculosis and skin disease) was a common affliction in all three areas, despite the varied socio-economic conditions, ethnicity and gender of the residents. Influenza outbreaks were detected in these areas in May–August 1959, October–November 1959 and March–April 1960.[181]

A notable outbreak in the early 1960s was the influenza pandemic in the Soviet Union and East Germany in January 1965. This led to a local outbreak with 114 hospital admissions and five deaths. A *Straits Times* report worried about the likelihood of another major outbreak in Malaysia (which then included Singapore) due to the large numbers of travellers from Japan and Europe. It wondered whether a mass vaccination campaign was necessary to prevent a repeat of 1957. The question was posed to three leading medical experts, Dr Ug See Yook (the Director of Medical Services), Dr Kandiah Kanagaratnam (the Deputy Director of Medical Services) and now-Professor Lim Kok Ann. The trio agreed that this was unnecessary, as vaccines were expensive (costing $4.60 a dose) and the virus had to be isolated. It would take at least two weeks to mount a major operation to immunise at least half a million people in Singapore. The Soviet outbreak lasted only about 10 days, Lim said, so such an operation could not be completed in time here.[182]

The 1957 influenza pandemic caught Singapore at a crossroads. The healthcare system was more developed than before the Second World War, owing to policy reforms under the aegis of British decolonisation. As the outbreak reached Singapore and grew, the system – from hospitals to rural clinics and mobile facilities – responded more effectively than in previous epidemics. Surveys of infected communities were carried out and virologists from the university isolated the virus. Nevertheless, the old public health limitations from the 1918 flu pandemic persisted. The Labour Front government did not have a policy to curtail the spread of influenza other than closing down some public places and urging ill people to stay home. The closure of schools addressed the problem of growing numbers of children in post-war Singapore, though it had been adopted in 1918. Work, trade and industry in the colony continued throughout the epidemic month of May, contributing to the spread of influenza. The wearing of masks and other containment measures were dismissed by government officials.

Despite the weak measures, the 1957 influenza pandemic was historically important. It showed a continuing belief that influenza outbreaks were impossible to stop. The LF government quickly conceded its role, while the political opposition did not dwell critically on its handling of the crisis. The epidemic revealed the decolonisation process to be uneven. The British had sought to nurture an elected government that would fulfil two criteria. One, this government would inherit a modified version of the colonial administration (including the health department) that the British deemed acceptable. Two, the government would represent the will of the people of Singapore, capable of protecting them from dangerous diseases while also able to obtain their support for public health interventions.

The LF government met the first but not the second criteria. It was a weak regime that had little support among the masses. Few people thought they were safe from influenza despite the official assurances. The working class in Chinatown and public housing estates responded to the epidemic in their own ways, seeking their own explanations for the outbreak and treatments for sickness. Lim Yew Hock's government was a historical anachronism as Singapore politics moved to the left throughout the 1950s. This was confirmed by the 1959 elections when the People's Action Party came to power. A large number of low-income people received little government assistance and suffered illness and the loss of livelihood during the outbreak. Emergency voluntary efforts had to be organised to compensate for the services that the state failed to provide. Despite achievements in other aspects of public health, the 1957 flu epidemic showed that a national health policy was still some years away. In the 1960s, self-governing Singapore continued its political evolution away from colonialism without an influenza policy.

## Notes

1  In 1951, Singapore's population reached a million people and its town was upgraded to the status of a city.
2  Paul H. Kratoska, *The Japanese Occupation of Malaya: A Social and Economic History* (London: C. Hurst, 1998).
3  MDAR 1946.
4  *Syonan Shimbun*, 13 September 1942, p. 6.
5  MDAR 1948, p. 24.
6  *Straits Times*, 31 January 1948, p. 7.
7  *Straits Times*, 7 August 1949, p. 9.
8  C.E. Gordon Smith and W.G. Thomson, 'An Outbreak of Influenza due to Type B Virus in a Residential Boys' School in Malaya', *Medical Journal of Malaya*, Vol. 10 No. 4, June 1956, pp. 332–337.
9  C.E. Gordon Smith, 'International Spread of Virus Diseases with Special Reference to Malaya', *Medical Journal of Malaya*, Vol. 10 No. 4, June 1956, pp. 63–68.
10  *Malaya Tribune*, 14 October 1947, p. 4.
11  Loh Kah Seng, *Squatters into Citizens: The 1961 Bukit Ho Swee Fire and the Making of Modern Singapore* (Singapore: NUS Press, 2013).
12  MOHAR 1946.
13  In 1946, the Malayan Union was formed, bringing all the Malay states, Penang and Malacca under British colonial rule. Two years later, the union was replaced by the Federation of Malaya.

14  Department of Social Welfare, *Five-Year Plan* (Singapore: Government Printing Office, 1949).
15  Ministry of Education, *Education Policy in the Colony of Singapore: Ten Years' Programme Adopted in Advisory Council on 7th August, 1947* (Singapore: Government Printing Office, 1948).
16  Singapore Improvement Trust, *The Work of the Singapore Improvement Trust 1927–1947* (Singapore: Singapore Improvement Trust, 1948).
17  Singapore, *Master Plan: Report of Survey* (Singapore: Printed at Government Printing Office, 1955).
18  Proceedings of the Legislative Council of Singapore, *The Medical Plan for Singapore*, 18 May 1948.
19  Loh Kah Seng and Hsu Li Yang, *Tuberculosis – The Singapore Experience, 1867–2018: Disease, Society and the State* (New York: Routledge, 2020).
20  *Singapore Free Press*, 13 May 1957, p. 1.
21  George Dehner, *Global Flu and You: A History of Influenza* (London: Reaktion Books, 2012).
22  *Straits Times*, 5 May 1957, p. 1.
23  MOHAR 1957, p. 93.
24  *Straits Times*, 4 June 1957, p. 4.
25  *Singapore Free Press*, 13 May 1957, p. 1.
26  'Influenza Epidemic (Statement)', *Official Reports of the Singapore Parliamentary Debates* (thereafter Hansard), 22 May 1957, https://sprs.parl.gov.sg/search/topic?reportid=014_19570522_S0006_T0023; MOHAR 1957; *Straits Times*, 6 May 1957, p. 7.
27  *Straits Times*, 23 May 1957, p. 8.
28  *Straits Times*, 15 December 1958, p. 4.
29  *Straits Times*, 10 May 1957, p. 1.
30  CCAR 1957.
31  *Straits Times*, 5 May 1957, p. 1.
32  MOHAR 1957, p. 90.
33  *Straits Times*, 7 May 1957, p. 1.
34  *Straits Times*, 5 May 1957, p. 1.
35  MOHAR 1957.
36  *Singapore Free Press*, 6 May 1957, p. 1.
37  *Straits Times*, 7 May 1957, p. 1.
38  *Nanyang Siang Pau*, 6 June 1957, p. 8.
39  *Singapore Free Press*, 7 May 1957, p. 1.
40  *Straits Times*, 7 May 1957, p. 1.
41  *Straits Times*, 8 May 1957, p. 15.
42  *Straits Times*, 8 May 1957, p. 15.
43  *Straits Times*, 7 May 1957, p. 1.
44  *Straits Times*, 15 May 1957, p. 1.
45  *Straits Times*, 17 May 1957, p. 1.
46  *Straits Times*, 17 May 1957, p. 1.
47  M. Yin-Coggrave and Z.N. Kadri, 'Type B Influenza in Singapore', *Singapore Medical Journal*, Vol. 6 No. 2, June 1965, pp. 71–74.
48  *Singapore Free Press*, 7 May 1957, p. 1; *Straits Times*, 10 May 1957, p. 1.
49  *Straits Times*, 8 May 1957, p. 15.
50  *Straits Times*, 9 May 1957, p. 1.
51  MOHAR 1957, p. 90.
52  'Influenza Epidemic in Singapore' (Statement by the Minister of Health), *Hansard*, 22 May 1957, https://sprs.parl.gov.sg/search/topic?reportid=022_19570522_S0004_T0015
53  *Singapore Free Press*, 7 May 1957, p. 1.

54 *Straits Times*, 10 May 1957, p. 1.
55 'Influenza Epidemic in Singapore' (Statement by the Minister of Health), *Hansard*, 22 May 1957, https://sprs.parl.gov.sg/search/topic?reportid=022_19570522_S0004_T0015
56 *Straits Times*, 15 May 1957, p. 1.
57 'Influenza Epidemic in Singapore' (Statement by the Minister of Health), *Hansard*, 22 May 1957, https://sprs.parl.gov.sg/search/topic?reportid=022_19570522_S0004_T0015
58 *Straits Times*, 10 May 1957, p. 1.
59 *Singapore Free Press*, 7 May 1957, p. 1.
60 *Straits Times*, 5 May 1957, p. 1.
61 *Singapore Free Press*, 6 May 1957, p. 1.
62 *Straits Times*, 22 July 1957, p. 6.
63 *Straits Times*, 11 May 1957, p. 1.
64 *Straits Times*, 11 May 1957, p. 6.
65 *Straits Times*, 6 May 1957, p. 7.
66 MOHAR 1957. This interpretation takes into account some people obtaining medical certificates to be absent from work on Mondays.
67 MOHAR 1957, p. 93.
68 'Influenza Epidemic in Singapore' (Statement by the Minister of Health), *Hansard*, 22 May 1957, https://sprs.parl.gov.sg/search/topic?reportid=022_19570522_S0004_T0015
69 *Straits Times*, 8 May 1957, p. 15.
70 Singapore government press statement, 'Singapore Gives Australia Advice', 31 May 1957.
71 *Straits Times*, 16 May 1957, p. 6.
72 *Nanyang Siang Pau*, 10 May 1957, p. 5.
73 *Straits Times*, 8 May 1957, p. 15.
74 *Straits Times*, 21 May 1957, p. 1.
75 *Straits Times*, 22 May 1957, p. 1.
76 CCAR 1957, p. 5.
77 *Straits Times*, 13 May 1957, p. 1.
78 *Straits Times*, 15 May 1957, p. 1.
79 *Straits Times*, 15 May 1957, p. 1.
80 CCAR 1957, p. 70.
81 CCAR 1957.
82 CCAR 1957, p. 70.
83 'Influenza Epidemic in Singapore' (Statement by the Minister of Health), *Hansard*, 22 May 1957, https://sprs.parl.gov.sg/search/topic?reportid=022_19570522_S0004_T0015
84 *Straits Times*, 16 May 1957, p. 1.
85 'Influenza Epidemic in Singapore' (Statement by the Minister of Health), *Hansard*, 22 May 1957, https://sprs.parl.gov.sg/search/topic?reportid=022_19570522_S0004_T0015
86 *Straits Times*, 20 May 1957, p. 7.
87 CCAR 1957, p. 11.
88 Sunil S. Amrith, *Decolonising International Health: India and Southeast Asia, 1930–65* (Basingstoke, Hampshire: Palgrave Macmillan, 2006).
89 *Straits Times*, 5 May 1957, p. 1.
90 *Straits Times*, 19 May 1957, p. 4.
91 National Archives of Singapore, Oral History Centre, interview with Lim Kok Ann, 3 February 1993; *Straits Times*, 25 May 1957, p. 4.
92 MOHAR 1957.
93 *Straits Times*, 31 May 1957, p. 6.

94    MOHAR 1957.
95    MOHAR 1957, p. 93.
96    *Singapore Free Press*, 11 May 1957, p. 1.
97    *Singapore Free Press*, 7 May 1957, p. 1.
98    *Straits Times*, 7 May 1957, p. 1.
99    *Straits Times*, 6 July 1957, p. 2.
100   MOHAR 1957, p. 90.
101   *Singapore Free Press*, 25 May 1957, p. 2.
102   *Straits Times*, 18 May 1957, p. 4.
103   Vernon Lee et al., 'Influenza Pandemics in Singapore, a Tropical, Globally Connected City', *Emerging Infectious Diseases*, Vol. 13 No. 7, July 2007, pp. 1052–1057.
104   MOHAR 1957.
105   'Influenza Epidemic in Singapore' (Statement by the Minister of Health), *Hansard*, 22 May 1957, https://sprs.parl.gov.sg/search/topic?reportid=022_19570522_S0004_T0015
106   MOHAR 1957.
107   CCAR 1957.
108   Michael Barr and Carl Trocki (eds), *Paths Not Taken: Political Pluralism in Postwar Singapore* (Singapore: NUS Press, 2008).
109   Loh and Hsu, *Tuberculosis: The Singapore Experience*.
110   The Malayan Communist Party was banned in Singapore and Malaya in 1948. Thereafter, communist cells operated underground in Singapore while the party fought a losing jungle war against the British and their allies.
111   *Straits Times*, 16 May 1957, p. 1.
112   *Straits Times*, 16 May 1957, p. 1.
113   *Straits Times*, 16 May 1957, p. 1.
114   *Straits Times*, 19 May 1957, p. 10.
115   *Straits Times*, 12 October 1957, p. 8.
116   *Singapore Free Press*, 20 May 1957, p. 5.
117   *Straits Times*, 23 May 1957, p. 11.
118   'Influenza Epidemic in Singapore' (Statement by the Minister of Health), *Hansard*, 22 May 1957, https://sprs.parl.gov.sg/search/topic?reportid=022_19570522_S0004_T0015
119   'Influenza Epidemic in Singapore' (Statement by the Minister of Health), *Hansard*, 22 May 1957, https://sprs.parl.gov.sg/search/topic?reportid=022_19570522_S0004_T0015
120   'Minister for Health's Visit to Japan (Benefit to Singapore)', *Hansard*, 22 May 1957, https://sprs.parl.gov.sg/search/topic?reportid=016_19570522_S0006_T0025; *Straits Times*, 23 May 1957, p. 11.
121   Niall Johnson, *Britain and the 1918–19 Influenza Pandemic: A Dark Epilogue* (London: Routledge, 2006).
122   *Nanyang Siang Pau*, 10 May 1957, p. 5.
123   *Singapore Free Press*, 14 May 1957, p. 16.
124   *Sin Chew Jit Poh*, 15 May 1957, p. 5.
125   *Straits Times*, 17 July 1957, p. 8.
126   *Straits Times*, 17 May 1957, p. 5.
127   *Straits Times*, 10 May 1957, p. 1.
128   *Straits Times*, 18 May 1957, p. 7.
129   *Straits Times*, 17 May 1957, pp. 1, 5.
130   *Straits Times*, 19 May 1957, p. 4.
131   CCAR 1957.
132   *Singapore Free Press*, 6 May 1957, p. 1.
133   *Singapore Free Press*, 13 May 1957, p. 4.
134   *Straits Times*, 20 May 1957, p. 6.

135   *Straits Times*, 13 May 1957, p. 1.
136   *Straits Times*, 17 May 1957, p. 1.
137   *Straits Times*, 15 May 1957, p. 1.
138   *Straits Times*, 17 May 1957, p. 5.
139   *Straits Times*, 16 May 1957, p. 1.
140   'Influenza Epidemic in Singapore' (Statement by the Minister of Health), *Hansard*, 22 May 1957, https://sprs.parl.gov.sg/search/topic?reportid=022_19570522_S0004_T0015
141   *Straits Times*, 22 July 1957, p. 6; N.W. Pirie, 'Radiation and Influenza Mutation', *Lancet*, 15 June 1957.
142   The Soviets conducted H-bomb tests in 1953 and 1955.
143   *Straits Times*, 8 May 1957, p. 15.
144   *Straits Times*, 26 May 1957, p. 7.
145   *Straits Times*, 26 May 1957, p. 7.
146   *Straits Times*, 26 May 1957, p. 7. The Angel of Mons was a series of rumours about supernatural forces (the 'angels') aiding outnumbered British troops against German forces at Mons, Belgium in 1914.
147   *Straits Times*, 17 June 1957, p. 6.
148   *Nanyang Siang Pau*, 15 May 1957, p. 6.
149   *Nanyang Siang Pau*, 8 May 1957, p. 14.
150   *Nanyang Siang Pau*, 7 May 1957, p. 5.
151   *Nanyang Siang Pau*, 7 May 1957, p. 6.
152   *Nanyang Siang Pau*, 20 May 1957, p. 6.
153   *Nanyang Siang Pau*, 6 June 1957, p. 5; *Sin Chew Jit Poh*, 22 May 1957, p. 8.
154   *Singapore Free Press*, 13 May 1957, p. 1.
155   *Nanyang Siang Pau*, 6 June 1957, p. 8.
156   *Sin Chew Jit Poh*, 12 May 1957, p. 8.
157   *Nanyang Siang Pau*, 8 May 1957, p. 14.
158   *Straits Times*, 12 May 1957, p. 1.
159   *Nanyang Siang Pau*, 6 June 1957, p. 8.
160   *Nanyang Siang Pau*, 8 May 1957, p. 14.
161   *Straits Times*, 9 May 1957, p. 1.
162   *Straits Times*, 11 May 1957, p. 1.
163   *Straits Times*, 9 May 1957, p. 1.
164   *Straits Times*, 23 May 1957, p. 8.
165   *Straits Times*, 16 June 1957, p. 7.
166   MOHAR 1957, p. 93.
167   *Straits Times*, 8 May 1957, p. 15.
168   *Straits Times*, 6 July 1957, p. 2.
169   *Singapore Free Press*, 18 July 1957, p. 2.
170   *Singapore Free Press*, 8 July 1957, p. 5.
171   *Straits Times*, 27 January 1958, p. 2.
172   *Straits Times*, 21 March 1958, p. 14.
173   *Singapore Free Press*, 31 May 1958, p. 5.
174   The PAP government continued to be responsible for healthcare in Singapore when the island was part of Malaysia between September 1963 and August 1965.
175   *Singapore Free Press*, 17 August 1959, p. 5.
176   *Singapore Free Press*, 21 August 1959, p. 5.
177   *Straits Times*, 28 August 1959, p. 4.
178   *Singapore Free Press*, 3 February 1960, p. 6.
179   *Singapore Free Press*, 17 March 1960, p. 12.
180   Dora S.K. Tan, 'A Review of Virus Infections of the Respiratory Tract', *Medical Journal of Malaya*, Vol. XIX No. 3, March 1965, pp. 201–212.

181   T.A. Lloyd Davies and Rosemary Mills, 'Survey of Sickness in Singapore, with Notes on Births, Deaths, Handicapped Persons, Puberty, Menopause, Immunisation, Incidence of Cough and Adoption', *Medical Journal of Malaya*, Vol. XV No. 3, March 1961, pp. 117–156.
182   *Straits Times*, 21 February 1965, p. 1.

# 9 Swine Flu to Bird Flu

## Epidemiology and Surveillance

Singapore unexpectedly left Malaysia in August 1965 to become an independent nation-state. In the next three decades, infectious diseases were largely regarded as a diminished public health threat. The narrative frame of post-colonial Singapore was, to use long-time Prime Minister Lee Kuan Yew's words, its spectacular rise from 'Third World to First'.[1] Standards of living rose for the majority of Singaporeans due to substantial state investments in healthcare and public health, and in environmental sanitation, modern housing and social amenities. They were also lifted more generally by the island's economic growth, which led to people's full-time employment in manufacturing, hospitality, advanced services and the civil service.[2]

This is not to say that Singapore's post-colonial pandemic history became uninteresting or non-existent. In light of contemporary developments, we now see that the years from 1965 to 2000 were a formative time. For one, the island was more globally connected than before. The growth of its export industries, built on foreign capital investment, and tourism in the age of mass air travel meant that dangerous diseases could still find their way into the republic.[3] One of these was influenza, though it remained an outlier as before. The People's Action Party government monitored various flu strains that caused periodic but mild outbreaks in Singapore without putting together an influenza policy. Still, two international flu outbreaks were historically significant. One was the threat of swine flu in 1976–1977, which precipitated an ultimately unsuccessful vaccination campaign on the island. The other was the 1997 bird flu outbreak in Hong Kong, which served as a warning for the 2003 SARS pandemic. This pair of flu events – scares more than outbreaks – began to change Singapore's response to influenza.

The change was gradual for a government that had been activist and single-minded in the development of Singapore. In its pursuit of nation-building goals, the leadership had forged a strong state, a vibrant export-oriented economy and a socialised citizenry. In the control of infectious diseases, there was a similar departure from the past. From the early 1970s, epidemiological surveillance replaced the quarantine system as the main means to protect Singapore from pandemic disease. The new approach was shaped by the global influenza surveillance programme launched by the World Health

DOI: 10.4324/9781003384014-10

Organization after the Second World War.[4] It was overseen in Singapore by a newly formed Ministry of the Environment (ENV), and coordinated by a little-studied Joint Co-ordinating Committee on Epidemic Diseases, which comprised representatives from the ENV and other ministries.

The British had talked about epidemiology, but the post-colonial version was more expansive. It was national in that it sought to survey an entire population and required the cooperation of doctors in the community and the community itself. The aim of epidemiology was not only to deal with diseases or to isolate the sick from the general population. It was also to ensure that the citizens were healthy so as to propel the nation-building project. To do this, social data had to be collected, and technology was indispensable. From the 1970s, there was growing sophistication in the ways Singapore's epidemiologists tracked infectious diseases. For example, tuberculosis was no longer the threat it used to be, but the Tuberculosis Control Unit continued to survey social trends, especially its prevalence among the vulnerable elderly.[5] Influenza variants were identified and monitored, not so much because illness was severe but because it was morbid. Socially, epidemiology was a new arm of public health that engaged the population to a far greater degree. It is not surprising that people in Singapore showed an increasing acceptance of biomedicine at this time.

Thus the period after 1965 was one of continuity and change. Singapore remained open to foreign industrialists and visitors, while increasing numbers of its citizens were travelling to countries where infectious diseases were endemic. Similarly, large numbers of low-wage migrant workers from such countries came to work in the city-state after 1970. Among the old trinity of diseases, the threat of plague and cholera fell and smallpox was eradicated worldwide at the end of the decade. But the threat of a pandemic remained real. Domestically, while Singapore's population growth plateaued in the 1970s to over two million people, it remained a dense, built-up city. The population was now rehoused in satellite towns far away from the old city centre. The latter was transformed into a business district, its remaining shophouses emptied of residents and conserved for offices and commercial establishments.

The high-rise public housing estates – the visible symbol of post-colonial Singapore's impressive development – remained a typology of high-density living. The limiting factor was the scarcity of land in the tiny city-state. The new flats, together with the flatted factories, government and commercial offices, and shopping centres where most Singaporeans lived, worked and mingled, constituted a new version of the island's historical urbanism. Despite the physical and socio-economic accomplishments, concentrated urban living and work still characterised the city's social rhythms. In 1971, for instance, medical practitioners reported a rise in influenza and colds in the densely populated public housing estates, though the MOH denied this amounted to an epidemic.[6] Post-colonial Singapore was still very much a 'hen coop' of sorts.

## The 1968 Flu Pandemic

After Singapore became independent, its first brush with mass influenza was a two-week outbreak that started in early August 1968 and peaked between the 16th and 25th.[7] The source of the pandemic was Hong Kong, where a major epidemic affected about half a million people in late July.[8] Tests showed the virus samples from the Hong Kong and Singapore outbreaks to be similar.[9]

As in other countries, Singapore's outbreak was mild. This was the MOH's view in mid-August, based on evidence from its outpatient services and general practitioners.[10] There had been significant increases in attendance at government outpatient clinics and dispensaries. At the height of the epidemic on 19 August, there was a 65 per cent jump in daily outpatient attendances from the norm of 6,052 to 9,966, of which 57 per cent were deemed to be for influenza.[11] Two days later, the MOH described the situation as being 'under control', as 'The infection has fanned through a large section of the community. It is now contained'.[12]

In a sense, this was a lesser version of the 1957 pandemic. The ministry did not make influenza notifiable and was thus unable to provide precise numbers of cases and deaths.[13] Lee et al. postulated 309 excess deaths and an excess mortality rate of 0.15 for the year for a population of just over two million people. The death rate was thus three times lower than the 0.47 per cent tabulated in 1957.[14] Unlike the earlier epidemic, the MOH decided not to close the schools or extend the school vacation. Its reasoning was that such moves were too late, with many people already infected. They were also counterproductive, since the closure of schools would only have 'the possible effect of lengthening the epidemic and delaying the development of "hurt immunity" [herd immunity]'.[15]

As in 1957, the University of Singapore undertook a clinical and a virological study to identify the virus and trace its epidemiology. The clinical study involved 522 students and 443 non-academic staff members and their family members. It concluded that unlike the Type B influenza responsible for an outbreak in 1963, the 1968 virus was more transmissible with an attack rate of 19.2 per cent. This was so especially among lower-income persons (an attack rate of 36.4 per cent), while children lacked resistance to the virus and suffered more severe symptoms. Though the outbreak was not serious, the study urged medical practitioners to be alert to flu-like symptoms in their patients and help prevent the outbreak's spread to other countries.[16] The virological study found the local virus to be similar to the A2/Hong Kong/68 virus despite having undergone an antigenic shift.[17]

Lee et al. viewed the 1968 outbreak as the last of the three influenza pandemics in 20th-century Singapore.[18] This was true on a global scale. But brief and mild, the 1968 event was not on the same level as the 1918 and 1957 pandemics for Singapore. It did not become an official point of reference for future flu outbreaks. In April 1970, the government attributed a rise in influenza cases over two weeks to a possible new wave of the 1968 Hong Kong flu.[19] In January 1973, when the island was again hit by an influenza wave from the West, a government pathologist declared that the strain was different from the one in 1968 and less virulent.[20]

After 1968, the MOH continued to monitor local influenza outbreaks sans an active policy. It did so by tracking the number of acute respiratory tract infections at government outpatient clinics, which were among the most common ailments in Singapore. Because the disease was so transmissible, the government decided to release public statements on influenza outbreaks. In 1974, a ministry spokesperson said, 'When there is an outbreak, we will inform you'.[21] The following year, the ministry reported epidemics caused by two variants of the Influenza A virus in April–June and the fourth quarter, causing a 40 per cent jump in attendances at outpatient clinics above the usual number.[22]

The unceasing monitoring of endemic influenza seemed an anomaly compared to the official position that no policy or notification for the disease was needed. The government held that 'Control of influenza through widespread vaccination of the general population is generally not advocated', except for vulnerable individuals in high-risk groups, such as the chronically ill and elderly. Flu vaccines were regarded as of dubious efficacy, especially against new variants.[23]

Nevertheless, the monitoring of outpatient attendances was clear evidence of the extensive reach of the Singapore state on public health. Through the influenza surveillance, the MOH utilised virological tools and gathered epidemiological datasets. This compiled a growing corpus of scientific – and also social – knowledge on influenza outbreaks and connected different variants – past and present, local and international. These were all requisite elements of an influenza policy and effective response.

In November 1973, the MOH launched an influenza surveillance programme to track weekly attendances for acute respiratory tract infections at the government's 26 outpatient clinics. Virus samples collected from patients were sent to the virology laboratory at the ministry's Pathology Department. The following year, the ministry established the A/Port Chalmers/1/73 virus to be responsible for the mild flu epidemic in Singapore between May and July.[24] Other viral agents were identified in subsequent outbreaks. The MOH learned that influenza epidemics often occurred in the second and final quarters of the year, though it was unsure why this would be so, as there were no significant changes in the weather at this time.[25]

### The Ascendancy of Epidemiology

Behind the scenes, paradigmatic and institutional changes to influenza surveillance were afoot in the republic. In September 1972, a new ministry called the Ministry of the Environment was formed to deal with matters of environmental health previously under separate portfolios. It combined the public health expertise of the MOH and the environmental engineering capability of the Ministry of National Development. It was an outfit run by doctors and engineers, whose joint expertise was applied to areas ranging from hawker surveillance and food safety to pollution and vector control.[26] The MOH, having fewer engineers and a small budget for engineering works, lacked the engineering expertise. By contrast, the ENV had the funding, expertise and manpower to carry out major environmental engineering and public health projects.[27] As Goh Kee Tai, a doctor who headed the Quarantine and Epidemiology Department (QED) in the ENV in the 1970s explained, the prominence of engineers sometimes contributed to an engineer's approach to infectious diseases, though doctors were the experts and more inclined to see the human side of the work.[28]

Part of the reason for the ENV's formation was that environmental public health was seen as the solution to the control of infectious diseases.[29] The answer lay in the surveillance and control of the total environment in which epidemics occur. In an early move, an Epidemiological Unit was formed within the ministry in 1973, charged with investigating and researching notifiable infectious diseases in Singapore other than tuberculosis and leprosy, which were handled by their own administrations. Interestingly, the unit surveyed diseases that were not notifiable but deemed significant. Influenza was one, in addition to other viral infections and dengue.[30] The unit obtained data and statistics on these diseases from doctors across the island.

As Goh later recalled, infectious diseases were still considered a serious problem in Singapore in the early 1970s, as they were endemic in the region. In his view, forming a new ministry where environmental sanitation and epidemiological surveillance could be applied to the problem was a far-sighted move. But the ENV did not have a smooth start: it was difficult to persuade doctors to join the new ministry due to the stigma against engineering and epidemiological work. The ENV's doctors were sometimes called *jam ban* ('toilet') doctors or mosquito doctors. Goh himself was seconded from the MOH to the ENV till 2003.[31]

The QED carried out epidemiological investigations and contact tracing into infectious disease cases and outbreaks in the 1970s and 1980s. The MOH by contrast was mostly concerned with laboratory investigations and treatment.[32] The QED had been formed in 1962 under a new Public Health Division that was created as a result of the reorganisation of the MOH when Singapore became a self-governing state.[33] At the time, the department's work was modest, concerned mostly with port and airport health quarantine for the trinity of plague, cholera and smallpox that were deemed to be threats in the region.[34] St. John's quarantine stations were still regarded as Singapore's 'first line of defence' against epidemic diseases.[35] With the formation of the ENV, the QED came under the new ministry. Epidemiology overtook quarantine and the scope of the department's work expanded substantially and paradigmatically.

As Goh noted, though first billed in the department's official title, quarantine was the poor cousin of epidemiology.[36] Officials like Goh deemed the strict quarantines of the past to be outdated and inferior to epidemiological surveillance.[37] The QED's work can be gleaned from its various publications:

its weekly bulletins, which were summarised in the monthly *Epidemiological News Bulletin* and the annual *Communicable Disease Surveillance in Singapore*. These publications contained detailed epidemiological data and statistics on disease outbreaks, notably measles and chickenpox in army camps, schools, homes, and the Changi International Airport.[38] The department also conducted special surveys on infections such as hepatitis and Legionnaires' disease. Influenza had a paragraph or two in these publications but otherwise received little attention. It was monitored not as a dangerous disease but a common one behind most upper respiratory tract infections in Singapore. The diseases that mattered to the department were contemporary ones: viral hepatitis, food poisoning, HIV/AIDS, vector-borne diseases and unresolved cases of sudden death among Thai migrant workers in the early 1990s.[39]

In Goh's view, the bulletins were successful in encouraging medical practitioners to notify cases of dangerous infectious diseases, serving as a bridge between them and the government.[40] The department also released public statements on any significant rise in the incidence of an infectious disease, so as to alert the practitioners and the public and enable them to take appropriate measures. It was aware of past outbreaks of influenza, using data to plot multi-year cycles of outbreaks.[41] Otherwise, the department compiled and furnished plenty of data and information that did not amount to an interesting read. But this was precisely the point. The aim was to outline the vigilance in Singapore's surveillance and to socialise doctors and citizens on how to behave and respond appropriately when sickness occurred. Repeatedly, the *Communicable Disease Surveillance in Singapore* reports stated that epidemiological surveillance was working and infectious diseases were being kept under control in the city-state.

Goh was also the secretary in another key surveillance body: the inter-ministerial group called the Joint Co-ordinating Committee on Epidemic Diseases formed in October 1973. The committee was a classic example of technocratic administration based on medico-engineering expertise. It initially comprised representatives from the MOH and the ENV (typically permanent secretaries, directors and department heads), before including those of other ministries and institutions.[42] The permanent secretary of the MOH was usually the chair of the committee with the counterpart from the ENV being the deputy.

The committee oversaw the 'coordination, formulation and evaluation of communicable diseases (CD) control policies and programmes in Singapore'.[43] It was to coordinate the work of the MOH and the ENV on epidemic diseases, conduct research on these diseases and present the information to the government and the public.[44] The committee was especially mindful to develop instruments of infection control in two issues relevant to an open city of trade and travel like Singapore. The first was to be aware of new pathogens emerging in other countries, while the second was to prevent the entry of drug- and insecticide-resistant diseases from the tropical region.[45] Thus the diseases of concern to the committee were both those that had been brought under control (tuberculosis, malaria, poliomyelitis, and diphtheria), and persistent or new illnesses (acute respiratory tract, sexually-transmitted and food-borne gastrointestinal infections). Together, these diseases were responsible for a third of outpatient attendances at government clinics in the early 1980s.

Like the QED, the committee emphasised public health education so that people could understand how infectious diseases spread and support the government's initiatives. This would address the paradox that successful quarantine and control would pose: it might leave an uneducated population lacking immunity vulnerable to local outbreaks or infection when they travel abroad.[46] The committee was also responsible for making decisions on Singapore's childhood immunisation programme and on the administration, manufacture and purchase of vaccines. Singapore kept emergency doses of common vaccines in reserve in the 1970s. But there were only 200 doses of influenza vaccines in reserve, compared to 5,000 doses of the smallpox vaccine; 2,000 doses of the yellow fever vaccine; 5,000 doses of the typhoid vaccine; and 5,000 doses of the cholera vaccine.[47]

The Joint Committee's work in the 1970s and 1980s supported that of the QED and reflected a strong engineering influence. The diseases of emphasis were hepatitis B, vector-borne diseases (including yellow fever), cholera, typhoid, HIV/AIDS and the national immunisation programme. The committee reconsidered and downplayed the surveillance of older diseases such as plague and smallpox, as these diseases declined in importance locally and internationally. The committee studied detailed epidemiological datasets on outbreaks of infectious diseases. As Singapore began to recruit large numbers of low-wage foreign workers from Asian countries at this time, it also monitored their screening for malaria, typhoid, tuberculosis and sexually-transmitted diseases.[48]

As mentioned earlier, influenza was monitored statistically and studied clinically, but was not a major concern. It was usually limited to two paragraphs in the monthly minutes of the committee's meetings; by comparison, the diseases of emphasis received much more substantial treatment and discussion. In most years, the committee reported that influenza did not reach epidemic proportions in Singapore.[49] The illness came under the category of acute respiratory tract infections caused by respiratory viruses, which were the leading cause of infectious disease morbidity in the country.[50]

The surveillance of influenza was based on the sheer number of attendances for such infections in outpatient clinics. At two of the dispensaries, 20 random throat swaps of patients were made weekly for virus isolation. In 1980, there was a proposal to increase the number of swaps to a hundred, but this was found to be impractical as it was difficult to supply even 20.[51] Based on data from the last five years before 1980, the committee found that influenza outbreaks often occurred two to four weeks after an increase in influenza isolations. Since such increases happened every year between April and June, the committee decided that the Ministry of Education and Ministry of Defence should warn school students and national servicemen against excessive physical activity if they had flu-like symptoms.[52]

The committee's work signified wider changes in the regimen of infectious disease control in Singapore. With the MOH and ENV providing expert advice and the latter also offering legal expertise, the list of notifiable diseases in the 1976 Infectious Diseases Act (the successor to the Quarantine and Prevention of Disease Ordinance) was reviewed and updated.[53] The trinity of plague, cholera and smallpox was retained, though the last would be removed from the list several years later. An important move was to make measles notifiable in 1980, while vaccination for rubella, though not notifiable, was monitored.[54] More than the MOH previously, the ENV was an enforcement agency to implement the provisions of the act. Besides disease notifications, it also carried out operations against illegal hawkers and tracked down infectious disease patients who defaulted on their treatment.[55]

In an internal review in 1981, the committee credited itself with revising the list of notifiable diseases in Singapore, adopting the WHO's clinical criteria for communicable diseases and conducting local research on typhoid, cholera and poliomyelitis. Its work had helped improve notification by general practitioners, although there were still doctors being swayed by pressure from their patients who wanted to avoid investigation by government officials.[56] But the committee's proposal to screen all food handlers in Singapore in 1974 for typhoid was controversial and mass screening was discontinued. Chronic typhoid carriers were banned from handling food the following year. In 1978, the committee conceded there was no fool-proof way to prevent the entry of yellow fever into Singapore. The quarantine of passengers for the disease ceased entirely, and arrivals from endemic areas without a valid certificate were to be vaccinated and quarantined for 24 hours.[57] The fear remained that an epidemic of yellow fever could occur if the virus were introduced into Singapore.[58]

The committee oversaw changes to the quarantine, surveillance and vaccination of the 'Big 3'. Plague remained on the radar for a time. In 1975, the committee was unhappy with the Ministry of Defence's decision to allow boats carrying Vietnamese refugees to berth alongside local wharves without being fumigated. A major move in 1979 was to refrain from classifying Singapore as an infected area for cholera unless two or more epidemiologically related cases were reported. In 1980, after the WHO declared the worldwide eradication of smallpox, the committee accepted an expert committee's recommendation to discontinue the vaccination of children for smallpox. This initially met with objections from the government, with the committee told to continue vaccination till all other ASEAN countries had lifted their vaccination programmes. In March 1981, as noted in Chapter 3, the cabinet finally approved the cessation of Singapore's smallpox vaccination programme.[59]

The review noted that the committee had 'matured over the years, and many bold steps have been taken', replacing the old quarantine system with epidemiological surveillance. The policies it had formulated were lauded as 'sound and rational'.[60] The review called for the committee to continue monitoring trends in communicable diseases in the region, including drug-resistant and especially vector-borne diseases, and to learn from developed countries about dealing with 'new' diseases.[61] But the question for us is how had the committee used information from epidemiological surveillance to deal with the threat of infectious diseases? Let us now turn to the influenza outbreaks in this period.

## The 1976 Swine Flu and Mass Vaccination

Rather than the 1968 pandemic, the first historically significant influenza event after Singapore's independence was the outbreak of swine flu in the US in January 1976. Singapore's response to the outbreak largely followed international and particularly American moves. These robust responses were due to the fear that the Influenza A/Victoria/3/76 virus responsible for the outbreak in Fort Dix, New Jersey[62] was similar to the Influenza A virus that had devastated the world in 1918–1919.[63]

Swine flu did not reach Singapore. A serological study found that 91.5 per cent of pigs in the country had antibodies to the virus. Among the general human population, sampled from blood donors and hospital patients, only those above 50 years of age had antibodies, as the swine flu virus was believed to be closely related to the Influenza A virus responsible for the 1918 influenza pandemic. These findings were similar to other countries. Among pig farmers and abattoir workers, however, 16.3 per cent of those under 50 had antibodies. Like those above 50, they were well. The study confirmed that swine flu infection was widespread among pigs in Singapore and had occasionally spread to humans, though with little ill effects.[64] It was subsequently established that the virus did not spread to the wider population.[65]

Despite this, the swine flu epidemic was a milestone in the global history of influenza. It was the first time a variant was identified early enough for a mass vaccination campaign to be implemented. This addressed previous arguments that influenza epidemics passed too quickly before vaccines could be delivered to the population on a large scale. Since the identification of the influenza virus in 1933 and especially during and after the Second World War, public health officials in the West had attempted to produce vaccines ahead of influenza outbreaks. They failed to do so during the pandemics of 1957 and 1968.[66] Now, the capacity to mass produce vaccines quickly had finally caught up with improvements in global influenza surveillance.

For Singapore, the swine flu outbreak was a historic event. As the US and other countries commenced mass immunisation programmes, Singapore, possessing the capacity to do so, likewise moved into action. The Minister for Health Dr Toh Chin Chye conferred with the newly formed working committee on influenza outbreaks and the Joint Co-ordinating Committee on Epidemic Diseases. The government quickly decided to immunise government employees in essential services.[67] Toh explained the rationale for the decision: 'if a fire breaks out and the firemen are down with flu, who is going to put out the fire?'[68]

In June 1977, a mass immunisation programme was rolled out for government employees 'liable to contract influenza' and 'those travelling abroad'. The government purchased 120,000 doses of a triple-flu vaccine for the swine, Victoria and Hong Kong flu variants. The vaccine was also made available to the public at $5 a dose. Whereas in the past only key personnel in the ministries and statutory boards like the Public Utilities Board and Port of Singapore Authority were vaccinated, all government employees would be immunised this time.[69] The first group to receive the vaccine was national servicemen based in military camps, deemed likely to spread influenza to their families when they went home. The government was willing to purchase more doses if there was sufficient demand from the public.[70]

For Singapore, the vaccination campaign was the first time a mass immunisation effort had been attempted for influenza. It ended decades of counter-arguments from political leaders and doctors that vaccines would take too long to manufacture or were simply ineffective. But the long memory of the 1918 influenza pandemic had as much to do with the change as medical expertise and technology. Interestingly, the triple-flu vaccination had taken place in the absence of a severe local outbreak. It anticipated a forthcoming pandemic that however failed to arrive.[71]

In the US, the mass vaccination push turned out to be a failure due to fears of the increased risk of Guillain-Barre Syndrome, a rare autoimmune response that could lead to paralysis in extreme cases. The anxiety stemmed from a study published in the *British Medical Journal* that suggested that those vaccinated for the swine flu were 7.5 times more likely than non-vaccinated persons to develop the syndrome. The vaccination programme came to a premature end. In the ensuing fallout, top American officials of the Department of Health Education and Welfare and the Centers for Disease Control and Prevention were blamed for the fiasco and fired.[72] Though rightly concerned about the risk of an influenza epidemic, they were wrong in thinking that the swine flu virus was easily transmissible. Just as important was the public health dimension: the officials had not communicated or managed the attendant risks of the vaccine well.[73]

Such concerns also abounded in Singapore, although no political fallout occurred as in the US. In July, an unnamed 'authoritative medical source' was quoted in the *Straits Times* as saying that the triple-flu vaccine was safe, being comprised of three vaccines and not just for swine flu alone. This was hardly reassuring to the public. The source added that the vaccine was as safe as those for measles, smallpox and diphtheria.[74] The government decided that the vaccine would be given on a voluntary basis, for the response was underwhelming.[75] Most of the excess doses had to be given to the Ministry of Defence to be stored before they expired.[76] General practitioners saw little public interest in the vaccine and did not make further orders. A common view among them was that the vaccine protected only against three variants out of over a hundred existing strains of influenza. Several vaccinated patients also reportedly returned to their clinic sick with influenza. Many doctors were sceptical. Why bother with the vaccine, one asked, if no permanent immunity was gained?[77] The 'limited use' perception of vaccines in the past persisted among doctors and the public.

A lasting effect of the swine flu outbreak was to establish a public health link between influenza and viral myocarditis. In early June 1976, two influenza patients – a female school student and a 29-year-old man – died from complications due to the latter.[78] The MOH cautioned recovering patients to refrain from strenuous physical activity to avoid heart complications. During the outbreak, mass physical activities of a strenuous nature were postponed.[79] The Singapore National Heart Association urged recovering patients against running and jogging within two weeks of infection.[80] In January 1977, a doctor with the Singapore Joggers' Association repeated the warning: while rare at about three per thousand persons, the influenza virus could affect the heart.[81]

Thus the 1976 mass vaccination effort in Singapore came to a disappointing end. But influenza surveillance continued in the 1980s and 1990s as around the world. Even as antibiotics and vaccines diminished or eradicated many of the old infections, the AIDS pandemic sustained interest in infectious diseases in the West, as did the emergence of drug-resistant tuberculosis and new diseases such as the Ebola virus. Added to this list was pandemic influenza.[82]

In Singapore, another outbreak between December 1977 and January 1978, caused by the A/Singapore/1401/77 virus, was found to be antigenically similar to that responsible for the 1890 pandemic. It had broken out among national servicemen based in army camps – a group of concern during the swine flu outbreak. From there, the outbreak had spread quickly to the general population.[83] There was an estimated 18 per cent increase in the number of people attending outpatient dispensaries, both young and elderly. The outbreak though was a mild one.[84] An unnamed medical expert believed that it was mild because the variant was similar to the 1968 pandemic strain. It had previously struck Singapore in 1948 and 1949, affecting mostly new-borns and young children, thus conferring them some immunity.[85] His reference to past outbreaks is interesting, as they had received little attention at the time, being attributed in part to the rainy season.[86] Between April and July 1979, another mild epidemic broke out among children and young adults and was found to be caused by the B/Singapore/222/79 virus.[87]

The 1980s saw the further evolution of influenza surveillance, supported by an emerging virology. In 1982, the MOH reported two different influenza strains as responsible for 41 per cent of all acute respiratory tract infections among attendances at outpatient facilities.[88] In 1984, the ministry received numerous inquiries about a US news report published in the *Straits Times* that people in Atlanta were being encouraged to be vaccinated against the B/Singapore/222/79 virus, especially those with chronic conditions. But the Department of Pathology at the SGH dismissed this as unnecessary, as Singaporeans had attained immunity during the 1979 outbreak caused by the virus.[89] In 1986, amidst another outbreak, a lengthy *Straits Times* article listed a series of recent epidemics in Singapore – in 1974, 1976 and 1979. It identified the strain of the ongoing outbreak as Influenza A (H1N1), noting that it had also been responsible for the 1957 pandemic.[90] In 1989, a 'mini flu epidemic' was held responsible for weakening people's resistance to a subsequent outbreak of chickenpox among young adults.[91]

Local virology tried to make sense of these outbreaks by considering various factors such as period of the year, climate and environment, as in colonial Singapore. In 1988, the influenza surveillance programme reported that the A virus was predominant in the first half of the year, while the B virus was prevalent in the second half.[92] A comparison was made between the causes of local outbreaks and those in temperate countries, where influenza would be more prevalent in winter. A government virologist suggested that weather fluctuations between April and June may lower one's resistance to the disease, though this was disputed by an official from the Meteorological Service, who noted that weather changes in mid-year were not extreme. The virologist also considered a more plausible factor: the high human density in Singapore. This was compounded by the presence of large numbers of visitors from all over the world and the prevalent use of air-conditioning in buildings that did not circulate fresh air.[93]

Rather than notification or mass vaccination, public health messaging was the main response to influenza events during the decade. Calls were made during outbreaks especially for children and the elderly to avoid crowded places and to cough or sneeze into tissue paper (rather than handkerchiefs).[94] The warning to refrain from strenuous exercise when ill was oft repeated. This was done with some emphasis after an apparently healthy national serviceman collapsed and died after a run in 1984. He was later found to have a 'flu-like' lung infection.[95]

The references to influenza strains, whether different or similar, are telling. They highlight a growing view in the 1970s and 1980s that scientific research on flu was newsworthy to the public – that influenza, while not notifiable, was a disease to be taken seriously. They also indicate greater rigour and self-confidence among local researchers, who regularly sent virus samples to disease control centres in the US and Britain. Two new strains were discovered in Singapore in the 1980s. These developments were part of advances in global influenza surveillance, which gradually recovered from the debacle of the 1976 swine flu. The local chapter of the WHO's global surveillance programme, the National Influenza Centre, continued to monitor influenza cases and trends in Singapore. In 1988, Singapore hosted its first international virology conference, the Asia-Pacific Congress of Medical Virology, attended by over 400 doctors and scientists from various countries.[96] The interest in influenza grew even though the *Epidemiological News Bulletin* reported few outbreaks in Singapore throughout the 1980s and 1990s.

## Prelude to SARS: The 1997 Bird Flu

Though it was a scare, the 1997 bird or avian flu epidemic in Hong Kong was a key event for Singapore like the swine flu. The outbreak sparked much concern among scientists in Hong Kong, who were alert to new deadly infectious diseases. The origins of avian flu lay in the development of industrial-scale poultry farms in south-eastern China. There, human workers were in constant close contact with large numbers of poultry farmed in 'chicken inns',[97] increasing the likelihood of bird-human disease transmission.[98] The culling of some 100–200 million birds in Hong Kong in 1997, at great cost to the industry and people's livelihoods, was a sign of this growing threat. The episode highlighted the need to include animal surveillance in the influenza surveillance programme.[99]

In a sense, the bird flu outbreak was a prelude to the SARS pandemic in the region six years later. Though caused by a different type of virus called a coronavirus, SARS demonstrated the dangers of zoonotic disease transmission and triggered vigorous responses in many countries. In Singapore, the 1997 bird flu scare highlighted what could be accomplished with good virology on the role of birds and other animals in the transmission of influenza to humans. During the outbreak, British and Singaporean scientists began to research new flu strains found on farms in China. An article in the *Straits Times* warned that these strains could infect humans through pigs and cause epidemics, even pandemics. It noted that the influenza pandemics of 1957 and 1968 – attributed to Asian or Hong Kong variants – had arisen this way.[100]

In March, when several Members of Parliament queried the government if the outbreak could spread to Singapore, the reply was that the island was safe.[101] But as the authorities in Hong Kong had begun culling large numbers of chickens on its farms in December, government departments in Singapore moved into action. There were only a small number of chickens reared in Singapore's farms, but the government was more concerned about imports from other countries, though Hong Kong was not a source of Singapore's chickens. The Primary Production Department, formed in 1959, inspected both local and imported poultry for the H5N1 strain responsible for the Hong Kong outbreak. Hospitals and general practitioners were instructed to notify the MOH of patients with flu-like symptoms, especially among those who had recently travelled to Hong Kong. Though assuring that the bird flu did not reach Singapore, the ministry nevertheless urged people to stay away from crowded places and to see a doctor if they were ill. Its influenza surveillance programme was expanded to include the H5N1 virus, but found no cases caused by the strain.[102] At this time, many scientists, including those at the WHO, did not think that human-to-human transmission of the virus was likely.[103]

The Hong Kong bird flu passed Singapore by, but things were coming to a head. In 1999, amid another influenza outbreak, a Member of Parliament asked the Minister for Health if it was caused by the Sydney or Hong Kong strain and whether vaccines were available for it. The minister pointed to the Sydney strain but gave the usual reply that vaccines were generally not used in tropical countries.[104] The following January, the A/Sydney H3N2 virus caused a global outbreak, affecting Europe and the US. In Singapore, the MOH urged locals travelling to these regions, especially the elderly, to have their flu shots and those returning with flu-like symptoms to see a doctor immediately.[105] When a writer to the *Straits Times* asked if the virus posed a threat to Singapore and if the authorities had a contingency plan,[106] the ministry replied that it was not a new strain but one that had been detected in Singapore in 1997.[107] Nevertheless, there was enough public consternation for over 5,000 flu shots to be administered during the month, causing supply to run out at two hospitals.[108]

There was at least one local expert who was aware of the growing threat of influenza and also cognisant of Singapore's history. In 1999, P.A. Tambyah, writing in the *Singapore Medical Journal* on the Nipah virus outbreak that year, warned, 'Perhaps the most important emerging zoonotic infectious disease of all is pandemic influenza'. He referred to the epidemics of 1918, 1957, 1968 and 1997. He added that general practitioners in housing estates are crucial in helping to detect cases in a new outbreak.[109]

At the end of the millennium, the developed city-state of Singapore stood at a crossroads in its pandemic history. The old system of quarantine seemed a thing of the past, as did many known infectious diseases. But there was still no influenza policy and the island was more plugged in to the outside world than ever and just as vulnerable to new diseases. After a long history of limited responses to influenza pandemics in 1890, 1918 and 1957, the post-colonial government had amassed the technical expertise and social capabilities for a robust response to a major epidemic. Its epidemiological surveillance system was able to track the movement of flu strains around the world and the number of infections among the local population. The government moved to vaccinate its employees during the 1976 swine flu scare, though this failed. The 1997 bird flu outbreak in Hong Kong provided further evidence that zoonotic diseases were on the horizon. The epidemic that occurred six years later was not due to influenza but another disease.

## Notes

1  Lee Kuan Yew, *From Third World to First: The Singapore Story: 1965–2000* (New York: HarperCollins Publishers, 2000).

2  Garry Rodan, *The Political Economy of Singapore's Industrialization: National State and International* Capital (London: Palgrave Macmillan UK, 1989).

3  W.G. Huff, *The Economic Growth of Singapore: Trade and Development in the Twentieth Century* (New York: Cambridge University Press, 1994).

4  George Dehner, *Global Flu and You: A History of Influenza* (London: Reaktion Books, 2012).

5  Loh Kah Seng and Hsu Li Yang, *Tuberculosis – The Singapore Experience, 1867–2018: Disease, Society and the State* (New York: Routledge, 2020).

6  *New Nation*, 8 May 1971, p. 3; *Straits Times*, 28 May 1971, p. 20.

7  Vernon Lee et al., 'Influenza Pandemics in Singapore, a Tropical, Globally Connected City', *Emerging Infectious Diseases*, Vol. 13 No. 7, July 2007, pp. 1052–1057.

8  *Straits Times*, 14 August 1968, p. 6; *Straits Times*, 2 December 1968, p. 12.

9  *Straits Times*, 18 August 1968, p. 2.

10  *Straits Times*, 14 August 1968, p. 6.

11  MOHAR 1957.
12  *Straits Times*, 21 August 1968, p. 22.
13  *Straits Times*, 25 August 1968, p. 16.
14  Lee et al., 'Influenza Pandemics in Singapore, a Tropical, Globally Connected City'.
15  *Straits Times*, 25 August 1968, p. 16.
16  Z.N. Kadri, 'An Outbreak of "Hong Kong flu" in Singapore', Part 1–Clinical Study, *Singapore Medical Journal*, Vol. 11 No. 1, March 1970, pp. 30–32.
17  M. Yin-Murphy, 'An Outbreak of "Hong Kong flu" in Singapore', Part 2–Virological and Serological Report, *Singapore Medical Journal*, Vol. 11 No. 1, March 1970, pp. 33–37.
18  Lee et al., 'Influenza Pandemics in Singapore, a Tropical, Globally Connected City'.
19  *Straits Times*, 10 April 1970, p. 4.
20  *New Nation*, 13 January 1973, p. 1.
21  *New Nation*, 4 December 1974, p. 1.
22  MOHAR 1975. The variants were the A/Port Chalmers/1/73 (responsible for the pandemic of 1974) and A/Scotland/840/74, a new variant.
23  *Epidemiological News Bulletin*, Vol. 1 No. 2 December 1974, p. 3.
24  K.T. Goh, *Epidemiological Surveillance of Communicable Diseases in Singapore* (Tokyo: Southeast Asian Medical Information Centre, 1983).
25  Goh, *Epidemiological Surveillance of Communicable Diseases in Singapore*.
26  ENVAR 1972.
27  Loh Kah Seng, interview with Goh Kee Tai, 16 February 2017.
28  Oral History Centre, National Archives of Singapore, Interview with Dr Sathiamoorthy Ramalingam Sayampanathan, Reel 7, 26 August 1999.
29  Goh, *Epidemiological Surveillance of Communicable Diseases in Singapore*.
30  ENVAR 1973.
31  Loh Kah Seng, interview with Goh Kee Tai, 16 February 2017.
32  Goh, *Epidemiological Surveillance of Communicable Diseases in Singapore*.
33  MOHAR 1962.
34  MOH 075/64, Minutes of the 7th Meeting of Officers of the Quarantine & Epidemiology Branch of the Public Health Division, 16 October 1964.
35  MOH 075/64, Minutes of the Meeting of Officers of the Quarantine & Epidemiology Branch of the Public Health Division, 20 March 1964, p. 2.
36  Loh Kah Seng, interview with Goh Kee Tai, 16 February 2017.
37  Goh, *Epidemiological Surveillance of Communicable Diseases in Singapore*.
38  ENV, *Communicable Disease Surveillance in Singapore 1984*.
39  ENV, *Communicable Disease Surveillance in Singapore 1990*.
40  Goh, *Epidemiological Surveillance of Communicable Diseases in Singapore*.
41  *Straits Times*, 19 May 1988, p. 15.
42  The full list of represented institutions included the MOH, ENV, the Department of Microbiology, National University of Singapore; Medical Services Headquarters, Ministry of Defence; and the Primary Production Division, Ministry of National Development. Goh, *Epidemiological Surveillance of Communicable Diseases in Singapore*.
43  Goh, *Epidemiological Surveillance of Communicable Diseases in Singapore*, p. xiii.
44  MOH 024/58/01–000 Vo. 13 A Review of the Work of Joint Co-ordinating Committee of Epidemic Diseases.
45  Goh, *Epidemiological Surveillance of Communicable Diseases in Singapore*.
46  Goh, *Epidemiological Surveillance of Communicable Diseases in Singapore*.
47  Goh, *Epidemiological Surveillance of Communicable Diseases in Singapore*.
48  MOH 024/58/01–000 Vol. 07 Minutes of the 67th Meeting of the Joint Co-ordinating Committee of Epidemic Diseases, 26 March 1981.
49  MOH 024/58/01–000 Vol. 09 Appendix 3, Virus Diseases Surveillance 1982.

50  MOH 024/58/01–000 V10 Appendix 3 'An Epidemiological Survey on Acute Upper Respiratory Infections and Air-Conditioning'.
51  MOH 024/58/01–000 Vol. 07 Minutes of the 63rd Meeting of the Joint Co-ordinating Committee of Epidemic Diseases, 31 July 1980.
52  MOH 024/58/01–000 Vol. 06 Minutes of the 62nd Meeting of the Joint Co-ordinating Committee of Epidemic Diseases, 20 May 1980.
53  MOH 024/58/01–000 Vol. 13 A Review of the Work of Joint Co-ordinating Committee of Epidemic Diseases.
54  Goh, *Epidemiological Surveillance of Communicable Diseases in Singapore.*
55  Loh Kah Seng, interview with Goh Kee Tai, 16 February 2017.
56  MOH 024/58/01–000 Vol. 11 Working paper, 'Notification of Infectious and Industrial Diseases', 1984.
57  MOH 024/58/01–000 Vol. 13 A Review of the Work of Joint Co-ordinating Committee of Epidemic Diseases.
58  Goh, *Epidemiological Surveillance of Communicable Diseases in Singapore.*
59  MOH 024/58/01–000 Vol. 13 A Review of the Work of Joint Co-ordinating Committee of Epidemic Diseases.
60  MOH 024/58/01–000 Vol. 13 A Review of the Work of Joint Co-ordinating Committee of Epidemic Diseases, p. 14.
61  MOH 024/58/01–000 Vol. 13 A Review of the Work of Joint Co-ordinating Committee of Epidemic Diseases.
62  MOHAR 1976.
63  *Epidemiological News Bulletin*, Vol. 2 No. 2, February 1977; Goh, *Epidemiological Surveillance of Communicable Diseases in Singapore.*
64  *Epidemiological News Bulletin*, Vol. III No. 2, February 1977; Goh, *Epidemiological Surveillance of Communicable Diseases in Singapore.*
65  MOH 024/58/01–000 Vol. 13 A Review of the Work of Joint Co-ordinating Committee of Epidemic Diseases.
66  Dehner, *Global Flu and You.*
67  MOH 024/58/01–000 Vo. 13 A Review of the Work of Joint Co-ordinating Committee of Epidemic Diseases, p. 6; Goh, *Epidemiological Surveillance of Communicable Diseases in Singapore.*
68  *New Nation*, 16 August 1977, pp. 10–11.
69  *Straits Times*, 20 May 1977, p. 13.
70  Hansard, 15 March 1977.
71  *New Nation*, 1 July 1977, p. 1.
72  Dehner, *Global Flu and You.*
73  Alfred Jay Bollet, *Plagues & Poxes: The Impact of Human History on Epidemic Disease* (New York: Demos, 2004); Niall Johnson, *Britain and the 1918–19 Influenza Pandemic: A Dark Epilogue* (London: Routledge, 2006).
74  *Straits Times*, 16 July 1977, p. 12.
75  MOH 024/58/01–000 Vo. 13 A Review of the Work of Joint Co-ordinating Committee of Epidemic Diseases.
76  MOH 024/58/01–000 Vo. 13 A Review of the Work of Joint Co-ordinating Committee of Epidemic Diseases.
77  *Straits Times*, 27 July 1977, p. 7.
78  *Straits Times*, 5 June 1976, p. 26.
79  Goh, *Epidemiological Surveillance of Communicable Diseases in Singapore.*
80  *New Nation*, 23 August 1976, p. 4.
81  *Straits Times*, 8 January 1977, p. 23.
82  Dehner, *Global Flu and You.*
83  Goh, *Epidemiological Surveillance of Communicable Diseases in Singapore.*
84  MOHAR 1977; *Straits Times*, 8 January 1978, p. 1; *Straits Times*, 12 January 1978, p. 1.

85  *Straits Times*, 23 January 1978, p. 5.
86  *Straits Times*, 31 January 1948, p. 7; *Straits Times*, 7 August 1949, p. 9.
87  Goh, *Epidemiological Surveillance of Communicable Diseases in Singapore*.
88  MOHAR 1982.
89  *Straits Times*, 1 December 1984, p. 13.
90  *Straits Times*, 20 April 1986, p. 9.
91  *Straits Times*, 20 December 1989, p. 32.
92  MOHAR 1988.
93  *Straits Times*, 20 April 1986, p. 9.
94  *Straits Times*, 23 April 1985, p. 10; *Straits Times*, 15 April 1986, p. 19.
95  *Straits Times*, 8 August 1984, p. 10.
96  *New Paper*, 3 November 1988, p. 6.
97  Dehner, *Global Flu and You*, p. 72.
98  Mark Honigsbaum, *The Pandemic Century: A History of Global Contagion from the Spanish Flu to COVID-19* (London: W.H. Allen, 2020).
99  Dehner, *Global Flu and You*.
100 *Straits Times*, 10 February 1997.
101 'Estimates of Expenditure for the Finance Year, 1 April 1988 to 31 March 1999', *Hansard*, 18 March 1998, https://sprs.parl.gov.sg/search/topic?reportid=004_19980318_S0002_T0003
102 MOHAR 1997; *Straits Times*, 10 December 1997.
103 *Straits Times*, 31 December 1997.
104 'Present Influenza Pandemic', *Hansard*, 11 February 1999, https://sprs.parl.gov.sg/search/topic?reportid=026_19990211_S0005_T0027
105 *Straits Times*, 15 January 2000.
106 *Straits Times*, 15 January 2000.
107 *Straits Times*, 18 January 2000.
108 *Straits Times*, 20 January 2000.
109 P.A. Tambyah, 'The Nipah Virus Outbreak: A Reminder', *Singapore Medical Journal*, Vol. 40 No. 5, 1999, p. 329.

# 10 The SARS Effect

Much has been written about the SARS episode in Singapore – the city-state's most serious epidemic since independence. To fully grasp its historical significance – as an event with a past and a bearing on the future – it is necessary to read between the lines in the official record and fill the gaps in the narrative. Most accounts have framed the 2003 outbreak as a senior journalist called it – a 'defining moment' that crystallised a unified response from Singaporeans under the government's leadership.[1] That moment has been widely commemorated in various books and other public media, symbolising Singapore's vigilance against infectious disease.[2] But themes of unity and leadership have tended to obscure deeper questions about mistakes made that could not be blamed on complacency by individuals or institutions alone.

Here, we treat SARS as a historical event. From this perspective, Singapore did well to contain the outbreak but made a number of mistakes underemphasised in most accounts. Chief of these was the lack of historical awareness in the SARS response. The epidemic has been likened to a crisis occurring out of the blue, catching Singapore by surprise. But as this book has shown, SARS had epidemic antecedents that could be traced from the historical record. There had been notable outbreaks within living memory: influenza in 1957, smallpox in 1959 and cholera in 1963. Worse epidemics had occurred before the Second World War that illustrated the colonial factor. Even in the post-colonial period, the Singapore government had recognised the threats posed by swine flu in 1976 and bird flu in 1997, while its epidemiologists had monitored influenza strains and outbreaks since the 1970s. The road to a more nuanced narrative of SARS begins by noting Singapore's first failure before the pandemic reached the island: the lack of a sense of history.

The other question from the SARS epidemic is its historical impact. The outbreak convinced the government of the threat posed by novel coronaviruses and demonstrated the need for a national response plan; indeed the long-needed influenza policy emerged in the aftermath. SARS also forced government agencies to figure out how to work across departmental lines to deal with an emergency health situation, though this had been preceded by the work of the Joint Co-ordinating Committee on Epidemic Diseases and other similar committees. The epidemic forged a closer collaboration between

DOI: 10.4324/9781003384014-11

the government, the healthcare system and the public. The crisis highlighted some continuities from the past, particularly in bringing back an adapted form of quarantine that had been dismissed as being outdated. These lessons from the SARS experience had a positive bearing on Singapore's response to the COVID-19 pandemic.

But because it had been framed as a unifying event, the SARS episode also had a negative impact. The government and healthcare system drew lessons from the outbreak in a way that was partial and flawed. SARS was only the most recent outbreak, one seen in largely positive terms. It was not understood as part of a long chain of epidemics in Singapore or told in a more nuanced narrative. The lessons drawn from SARS were overly focused on the events of 2003. Even then, the government's efforts were emphasised while social differences were obscured by the unity story; the response plan drafted in the aftermath was based on science with little input from the social sciences and humanities. From hindsight, the narrow lessons affected Singapore's early response to the COVID-19 pandemic. SARS is a cautionary tale of how lessons should and should not be drawn from the past.

## Forgotten Past, Unprepared Nation

A common claim made about SARS was how unprepared Singapore was. The Tan Tock Seng Hospital (TTSH) publication, *The Silent War*, claimed that 'The enemy gave no warning'.[3] Admittedly, there was some basis for this claim with coronavirus, the microbial agent behind the outbreak. There had been a growing awareness in scientific circles of avian influenza, the Nipah virus and Ebola virus at the end of the 20th century. But coronaviruses were still under the radar. They are a large family of viruses so named because of the 'crown' of spikes that protrude outside the virus particles. They have been known to cause respiratory or gastrointestinal illnesses in a large variety of mammals and birds. Hitherto they had been the 'Cinderellas' of pathogens, originally associated with the mild common cold in humans.[4]

It was only from 2002 that three epidemic coronaviruses capable of causing severe illness in humans appeared. These were the Severe Acute Respiratory Syndrome coronavirus (SARS-CoV-1), the Middle East Respiratory Syndrome (MERS) coronavirus, and the coronavirus responsible for the COVID-19 pandemic, SARS-CoV-2. As in other affected countries, in the early stages of the pandemic, Singapore had to fumble its way while a clinical understanding of SARS-CoV-1 was being put together.

Less tenable, however, was the bigger claim with respect to emerging infections as a whole. As we saw in the previous chapter, though the 1997 bird flu outbreak in Hong Kong did not reach Singapore, it was a portent of what was to come. That outbreak, and that of the Nipah virus two years later (which did affect Singapore), highlighted the rising threat of zoonotic diseases due to increasing contact and disease transmission between humans and animals.[5] Dr Leo Yee Sin at the TTSH had deemed the Nipah outbreak as a 'small test' and 'appetiser' for SARS.[6]

It should also be noted that Singapore has a long history of infectious disease outbreaks and responses. Epidemiologically, SARS differed from infectious diseases in the past: it was spread mostly by professionals and businesspeople in the age of air travel, rather than deck passengers huddled close together onboard ships.[7] But as documented in the previous chapter, epidemiological surveillance of infectious diseases had been a mainstay of public health in Singapore since the 1970s. The underlying premise was to develop a set of strong 'home defences' against epidemic disease through a combination of epidemiological surveillance, environmental sanitation, public education and mass vaccination. These defences had been tested albeit on smaller scales in minor outbreaks of cholera, influenza and the vector-borne diseases in the late 20th century. On the claim that SARS caught Singapore unprepared, this was true in either one or both of two ways: that the authorities were unaware of this history, or that inadequate attention had been given to the threat of new infectious diseases.

Many of the practical measures put forward by the government and healthcare officials were fairly straightforward, to be expected from capable leaders and officials. Singapore's leaders and officials were capable. They performed well, though not as well as they could have. To take an example, the mini-outbreaks at the hospitals and in the community could have been averted with better preparedness and decision-making, particularly to respect the initially unknown properties of the SARS-CoV-1. There were extenuating circumstances why these and other mistakes occurred, but it is important to acknowledge and learn from them.

Singapore's hospitals were also poorly equipped for SARS after years of under-investment in the control of infectious diseases. The ageing Communicable Disease Centre, built in 1913, had not been replaced despite proposals since the early 1990s. It had only 36 isolation rooms, no support facilities like an X-ray service, a dark room to process films, or computers at nursing stations to monitor the patients.[8] To keep potential SARS cases away from the TTSH (the parent hospital) at the onset of the outbreak, the CDC served momentarily – for a fortnight – as a screening centre before this work was also taken over by the TTSH.

In this period, the CDC's AIDS ward was emptied out for the isolation of probable and suspected SARS cases, as for several months there was no specific laboratory test to diagnose infection by SARS-CoV-1.[9] Four emergency container wards were hastily built at the centre and used for suspected, probable and confirmed SARS cases. Still, many SARS patients warded at the CDC demanded to be treated in a modern hospital. CDC nurse Akhterun Nisha deemed the SARS epidemic the most challenging in her career, with patients asking, 'What place is this?'.[10] With several exit points, the CDC's security was also lax and a SARS patient managed to escape by walking out the gate together with the staff.[11]

There was an overall lack of isolation beds in Singapore, even at the new TTSH campus that was built in 1999, which took the SARS outbreak to rectify. As the hospital's CEO admitted after the epidemic, even the existing plans for a new CDC were inadequate to cope with a disease such as SARS.[12] There was no stockpile of personal protective equipment (PPE: the mask, gloves, googles and gown), which were then regarded as unnecessary in the management of most infectious diseases. The small supply that existed was a holdover from the treatment of tuberculosis.

The SARS outbreak also coincided with a little-known development at the time: the ENV's longstanding public health and epidemiological capabilities were being migrated to the MOH at the time. The transfer had started at the end of 2002 and was completed the following April.[13] Thus it was the MOH and not the ENV that led the response effort. The outbreak occurred at the worst possible timing for Singapore in the midst of this transition.[14]

Some background on SARS is useful for perspective. It was not an extremely transmissible disease. Each case was estimated to infect two to four close contacts on average, though a small number of 'super-spreaders' could transmit the disease to many others. In Singapore, five such super-spreaders accounted for 121 out of the initial 206 cases. The index case and the six clusters linked to her accounted for all the cases except eight. Virtually all infected persons were symptomatic and infectious only after the onset of symptoms. The outbreak could thus be contained by rapidly isolating infected persons and quarantining their close contacts. SARS was largely a nosocomial illness with limited spread in the community; it was easier to contain than a disease like COVID-19. Moreover, SARS patients were infectious only when they had symptoms, though the few patients with atypical symptoms caused further outbreaks and prolonged the course of the epidemic.[15] With effective contact tracing and quarantine, it was possible to ringfence the clusters caused by the super-spreaders. Ultimately, the SARS crisis in Singapore was a small one. This was due in part to the response of the government but also to the clinical nature of the disease.

## Mystery Outbreak at the TTSH

The SARS epidemic in Singapore began on 1 March when the index case was admitted to the TTSH for a persistent fever. She had travelled to Hong Kong on 20 February, staying in the Metropole Hotel where she had contracted the disease from another occupant. Both her travel companions were also infected, but recovered uneventfully at SGH without transmitting the infection to others. It is noteworthy that the super-spreading event on the 9th floor of the hotel resulted in the spread of SARS to Singapore, Vietnam and Canada.

The TTSH soon experienced an outbreak among its staff and patients – this had happened with outbreaks of influenza and other infectious diseases throughout Singapore's history. It was only on 6 March that the MOH was informed about the three cases warded for atypical pneumonia, who had all travelled to Hong Kong the previous month. At the time, the doctors thought they might be dealing with an environmentally-borne disease like Legionnaire's.[16] On the same day, the WHO informed the ministry of similar cases of pneumonia in Hanoi. A week passed.

On 13 March, the WHO despatched a global alert on SARS and the Singapore government responded immediately by issuing a directive to isolate all cases of atypical pneumonia and an advisory against travelling to affected countries. At the TTSH, *The Silent War* book commissioned by the hospital was candid on the myriad problems faced in coming to terms with the unknown disease. The WHO alert finally made the hospital's management consider the pneumonia cases a priority issue. The trio of pneumonia cases were isolated but not before the index case at TTSH had infected 22 people, among them ten healthcare workers. The CEO was informed on 14 March but decided that the Dinner & Dance planned for the staff that night would go ahead. It was fortunate that the nurses who cared for the index patient and attended the event did not spread the infection to others.[17] The thought then, as the Director of Medical Services Professor Tan Chorh Chuan recounted, was that it was bird flu. WHO officials thought so too. But this was quickly quashed when the mysterious disease was found capable of infecting other people, something that bird flu could not do.[18]

The MOH scrambled to put together what was later known as the 'prevent-detect-isolate-contain' strategy. The phrase is nice but confusion reigned at the MOH and the TTSH at the time. The strategy entailed reviving a modified form of quarantine. When Tan Chorh Chuan first broached this to his colleagues, it was thought of as being antiquated.[19] At this stage, the MOH was severely hampered by the lack of information about the novel infection and a reliable diagnostic test.[20]

Two days after the WHO alert, the MOH formed a SARS Taskforce, comprising hospital management, infectious disease physicians and other experts, to provide the medical services and public health measures required to contain the outbreak. An operations centre was set up at the TTSH to deal with the emerging crisis on the same day, which provided updates on the daily situation in the hospital. On the 16th, the ministry instructed emergency departments, as the first point of patients' contact with the hospitals, to adopt the triage system to separate febrile patients from others. The following day, in a key move, SARS was made a notifiable disease.

A week later, on 22 March, the MOH designated the TTSH as the sole hospital to treat SARS cases. All possible cases were to be transferred there and the hospital would empty out other patients. The intention was to isolate all SARS cases at the TTSH and keep other hospitals safe from the epidemic.[21] Infection control measures were implemented in high-risk areas in hospitals to prevent the spread of the disease, including the use of PPE and regular temperature-taking for hospital staff. The supply of PPE was initially very small. Limits were also placed on visitors to the hospital (visitation ceased altogether on 29 April), in-patient transfers and readmissions.

At this stage, the MOH was still leading the SARS response. But it was being overwhelmed by the scale of the measures. The morale of staff at the TTSH was dropping and there was widespread fear about the risk of infection among them, especially those working in the ICU ward.[22] Many nurses faced pressure from their families to quit their jobs.[23] At the CDC, some foreign nurses from the Philippines and China wanted to return home and had to be persuaded to stay.[24]

School closure had occurred in several of Singapore's influenza epidemics. This was a contested issue during SARS. On 21 March, the Minister of Health Lim Hng Kiang told his cabinet colleagues there was no need to close the schools, which were in the midst of a week-long break. They subsequently reopened, but parents were notably anxious about their children's health. On 26 March, the Acting Prime Minister Lee Hsien Loong, along with Lim and the Minister for Education Teo Chee Hean, conferred and decided to err on the side of caution. Schools were closed the following day, bringing relief to many parents, and reopened in early April in phases.[25] At the end of April, it remained mandatory to monitor school children's temperatures twice a day.

On 4 April, the MOH was stunned by an outbreak of SARS at the Singapore General Hospital, involving 13 healthcare workers deployed in two wards. In one of the wards was, unknown to the hospital, a patient who had contracted SARS while sharing the same ward with the index case at the TTSH. This patient, who had chronic kidney disease, was discharged from the TTSH as the policy was to send away non-SARS cases, but subsequently admitted to the SGH for a foot infection. A frenzy of efforts saw the SGH cluster contained within 10 days, without the hospital – Singapore's largest – needing to be shut down. Two entire wards of patients and a surgical team were transferred over to the TTSH at this time.[26]

The SGH received much public criticism for its outbreak. After all, it seemed to have let the healthcare system down. The hospital was accused of being complacent, lacking the discipline to implement effective infection control. Journalist Chua Mui Hoong's commissioned book on SARS even imagined a mock trial on the hospital's culpability.[27] Admittedly, the SGH had failed to recognise that its patient had stayed in the TTSH and act accordingly. In the context of the outbreak, the hospital should have been more vigilant towards new admissions.

However, the SGH outbreak should also be seen in a broader perspective beyond the failings of individuals or the absence of moral qualities. We also have to reckon with the clinical nature of SARS and the decision to designate a single hospital for it. The decision in itself was probably not a wrong one. But in practice, it left little margin for error with a disease that was not fully understood. Though the SGH should have been more alert, some SARS patients did not present with the typical symptoms of the affliction. It was a collective mistake – Singapore's mistake. Tan Chorh Chuan acknowledged that the epidemic would have been shortened if 'more aggressive measures had been introduced in TTSH on 15 March, specifically if all discharges from the hospital were stopped and no visitors to the hospital allowed'.[28]

After the SGH outbreak, the MOH set up a web-based system to give all hospitals access to information that had been missed: updated lists of suspect and probable SARS cases, contacts, persons under quarantine and recent hospitalisation records. The ministry also required that all in-patients with chronic medical conditions warded in the TTSH and SGH be placed on home quarantine for 10 days upon their discharge.[29] Singapore, the SGH outbreak showed, was prompt at learning from specific mistakes during the epidemic.

## The Government at the Helm

In early April, the government assumed control of the situation. Several ministers realised that the MOH was struggling to cope. Public health doctors were ill-prepared to formulate a national response to SARS or communicate it effectively to the public. On the 3rd, Prime Minister Goh Chok Tong met the Minister for Home Affairs Wong Kan Seng (anointed 'troubleshooter' in the cabinet) about activating the Executive Group comprising the permanent secretaries to manage the outbreak. The group had been formed in 1986 in response to the collapse of a local hotel and dealt with major crises in recent Singapore history.[30] The two ministers agreed to activate the Executive Group. On 7 April, after news of the SGH outbreak broke, they decided to form an inter-ministerial committee to direct the group.[31]

The nine-member inter-ministerial committee was chaired by Wong and had representatives from the Health, Education, National Development, and Manpower ministries. This was to provide a high-level oversight on the management of the crisis, including its social and economic impact, and to facilitate cross-ministry efforts.[32] It was also to provide assurance to the public that the epidemic was capably managed.

The ministerial committee was supported by other high-level groups. The Executive Group was to direct the implementation of containment measures by the civil service and draw up plans for different scenarios. A Ministerial SARS Combat Unit was formed on 20 April, headed by the Minister of Transport and Information, Communications and the Arts Khaw Boon Wan. It worked closely with the hospitals to implement infection control and contain the outbreaks.[33] In the unit were three Ministers of State who were doctors in order to 'blood' the junior ministers and give 'teeth' to the infection control efforts in the hospitals.[34] The creation of both groups showed that beyond a certain point, major epidemics could not be siloed as a purely health issue.

On 8 April, the MOH issued a directive under the Private Hospitals and Medical Clinics Act requiring hospitals and nursing homes to adopt protocols on triage, isolation of cases, use of PPE, and infection control. The following day, air passengers arriving in Singapore were required to complete a health declaration card while locally built thermal scanners were deployed at the Changi Airport to detect instances of fever. On 11 April, low-wage foreign workers arriving in Singapore had to serve a two-week quarantine while those who had visited infected countries would not be allowed entry. In contrast, foreign professionals and Singaporeans who had visited infected countries were simply asked to quarantine themselves voluntarily for ten days.

Due to the fear of super-spreading events, the MOH cast a 'wide net' in the surveillance, isolation and quarantine of SARS cases and contacts.

Epidemiology had a key role to play, providing needed information on the transmission of the disease. Initially it was beyond the ministry's capability, and personnel from a grassroots statutory board, the People's Association, had to be roped in to do contact tracing.[35] The force was later bolstered by national servicemen from the Ministry of Defence. The criteria used was broad and the yield low among the large numbers of people traced and quarantined, but the epidemiological work succeeded in getting many probable SARS cases isolated at an early stage. Tan Chorh Chuan later acknowledged the need for more sensitive tests for SARS that would reduce the number of people quarantined.[36]

Over 12,000 contacts were placed under home quarantine or telephone surveillance under the provisions of the Infectious Diseases Act. Home quarantine in particular entailed a high degree of restriction and surveillance: video cameras were installed in the house and the quarantined person had to appear in front of them daily. Those found to have transgressed quarantine orders had to wear an electronic tag that would sound an alert should they leave the home. The ministerial committee discussed the question of civil liberties but quickly dismissed it; public health took precedence. Minister Wong later joked,

> You better quarantine him [the contact]. Otherwise, he'll get more freedom after that but he may be dead. Or he's infecting other people and causing them great disasters.[37]

The measures appeared to work. But 'leakages' from the TTSH and SGH outbreaks continued to occur. The period from 19 April to 4 May saw an alarming case of community spread. The Pasir Panjang Wholesale Centre witnessed an outbreak traced to a worker there who was the brother of the SGH index case. The centre was closed for 15 days while contact tracers, including People's Association personnel, located 1,917 people and placed them under home quarantine. The National Environment Agency also conducted daily temperature-taking for stallholders and workers at other markets in Singapore.[38]

But even though the Pasir Panjang outbreak was a small one, again mistakes were made. The police swiftly cordoned off the centre and sent the stallholders and workers home. This made it difficult to trace them afterwards for quarantine. At this time, the lack of an integrated computer database for contact tracing became obvious. The MOH's contact tracers were still using spreadsheets or even paper copies. It was difficult to obtain information on staff movement, people's contact numbers, the identities of people being isolated or quarantined, and case management. The centre's closure also temporarily disrupted the supply of fresh vegetables in Singapore, while causing financial difficulties for stallholders and their assistants. The government gave them and others under home quarantine allowances for the period of closure.[39]

On 28 April, as contact tracing and home quarantine grew, the government reinforced the provisions of the Infectious Diseases Act, stipulating penalties for those who broke quarantine. The MOH had invoked the Act to quarantine SARS patients and suspected cases discharged from hospital a month ago. However, the Act did not contain penalties for those who violated quarantine. As Ooi et al. intimated, the quarantine move was not so much backed by scientific evidence as by the pressure to prevent community spread of a disease with no effective treatment or vaccine.[40]

The first worker who contracted SARS at the Pasir Panjang Wholesale Centre caused an outbreak at the National University Hospital where he was treated. Again, he had been missed. Eventually the disease spread to several other public hospitals. These mini-outbreaks would have been serious if SARS was a more transmissible disease. The period from the beginning of May to mid-July witnessed much contact tracing and quarantine as a result, affecting many people's daily lives. But no new cases of SARS were uncovered. From the middle of July, the measures were scaled back. The SARS epidemic ended within three months. It had infected 238 people in Singapore, of whom 33 died, giving rise to a mortality rate of 13.9 per cent.

As in the pandemics of the colonial era, the SARS outbreak spurred the government to renew efforts to improve the general state of sanitation. A public campaign was launched during the epidemic to urge people to wash their hands thoroughly and maintain a high level of personal hygiene. This would be replicated during the COVID-19 pandemic.

## The SARS Metaphor

The SARS experience illustrated most people's support for the containment measures. This was a key factor in Singapore's ability to manage the outbreak. It departed from a long history of avoidance and non-notification during the epidemics of the colonial period. Government and health officials hailed the people's support in controlling SARS, while sociological surveys found a general willingness to accept restrictive measures such as prevention and quarantine.[41] A key factor in people's support was the official discourse on the threat of SARS and the measures adopted to combat it.

Much of the research on the official discourse has centred on two differing themes. One was the transparency and clarity of information communicated by the government to the public. This was an area where Singapore received much praise from the WHO, compared to other countries in the region that initially tried to cover up their outbreaks.[42] The MOH held press conferences chaired by the Minister for Health on the daily situation. A SARS television channel was launched to convey information to the people in various languages and dialects, though viewership not surprisingly was low.

Tan Chorh Chuan credited the open and frank communication for channelling people's fear of disease into support for the control efforts.[43] Other (usually local) scholars have endorsed the government's call for people to be cooperative and socially responsible, such as in maintaining personal hygiene.[44] This was exemplified by Prime Minister Goh's open letter to the people on 22 April. He beseeched them to be socially responsible, provide relevant personal information to the authorities and support the containment measures.[45]

Several surveys revealed Singaporeans' understanding of SARS and the government's response. People were less clear about certain aspects of the disease, such as how it was transmitted and the appropriate infection control measures.[46] While this was expected for a new disease, it did suggest that people's support for the measures was due less to an understanding of the science, but their trust in the government and public institutions.[47] By and large, Singaporeans wanted the government to tell them what to do during the crisis rather than have to figure it out for themselves.

The official discourse had a flip side. If community cooperation was required, it rendered those who contravened the containment measures into anti-national and anti-social figures. These persons found the social stigma against SARS transposed onto them.[48] The name of the index patient was published in the newspapers, as was that of a 50-year-old man who was convicted of repeatedly breaking his quarantine.[49] In his open letter, Prime Minister Goh used similar cases to emphasise the importance of cooperation. He criticised the worker at the Pasir Panjang Wholesale Centre for going to work despite having as fever and sparking off another outbreak. He also deemed socially irresponsible a family who took off their masks and went to a food centre instead of waiting for an ambulance to bring them to hospital.[50] They became known as 'The Family of Eight', facing public ostracism for putting the community at risk.[51] Such naming and shaming was one thing the majority of Singaporeans (64 per cent in one survey) seemed to disagree with.[52]

The second theme about the SARS discourse was that it was overly strident. Some critics alleged that the government worked hand in hand with the mainstream media to propagate a rejuvenated form of Confucianism (first used in the 1980s) to mobilise the citizenry and forge social consensus.[53] In a newspaper editorial, Chua Mui Hoong pointed out the lack of checks in the government's robust response to SARS.[54]

The SARS discourse has also been criticised for its militaristic language. The TTSH's COO was a former army officer, and much of the language and manner of the official response was couched in military terms.[55] The hospital's commissioned book, titled 'The Silent War', was replete with military metaphors such as 'ground zero', 'the first line of defence' and 'trench warfare'.[56] As Yasmin Ibrahim pointed out, the use of military metaphors is common in the history of medicine, most recently during the AIDS pandemic in the 1980s.[57] In Singapore, some scholars have attributed the SARS discourse to the national culture of perpetual vulnerability. When the country became independent in 1965, it was not assured of its survival as a nation, and this sense of vulnerability to both external and internal threats has persisted in the government's outlook and policies.[58] A pandemic presents an external danger, but equally perilous was the apathetic or uncooperative populace. A war discourse is deemed to be necessary to rouse the citizens in this situation. Singapore's state-owned newspapers duly did so, likening the SARS outbreak to recent military events still fresh in people's memories, such as 9/11 and the war in Iraq.[59]

As Ibrahim explained, the war metaphor worked by narrowing the frame of people's reactions to a pandemic, subtly inserting implicit values into what appeared to be a rational or practical response.[60] In a war, the enemy was an absolute threat and coming together against it was unconditional. A war metaphor not only galvanises the population to support the government's measures, but also undercuts any countervailing criticism, opposition or proposal of alternative action.

On the other hand, the war discourse could place additional strain on the populace and create social divides. A nation could not be expected to agree on all aspects of a policy even during a crisis. Singaporeans held varying, even contradictory views on the disclosure of personal information during SARS. While they largely agreed that the public good came before the right to privacy during an epidemic, they were also fearful of being ostracised should knowledge of their illness become known to their employers and the public.[61]

Teo et al.'s survey found considerable minority disagreement on several such measures, for example publicising the names of those under quarantine orders, the use of home video surveillance and the requirement for students to be sent home if they had a temperature.[62] The last was not an issue of rights, but a practical matter, with parents struggling to make childcare arrangements. History, too, makes a clear distinction between war and its metaphors. A 70-year-old cobbler who had lived through the Second World War and the Japanese Occupation made light of the metaphor during SARS:

> War is definitely more scary. If you got bombed, you died. If the Japanese didn't like your face, they killed you. With SARS, at least you stood a chance of surviving.[63]

His remarks provide a glimpse into how differentially the older generation would respond in a pandemic. This would become clear during the next coronavirus pandemic in 2019.

The mainstream narrative forged in the aftermath of the SARS episode contained fragments of anti-social behaviour that were overcome by a nation closing ranks and coming together. There were numerous anecdotes of nurses being evicted by their landlords, taxis refusing to stop at the hospitals or families under quarantine shunned by their neighbours.[64] In the SARS story, wrongdoers were not on the 'right' side of the struggle – doctors, by contrast, were portrayed as typically selfless and heroic. Anecdotally, there were senior doctors who sent their juniors to see the patients. We know this by working backwards from sources: the MOH quietly learned from the experience and when the National Centre for Infectious Diseases (NCID) was built, it was made clear that all staff regardless of seniority had to deal with infectious disease outbreaks.

Like *The Silent War*, Chua Mui Hoong's journalistic account, *A Defining Moment: How Singapore Beat SARS*, typified the main narrative. Based largely on interviews with political leaders and senior doctors, it foregrounded their perspectives and experiences, such as Minister Wong's anecdote about how he chanced upon the idea of home video surveillance, or the doctor who gave very public dressing downs to colleagues who did not follow the infection control measures. Where the book contained interviews of ordinary people, these were careful curations: a sample of individuals who freely volunteered their services to the cause or found creative micro-solutions. They all expressed the 'kampong spirit' – Singapore's quintessential term for a close community. None related to the dilemmas of people who shunned the SARS patients and healthcare workers.

Nevertheless, Chua's access to political leaders, healthcare officials and civil servants makes her book a valuable document on Singapore's response from above. She is to be credited for highlighting some major mistakes made, such as the amount of time it took for the government to take control. We know from the book there were dissenting views within the cabinet on school closure and civil liberties, as well as the existence of the hitherto little-known Executive Group, which tells us about Singapore's preparedness for emergency situations. Another interesting titbit was provided by a senior administrator, who accused middle bureaucrats of being guided by self-interest, which says something about the state of the civil service at the time.[65] Some of the intellectual honesty in the book probably owes to long-time civil servant and diplomat Tommy Koh, who headed the advisory panel for the project.

## Learning from SARS and the H1N1 Test

The social and economic effects of SARS, though short-term, were severe. The outbreak hit Singapore's service industries particularly hard, as consumer demand fell in the tourism and hospitality sectors. This was worsened by the arguably unnecessary travel restrictions recommended by the WHO, which hurt many Asian economies while having little effect in stemming the spread of the disease.[66] Local services such as retail, taxis and food and beverages also suffered. Together with the economic fallout from the Iraq War, the retrenchment and social distancing measures during SARS saw employment fall by its worst quarterly decline since the 1985 recession. The plummet was particularly steep in the services, construction and manufacturing.[67]

In this context, the government introduced remarkable efforts to boost consumer, public and investor confidence during and after the crisis. The strategy was to promote the island as 'SARS-free' and distinguish it from other pandemic-hit countries in the region. Measures such as temperature screening were added to the usual repertoire of environmental sanitation work.[68] To stave off a likely recession, the government urged tourists to return to Singapore, while a 'Step Out Singapore' campaign encouraged locals to go out to shopping malls and other public places. Conversely, Singaporeans were told to be socially responsible – to monitor their temperatures daily and avoid public places if they were unwell.[69]

These messages have a long history reaching back to the colonial era, especially during the influenza outbreaks. But now there was an added dimension of assuring foreign investors and visitors that Singapore was safe to return to. These efforts did create tension between the aims of pandemic control and economic recovery. As doctors K.U. Menon and Goh Kee Tai pointed out, the government was encouraging tourists to visit Singapore at the same time restrictions were imposed on those arriving from infected areas. It was also urging locals to stay away from crowded places while resuming their normal lives.[70]

The government formed an International Image Task Force to correct erroneous reports about the local situation and maintain Singapore's global image. An interesting move was to dispel the misconception that many locals were wearing masks. On 3 May, amid the flurry of contact tracing, the cabinet had discussed whether people should wear masks. There were both advocates and dissenters, but the decisive factor was the government's wish to differentiate Singapore from Hong Kong, Taiwan and China where masks were commonly worn. As in the 1957 influenza epidemic, the government decided that masks need not be worn unless if one was sick and went to see a doctor.[71]

Less obvious was the psychological impact of SARS, but this was also considerable. It was expected that the government would announce financial support packages for people placed under home quarantine and industries hit by the reduced consumer demand. Similarly, the unions worked within the established tripartite system to save jobs and minimise retrenchment by getting workers to accept wage cuts.[72] But it was more difficult to deal with problems in the private realm.

As George Bishop noted, the psychological legacy of SARS was out of proportion to the number of people who contracted the disease. The epidemic created much social anxiety and even panic about the risks of infection, especially in the early weeks. The stigma against healthcare workers and people under quarantine also robbed them of the community and neighbourly support they most needed at the time.[73] Among SARS survivors, fear-induced loneliness and discrimination from others were embedded into their experiences of hospitalisation and recovery, worsening their mental distress. The use of PPE by healthcare workers, though scientifically justified, made many patients feel 'ostracised' and 'dirty'. Some discharged patients indeed practised self-stigmatisation, avoiding contact with their family members on their own accord. The protocols of home surveillance continued to remind them that they were a threat to the community. In general, SARS patients and contacts felt hapless and discriminated, unable to control their circumstances during and after the outbreak.[74]

In the wake of SARS, Tan Chorh Chuan provided astute reflections on how Singapore had fared. Given the peculiar nature of the disease, the surveillance, isolation and quarantine measures that had worked would be ineffective if infectious patients could be asymptomatic (as with COVID-19). He acknowledged that the nation-wide temperature screening had little effect – none of the school children who had SARS were detected this way – but thought that the assurance it gave the parents and the public was valuable.

Likewise, the much vaunted and expensively assembled thermal scanners did not pick up any SARS cases at the airport.[75] The five imported SARS cases subsequent to the index case developed fever only after leaving the airport. Both measures were adopted during the COVID-19 pandemic.

Tan highlighted several key lessons from SARS – and the central problem – for Singapore. It was crucial to have standardised criteria and processes to collect information and inform the stakeholders in a timely manner. At the same time, any planned response to a future epidemic had to be flexible to adapt to rapidly evolving circumstances. People could not simply rely on the protocols; they had to be prepared to accept that these may need to be replaced by new ones.[76]

As would be expected of an efficient state, Singapore duly recognised the lessons of the SARS epidemic, albeit too specifically and narrowly. The SOPs (standard operating procedures) that had been missing were now in place. In the aftermath of SARS, the MOH developed an integrated IT system called the Infectious Disease Alert and Clinical Database to support surveillance, contact tracing, isolation, and quarantine efforts.[77] The system was used in September 2003 for contact tracing work when a local researcher was infected with SARS. The ministry also established a contact tracing centre and stockpiled a six-month supply of PPE. These improvements leaned heavily on the SARS experience.

In one aspect though, learning from SARS was not narrow. It involved an interesting turnaround: it had taken a coronavirus outbreak to alert the government to the threat posed by influenza. A National Influenza Pandemic Readiness and Response Plan was drawn up, acknowledging that the government can and should actively deal with influenza outbreaks. Residents in nursing homes and at the Institute of Mental Health, which had experienced a scare during SARS, were vaccinated for influenza. The flu vaccine was also offered to public healthcare workers.[78]

Tan also noted the lack of manpower, especially contact tracers and ICU staff, as well as isolation rooms when an outbreak created a surge in demand for them.[79] This was not a new problem, but one that Singapore's medical officials had recognised in the 1950s. An infectious disease epidemic would place extraneous demands on the healthcare system that would not exist in normal times. In the wake of SARS, a community hospital next to TTSH was converted into the Communicable Disease Centre 2, which had 39 isolation beds and 18 ICUs.[80] But the original CDC at Moulmein Road remained, in name at least, the main isolation hospital for infectious diseases.

The SARS episode also saw the formulation of a four-coloured response system, ranked according to the severity of the outbreak. At the Yellow alert level, the focus would be to prevent imported cases and detect local cases quickly. If the outbreak worsened, the colour would be raised to Orange and finally Red, signifying enhanced containment measures, such as infection control in hospitals, isolation and quarantine. In the case of a Red alert, schools and other public institutions would be closed.[81]

These protocols were apparently validated in a simulation drill of a SARS-like respiratory disease outbreak across the MOH several months later.[82] But a better test of Singapore's learning from the epidemic was during the H1N1 swine flu outbreak in 2009, caused by the novel influenza A (H1N1)pdm09 virus. The virus was responsible for 1,301 cases in Singapore and the disease was made notifiable. The comprehensive response based on the SARS experience was mobilised for the new outbreak. It was led by a Homefront Crisis Management System at the helm, consisting of an inter-ministerial committee chaired by the Minister for Home Affairs. The committee was, again, supported by an executive group of permanent secretaries taking charge of various policy areas. As in 2003, the political leaders presided over the H1N1 Taskforce led by the permanent secretary of Health and the Director of Medical Services. This was supported by the H1N1-2009 Clinical Group, which dealt with clinical and public health matters.[83]

Many of the measures implemented during the H1N1 episode had their origins in 2003: the use of PPE, triage at emergency departments, expansion of the Infectious Diseases Act to require notification of cases, isolation and quarantine of cases and contacts, infection control in hospitals, restrictions on movements of staff between hospitals, regular temperature checks and partial closure of classes, thermal scanning at the airports and a mass media campaign to inform the people.[84] These measures showed the benefits of learning from SARS.

Yet there were significant differences between the events of 2003 and 2009. For one, influenza A (H1N1)pdm09, while also a novel virus, was not as virulent as SARS-CoV-1.[85] Evidence that the disease was milder than expected led the MOH to depart from the WHO's system of pandemic phases and focus on the disease's severity instead of its spread. Healthcare institutions in Singapore stepped down their responses to focus on mitigating rather than containing the outbreak, in effect shifting the burden of response from hospitals to the community. There was no designated hospital for H1N1; instead Pandemic Preparedness Clinics (that is, designated GP clinics in the community) dealt with most cases.[86]

The H1N1 epidemic was a good test run for the SARS-based plan. It showed that the plan had to change and accommodate new outbreaks. As Joanna Tay et al. noted, Singapore had not anticipated a virus that was highly transmissible but low in morbidity, leading to longer waves of outbreaks. Singapore also made gradual transitions in alert levels that helped the public understand how the situation was changing, but these small changes confused healthcare workers used to clearer distinctions.[87] Some of the measures implemented during H1N1 anticipated those that became commonplace during the COVID-19 pandemic: monitoring developments in and learning from other cities, and social distancing measures adopted by businesses and the community.

SARS was a historic event for Singapore in many ways. Though a mini-epidemic, it had an effect out of proportion to its scale and severity. It demonstrated at the start of the new millennium that the threat of infectious disease, in the form of zoonotic infections, was very much alive. This had been anticipated by health officials and epidemiologists since the 1970s. Singapore's leaders and officials tried to learn from SARS to prepare for the next big outbreak. They were ready to use quarantine and epidemiological surveillance together, rather than choose between them, to control the outbreak.

But it is clear now that the lessons of SARS were imperfectly drawn. The administration attempted to prepare for a future threat without studying those outbreaks that predated SARS. The singular focus on the events of 2003 produced a response plan that was too narrow and rigid. Such a plan could not be fully applicable in a different historical context. It would have benefited from a larger sample of infectious diseases and epidemics in Singapore history, which tells us equally about the successes, failures and mistakes made.

At the same time, the SARS narrative reinforced the official belief that only specific lessons needed to be learned. The government acknowledged that mistakes had been made, but these were in the main attributable to the failings of individuals or institutions. Deeper reflection on mistakes was overlaid by the metanarrative of national unity: that Singapore had fought a dangerous enemy and (largely) won. But when failings are not properly acknowledged – and there is an argument to be made that the post-mortem should take place as a public discussion rather than narrowly amongst political leaders and medical experts – it is likely that the full lessons of SARS would not be learned.

## Notes

1 Chua Mui Hoong, *A Defining Moment: How Singapore Beat SARS* (Singapore: Ministry of Information, Communications and the Arts, 2004).
2 Liew Kai Khiun, 'Terribly Severe Though Mercifully Short: The Episode of the 1918 Influenza in British Malaya', *Modern Asian Studies*, Vol. 41 No. 2, March 2007, pp. 221–252.
3 Tan Tock Seng Hospital, *The Silent War, 1 March–31 May 2003* (Singapore: Tan Tock Seng Hospital, 2004), p. 9.
4 Mark Honigsbaum, *The Pandemic Century: A History of Global Contagion from the Spanish Flu to COVID-19* (London: W.H. Allen, 2020).
5 Alfred Jay Bollet, *Plagues & Poxes: The Impact of Human History on Epidemic Disease* (New York: Demos, 2004).
6 Loh Kah Seng, Interview with Leo Yee Sin, 10 June 2019.
7 Bollet, *Plagues & Poxes.*
8 Tan Tock Seng Hospital, *The Silent War.*
9 Loh Kah Seng, Interview with Dorothy Gomez, 29 May 2019.
10 Loh Kah Seng, Interview with Akhterun Nisha, 11 March 2019.
11 Tan Tock Seng Hospital, *The Silent War.*
12 Tan Tock Seng Hospital, *The Silent War.*
13 Loh Kah Seng, Interview with Goh Kee Tai, 16 February 2017.
14 Loh Kah Seng, Interview with Ooi Peng Lim, 6 June 2019.
15 Tan Chorh-Chuan, 'SARS in Singapore – Key Lessons from an Epidemic', *Annals – Academy of Medicine Singapore*, Vol. 35 No. 5, May 2006, pp. 345–349.
16 Chua, *A Defining Moment.*
17 Tan Tock Seng Hospital, *The Silent War.*
18 Tan Chorh-Chuan, 'Public Health Response: A View from Singapore', in Malik Peiris et al. (ed.), *Severe Acute Respiratory Syndrome* (Malden, MA: Blackwell Publishing, 2005), pp. 139–164.
19 Loh Kah Seng, Interview with Tan Chorh Chuan, 4 August 2021.
20 Tan, 'Public Health Response'.
21 Tan, 'SARS in Singapore'.
22 Tan Tock Seng Hospital, *The Silent War.*

23 Tan Tock Seng Hospital, *The Silent War*.

24 Loh Kah Seng, Interview with Harbhajan Singh, 21 March 2019.

25 Chua, *A Defining Moment*.

26 Singapore General Hospital, 'Never Again', 29 June 2022, www.sgh.com.sg/news/lighternotes/never-again

27 Chua, *A Defining Moment*.

28 Tan, 'Public Health Response', p. 152.

29 Tan, 'Public Health Response'.

30 Sumiko Tan (ed.), *In This Together: Singapore's COVID-19 Story* (Singapore: Straits Times Press, 2022).

31 Chua, *A Defining Moment*.

32 Tan, 'SARS in Singapore'.

33 Tan, 'Public Health Response'.

34 Chua, *A Defining Moment*, p. 59.

35 Chua, *A Defining Moment*, p. 137.

36 Tan, 'SARS in Singapore'.

37 Chua, *A Defining Moment*, p. 137.

38 Tan, 'Public Health Response'.

39 Chua, *A Defining Moment*.

40 Peng Lim Ooi, Sonny Lim and Suok Kai Chew, 'Use of Quarantine in the Control of SARS in Singapore', *American Journal of Infection Control*, Vol. 33 No. 5, June 2005, pp. 252–257.

41 G.M. Leung, S. Quah, Ho L.M., Ho S.Y., A.J. Hedley, Lee H.P. and Lam T.H., 'Community Psycho-Behavioural Surveillance and Related Impact on Outbreak Control in Hong Kong and Singapore during the SARS Epidemic', *Hong Kong Medical Journal*, Vol. 15 Suppl. 9, 2009, pp. 30–34.

42 Khai Leong Ho, 'SARS, Policy-making and Lesson-drawing', in Tommy Koh, Aileen Plant and Eng Hin Lee (eds), *The New Global Threat: Severe Acute Respiratory Syndrome and Its Impacts* (Singapore: World Scientific Publishing, 2003), pp. 195–208.

43 Tan, 'Public Health Response'.

44 Pheng-Soon Lee, 'SARS – Lessons on the Role of Social Responsibility in Containing an Epidemic', in Koh et al., *The New Global Threat*, pp. 273–282.

45 Goh Chok Tong, Singapore government press release, 'Fighting SARS Together', 22 April 2003.

46 Lim, 'War with SARS'.

47 M. Deurenberg-Yap, L.L. Foo, Y.Y. Low, S.P. Chan, K. Vijaya and M. Lee, 'The Singaporean Response to the SARS Outbreak: Knowledge Sufficiency Versus Public Trust', *Health Promotion International*, Vol. 20 No. 4, June 2005, pp. 320–326.

48 Peggy Teo, Brenda S.A. Yeoh and Shir Nee Ong, 'SARS in Singapore: Surveillance Strategies in a Globalising City', *Health Policy*, Vol. 72, 2005, pp. 279–291.

49 Catherine Tay Swee Kian, *Infectious Diseases Law & SARS* (Singapore: Times Media, 2003).

50 Goh, 'Fighting SARS Together'.

51 'Remembering: A Straits Times SARS Special', *Straits Times*, 22 July 2003.

52 Vivien K.G. Lim, 'War with SARS: An Empirical Study of Knowledge of SARS Transmission and Attitude Toward Working with SARS Victims Among Singaporeans', Research paper #03–15, Faculty of Business Administration, National University of Singapore, 2003.

53 Ian Weber, Tan Howe Yang and Law Loo Shien, '"Triumph over Adversity": Singapore Mobilises Confucian Values to Combat SARS', in John H. Powers and Xiaosui Xiao (eds), *The Social Construction of SARS: Studies of a Health Communication Crisis* (Amsterdam: John Benjamins, 2008), pp. 145–162.

54 *Straits Times*, 10 May 2003, p. H11.

55 Chua, *A Defining Moment*.
56 Tan Tock Seng Hospital, *The Silent War*.
57 Yasmin Ibrahim, 'SARS and the Rhetoric of War in Singapore', *Crossroads: An Interdisciplinary Journal of Southeast Asian Studies*, Vol. 18 No. 2, 2007, pp. 90–119.
58 Teo at al., 'SARS in Singapore'.
59 Ibrahim, 'SARS and the Rhetoric of War in Singapore'.
60 Ibrahim, 'SARS and the Rhetoric of War in Singapore'.
61 Lim, 'War with SARS'.
62 Teo at al., 'SARS in Singapore'.
63 'Remembering: A Straits Times SARS Special', p. 8.
64 Chua, *A Defining Moment*; 'Remembering: A Straits Times SARS Special'.
65 Chua, *A Defining Moment*.
66 Paul Ananth Tambyah, 'The Infection Control Response to SARS in Hospitals and Institutions', in Koh et al., *The New Global Threat*, pp. 243–272.
67 Grace O.M. Lee and Malcolm Warner, *The Political Economy of the SARS Epidemic: The Impact on Human Resources in East Asia* (London: Routledge, 2008).
68 Chua, *A Defining Moment*.
69 Chua, *A Defining Moment*.
70 K.U. Menon and K.T. Goh, 'Transparency and Trust: Risk Communications and the Singapore Experience in Managing SARS', *Journal of Communication Management*, Vol. 9 No. 4, 2005, pp. 375–383.
71 Chua, *A Defining Moment*.
72 Chua, *A Defining Moment*.
73 George D. Bishop, 'SARS: A Psychological Perspective', in Koh et al., *The New Global Threat*, pp. 209–220.
74 Nicholas Chew Wuen Ming, *Psychological Distress and Coping in Severe Acute Respiratory Syndrome*, unpublished thesis, Faculty of Medicine, National University of Singapore, 2004, p. 55.
75 Tan, 'SARS in Singapore'.
76 Tan, 'SARS in Singapore'.
77 Tan, 'SARS in Singapore'.
78 Tan, 'Public Health Response'.
79 Tan, 'Public Health Response'.
80 Tan, 'Public Health Response'.
81 Tan, 'Public Health Response'.
82 Tan, 'SARS in Singapore'; Loh Kah Seng, Interview with Chen Jing, 26 August 2021.
83 Joanne Tay, Yeuk Fan Ng, Jeffery Cutter and Lyn James, 'Influenza A (H1N1-2009) Pandemic in Singapore – Public Health Control Measures Implemented and Lessons Learnt', *Annals – Academy of Medicine Singapore*, Vol. 39, 2010, pp. 313–324.
84 Tay et al., 'Influenza A (H1N1–2009) Pandemic in Singapore'.
85 George Dehner, *Global Flu and You: A History of Influenza* (London: Reaktion Books, 2012).
86 Tay et al., 'Influenza A (H1N1-2009) Pandemic in Singapore'.
87 Tay et al., 'Influenza A (H1N1-2009) Pandemic in Singapore'.

# 11 COVID-19

## A Culmination and a Departure of Sorts

If SARS was a case of Singapore not knowing its history, the COVID-19 pandemic highlighted the consequences of leaning on the most recent event. The government took heed of the experience of 2003 in preparing the pandemic response plan. But because COVID-19 was a very different disease, using a sample of one was likely to confound and mislead. As Defence Minister Ng Eng Hen admitted during the pandemic, 'many unknowns and many assumptions [were] made because of our experience with SARS and H1N1'.[1] The government's efforts in the early months of COVID-19 seemed to be trying to fight the SARS epidemic again. In the decade and a half since SARS, the history of Singapore's pandemics had not received any official interest.

In this chapter, as for SARS, we look at COVID-19 through a historical lens, contextualising the current crisis as a culmination of previous outbreaks and (hopefully) as a departure of sorts. At the state level, the government's response, even more so than in 2003, was characterised by strong leadership and mobilisation of the people. The British had attempted quarantine and surveillance measures during the colonial period, but lacked comparable political commitment, resources, expertise and social reach. They (and the Labour Front government in 1957) allowed influenza outbreaks to burn out.

The social history of COVID-19 in Singapore also showed continuity and change, as with other pandemics in the past. The government's safe management measures and mass vaccination programme were largely effective, accepted by the majority of the population, but there were some who resisted or struggled to follow them. These difficulties are not new: immigrants in colonial Singapore had long been unwilling to report infectious disease to the authorities or accept immunisation for smallpox. This had begun to change after the Second World War and particularly after Singapore became an independent state. But the reasons for ingrained resistance in the present day have remained of a practical and social nature.

As in previous outbreaks, COVID-19 hit the vulnerable groups hardest: the elderly, low-income families and migrant workers. This was due to the nature of the epidemic itself but also the public health measures, which affected people's lives and livelihood. To stand in the shoes of the socially vulnerable, we sought to read official and media sources carefully (sometimes against the

DOI: 10.4324/9781003384014-12

grain), while also drawing upon sociological studies and our oral history interviews with migrant workers. Political leaders and senior doctors have been given prominent coverage in the mainstream media. The 2022 *Straits Times* publication edited by journalist Sumiko Tan, *In This Together: Singapore's COVID-19 Story*, offers some useful insights into the government's response.[2]

Media accounts are, however, less useful for a social account of an epidemic. *In This Together* contains curated interviews of healthcare workers and ordinary people, but unanchored to a set of research questions. They float about in the story as heart-warming soundbites to add colour to the narrative of a shared national experience.[3] Through our interviews with migrant workers, we were able to uncover the struggles of a marginal group not unlike the coolies of colonial Singapore. Testimonies of migrant workers and field interviews with vulnerable Singaporeans deepen our understanding of COVID-19's social impact. They reveal underlying issues that had long existed – historically, quarantine and surveillance have had adverse social effects in the colonial period, and the working class in Chinatown had been hard-hit by the 1957 influenza epidemic. The story of COVID-19 would be incomplete without social and historical perspectives. Singapore's policymakers have struggled to come to terms with both the public health aspects of a fast-evolving outbreak and the socio-economic repercussions for vulnerable groups.

## The Shadow of SARS

As Tan Chorh Chuan, the Director of Medical Services in 2003 and Chief Health Scientist at the MOH since 2018, related in an interview with us in 2021, senior health officials took SARS as their frame of reference when formulating the early response to COVID-19.[4] The government's White Paper on the COVID-19 pandemic, published in March 2023, called the first three months between January and March 2020 'early days of fog'.[5] As the new coronavirus was then not well understood, the government initially adopted a strong 'Zero COVID' policy as it did for SARS. The collapse of healthcare systems in Wuhan, China and northern Italy reinforced this decision. As with SARS, the 'Zero COVID' policy entailed an unrelenting attempt to stamp out the disease by isolating patients, quarantining close contacts, protecting the healthcare system, and preventing transmission in the community.

But COVID-19 turned out to be a very different type of disease. Its key clinical features were only discovered later: unlike SARS, it could cause severe illness but was mild for the majority of infected persons, while it could be transmitted to others up to two days before any symptoms appeared. This made it highly infectious, much more difficult to ringfence and capable of spreading widely in the community. SARS-CoV-2 – the virus behind COVID-19 – resembles the existing human coronaviruses that cause the relatively harmless common cold, rather than the zoonotic coronaviruses of the 20th century – SARS-CoV and the Middle-East Respiratory Syndrome coronavirus (MERS-CoV) that spread mainly in nosocomial or household settings.

Officially, Singapore's 'Zero COVID' policy lasted for close to 15 months till mid-2021, when the appearance of the vaccines enabled the government to adopt an alternative policy. Technically, it could be said to have ended in April 2020 when the circuit breaker was announced. With the lockdown, the government adopted a 'Low COVID' policy to limit the spread of SARS-CoV-2 through a combination of physical distancing, epidemiological surveillance and quarantine till the decision was announced in 2021 that Singapore should live normally with COVID-19.

Historically, many infectious diseases in Singapore continued to circulate in the community long after the initial outbreak. Tuberculosis has remained endemic despite robust efforts at case-finding, treatment, vaccination, and elimination after the Second World War. A national elimination programme was implemented in 1997, but has also not achieved its aims.[6] We agree that an initial outbreak should be met by a robust response, but subsequent measures might shift from strong quarantine and isolation to regular epidemiological surveillance to prevent another explosive outbreak. This had been the practice in the surveillance of influenza, cholera and tuberculosis since the 1970s. With COVID-19, the government was right to minimise the initial impact of a disease that could cause severe illness and spread widely. Its calibrated response, taking into account changing circumstances both local and global, was well-suited for adapting to COVID-19 and its variants over the long term. But a more nuanced response thereafter would have mitigated the impact of restrictions on migrant workers, the elderly and low-income families.

In the final days of December 2019, MOH officials began to hear about cases of atypical pneumonia in the city of Wuhan. On 2 January 2020, as countries in the region increased their surveillance for the mystery disease, a workgroup at the ministry headed by Deputy Director of Medical Services Kenneth Mak decided to do the same. The MOH sent out an advisory to doctors to look out for patients with atypical pneumonia who had recently travelled to Wuhan, while arrivals at the airport had their temperature screened. On 21 January, Singapore raised the DORSCON (Disease Outbreak Response System Condition) level from green to yellow, indicating an increased threat of transmission. Two days later, the index case appeared: a tourist from Wuhan who was visiting Singapore.

The SARS influence was apparent when the government formed a Multi-ministry Task Force (MTF) to lead a whole-of-government response a day earlier, on 22 January. The 10-member group was headed by two co-chairs: Gan Kim Yong, the Minister for Health, who had initiated discussions with Senior Minister Teo Chee Hean, and Lawrence Wong, the Minister for National Development. The MTF was advised by Deputy Prime Minister Heng Swee Keat and had ministerial representatives from Trade and Industry, Education, Manpower, Communications and Information, Environment and Water Resources, Social and Family Development, and Transport.[7] Following a cabinet reshuffle in May 2021, the group had three co-chairs, Gan (now the Minister for Trade and Industry), Wong (the Finance Minister) and Ong Ye

Kung (the new Health Minister). As the MTF led the government's response, Prime Minister Lee Hsien Loong was kept informed and limited his public role to a number of televised speeches on key changes and developments, such as announcing the circuit breaker on 7 April 2020.

The MTF, as during SARS, was intended as a closed forum for members to submit the strongest possible argument on behalf of their ministry. As Lee Hsien Loong explained, it was especially important to have the ministers for health and trade and industry articulate their respective positions and enable the MTF to make informed decisions in the national interest of Singapore:

> The difficulty is not that you had ministers fighting one another. The difficulty is to articulate strongly enough all these different perspectives and make sure that important perspectives are not neglected.[8]

Lee's comments suggest that the members of the MTF were conciliatory rather than fractious, thus avoiding the scenario of serious infighting or even deadlock in a divided government. It was primarily a matter of assessing the trade-offs. If so, the issues that surfaced subsequently with respect to vulnerable Singaporeans and migrant workers raised questions about the role of the ministries responsible for their interests.

The primary contention would have been between the public health and economic imperatives, as was the case in many countries and historically in Singapore. But this did not appear to have been a very difficult issue for the MTF. Senior Minister Tharman Shanmugaratnam, an economist, related that Singapore did not try to balance the two imperatives, but prioritised public health. He reasoned that if the pandemic had gone out of control, the economy would not be spared either. The government also had a responsibility to protect the weakest members of society who were likely to be worst hit by the outbreak.[9]

On 22 January, the government also activated the Homefront Crisis Executive Group that had operated during SARS and Singapore's previous crises. It was led by the Permanent Secretary of Home Affairs and comprised senior civil servants from other ministries and statutory boards. The group reported to the MTF, which in turn reported to the cabinet.[10]

In the early months, the official response was clearly shaped by the SARS experience. On 27 January, the MTF began the first of its daily media conferences patterned on the practice during 2003. They were usually chaired by the MTF co-chairs, with Kenneth Mak fielding the medical inquiries. As Gan Kim Yong recounted, 'we were prepared to be frank and upfront when we answered the questions'.[11] The data the cabinet received was published publicly in the daily situational reports. The government's openness to the medical data and situation was a positive influence of the SARS episode.

Singapore's response to the pandemic was, as Lee Hsien Loong intimated, data-based.[12] It was calibrated and pragmatic, taking into account international and local developments. The MTF and health officials closely followed the science of COVID-19 and drew conclusions from the experiences of other countries. But science by itself was insufficient; indeed, overreliance on it could be deleterious. Good science should take into account the local context: safe distancing and vaccination would mean very different things to members of two different socio-economic groups. As the outbreak unfolded in Singapore, it became clear that COVID-19 was a socio-economic, political and historical crisis in addition to being a public health emergency.

In contrast to science, the government viewed history as a record of human failure. As Lee recounted in a December 2020 interview, the government's decision to ringfence COVID-19 differed from how past pandemics were allowed to burn through the population. Speaking of the 'Zero COVID' policy, he said,

> In other words, we are not trying to wipe out the disease, it's going to burn through your population, but let it burn slowly so I don't overwhelm my hospitals ... That's what happened with the great flu pandemic [of 1918] and previous diseases because, in those days, people had no choice. You just made the best of it and waited till the pestilence passed ...
>
> We decided that very early. I told Gan Kim Yong, 'We do not flatten the curve. We do not want to climb this mountain. We keep it down. We keep our people safe'.[13]

Singapore's history of pandemics offers a more complex and useful picture. While influenza was allowed to burn through Singapore in 1918 and 1957, the country's responses to the disease since the 1970s, and to the trinity of plague, cholera and smallpox, were much more robust and science-based.

The MTF's data-based approach was undermined by the partial early understanding of COVID-19 and the limits of scientific knowledge. It led to Singapore's first mistake in January 2020: to discourage the wearing of masks by the public unless one was sick. Masks were reserved for COVID-19 patients and healthcare workers. This was based on the WHO's recommendation at the time – that for a disease spread by droplets, handwashing was a better way to prevent infection while masks might cause a false sense of security or even increase the likelihood of infection.[14] In practical terms, there were insufficient masks for the entire population, though reusable masks could be a stopgap while disposable masks were procured. During the SARS epidemic, the wearing of masks had also been discouraged unless one was ill, for it was seen to impede Singapore's public image and economic recovery.

The decision stood despite a letter written by several doctors in early February urging people to wear masks outside.[15] It was reversed when it became demonstrably clear that asymptomatic cases could transmit the virus. On 14 April, wearing masks in public places became mandatory. Once taken, the decision was enforced robustly. The issue had taught the MTF a lesson about being flexible and adapting to new data. Kenneth Mak likened the change to sailing a ship: the destination remained the same though the course changed with the winds.[16]

The wearing of masks has since largely been accepted in Singapore, which had not seen the widespread resistance that occurred in some Western countries. The bigger issue has been the difficulty of compliance among elderly people, blue-collar and manual workers, such as hawkers. This was illustrated in the outbreak among port workers and customers at the Jurong Fishery Port in July 2021, which spread into the community and grew into Singapore's biggest cluster at the time.[17]

The early measures seemed to work throughout February 2020 and the number of cases remained stable. But it was a matter of time before the highly transmissible virus slipped through epidemiological surveillance. As thousands of overseas Singaporeans returned home in March, the number of community cases began to climb. Lee Hsien Loong acknowledged this:

> Unfortunately, we were not tight enough early enough on the SHNs (Stay Home Notices) and quarantine arrangements for them. So the cases spread into the community and, by the end of March, we could see the community numbers going up.[18]

It was unlikely that the community spread could have been averted by greater vigilance, in the same way that the outbreak at the Singapore General Hospital during SARS could have been prevented. It was not human failure that led to community transmission but the transmissibility of the disease.

In September 2019, several months before the pandemic, the ageing CDC had been replaced as the infectious diseases hospital by the new National Centre for Infectious Diseases. In a departure from 2003, the NCID was not designated the COVID-19 hospital as the TTSH had been for SARS, although the majority of COVID-19 cases were initially isolated there. The MOH decided against this at an early stage because, as Kenneth Mak explained, 'We didn't want to load the NCID right from the onset'.[19] Developments in China at the time also suggested that outbreaks in Singapore could exceed the total bed count of the NCID. In addition, the staff had to familiarise themselves with infection control protocols and equipment at the new facility, though they had managed well a measles outbreak among migrant workers in 2019.[20] Instead, COVID-19 cases were treated at all hospitals, while the NCID also monitored international developments on COVID-19 and formulated clinical care protocols. As the epidemic spread widely in the community, this move turned out to be the right one.

On 7 February, Singapore further raised its DORSCON level to Orange, precipitating frenzied buying of household goods such as toilet paper. Four days later, the WHO identified the coronavirus and gave it a name: SARS-CoV-2. But the new disease was still little understood. On 15 February, a dinner gathering at the Joy Garden Restaurant resulted in a cluster of 47 cases. This showed that unlike SARS, COVID-19 could spread widely. As Tan Chorh Chuan admitted, the government had underestimated the rapid transmission due to imported cases in the community and subsequently the migrant worker dormitories.[21]

## The Circuit Breaker

Throughout March, cases rose in the community and more control measures were implemented. On 26 March, amendments made to the Infectious Diseases Act sanctioned a slew of safe management measures. These included safe distancing in public places, limits on group sizes and public events, periods of isolation and home quarantine for COVID-19 patients and close contacts respectively. The home quarantine used during SARS was reinstituted, and isolation and quarantine facilities were established for large numbers of patients and suspected cases.[22] On a much larger scale than in 2003, extensive contact tracing efforts, both manual and digital, were made as part of the 'Zero COVID' policy. The MOH's contact tracers were augmented by officers seconded from other ministries, such as the Singapore Armed Forces, and airline cabin crew, whose work had ceased due to travel restrictions. But the outbreak could not be ringfenced.

On 7 April, the government decided to implement what it called a 'circuit breaker' – Singapore's term for the lockdown. This entailed a temporary cessation of public activities to arrest the community outbreak and bring down the number of cases. Only businesses providing essential services were allowed to operate, while non-essential employees were to work from home. In schools, learning was made home-based between 8 April and 4 May. Much of the work and economic activity moved online, utilising digital tools such as Zoom and e-delivery platforms. The circuit breaker lasted two months till 1 June.

The borrowing of a term from physics for the lockdown is telling, reflecting the scientific bent of the government's response. It was coined by Gan Kim Yong, an electrical engineer by training, who stumbled on the term by accident. The MTF accepted the term as it distinguished Singapore's policy from the word 'lockdown', which was used loosely worldwide and meant different things in different places.[23] To the government, a circuit breaker offered the flexibility – via a series of brakes – to make continuing adjustments to the safe management measures.[24] Nevertheless, the first iteration of the circuit breaker in Singapore was more or less a full lockdown in the general sense of the word.

More interesting was the revelation made by Lee Hsien Loong that the circuit breaker was taken as a last resort. It was first broached in the cabinet on 1 April and took another meeting the following day for the decision to be made. Several ministers wanted to wait longer. The Executive Group as a whole also preferred to avoid a lockdown that would have major social and economic implications. Other ministers, including Lee himself, 'would rather overreact than underreact' and 'frontload strong intervention'.[25] Nevertheless, even the advocates viewed the circuit breaker as a temporary move that could not be sustained for a lengthy period. Lee noted that 'once you lock down, the clock is ticking'.[26]

When the circuit breaker was lifted on 2 June, Singapore moved into a three-phase easing of restrictions. Over a period of six months, more businesses such as restaurants and hair salons reopened and more workers were able to return to office.[27] But this transition was marked by a constant tinkering of rules and figures, such as the number of people who could visit their elders or dine together. On 5 June, the opposition Workers' Party called for a review of these 'piecemeal announcements, U-turns and positions that did not gel intuitively'.[28] The government waived the call, but this was a sign of how the data-based approach, implemented as a series of brakes, could cause intermittent confusion and disruption for many people.

Technology played a key role in Singapore's emergency response. As community transmission surged in March, the MTF's press conferences were held virtually via the digital app Zoom at the end of the month. The government also used other digital and social media apps such as Facebook and WhatsApp to publish data and communicate safe management measures to the public.[29] But the use of digital technology and social media was not the monopoly of the government. Such tools, along with online forums and apps that enabled the formation of interest-based communities, were also used by different groups of people, as discussed later in the chapter.

Digital technology was an important means of epidemiological surveillance for a big community outbreak. Singapore developed two Bluetooth-based digital tools to study, analyse and contain COVID-19 clusters. SafeEntry, which documented the places a person visited, was introduced in March 2020 and became mandatory two months later for access to shopping malls, schools and offices. In April 2021, a new app called TraceTogether allowed the government to track a person's physical proximity to a COVID-19 case. The two apps were eventually combined into one. They reduced the reliance on people's memory, especially among elderly people, the group most resistant to contact tracing efforts.[30] As an alternative to the app, TraceTogether tokens were issued to adults and children. When Singapore moved to a 'Living with COVID-19' policy in mid-2021, contact tracing focused on unvaccinated persons and other vulnerable groups.[31]

The use of tools that could systematically collect private information on people's whereabouts and movements raised ethical issues. The WHO recommended that the use of contact tracing apps be guided by privacy guidelines. In Singapore, the use of TraceTogether, which stored information temporarily on the government's server, sparked some controversy in January 2021. The Minister for Foreign Affairs Vivian Balakrishnan, who also helmed Singapore's Smart Nation programme, had previously assured that the app would only be used for contact tracing. A backlash occurred when it emerged that the data could also be used for cases of serious crime.[32]

The circuit breaker was relatively short but severe and long-lasting in its impact. It revealed issues that had existed in Singapore society. Anxious about the uncertainty of the future, more people made calls to mental health helplines.[33] For vulnerable groups, many of their difficulties did not end with the circuit breaker. The lockdown increased financial and mental distress for the elderly, with 154 cases of suicide in 2020 among persons aged 60 and above, the highest figure since 1991.[34]

The community development NGO, Beyond Social Services, conducted a study of financial assistance applicants spanning the period of the circuit breaker and the immediate aftermath. It concluded that '2020 was a harrowing year for many families'.[35] The chronic difficulties facing low-income families were not fully ameliorated by the government's assistance efforts. During the circuit breaker, they encountered multiple forms of insecurity – for jobs, food, health, and legal status:

> Not only did many households see their incomes vanish entirely or drastically reduce, everyday life was disrupted in unforeseen ways: during the circuit breaker, schools and childcare centres closed, digital access became a necessity, grocery shopping was unpredictable and stressful, and families were forced to spend most of their time at home, often in overcrowded conditions. Staying safe comfortably, eating regularly and healthily, working from home (and getting paid): these are marks of privilege, and out of reach for many lower-income families.[36]

The epidemic exacerbated pre-existing forms of precarity. The breadwinners in low-income families had little job security, typically employed as blue-collar workers or freelancers in the service or gig economy. The loss or shrinking of their incomes (as much as by over two-thirds) led to rental arrears and difficulty in paying for food. Stressful for many middle-income families, working from home for low-income families with more dependents was additionally difficult. Their smaller homes could not easily accommodate the larger number of family members working or studying at home. Physical restrictions also separated low-income families from their extended family and social support networks. In one case, a single mother, who suffered from severe depression, was unable to find a job during the circuit breaker and constantly worried about her two children and herself contracting COVID-19.[37]

These forms of insecurity persisted after the circuit breaker and in the present state of economic stagnation and high inflation. Further studies by Beyond Social Services in 2021 showed that low-income families continued to face healthcare and food insecurities.[38] The NGO proposed reforms that would address these deeply entrenched issues: to strengthen labour rights and protections, reduce housing rents and provide debt relief.[39] Low-income families shared the same need for social protection with another vulnerable community that was badly hit by the pandemic: migrant workers.[40]

## Inside the Dormitories and Beyond

The circuit breaker coincided with an alarming outbreak of COVID-19 in the migrant worker dormitories at the end of March 2020. Some 200,000 low-wage Asian migrant workers – about a quarter of the total number – lived in 43 purpose-built dormitories in Singapore. An additional 100,000 workers were housed in some 1,200 factory-converted dormitories. The catalyst for the outbreak was migrant workers continuing to work despite being ill and transmitting the disease to others at the worksite who lived in different dormitories. This had occurred in many of Singapore's epidemics during the colonial era.

By early May, there were more than 15,000 cases among migrant workers, which more than doubled a month later. The government and particularly the Ministry of Manpower were much criticised for the continuing neglect of living conditions in these vast and densely populated dormitory complexes with shared rooms.[41] In 2015, the Foreign Employee Dormitories Act had been passed, stipulating basic requirements, including healthcare and environmental sanitation. But enforcement had weakened in the intervening years.[42] It is unlikely that the outbreak could have been averted, given the dense living conditions in these dormitories.

The outbreak had also occurred because the dormitories were a blind spot for the government, then focused on bringing overseas Singaporeans home. On hindsight, the two measles outbreaks involving six and five migrant workers living in dormitories in 2019 had been warning shots – the number of cases in each outbreak was small only because the majority of workers had either been vaccinated or previously infected by the disease. As Singapore began a vigorous response to the COVID-19 outbreak in February 2020, little comparatively was done to protect the workers. This was limited to identifying workers with symptoms, disinfecting the premises and preparing a small number of isolation rooms. The science was still inconclusive on asymptomatic cases, but the government also ignored warnings from migrant worker advocacy group Transient Workers Count Too (TWC2) about the risk of a vast dormitory outbreak.[43]

Although the government had been reluctant to contemplate this massive undertaking, the dormitories were quickly locked down on 5 April. The lockdown was an enormous administrative and logistical operation that tested the government's emergency response capacity. It took a month to fully implement. Minister Teo Chee Hean assigned an army general, Brigadier-General Seet Uei Lim, the Chief Guards Officer, to head the cross-ministry Joint Task Force to manage the operation. The task force comprised the MOH (for healthcare), SAF (manpower, command and planning), Home Team (dormitory security), Ministry of National Development, Ministry of Communications and Information, Building and Construction Authority, and National Environment Agency. Forward Assurance and Support Teams (FAST) teams comprising personnel from these agencies were formed to cater to the medical care and daily needs of the workers, and sanitation of the dormitories.[44]

Migrant workers with mild illness and their close contacts were initially isolated within the dormitories and in quarantine and isolation facilities elsewhere, such as the converted exhibition complex at the Singapore Expo, and the CDC itself, briefly reprising its role as an isolation facility.[45] Although the average migrant worker was young and in fairly good health, there were older workers with chronic health conditions who had worked in Singapore for many years. The government segregated them from the younger workers.[46]

It was several months before the dormitories were declared free of COVID-19 on 19 August 2020.[47] This occurred two months later than the lifting of the circuit breaker on 2 June, and while migrant workers had been allowed to resume work in mid-June, this was a slow, intermittent process.[48] In 2020, over 90 per cent of COVID-19 cases in Singapore were migrant workers, though there were only two deaths among them that year. In an interview after the dormitory outbreak, Lee Hsien Loong admitted that the government had not prepared adequately for the eventuality.[49] Given Singapore's reliance on migrant labour, this was a major failing in the emergency planning for an infectious disease outbreak since the SARS episode.

On 22 August, the Joint Taskforce handed its operations over to the Assurance, Care and Engagement (ACE) Group, a new and permanent Ministry of Manpower (MOM) Division established to prevent further public health threats to migrant workers living in dormitories, including a possible resurgence of COVID-19. In doing so, the government recognised that the living conditions of the dormitories posed a continuing threat to the health of migrant workers. This points to a policy narrative of an initial government oversight followed by robust action to compensate for it. But such an account is inadequate without the voices of the migrant workers themselves. To complete it, we have to peer inside the dormitories and view the lockdown as experienced by the workers.

At the onset of the lockdown, a landscape of confusion and fear reigned at the dormitories. Many workers did not initially understand COVID-19 or the government's measures, others received conflicting information from their families or other sources, while some were confused why other dormitories did not seem to be closed.[50] Information from the MOM was often not forthcoming on what the lockdown entailed and how the workers would be protected. The fact that the disease could be asymptomatic caused much distress. They could see fellow infected workers being taken away in ambulances but did not know if they were seriously ill or if oneself had been infected. There was also great anxiety about their families at home, where outbreaks of COVID-19 were often more serious.[51]

As migrant worker advocacy group Humanitarian Organisation for Migration Economics (HOME) stated in its pandemic report, the impact on migrant workers was 'catastrophic, and long-lasting'.[52] Many of them lost their jobs or had their wages slashed. This was even though the government had announced that workers would receive their salaries during the circuit breaker. The administration also provided wage subsidies to employers and waived the foreign worker levy. But migrant workers were not unionised and received no protection from the National Trades Union Congress, which was trying to prevent unemployment among locals. During the lockdown, migrant workers received less access to medical and mental health care and welfare services, with NGOs having to close their services or move them online. Workers living outside the dormitories also faced reduced access to shelter. The relative power of employers and lack of social protection for migrant workers were not new problems but deeply rooted in the migrant worker experience.

Workers' fears were not unfounded. In practice, the lockdown did more to ringfence the dormitory outbreaks rather than protect migrant workers from infection. The safe distancing measures that worked in the wider community and in homes for semi-nuclear families were not practicable inside dense complexes with thousands of workers. It was virtually impossible to isolate multiple workers sharing a room, showers and toilets. Neither could contact tracers keep pace with the rapid spread of infection in these enclosed spaces.[53]

Feeding the dormitory workers was a major difficulty and one that was widely known. It was also a historical problem that could be traced to the food served at hospitals and quarantine facilities in colonial Singapore. At the start of the lockdown, airline and other generic food was hurriedly packed and delivered to the dormitories. Many workers, especially those from South Asia, threw away the food as being unsuitable. It might seem that food should not be a priority during an emergency. However, as a basic necessity, food was a marker of health and social protection in the context of a pandemic. Just as unwilling patients in colonial Singapore had complained about the quality and type of food, migrant workers rejected the airline food because apparently their welfare was again being neglected. More palatable food arrived subsequently, but the lack of variety was a continuing reminder of migrant workers' marginal place in Singapore society.

From a historical viewpoint, the dormitory outbreak was a case of failing to heed the lessons of history. There had been epidemics of cholera, smallpox, influenza, and tuberculosis in the town during the British colonial era.[54] The town's shophouses then also housed large numbers of single male immigrants in tiny shared cubicles. These were sites for the easy transmission of infectious disease, places that existed beyond the pale of colonial sanitary governance and epidemiological surveillance.[55] In the new millennium, though the Singapore government possessed the means to improve the living conditions of the dormitories and the health of the residents, these had not been accomplished. The hope is that the COVID-19 pandemic would finally move the authorities to do so.

The S11 dormitory complex in Punggol, the scene of the largest migrant worker outbreak, is an instructive case study. The outbreak came to the attention of the regional hospital, the Sengkang Hospital, when the staff began to see migrant workers reporting sick. Dr Ong Biauw Chi, the chair of the hospital's Medical Board, decided to move the hospital's screening work inside the dormitories. Visiting the complex for the first time, she was stunned by its sheer size and the number of workers it housed – some 14,000 people.[56] It had set aside only about 50 rooms for isolation. S11 Capital Investments Pte Ltd, the dormitory operator, worked with the MOH and FAST teams to lock down the complex and provide for the workers' needs. As the business development director quipped, he learned how to run a hospital during the lockdown while Ong learned how to run a dormitory.[57] Ong's small team attempted to swab the workers and isolate the cases within the dormitories. But they could not keep pace with the outbreak.[58]

The majority of the workers at the S11 complex were Bangladeshi construction workers, followed by smaller groups of Indians, Chinese, Thais and Burmese. Many did not wish to be swabbed, fearing they would be moved to isolation facilities; they wanted to continue to work. Unable to leave the premises, the worried workers were almost like 'trapped animals trying to get out', as Ong put it.[59] Bangladeshi workers who were ill preferred to visit the Shifa clinic in Little India where they usually went instead of an unknown hospital.[60] According to Ong, the Chinese workers, apparently more knowledgeable about the disease than the others, did not want to remain inside the dormitories with the positive cases.[61]

Among the Chinese was construction worker Tang Zuoting, who had worked in Singapore for 20 years. For him, the lockdown did not cause the distress that many of his fellow residents endured. He found the food acceptable though lacking in variety and did not expect better housing. Still, he had difficult experiences as well. A cough was something he feared, for it might mean a COVID-19 infection, a period of quarantine and a loss of income. For him, there was no discernible difference between the circuit breaker and its long aftermath punctuated by routine tests and restrictions. He felt weaker physically and psychologically throughout the pandemic. The main concern of the Chinese workers, he said, was to be able to work safely without the fear of infection and quarantine.[62]

The Bangladeshi workers have been candid about their experiences. Zakir Hossain, who had worked in Singapore for 19 years, lived in a dormitory of some 4,000 workers in Sembawang. When the lockdown occurred, the physical demands were impossible to meet. Safe distancing was mandated though there were a dozen persons sharing a room, and the wearing of masks was decreed but there were none for a time. As their roommates and fellow workers successively fell sick, many workers experienced depression for the first time in their lives. Hossain contracted COVID-19 but his symptoms were initially dismissed by the security personnel, who told him to return to his room. His recovery proved an arduous experience, from being treated at a hospital to being moved to a tent in an army camp, enduring the sweltering heat and a rude doctor, and then to a hotel before he finally returned to the dormitory.[63] In a poem he wrote, he likened migrant workers' fears of being infected by COVID-19 to being matched by that of speaking out about their hardship and grievances during the pandemic.[64]

Ripon Chowdhury was a Bangladeshi marine worker who lived in a dormitory in Jurong and had been in Singapore for 12 years. As he surmised, 'social distancing is a joke', unenforceable unless the number of people in a room was reduced. He volunteered for the 'Here with You' helpline during the epidemic, translating calls from Bangladeshi workers to the counsellor. The issues they raised ranged from salary matters and their families asking for money to be remitted to their own stress and suicidal tendencies. The food issue was 'the worst thing during the lockdown'. From his long time in Singapore, Chowdhury had accepted local food, but it was difficult to eat the same food (white rice with egg and chicken) for a month.[65] In a Facebook post, he explained why many migrant workers could not easily adapt to their diet: 'Surprisingly, waking up at five in the morning, returning from work at eight at night, taking a bath, washing clothes, and cleaning the room, doing all this it becomes the time to sleep'.[66]

Chowdhury's account revealed that the end of the lockdown did not bring relief to migrant workers. They remained confined within the dormitories except for short periods of 'yard time' inside the premises and brief weekly trips outside to designated recreational centres. But as he pointed out, the limited number of slots for going out, the need to take an Antigen Rapid Test before they could do so, and the huge demand kept many workers inside the dormitories long after the lockdown. Most of them were glued to their phones, at the mercy of the weak Wifi, with little opportunity to exercise.[67] The lengthy isolation gave rise to 'tensions, tempers and anxieties',[68] and to cabin fever, unruly behaviour, fights and depression.[69]

The continuing physical confinement was tantamount to an extended period of quarantine. It was a source of mental anguish, as it was clear to the workers that the dormitory outbreak had ended and the general population was going out and returning to work to a larger degree. As Bangladeshi worker Islam Rafiquil aptly described the effect of persisting restrictions, 'My mind does not feel free'.[70] The confinement and concerns about work and family caused many workers to experience psychological distress, but unable to express it or speak to a counsellor. Many could not tell their families when the next remittance would be.[71]

Our interviews revealed economic sources of mental distress. Between May and June 2020, the government waived the work permit levy of $750 for employers and provided rebates to keep their workers in employment. But it was difficult to ensure that the employers paid their employees, both local and migrant, the full wages.[72] From July, the levy was reinstituted at half the amount. Many migrant workers received their basic salary of $400–$500 during the lockdown, less than half of what they usually received.[73] Several interviewees told us that migrant workers were unhappy about not having received the waived levy or rebates; in their view, these were sums of money that rightfully belonged to them.[74]

In October 2021, riot police arrived at a dormitory in Jalan Tukang, fearing an outbreak of violence there that did not occur. The workers, mostly mainland Chinese who had recently arrived, claimed that they were dissatisfied about not being treated or moved to isolation facilities when they tested positive for COVID-19. Again, they voiced complaints about the poor quality of food. It transpired that the workers had not been vaccinated and were concerned for their health, as the MOM had yet to implement safe management measures at the facility.[75]

On the Chinese messaging app WeChat, the workers made a series of posts about not being able to see a doctor, isolate safely from those who had contracted the disease and not being able to use vaccines manufactured in China.

One post exclaimed, 'I don't feel that lives are protected here, and this even infringes on our dignity', while another alleged, 'the food has no nutrition and no variety; the quantity is also too little'.[76] Subsequent posts noted that the situation had improved and beseeched the workers to remain calm. TWC2 has highlighted an underlying factor in the Jalan Tukan incident: that employers and dormitory operators had been struggling to fulfil their increased responsibilities to provide for migrant workers during the pandemic.[77]

Outside the dormitories, other groups of migrant workers faced variations of these problems. Those living in employer-rented housing were also locked down and ordered to remain home during the circuit breaker. Lacking the healthcare and welfare services provided at the dormitories, this group of workers was even more dependent on their employers and could have fared worse in some cases. HOME picked up many homeless workers evicted by their landlords and reduced to sleeping in the streets, while others had to pay higher rental fees (which increased by 20 per cent in 2020) charged by opportunistic landlords.[78] HOME, TWC2, other volunteer groups and volunteers strove to provide masks and hand sanitisers to migrant workers and set up hotlines to advise on employment, health and mental health issues.

Fazley Elahi Rubel was a Bangladeshi safety coordinator in a construction company who had worked in Singapore for 12 years. He lived in temporary housing at a construction site in Orchard Road. At first, the lockdown seemed 'like a fantasy' to him – for a migrant worker to be paid without having to work. But mental fatigue soon set in. He was still able to move about as a volunteer with TWC2, delivering food, hand sanitisers, masks, and phone cards to the dormitory workers. Some of the food he brought to his friend and compatriot, A.K. Zilani, an IT technician who had been in Singapore for 11 years and was residing in a shophouse. The dwelling was employer-rented and shared with other migrant workers, making safe distancing difficult. Both men believed that in all aspects other than cleanliness, employer-rented housing was more suitable as housing than purpose-built dormitories. When he contracted COVID-19, Zilani was quarantined in a hotel for a long time, with his 14-day quarantine order repeatedly renewed. The comfort provided by the air-conditioning, Wifi and television lasted only a few days before his mental health suffered. 'Luxury without freedom is crap', he laughed. Rubel and Zilani's employers were kind and checked in on their well-being regularly, but the Bangladeshis still lost wages during the lockdown, which distressed them and their families.[79]

The pandemic affected over 260,000 domestic workers in Singapore who lived with their employers. Many had a hard time financially when they were not paid their salaries or had their pay cut. The circuit breaker alienated domestic workers from friends whom they often met on their off days and comprised their social support network. In addition, as most employers and their children began to work and study at home during the circuit breaker, there was more cleaning to be done or such work had to be done at night when the regular work day ended. The increased number of people at home was stressful in another sense: the powerless 'maid' in the house could be a convenient target for verbal abuse and conflict. Robina Navato, a domestic worker from the Philippines who had worked in Singapore for 25 years, was a volunteer at HOME. She revealed that many domestic workers ran away from their employers during the circuit breaker and sought sanctuary at HOME or called its hotline for help.[80] In 2020, domestic workers made a quarter more calls to the hotline, seeking emergency accommodation or economic assistance due to unemployment, reduced or unpaid wages. Others requested protection from employer abuse or increased surveillance, and from overwork as some employers demanded that they continue to work on their off days.[81]

The increased proximity between employers and their domestic workers had various consequences. They had to pretend they were well – 'put on a happy face' – even if they were worried about the health and financial status of their families in their hometown, where the pandemic might be worse than in Singapore.[82] As Navato related, because she felt more scrutinised by her at-home employer (even when this was objectively not the case), she responded by cleaning more. Domestic workers were also worried about being fined by safe distancing ambassadors when they took the employer's children outside, as they might not be able explain their actions fluently or make the ambassadors understand them.[83]

For Indonesian domestic worker Endah Purnamasari, who had worked in Singapore for 12 years, the circuit breaker encapsulated the travails of working from home, having to share the house with the employer's family throughout the day. She noted that it was difficult for many Indonesian domestic helpers to voice their distress, stand up to their employers, or seek help at an NGO, as these were actions they were not used to doing, or could not do well in English. The travel restrictions during the pandemic likely did not give domestic workers greater leverage vis-à-vis the employers. Purnamasari changed employers thrice within two weeks in 2021 before she found a reasonable one. This showed the lack of labour protection for domestic workers despite her favourable outcome. Their experience was hugely dependent on the employer who hired them.[84]

Crises often have an epiphanic effect, as in the case of Heidee Roiles from the Philippines. She felt 'reborn during the pandemic', finding the impetus to write poetry and do theatre – an interest in her early life. Even so, her mental health suffered as she would overthink her employer's comments and feel depressed. She was also worried about her family in Cebu, where the pandemic was more serious than in Singapore. Her father had told her he would not want to go to a hospital there where he might contract COVID-19. A handyman, his income had dwindled because he was unable to go to his clients due to the COVID-19 restrictions, while Roiles' mother had lost her job as a childcare teacher.[85]

Singapore's migrant workers were not a hapless group. They had made commendable efforts to improve their working conditions and well-being. Many of them, especially male workers like Fazley Elahi Rubel who did not live in the dormitories, and domestic workers, tried to help their fellow workers by volunteering at NGOs or forming their own support groups to canvas donations, medicines, masks and hand sanitisers. During the pandemic, Zakir Hossain and other migrant activists continued to organise poetry, storytelling, photography and theatre events for migrant workers. These efforts often involved collaboration with local poets, literary and theatre groups and utilised social media platforms. Robina Navato was 'Madam' to her younger followers on TikTok, using dance videos to provide practical information such as how to transfer to another employer.[86]

Migrant activists also set up Facebook groups for workers to express how they felt and upload their images of the pandemic. These groups are archives of migrant pandemic lives and activism. The cultural activism sought to address the underlying issues migrant workers faced in Singapore; it was not political or anti-government. Activism boosted the self-confidence of workers like A.K. Zilani and Endah Purnamasari. Heidee Roiles performed in a series of plays before and during the pandemic as part of the Birds Migrant Theatre, in collaboration with the local theatre company The Necessary Stage.[87] The cultural work was useful in inspiring migrant workers to form more positive images of themselves.

These efforts also communicated the workers' plight to a wider public, so building bridges between locals and a large group of foreigners who were largely unseen to the public eye. Ripon Chowdhury observed that to know about migrant life was not to read blogs or books, but to know the workers as people and as friends. A common belief among locals who did not know them was that they were well-to-do, able to pay their way to Singapore.[88] As Hossain pointed out, the pandemic was a reminder that migrant workers were part of the community, rather than a group apart.[89] But these efforts were not enough by themselves nor could they reach the majority of migrant workers, especially those who did not speak English.

Not all migrant workers had adverse experiences during the pandemic. For some like Roiles, it spurred them to self-realisation and inner growth, while others were able to save more from their earnings during the circuit breaker.[90] In general, however, the crisis highlighted the precarious nature of all low-wage labour – migrant and local – and the implications for one's health and mental health. As Ambassador Tommy Koh pondered in the foreword to this book, 'I wonder if the huge outbreak could have been avoided if the dormitories were less crowded, better ventilated, cleaner and more hygienic'. The government has made welcome announcements that it would continue to improve living conditions in the dormitories. The guiding principle is to recognise migrant workers as a vulnerable group who are heavily reliant on their employers. They are similar to other such groups such as elderly people, low-income families or the coolies of colonial Singapore.

Deeper reforms are needed not only to deal with problems specific to the pandemic, but also underlying issues migrant workers have faced in what the BBC called 'a pandemic of inequality'.[91] TWC2 noted that new government standards for the dormitories published in September 2021 were concerned primarily with the control of COVID-19, rather than the root problems of overcrowding and lack of green areas.[92] As HOME urged in its report, it is crucial to recognise the basic right of migrant workers to switch employment freely. Other pressing issues were wage protection (such as through a minimum wage), freedom of movement and improved access to health and mental health services. Basic to these reforms was the recognition for labour rights.[93]

## Social Strains of Living with COVID-19

The arrival of the vaccines heralded a turning point for the 'Zero COVID' policy. As Lee Hsien Loong announced, 'Now that vaccines are becoming available, we can see light at the end of the tunnel'.[94] From the end of December 2020, Singapore embarked on an extensive vaccination programme using the new mRNA vaccines manufactured by Pfizer-BioNTech and Moderna. The vaccines were offered first to healthcare workers, followed by elderly people aged 70 and above and then to progressively younger age groups in the population. Vaccination was strongly encouraged, free but voluntary. But individuals who were eligible but chose to remain unvaccinated were barred from indoor public spaces (shopping malls, restaurants, hawker centres, cinemas and sports halls). These 'vaccination-differentiated measures' were implemented in August 2021 to encourage the unvaccinated to be immunised.

However, from late April 2021, the arrival and spread of the highly infectious Delta variant of SARS-CoV-2, which could also cause more severe illness, forced a government rethink. As it became the dominant strain, Delta affected a wide range of places in the community, from a major fishery port to food centres and nursing homes. More people, especially the elderly, experienced severe illness. The number of deaths from COVID-19 jumped from 29 to 726 by the end of the year. The healthcare system came under tremendous strain.[95]

Delta ultimately forced the government to follow many other countries in officially abandoning the 'Zero COVID' policy for a more realistic approach. The decision to accept 'Living with COVID-19', rather than implement a second circuit breaker, was debated within the MTF. It was quickly decided that a series of smaller changes was better. The ministers wanted to reduce the impact a circuit breaker would have on the economy, as well as the risk of infection for the populace, such as when people were not wearing masks. The ability to do mass testing for COVID-19 and trace contacts also gave the MTF confidence that it could manage the Delta wave. Medical doctors and health officials also supported the idea of living with COVID-19.[96]

As Delta infection rates began to stabilise, the MTF co-chairs penned an op-ed. piece in the *Straits Times* on 24 June titled, 'Living normally, with COVID-19'. Using the example of influenza as an endemic disease, the ministers announced their intention for Singapore to co-exist with COVID-19. This would be made possible by mass vaccination, targeted testing and improved therapy. In accepting COVID-19 as an endemic illness,

Singaporeans would have to be socially responsible about their health and that of others. The extensive contact tracing done under the 'Zero COVID' policy would come to an end, while most patients with mild illness would recover at home. Safe management measures would be progressively relaxed, while large gatherings and overseas travel would be permitted with targeted testing. At the end of the piece, the ministers wrote, 'History has shown that every pandemic will run its course'.[97] This was a different interpretation from Lee Hsien Loong's warning about past pandemics being allowed to burn through the population half a year earlier.

Living with COVID-19 was the right strategy. It recognised the disease in its own right and departed from the 'Zero COVID' approach influenced by SARS. However, the road to the goal was bumpy, partly because the government's method was still based more on science and less on sociology. An outbreak of Delta at the Jurong Fishery Port in July led to a reversal in the easing of restrictions. The move was much debated in the MTF, with some ministers arguing against tightened restrictions as infection rates would naturally rise with their easing. But the decisive argument was the vaccination rate, which stood then at 50 per cent and was particularly low among the elderly.[98]

On 6 August, the MTF outlined a four-stage plan to achieve the goal of a COVID-19-resilient nation. But the plan had to be modified as infection rates rose again, causing many patients to seek help at the emergency departments of hospitals and straining the healthcare system. The MOH announced in September that vaccinated patients under the age of 50 would be able to recover at home instead of in a hospital. This heralded a new social role for the populace. Most people, particularly those who were vaccinated or younger, would now shoulder the responsibility for their own health and that of the community.[99]

Home recovery was another exercise the government was initially not prepared for. Many patients told to recover at home were confused about what to do and frustrated at the lack of instructions from the MOH. Elderly patients with underlying health conditions needed specialised care, and even younger people in good general health worried about infecting their family members or burdening them with caregiving.[100] As home recovery patients were not issued a discharge memo, some of those who had recovered had difficulty resuming their life and work because the TraceTogether app continued to show an infected status.[101] The government was criticised for not having planned adequately for home recovery or an upsurge of cases if Singaporeans were to live with the coronavirus. Its approval rating dropped to its lowest – 59 per cent – during the pandemic in early October. The MTF had to second manpower from the SAF to man MOH hotlines for patients recovering from home.[102]

The underlying problem with home recovery was enforcing public health measures that made sense within the private sphere of the home. The circuit breaker had confined healthy adults and children. But in home recovery, living arrangements differed substantially between homes, making it difficult for some households to adhere to quarantine and safe distancing protocols. A vaccinated elderly man who contracted COVID-19 ignored his family's pleas to heed the protocols. He was frustrated by what he probably felt as controlling actions by his family members, who in turn were exasperated by his behaviour. The MOH suggested that they call the police on the elderly man. His daughter said, 'I felt that we were one of the families that had been forgotten. Nobody checked on my dad or monitored his condition'.[103]

The new policy became synonymous with a long series of tweaks to restrictions and rules, often confusing and exhausting to business owners, families and individuals alike. The MTF focused on the national scale, expecting people to accept finely calibrated transitions and new rules. But the rules had different effects for different groups of people. Consider hawkers and other business operators, for example, who could not adapt to continuing changes at short notice. For the general population, the constant tweaking of numbers seemed arbitrary or even contradictory, such as preventing families of more than five persons from dining together at a restaurant. As Ong Ye Kung admitted, 'Some people tell me that they are more afraid of these rules than COVID-19 itself'.[104]

Ong was obviously frustrated when over a thousand unvaccinated elderly people contracted COVID-19 between 12–29 October 2021:

> We kept telling them to get vaccinated, they didn't. Then we told them, at least stay home ... and they still went out before restrictions set in. There was a sudden surge of activities among this group and they got infected. It's just very sad.[105]

In Ong's view, the failing was a personal one: the elderly infected were irresponsible. But there were other factors – countervailing emotions and social influences – that guided people's actions. While the figures and rules were based on data, science was not the only force at play. Elderly people might not understand or accept the science, or were in greater need of physical mobility or social interaction. This shows a fundamental issue in public health: it is not enough to deliver a message and provide the evidence for it. What is equally important is to find a common starting point to convince people with differing views and priorities, or to find a middle ground where understanding on both sides could take place. Living with COVID-19 required knowing the personal circumstances, value systems and social needs of different groups of people.

There was much evidence that measures should be guided by social as much as scientific data. Community workers pointed out that elderly Singaporeans were a unique group with a range of personal circumstances, motivations and belief systems; they should not be judged by a universal yardstick meant for the younger population or dismissed as recalcitrant 'boomers'. Some elderly people lived alone and had no need to be vaccinated to protect their family members, while those with mobility issues might not see why they had to do so. Others were fatalistic in outlook, to whom the language of social responsibility meant little; one of them asked, 'I'm already old and dying. So what's the point?'.[106] Others with underlying health conditions were legitimately worried about the risks of receiving the mRNA vaccines.[107]

Such social issues could be gleaned from history. The past is a valuable resource for attaining empathy with those who had different viewpoints or ways of life. As we saw with smallpox in colonial Singapore, notification and vaccination for disease were often hindered by non-cooperation from the Asian population. These responses were driven by practical considerations – how reporting smallpox hurt one's self-interests – or cultural ones, where Western biomedicine diverged from customary views of health and sickness. These differences could be dismissed as irrational by officials used to a scientific line of work. Worse, they became political issues when the colonial administration held the power to judge and punish non-cooperation without entering into a dialogue with the people. However, history also shows that Asian reluctance could be resolved. In the post-war period, vaccination for smallpox, tuberculosis and other infectious diseases became widely accepted, partly due to extensive public education and partly to the demonstrable benefits of the vaccines.

The government soon realised that the vaccines were not the solution they were thought to be. Many 'breakthrough infections' (vaccinated people contracting the illness) caused by Delta occurred. Continuing changes to safe management measures were made throughout 2021 and early 2022. They showed that Singapore was still operating under the rubric of a circuit breaker, applying a series of brakes on the easing up as required. It had learned from developments in countries such as Britain and Israel where substantial relaxation of restrictions caused new waves of infection.[108] But while the brakes reduced the infection rates, they also had an adverse impact on the economy.

The pandemic caused Singapore's economy to shrink by nearly 6 per cent in 2020. As with SARS, worst hit were the tourism, hospitality, retail, and food and beverages sectors. Until a large proportion of locals were vaccinated, the tourism industry was shuttered for much of 2020 and 2021. Quarantine-free vaccinated travel lanes were introduced only on 8 September 2021. The economic impact was especially acute during the circuit breaker, but the tweaking of restrictions afterward up to mid-2022 was also difficult for many business owners.[109] In November 2021, the number of people who could dine together at restaurants and food centres was increased from two to five. But for the owners, having to ensure that a group was from the same family meant additional work and costs they could ill afford.[110] As many businesses went online and adopted e-commerce, a tech gap appeared those with the ability to do so and others that did not. Smaller businesses and older hawkers with limited means had difficulty affording the commissions charged by food delivery platforms.[111]

An interventionist administration, the government passed five major fiscal packages totalling nearly $100 billion in 2020 to ameliorate the socio-economic impact of the pandemic. The unprecedented sum was drawn from Singapore's reserves.[112] The packages were based on the prevailing pro-business philosophy, instead of alternative schemes in the West such as unemployment relief or furlough. After an initial package provided temporary relief to people whose livelihoods were affected by the pandemic, the bulk of the assistance went to help businesses pay their workers and keep them in employment. The fiscal packages also sought to create new jobs and retrain workers. These efforts had the support of the NTUC, as was the case during SARS.

The government complemented the pro-business policy with specific assistance for vulnerable groups. As the pro-business policy was integral to the government's economic policy, help for the vulnerable was part of its welfare policy. As Tharman Shanmugaratnam indicated, a key concern was to keep mature workers in employment or equip them with new skills through retraining. But it was not always easy, he admitted, to match jobseekers and jobs. While it was plausible to temporarily assign airline crew as public health ambassadors and contact tracers, getting older workers to discard their expertise and take up a new vocation was altogether quite different. Additional assistance was also given to lower- and middle-income families.[113]

Nevertheless, evidence suggests that applying established economic and welfare policies in the context of a crisis was not fully successful. Vulnerable groups who needed help most were not fully shielded from the economic impact of COVID-19. While there are no general unemployment figures in Singapore, an undetermined number of jobs were lost during the pandemic.[114] Although there is a tripartite system based on consensus between labour, management and the government, retrenchment was still largely a business decision that could be undertaken unilaterally by struggling firms. Many salaried workers were not unionised while those in the gig economy inherently lacked protection from unfair dismissal or work practices. In the general elections in July 2020, one of the reasons for the government's underwhelming performance was the economic grievances of middle-aged workers and the private property-owning middle class, whose respective incomes and businesses had been hit by the pandemic.[115]

Living with COVID-19 was also a divisive social issue, reflecting the existence of communities in Singapore with widely differing views. The question of vaccination was acute. In several Western countries, anti-vaccination movements claimed the vaccines to be unsafe and upheld the sanctity of individual rights. Singapore, which had long contrasted itself to the individualism in Western societies, was not fully spared either. While the majority of Singaporeans accepted the mRNA vaccines, a minority preferred to wait for traditional vaccines using an inactivated virus, particularly those manufactured in China such as Sinovac. The latter was only available in October 2021, ten months after the start of the vaccination programme. This reflected the influence of China's mass media on some Chinese-educated Singaporeans. Arguments over vaccination caused rifts between family members.[116]

Another minority, possibly influenced by the religious right, rejected vaccination altogether. Groups such as *Truth Warriors* used Telegram and other e-platforms to exaggerate the risks of vaccination and recommend the use of alternative remedies such as ivermectin, as US President Donald Trump did.[117] The ironically named Healing the Divide was another group that petitioned against the government's vaccination-differentiated measures. In October, the group called upon some 2,000 followers on Telegram to call and overwhelm public hotlines.[118] Ong Ye Kung thought that while people could make their own choices, they should not organise a movement against vaccination.[119] The existence of anti-vaxxer groups was a serious issue on social media. They were online communities of knowledge with alternative sources of authority, resisting accepted views on medicine and science.

Again, one solution is to build bridges to the opposing side. As two doctors noted, while vaccination-differentiated measures were useful from a public health standpoint, they were socially and ethically contentious.[120] Three academics pointed out that the measures contradicted the government's decision not to make vaccination mandatory. Instead of dismissing the unvaccinated as 'COVIDiots', it would be more productive to understand why people would be concerned about the risks of vaccination or influenced by anti-vaxxer claims, particularly on social media. It was important for family doctors to reassure them that the vaccines were safe, for the media to be circumspect in reporting side effects, and for the government to publish data showing the greater risks of infection and severe illness for the unvaccinated.[121] From Singapore history, we know that the fear of viral myocarditis was a major factor in the failure of vaccination against swine flu in 1976, while the crude way that inoculation against smallpox was practised on children at the beginning of the 20th century had caused resistance among parents.

Two and a half years on, the Omicron variant and subvariants that appeared since late November 2021 have caused a massive surge in the number of cases in Singapore. Initially, they further strained the healthcare system as numerous patients sought help at hospitals and general practitioners.[122] By August 2022, about 70 per cent of people in Singapore had caught COVID-19, mostly from Omicron.[123] But the wave had subsided and the number of COVID-19-related deaths, at 1,711 at the end of the year, had been very low, mostly among elderly people: 96 per cent of the eligible population had been vaccinated (including with a booster dose).

Severe disease and new safe distancing restrictions did not return to Singapore, and the MTF remained committed to living normally with COVID-19 as an endemic disease. In March 2022, masks were no longer mandatory outdoors and from 29 August, they were optional both outdoors and indoors except on public transport and in healthcare settings. These remaining restrictions were finally lifted in February 2023, when the Multi-ministry Task Force was also stood down. Crowds returned to public places and workers to their offices. But living with COVID-19 in Singapore remained an uneven process while underlying social issues persisted.

The double whammy of stagflation in 2022 from Russia's invasion of the Ukraine and high oil prices continued to hurt livelihoods, particularly for low-income families affected by COVID-19. The pandemic called attention to vulnerable groups who required solutions specific to their needs and demographic. Though migrant workers' physical restrictions were slightly relaxed from September 2021, the easing was slower than the rest of the population and fell short of what was required. Without adequate labour protection, migrant workers continued to face serious mental health, health and financial issues.[124] Sex workers and people with disabilities were two other minority groups that were disproportionately affected by the pandemic while receiving little public assistance.[125] Some Singaporeans resigned from their jobs or sought new forms of employment due to stress-related reasons triggered by the pandemic, akin to the Great Resignation in the West.[126] Healthcare workers had been physically and emotionally exhausted by the protracted fight against COVID-19, with foreign staff unable to return to their home countries till late 2021.[127]

The White Paper on COVID-19 released in early 2023 recognised many of these issues. It was a fairly balanced appraisal of the successes and mistakes in the government's response to the pandemic. The report admitted that the initial efforts to keep the dormitories safe were inadequate, while the continued restrictions on migrant workers affected their mental health. It also acknowledged that the safe management measures were overly calibrated and became impractical, while the transition to living with COVID-19 was uneven. But the White Paper has not gone far enough to delve into the deeply rooted socio-economic issues faced by vulnerable communities.[128]

These issues call for reform and change, something not discussed in the White Paper. It was not necessary to have to wait for a pandemic like COVID-19 to be aware of them. The history of pandemics in Singapore was always there to be studied, as it should have been post-SARS. The past is not an account of human folly of no relevance to present predicaments. True, the 1890, 1918 and 1957 flu pandemics highlighted the inertia of the colonial system and the limits of decolonisation, which may not seem useful to today's policymakers. The British also paid too much attention to plague, cholera and smallpox to the neglect of other infectious diseases. But a record of failures points to deeply rooted social cleavages and inequalities that may have persisted over time.

The history of epidemiology tells us about the places where epidemics broke out and spread – in the colonial town's overcrowded cubicles in particular. A big gap divided colonial health and the socio-cultural dynamics of the coolie town. Outbreaks of influenza, smallpox and tuberculosis occurred there not only because of people's insanitary habits or ignorance, but also because the colonial regime had little control over Asian dwelling spaces. This was a result of little interest in – and empathy for – the hearts and minds of the labouring poor. These historical failings provide a lesson for the massive dormitory outbreak in 2020 and the impact of continuing restrictions for migrant workers. Arguably, any improvements to be made in this respect must be of a fundamental nature. They should involve migrant workers themselves, whose community leaders have shown themselves to be intelligent and constructive.

What, then, did we learn from the current pandemic? As Peter Furtado observes, like the influenza of 1918, COVID-19 is a destroyer but also a teacher.[129] The Singapore government has managed the present crisis better than the colonial state did in the past and many countries in the world today. Success, though, was not due primarily to robust measures or biotechnology but to people's support and cooperation – something that has been built up in the last 70 years. The government's response had also not been flawless. Lee Hsien Loong has rightly spoken about the need to continue to learn from the pandemic;[130] reverting to the status quo ante is not an option.[131] The deeply rooted issues serve as a reminder that Singapore, despite its development and wealth, remains an open city-state with a diverse population and vulnerable social groups at the margins.

The other lesson is that the island will remain susceptible to pandemic disease, which might come in a different form from the last. A plan to prepare for the next threat should be able to adapt to the new circumstances that may have emerged then. Equally, the plan has to incorporate sociological and historical perspectives – on why most people in Singapore supported the official measures while a minority struggled or refused to do so. People are the social resource that the country will need to confront the next pandemic. In addition, the plan should include provisions for the safety and interests of vulnerable groups – something that also requires intervention from the humanities and social sciences. When the Minister for Health Ong Ye Kung announced a five-year research plan in November 2022, he emphasised scientific data and methods, though he did note the need for multi-disciplinary research.[132]

The White Paper on COVID-19 has said the right things about learning from the pandemic. It acknowledged that the next crisis would be different, so Singapore would need to find new solutions when previous ones did not work. But this was unfortunately the same perspective adopted after SARS: the last pandemic was taken as the point of reference while it was urged that the pandemic response had to be flexible enough to deal with a different disease. The SARS experience was still viewed in largely positive terms, allowing the government to 'avoid a cold start and hit the ground running'.[133] The White Paper outlined seven lessons from COVID-19: the need to adapt, to enhance social resilience, to better collaborate with the people and private sector, to develop public health expertise and organisational capacity, to better utilise science and technology, to improve forward planning, and to maintain clear and transparent communication with the public. These lessons, the White Paper stated, were reasonably obvious to the government.[134] They were also narrow, predicated on present experience.

For too long, Singapore has ignored its own history of pandemics. The government's early response to COVID-19 was unnecessarily weighed down by the SARS experience and narrative. By the same token, the present pandemic should not be taken as the primary case study and basis of a revised pandemic plan. It may be a mistake to over-state the threat of novel coronaviruses. Instead, a social history of pandemics, covering a wider group of significant diseases, outbreaks and scares, offers a broader canvas from which a more flexible and socially inclusive plan may be drawn. The way forward is not merely to scan ahead for new biotechnology or management measures, but also to look backwards to interpret, reflect and learn from the past. If this does happen, the COVID-19 pandemic may yet contribute to a new beginning for Singapore.

## Notes

1  Sumiko Tan (ed.), *In This Together: Singapore's COVID-19 Story* (Singapore: Straits Times Press, 2022).
2  Tan, *In This Together*.
3  Tan, *In This Together*.
4  Loh Kah Seng, Interview with Tan Chorh Chuan, 4 August 2021; Loh Kah Seng, Interview with Leo Yee Sin, 25 August 2021.
5  Prime Minister's Office, *White Paper on Singapore's Response to COVID-19: Lessons for the Next Pandemic* (Singapore: Prime Minister's Office, 2023).
6  Kah Seng Loh and Li Yang Hsu, *Tuberculosis – The Singapore Experience, 1867–2018: Disease, Society and the State* (New York: Routledge, 2020).
7  Tan, *In This Together*.
8  Tan, *In This Together*, p. 50.
9  Tan, *In This Together*.
10  Tan, *In This Together*.
11  Tan, *In This Together*, p. 45.
12  Tan, *In This Together*, p. 46.
13  Tan, *In This Together*, p. 56.
14  Tan, *In This Together*.
15  Tan, *In This Together*.
16  Loh Kah Seng, Interview with Kenneth Mak, 13 August 2021.
17  CNA, 7 September 2021, www.channelnewsasia.com/singapore/jurong-fishery-port-biggest-community-cluster-closes-COVID-19-2155351
18  Tan, *In This Together*, p. 58.
19  Tan, *In This Together*, p. 116.
20  Loh Kah Seng, Interview with Margaret Soon, 26 August 2021; Loh Kah Seng, Interview with Leo Yee Sin, 25 August 2021.
21  Loh Kah Seng, Interview with Tan Chorh Chuan, 4 August 2021.
22  Loh Kah Seng, Interview with Kenneth Mak, 13 August 2021.
23  Tan, *In This Together*.
24  Tan, *In This Together*.
25  Loh Kah Seng, Interview with Kenneth Mak, 13 August 2021.
26  Tan, *In This Together*, p. 58.
27  Tan, *In This Together*.
28  *Straits Times*, 5 June 2020.
29  Tan, *In This Together*.
30  Loh Kah Seng, Interview with Shafiq Sahib, 30 September 2021.
31  Loh Kah Seng, Interview with Jayne Lim, 29 September 2021.
32  *Straits Times*, 2 February 2021.
33  CNA, 15 April 2020.

34   *Straits Times*, 8 July 2021.
35   Beyond Social Services, *Mind the Chasm: COVID-19 & Deepening Inequalities in Singapore* (Singapore: Beyond Social Services, 2021), p. 8.
36   Beyond Social Services, *Mind the Chasm*, p. 8.
37   Beyond Social Services, *Mind the Chasm*.
38   Beyond Social Services, *Stretched at Work, Stretched at Home, Thinking Twice Before Seeing Doctor: Healthcare Capacities of Lengkok Bahru Residents* (Singapore: Beyond Social Services, 2021); Beyond Social Services, *'People Give, Just Take and Eat': Food Insecurity and Food Aid in a Public Rental Neighbourhood in Singapore* (Singapore: Beyond Social Services, 2021).
39   Beyond Social Services, *Mind the Chasm*.
40   Stephanie Chok and Isaac Neo, 'Crisis and Inequality: Social Protection Gaps in Pandemic Singapore', forthcoming book chapter.
41   Tan, *In This Together*.
42   Tan, *In This Together*.
43   Tan, *In This Together*.
44   Tan, *In This Together*.
45   Loh Kah Seng, Interview with Leo Yee Sin, 25 August 2021.
46   Tan, *In This Together*.
47   Tan, *In This Together*.
48   Humanitarian Organisation for Migration Economics (HOME), *COVID-19 Impact Report 2020* (Singapore: HOME, 2020).
49   Tan, *In This Together*.
50   Loh Kah Seng, Interview with Letchumanan Muralidharan, 11 August 2021.
51   Tan, *In This Together*.
52   HOME, *COVID-19 Impact Report 2020*, p. 3.
53   HOME, *COVID-19 Impact Report 2020*.
54   Loh and Hsu, *Tuberculosis – The Singapore Experience, 1867–2018*.
55   Brenda S.A. Yeoh, *Contesting Space in Colonial Singapore: Power Relations and the Built Environment* (Singapore: Singapore University Press, 2003).
56   Loh Kah Seng, Interview with Ong Biauw Chi, 16 August 2021.
57   Loh Kah Seng, Interview with Lawrence Lee, 11 August 2021.
58   Loh Kah Seng, Interview with Ong Biauw Chi, 16 August 2021.
59   Loh Kah Seng, Interview with Ong Biauw Chi, 16 August 2021.
60   Loh Kah Seng, Interview with Jajala Thirupathi and Noelle Heng, 25 July 2021.
61   Loh Kah Seng, Interview with Ong Biauw Chi, 16 August 2021.
62   Loh Kah Seng, Interview with Tang Zuoting, 20 November 2021.
63   Loh Kah Seng, Interview with Zakir Hossain, 10 July 2021.
64   Zakir Hossain, 'First Draft', *ArtReview*, https://artreview.com/the-poetry-of-singapore-migrant-workers/
65   Loh Kah Seng, Interview with Ripon Chowdhury, 30 August 2021.
66   Ripon Chowdhury, Facebook post, 23 April 2020, www.facebook.com/staywithMWS/posts/664083137504192
67   Loh Kah Seng, Interview with Ripon Chowdhury, 30 August 2021.
68   HOME, *COVID-19 Impact Report 2020*, pp. 5, 9.
69   Loh Kah Seng, Interview with Lawrence Lee, 11 August 2021.
70   Tan, *In This Together*, p. 190.
71   HOME, *COVID-19 Impact Report 2020*.
72   HOME, *COVID-19 Impact Report 2020*.
73   Tan, *In This Together*.
74   Loh Kah Seng, Interview with Zakir Hossain, 10 July 2021.
75   *Straits Times*, 21 October 2021.
76   新加坡万事通, 12 October 2021, https://mp.weixin.qq.com/s/zvkKy9TzCHN7bdEG0F-J4w

77  TWC2, 'COVID-19 crisis at Jalan Tukang dormitory — some immediate comments from TWC2', 15 October 2021, https://twc2.org.sg/2021/10/15/COVID-19-crisis-at-jalan-tukang-dormitory-some-immediate-comments-from-twc2/

78  HOME, *COVID-19 Impact Report 2020*.

79  Loh Kah Seng, Interview with Fazley Elahi Rubel and A.K. Zilani, 6 September 2021.

80  Loh Kah Seng, Interview with Robina Navato, 13 November 2021.

81  HOME, *COVID-19 Impact Report 2020*.

82  Loh Kah Seng, Interview with Lydia, 5 September 2021.

83  Loh Kah Seng, Interview with Robina Navato, 13 November 2021.

84  Loh Kah Seng, Interview with Endah Purnamasari, 29 August 2021.

85  Loh Kah Seng, Interview with Heidee Roiles, 17 October 2021.

86  Loh Kah Seng, Interview with Robina Navato, 13 November 2021.

87  Loh Kah Seng, Interview with Endah Purnamasari, 29 August 2021; The Birds Migrant Theatre, Facebook page, www.facebook.com/profile.php?id=100057598802984

88  Loh Kah Seng, Interview with Ripon Chowdhury, 30 August 2021.

89  Loh Kah Seng, Interview with Zakir Hossain, 10 July 2021.

90  Loh Kah Seng, Interview with Siti Mujiati, 20 July 2021.

91  BBC, 18 September 2020, www.bbc.com/news/world-asia-54082861

92  TWC2, 'Government announces new standards for control of virus, packaged as new dorm standards', 30 September 2021, https://twc2.org.sg/2021/09/30/government-announces-new-standards-for-control-of-virus-packaged-as-new-dorm-standards/

93  HOME, *COVID-19 Impact Report 2020*.

94  Tan, *In This Together*, p. 62.

95  Lee Hsien Loong, Foreword, in Tan, *In This Together*.

96  Tan, *In This Together*.

97  *Straits Times*, 24 June 2021.

98  Tan, *In This Together*.

99  Tan, *In This Together*.

100  CNA, 22 September 2021, www.channelnewsasia.com/singapore/COVID-19-home-recovery-quarantine-art-self-test-kit-telegram-support-group-2191691

101  *Straits Times*, 4 October 2021.

102  Tan, *In This Together*.

103  *Straits Times*, 4 October 2021.

104  Tan, *In This Together*, p. 73.

105  Tan, *In This Together*, p. 125.

106  *Straits Times*, 12 July 2021.

107  Edoardo Liotta, 'I Work with Seniors, and This Is Why Some Aren't Getting Vaccinated', *Rice*, 28 July 2021, www.ricemedia.co/features-seniors-not-vaccinated/

108  Tan, *In This Together*.

109  *Straits Times*, 21 October 2021; *Straits Times*, 14 October 2021.

110  CNA, 17 November 2021, www.channelnewsasia.com/singapore/dine-cap-two-persons-simpler-easier-logistical-challenges-coffeeshop-operators-2318996

111  Peter Guest, 'The pandemic didn't kill Singapore's UNESCO-listed food stalls. Delivery apps might', *Rest of World*, 19 July 2021, https://restofworld.org/2021/singapore-hawkers-delivery-apps/

112  Tan, *In This Together*.

113  Tan, *In This Together*.

114  Tan, *In This Together*.

115  Tan, *In This Together*.

116  CNA, 27 October 2021, www.channelnewsasia.com/commentary/COVID-19-vaccine-antivax-conspiracy-family-conflict-fight-tips-resolve-therapy-2269127

117  Tan, *In This Together*.

118   *Straits Times*, 25 November 2021.

119   Tan, *In This Together*.

120   CNA, 5 August 2021, www.channelnewsasia.com/commentary/COVID-19-corona virus-mandatory-vaccine-phase-2-restriction-rule-dine-travel-passport-2088856

121   CNA, 18 August 2021, www.channelnewsasia.com/commentary/why-people-ha ve-not-taken-COVID-19-vaccine-hesitancy-reasons-2115446

122   CNA, 11 February 2022, www.channelnewsasia.com/singapore/healthcare-workers-describe-struggles-patients-flood-emergency-rooms-amid-omicron-wave-2492571

123   Ong Ye Kung, Speech at COVID-19 Multi-Ministry Taskforce Press Conference, 24 August 2022, www.moh.gov.sg/news-highlights/details/opening-remarks-by-m inister-for-health-mr-ong-ye-kung-at-COVID-19-multi-ministry-taskforce-p ress-conference-on-24-august-2022/

124   CNA, 22 November 2021, www.channelnewsasia.com/singapore/COVI D19-restrictions-dormitory-migrant-workers-community-visits-2324641

125   Chok and Neo, 'Crisis and Inequality'.

126   CNA, 9 November 2021, www.channelnewsasia.com/commentary/job-quit-le tter-boss-employer-great-resignation-wave-work-life-balance-2298456

127   Lenny Chua, 'Singapore Nurses Are Drained and Looking for an Out', *Rice*, 15 November 2021, www.ricemedia.co/singapore-nurses-are-exhausted/; CNA, 1 November 2021, www.channelnewsasia.com/singapore/resignation-rates-am ong-healthcare-workers-singapore-year-moh-increase-icu-capacity-2282766

128   Prime Minister's Office, *White Paper on Singapore's Response to COVID-19*.

129   Peter Furtado (ed.), *Plague, Pestilence and Pandemic: Voices from History* (London: Thames & Hudson, 2021).

130   CNA, 12 April 2022, www.channelnewsasia.com/singapore/government-did-not-ge t-every-call-right-COVID-19-pandemic-pm-lee-2621611

131   CNA, 24 April 2022, www.channelnewsasia.com/singapore/pm-lee-hsien-loong-sgh-COVID-19-2644406

132   CNA, 3 November 2022, www.channelnewsasia.com/singapore/programme-resea rch-epidemic-preparedness-and-response-prepare-official-launch-tackle-future-pa ndemic-3039981

133   Prime Minister's Office, *White Paper on Singapore's Response to COVID-19*, p. 30.

134   Prime Minister's Office, *White Paper on Singapore's Response to COVID-19*.

# Conclusion

Living in the midst of the COVID-19 pandemic has brought home the fact that so little is known about Singapore's past encounters with deadly pathogens. Pandemics have long been part of the city-state's history but their significance and relevance remain to be unearthed and recognised. Historical research – from plague to coronavirus, quarantine to epidemiology – helps to explain the present state of affairs while offering a guide to future action. We can ill afford to wait till the next pandemic to do this.

Here are our findings from Singapore's long and varied experience with infectious disease pandemics. Some of these are in the form of lessons that have a bearing on policy and can be included in a pandemic response plan. Others are issues and insights gleaned from the study of disease outbreaks – here, the application is less clear but equally important perhaps is the need to re-examine our assumptions about pandemics and history. Together, the lessons, issues and insights serve as a guide for reflection and action in the age of COVID-19.

*History raises further policy questions.* The history of pandemics in Singapore offers general lessons to help us prepare for future infectious disease threats and outbreaks. These lessons are general rather than specific because history is not a repository of facts from which we can find ready-made solutions. We also need to be self-aware about how we conduct historical research and accept that our findings will be tentative.

The study of contexts – historicism – is integral to the historian's craft. A historical event is situated within its times, part of a bigger whole. For our purpose, a pandemic is an event of a certain time and place as well as one in a series of outbreaks. It is necessarily local. Historicism cautions us not to take a pandemic out of its context and draw a simple but likely misleading parallel with a present outbreak. By the same token, a future pandemic should not be shorn of its context, which will invariably be different, and likened to a precedent. The next pathogen may be different but more important are the differences in the political, economic, social and cultural contexts in which it causes an epidemic.

The task of the policymaker and health official is to distil general historical lessons and adapt them to a pandemic plan. As Singapore understood after the SARS epidemic and learnt during the COVID-19 pandemic, such a plan must allow for the flexibility needed to deal with different types of diseases

DOI: 10.4324/9781003384014-13

and contexts. It makes sense to pattern aspects of the plan based on the last outbreak if it is caused by a similar pathogen or disease. But it would be a mistake to persist with such a plan when new information emerges. Needless to say, for a plan to be flexible yet still useful as a guide for action is exceedingly difficult. What this means is that learning from the past is inquiry- rather than solution-oriented. It is really an exercise to ask further questions about how pandemic plans can be refined by adapting the historical evidence, while remaining clear-eyed about the different contexts between various outbreaks.

*Singapore can best aim to minimise the impact of a pandemic.* Two deeply rooted and long-term factors have been behind the pandemics in Singapore history: the island's openness to international trade, capital investment, immigration and tourism, and the dense concentration of the population in a small urban space. Since the beginning of East India Company rule, the population has mostly dwelt in a tiny slice of municipal land around a pair of primary trading zones: the Singapore River and the Singapore Port. Epidemics have in the main occurred in these zones. They worsened when Singapore became a coolie town of mostly single, working-class men from the late 19th century due to large-scale immigration; in 1951, the town became a city of a million people. Cholera is a good example of the public health consequences of Singapore's urbanity: a quintessentially urban disease imported by infected ships into the town. It led to frequent outbreaks there because the municipal government failed to provide safe drinking water and environmental sanitation.

The popularity of air travel after the Second World War created a new entry point for infectious diseases. Most recently demonstrated by the SARS, influenza A(H1N1)-2009 and COVID-19 pandemics, this is an extension of the city-state's heavy reliance on global trade and travel that has its roots in the entrepôt trade and mass immigration of the British years. After Singapore attained self-government in 1959, the population of the town and surrounding urban kampongs were dispersed to outlying new towns built by the Housing and Development Board. The housing was superior but the new nation remained a city-state, with its populace residing in high-density apartment blocks. Immigration also resumed in the 1970s, exemplified by the recruitment of large numbers of low-wage migrant workers not dissimilar to the coolies of the colonial era. These workers have been vulnerable to outbreaks of infectious diseases throughout history in view of the circumstances under which they lived and worked, including El Tor cholera, tuberculosis, influenza and, of course, COVID-19.

Given Singapore's hyper-urban physical environment and its need for global commerce, investment, tourism and foreign workers (both professional and low-wage), the island will continue to face outbreaks of highly transmissible diseases. When a specific outbreak is contained, as in the case of SARS, it should be seen within a realistic perspective. This means recognising the limits of governance, science and medical technology among policymakers, health officials and the public. Short of a major paradigm shift, what should be done is to minimise the social, economic and public health impact of an outbreak. The drawn-out nature of COVID-19 is a validation of these limits, as is Singapore's long history of endemic diseases discussed in this book.

*Quarantine and epidemiological surveillance need to be more agile and people-focused.* How had the city-state's previous policymakers reckoned with these underlying factors? Singapore's pandemic record is mixed. The colonial and municipal governments focused on the trinity of dangerous infectious diseases – bubonic plague, cholera and smallpox – though their efforts to prevent and control them were not always successful. The 'Big 3' were considered especially menacing because they were endemic in the region. In 1913, the Municipal Commission built a new infectious diseases hospital at Moulmein Road primarily to treat and isolate cases of these illnesses, but the facility struggled to deal with other diseases that were more prevalent, such as diphtheria, poliomyelitis and, at times, influenza. The attention given to plague, from the constant maritime quarantine to the development of theories about how the disease was transmitted locally, contrasted with the relatively small numbers of cases and outbreaks. Plague was first detected in the town in 1900 and recurred there in small numbers for under three decades. Two of the 'Big 3' – plague and cholera – are still notifiable in Singapore today, though smallpox has been eradicated.

The emphasis on the trinity relegated other major infectious diseases to secondary importance. As a disease that seemed to break out and end suddenly, influenza is a good example. It was not made a notifiable disease throughout Singapore's history (except briefly in 1918–1919) and allowed to burn through the population during the epidemics of 1890, 1918 and 1957. In 1918, the first wave of the global flu reached Singapore while the port health authorities were scanning the horizon for cerebrospinal meningitis. In 1957, the Labour Front government deemed the quarantine of ships for influenza to be impracticable for an open port city like Singapore. Also long dismissed as impossible was the use of a vaccine for influenza till the outbreak of swine flu in the US in 1976, when the Singapore administration attempted to immunise government employees; this failed due to fears of viral myocarditis. The island had no influenza policy throughout its history till after the SARS outbreak of 2003. What was done in post-colonial Singapore was that epidemiologists incorporated influenza into the surveillance system as a disease of concern. They studied the variants and monitored the number of local acute upper respiratory infections. The technical expertise, data and technology for an influenza policy had long existed.

The quarantine system was established to prevent disease outbreaks highlighted these issues. It developed gradually due to competing interests and changed slowly in response to new threats. Initially, it took two pandemics for the colonial government to improve the quarantine system. The 1873 cholera epidemic, believed to have originated in Bangkok, led to the rudimentary Quarantine Ordinance, while the scare caused by the 1894 plague outbreak in Hong Kong spurred the building of a hospital for the disease on St John's Island and the inspection of ships from infected ports. This showed that the colonial government was willing to learn from international developments. However, the history of quarantine was beset by a longstanding dispute between the colonial and municipal administrations that was not resolved till 1907, as well as by competing economic and public health interests that were never fully reconciled during the colonial period. The British belief that Singapore should not be a walled city contributed to the poor state of quarantine facilities on St John's till 1912, while the underinvested port health department was unable to carry out effective surveillance in the rural areas.

Quarantine was superseded by epidemiological surveillance in post-colonial Singapore with the establishment of the Ministry of the Environment in 1972. Two government units, the ministry's Quarantine and Epidemiology Department and the inter-ministerial Joint Co-ordinating Committee on Epidemic Diseases, commenced crucial work in epidemiological surveillance. The new system worked alongside a number of other complementary measures in this period: a national notification system superior to its colonial predecessor, mass vaccination (particularly for smallpox, tuberculosis and childhood diseases such as measles), environmental sanitation and public education.[1] Still, new forms of quarantine were reinstituted alongside epidemiology in the early 21st century during the SARS and COVID-19 pandemics.

Despite significant improvements, it is important to recognise that the quarantine system had been slow to change. Singapore still treats plague and cholera as dangerous infectious diseases – a view that traces to the colonial period when the way to control these diseases was through quarantine. To deal with the threat of emerging infectious diseases in the 21st century, what is needed is an agile system of quarantine and surveillance informed by new data and social circumstances.

Quarantine and epidemiology should equally be mindful to treat people with empathy and dignity. The extended restrictions on the physical movement of migrant workers during COVID-19 amounted to an unnecessarily prolonged period of quarantine that caused them much distress. So did home quarantine for vulnerable groups of locals, both during the circuit breaker and in the efforts to live normally with the coronavirus afterward. Lest we forget, Singapore history tells us what happens to notification, cooperation and contact-tracing when patients and contacts were treated poorly by colonial officials.

*The history of influenza needs to be rewritten.* Looking back, most governments throughout Singapore history were passive about the threat of influenza, as in many other countries. They dismissed key questions about quarantining ships, controlling outbreaks and vaccinating vulnerable people. It is true that vaccination was hampered by technological constraints and antigen shift in influenza viruses. Conversely, the early post-colonial government did attempt to keep track of flu cases and strains. Nevertheless, for too long a time influenza was not thought to be a serious illness except for vulnerable people like the elderly. This led to the absence of an influenza policy till recently (in Singapore, after the SARS crisis).

This does not mean that we should expect to deal with influenza as we had done with the quarantinable diseases. What we do should depend on the severity of the strain, socio-economic considerations and other factors. What historians can do is to establish the context of an outbreak: find out why influenza was neglected in a specific time and place, and what the outcomes and costs were. In Singapore, the colonial factor was a long-term influence, even up to the 1957 influenza pandemic when the country was on its way to self-rule. In contrast, the British acted with more vigour in the quarantine of plague, cholera and small-pox, and in their attempts to control outbreaks of these diseases in the face of widespread non-cooperation. The neglect of influenza was similar to that of tuberculosis, though a colonial policy to control the latter was developed and implemented in the 1950s.

Reassessing the history of influenza is an example of the relationship between past and present. The relationship is dynamic and dialogic, and not in one direction only. As E.H. Carr observes, 'To learn about the present in the light of the past means also to learn about the past in the light of the present'.[2] Just as our desire to learn from history is motivated by the present crisis, our interpretation of the past can be shaped by contemporary issues. COVID-19 has brought home the fact that the general population may need to be kept safe from dangerous infectious diseases through strong forms of quarantine and epidemiology.

*The Singapore government should continue to learn from past mistakes.* The present administration has had greater political will and resources, and enjoyed greater success, than the colonial regime in dealing with infectious diseases. But there have been mistakes and blind spots in its efforts. There are countless examples of British failure due to the lack of political commitment, administrative rivalry, economic priorities and sound epidemiology. To take the example of cholera, the 1851 outbreak led to a protracted process to build Singapore's first reservoir, the Impounding (later MacRitchie) Reservoir, but this was only completed 16 years later. Even then, safe drinking water eluded most of the town's working class who had to rely on insanitary wells.

In contrast, the post-colonial government responded well to the emergence of El Tor cholera in the region, carrying out mass vaccination campaigns in 1961 and again two years later when the local outbreak occurred and was contained.[3] The effective control of cholera, along with the use of oral rehydration therapy, aided the government's efforts to make Singapore a garden city in the 1970s. Similarly, the Labour Front government and City Council were able to ringfence the 1959 smallpox outbreak, showing what late-colonial administrations could achieve. Two decades later, the Joint Co-ordinating Committee on Epidemic Diseases and Expert Committee on the Immunisation Programme agreed to cease the compulsory vaccination of children for smallpox, after careful deliberation on the scientific data.

However, the post-colonial government should also learn from the mistakes it has made, particularly in dealing with influenza and novel coronaviruses. In the flu outbreaks of 1890, 1918 and 1957, British responses really existed only on paper. Many of the measures declared were tokenistic and ineffectual (street watering, removal of dust and blaming the weather). The injunction for people to avoid crowded places was largely ignored, not only by Europeans but also the Asian working classes for whom the loss of income could be a personal calamity. Compared to its efforts against smallpox in 1959, the Labour Front government's response to the 1957 influenza epidemic was markedly similar to those of the colonial regime in previous flu outbreaks. This showed the limits of decolonisation in managing influenza, a disease that seemed to erupt suddenly and disappear such as quickly.

But there were also continuities from the colonial era that should make us pause for reflection. The wearing of masks was not encouraged by the government during all the influenza outbreaks in Singapore's history; it was expressly discouraged in 1957. This happened again with coronavirus: during SARS and in the first few months of COVID-19. The mass use of a flu vaccine occurred only once as a government policy prior to COVID-19 – during the 1976 swine flu outbreak, which failed due to widespread fears of possible side effects. In its thinking on influenza and coronaviruses, the post-colonial government has largely followed the rest of the developed world and WHO. This can be an issue when scientists and health officials worldwide have found it difficult to deal with emerging and zoonotic diseases.

Something ought to be said about the role of an infectious diseases hospital in Singapore. The colonial iterations were plagued by chronic under-investment, and also by the continuing reluctance to give due attention to influenza, diphtheria and poliomyelitis. The first such hospital at Balestier Road was without exaggeration a slaughterhouse, and its replacement at Moulmein Road owed much to the efforts of the Asian middle class, who wanted a hospital commensurate to their desired level of comfort, privacy and safety. But the building of the Moulmein Road Hospital was long hampered by 'hanging fire', as the colonial and municipal governments haggled and passed the buck back to each other before the Governor substantially cut the budget. Amid the expansion of the healthcare system after the Second World War, the plan for a second infectious diseases hospital was shelved, with the Middleton Hospital given only a new cubicle ward in 1956.

Some of these issues persisted after Singapore became independent. The Middleton Hospital became the Communicable Disease Centre of the Tan Tock Seng Hospital in 1985, reflecting the lower priority given to infectious diseases at this time. Its ageing wards for the Big 3 were adapted to new uses: for patients of HIV/AIDS, chickenpox and skin diseases. A new CDC had been proposed in the early 1990s, but was unbuilt, leaving Singapore unprepared for SARS. The CDC lacked isolation beds and served as a screening centre for SARS cases only for two weeks before the bulk of the work passed to the TTSH. The National Centre for Infectious Diseases replaced the CDC in September 2019, less than half a year before the COVID-19 pandemic reached Singapore. However, the centre was not pandemic-ready at the outset and it took time, with resources and manpower from the TTSH and MOH, to be fully utilised. The dilemma facing the post-colonial government over the infectious diseases hospital is a longstanding one. Post-war doctors and health officials had anticipated it 70 years ago: that the hospital would be expensive to maintain in normal times and would prove its worth only during an epidemic. COVID-19 is an urgent memo that a resolution to the dilemma needs to be found quickly.

*Living with endemic disease has been the default experience.* Most of Singapore's pandemics prior to the 20th century were eventually forgotten by the authorities and had little influence on the course of the next outbreak. The typical pandemic had little discernible effect on colonial healthcare, quarantine, epidemiology and public health. In the aftermath of the 1890 influenza pandemic, the Municipal Commission waived aside a proposal to improve the notification system. This helps explain the chronic non-cooperation among Asians throughout the colonial period. For example, municipal health officers were often frustrated in their attempts to trace the addresses of smallpox patients. During the SARS and COVID-19 pandemics, Singapore's officials were candid about their lack of local historical knowledge, but this has been a long-term institutional amnesia.

There were a few examples to the contrary that might give hope that we can keep the memory of pandemics alive. Singapore has on occasion remembered its last outbreak, either for its exceptional nature (such as SARS) or as evidence of a continuing threat (such as the 1851 cholera outbreak). The memory of the second deadly influenza wave of 1918 also worried doctors and the public experiencing the 1957 flu epidemic. One of the findings of our research is that in addition to official memory, there had been strands of social memory in the aftermath of pandemics. We found a small collection of personal recollections, editorials and advertisements for supposed remedies in the newspapers. A handful of European doctors – and in the post-colonial period local doctors like Goh Kee Tai and Lee Yong Kiat – wrote about the history of Singapore's epidemics. Unfortunately, these individual efforts had little outreach and impact on policy or public memory.

Historical amnesia also means that living with an endemic disease – the current policy for COVID-19 – has in fact been the default experience throughout Singapore's history. Plague was deemed in some official quarters as an 'endemic Sinbad' in 1927 – as an imported disease that had become endemic locally. This perception arose because while few major outbreaks of the disease occurred, a small number of cases continued to surface in the same parts of the town. But the best example of endemicity is influenza, where major epidemics in 1890, 1918 and 1957 were followed by a series of smaller outbreaks in a long aftermath.

What was the nature of Singapore's endemic experiences? They were often ambivalent, though there has also been some improvement. During the colonial era, living with a deadly disease often increased one's chances of contracting and dying from it, particularly among the Asian working class. Non-cooperation with the authorities, rejection of biomedicine (including vaccination) and belief in community medicine, cosmological explanations and miracle cures – these were all facets of a trying attempt to live with infectious disease. After 1959, however, co-existence with an endemic disease has become more synonymous with improved standards of health, environmental sanitation and a general acceptance of biomedicine and government measures. In the 21st century, the challenge is how to learn from both these positive and negative experiences in coping with emerging diseases such as COVID-19.

*Avoid the most obvious precedent.* It can be misleading to base a pandemic plan chiefly on the most obvious precedent or the most recent one. This is illustrated by the influence of the SARS experience on Singapore's pandemic planning and initial response to COVID-19. Worldwide, there has been a tendency during the current pandemic to look for lessons from the 1918 influenza pandemic, which had a similar scale and severity. In both cases, the contexts have changed drastically between 1918 and 2019, or even between 2003 and 2019. Singapore has become a nation, the quarantine system has yielded to epidemiological surveillance and the science has improved. The demographics and social circumstances have also changed: the population is now settled, comprised of nuclear families and responsive to biomedicine. Because of these changes, the 1918 pandemic should not be seen as a foil to differentiate contemporary efforts from 'bad history'. The British fared poorly then, but this was largely due to the nature of a colonial system that no longer exists, as well as scientific understanding of influenza that is dwarfed by what we know today. Using the past as a foil is based on a view of history as antiquarian and unhelpful for modern times. But history offers much more.

A better way is to undertake a study of all the major or historically significant threats and outbreaks throughout Singapore's history. It should include complex or even contradictory case studies, which will offer a measure of the flexibility that a good pandemic plan needs. The Labour Front government struggled to cope with the 1957 influenza pandemic, but did better to stem the smallpox mini-outbreak two years later – this tells us something about the potential and limits of a government on the cusp of self-government. The multiple immunisation campaigns for smallpox, cholera, poliomyelitis, and tuberculosis, which took place during Singapore's transition from colonialism to independence, may offer insights into how social resistance to future mass vaccination can be overcome.[4] Though Singapore has co-existed with endemic diseases to varying degrees, the experiences of living with the trinity of infectious diseases and with influenza have been quite different. Historical comparisons and inferences such as these are important if we are to avoid repeating the error of SARS with COVID-19. While prolonged and severe, the latter still remains one in a series of pandemics in Singapore. It should be treated as an event of its times, rather than the primary crisis upon which the next iteration of the pandemic plan would be based.

*Social and cultural contexts are crucial.* Pandemics were not only public health emergencies but also political, economic, social and cultural flashpoints. Local circumstances greatly influenced how a pandemic unfolded and how well it was contained. During the colonial period, the relationship between the British administration and the Asian population was that of foreign rulers and Asian subjects. Both distrusted each other. The Europeans viewed their subjects as insanitary, unruly and superstitious. A common experience of Asian patients and contacts was to have their belongings destroyed (even their homes burned down), to be roughly handled like criminals, before having to endure poor quarantine facilities on St John's and at the infectious diseases hospital. In 1910, Chinese cholera contacts being hauled to the quarantine station had their queues tied together to prevent them from escaping, while even Chettiars were publicly marched under a police guard to the jetty during the smallpox outbreak the following year. Locals probably feared the authorities as much as infectious disease as a result.

A word should be said about the question of food in the pandemic experience. There is a long history of poor or inappropriate food being served to Asian patients and contacts. Prior to the 1912 Quarantine Commission, contacts of better means who were held at St. John's complained about the lack of cooking facilities and poor quality of food. There were numerous cases throughout Singapore history where the food was rejected for not being appropriately prepared (not halal or unsuitable to a caste). Underlying the question of food was disregard for one's diet and custom. The food issue for migrant workers during COVID-19 was not incidental, but rooted in colonial quarantine practice in Singapore. The British had viewed Asians as an undifferentiated mass of uneducated people, rather than as distinct communities with their own cultures and needs. Resolving the food issue entails acknowledging the social and cultural dimensions of a pandemic response.

The social history of pandemics is of utmost importance to the historical account. It throws light on the impact of an outbreak, particularly on vulnerable groups, as well as the cleavages between the state and society that would have shaped the outcome. It was frequently the working class, elderly, poor and other vulnerable groups who were most adversely affected by an outbreak. During the colonial era, the Asian coolie was at great risk both from death from illness and from the loss of income due to quarantine. James Warren's deep dive into the lives of Chinese rickshawmen revealed how cholera was a scourge upon their lives and livelihoods.[5] Smallpox killed disproportionately more of those who were unvaccinated, who were usually Asians. Influenza is often seen as a universal disease that strikes people of all social classes. But it undoubtedly hit the vulnerable groups harder, such as the elderly population in 1890. In the 1957 epidemic, influenza struck the working classes in Chinatown with such severity that an emergency clinic was formed there by volunteer doctors and nurses.

The colonial regime often blamed Asians, including those who were wealthy and educated, for making worse the spread of an infectious disease. In the pages of the colonial archives, many government and municipal health officials accused Asians of failing to report cases of infectious disease, withholding epidemiological information, dumping bodies in the streets or fleeing to another part of the town. But such allegations say more about the effects of colonial measures than they do about Asian culpability. People's acts of passive resistance constituted what James Scott called the 'weapons of the weak', undertaken as the last resort by those who were unable to mediate colonial policy.[6]

In the 19th and early 20th centuries, most Asians subscribed to a customary system of medicine or cosmological explanation for illness. The Chinese and Indians carried out elaborate exorcism rituals when a smallpox outbreak occurred, while the Malays relied on their bomors or cared for the sick within the kampong. Miracle herbs and fruits sold well during the influenza pandemics of 1890, 1918 and 1957. History also reminds us that it was not only uneducated Asians who leaned towards fake medicines or unruly rituals, for commercial 'pink pills' and other cold remedies touted by European chemists and pharmacies also profited from their Western-educated clientele. European and Asian views of infectious disease could mix and intertwine: the widespread rumours that the 1957 influenza virus was a result of H-bomb tests was first proposed by two European doctors. They were a mark of the Cold War, the arms race and living with mutual assured destruction.

Underneath the gulf between colonial science and Asian beliefs was the unequal nature of the political system at the time. While they did not do enough to stamp out the epidemics, the British held the power to rule their subjects, including on matters of health and disease. Race was a central symbol and factor in colonial governance, and many infectious disease outbreaks were unhelpfully racialised. The racial discourses that emerged in the course of an epidemic deflected attention from the failings of British measures. They legitimised the perpetuation of imperial dominance. Thus, congested housing, environmental insanitation and social vulnerability – issues that explained how epidemics occurred, spread and killed – could remain ignored partly by categorising a diverse population into races.

In the colonial perspective, epidemics demonstrated unequivocally the inequality of races and the theory of racially determined immunity. During the 1918 influenza pandemic, South Indians were deemed to be especially susceptible to pneumonia, the Europeans and Chinese to enteric fever, and native South Africans to influenza. As late as the 1957 influenza pandemic, a widely held belief among officials was that unlike Asians, Europeans were virtually immune to the disease. In the British reckoning of a 'Mohammedan problem' in smallpox, it was irrational for Malays to view the hospital as a death trap and prefer their bomors, while more unvaccinated than vaccinated people were dying of the disease. But history has shown that Malays and other Asian groups had increasingly accepted biomedicine after the war, producing generations of vaccinated people. Communities have a key role to play in the success of a pandemic plan.

*Give more support to the humanities and social sciences.* In addition to science and biomedicine, intervention from the humanities and social sciences is vital. History is useful because it combines aspects of both the humanities and social sciences. As Carr also reminds us, there are similarities between history and science that transcend the disciplinary divide:

> [The] historian and physical scientist are united in the fundamental purpose of seeking to explain, and in the fundamental procedure of question and answer. The historian, like any other scientist, is an animal who incessantly asks the question 'Why?'.[7]

Our book has tried to explain why Singapore's pandemics were often more severe than they should have been, and why locals behaved in ways that diverged significantly from what the colonial officials and doctors prescribed. History, like sociology and anthropology, enables us to discern that a population is made up of distinct groups based on class, age, gender and ethnicity. Policymakers, scientists and medical doctors should pay heed to these social categories. We have seen in history that many colonial doctors were not objective or politically neutral. They subscribed to the superiority of Europeans and the colonial system, racialising the people they were meant to be protecting from disease. Even when the science behind biomedicine has a legitimate basis, ignoring the social impact of pandemic measures or locals' views of sickness may come at a great cost to a society.

Studying the past yields historical empathy, a way of thinking about others that the humanities and social sciences can offer to scientists, doctors and policymakers. Historical empathy provides additional tools to deal with the socio-cultural and economic dimensions of a pandemic. During the COVID-19 outbreak, the regimen of safe management brakes caused social frustrations, economic hardship and mental distress for both Singaporeans and migrant workers. History helps us to understand these issues without prejudging them, as we stand in the shoes of people with very different worldviews and circumstances from those in positions of power or expertise. The key here is to focus less on people's acts of resistance and more on the thinking and situations behind those acts. When we begin to understand why historically Asians had not reported cases of infectious disease or sought help at a hospital, we can formulate solutions that address people's concerns and gain their support and cooperation in the present time.

*Our book's relevance beyond Singapore.* We acknowledge the limits of generalisation insofar as if one was looking to simply apply lessons from Singapore. The study of the island's pandemics is the history of a tiny city-state with an open economy, a strong government and a diverse, mostly Asian population. It is a classic example of a micro-urban history. Most nation-states are far larger in size and population and even individual cities often have a substantial hinterland. Compared to Singapore, other countries may have a weaker government or layers of government. They may also have a homogenous population or a predominantly non-Asian population.

Likely, too, these countries have their own histories of pandemics. Typically, Western countries did not have a colonial history of disease or had an encounter with a different form of colonialism, such as the US. Even among Asian countries, some (notably China and Thailand) were semi-colonial while nominally independent. Most countries outside East and Southeast Asia did not experience the SARS outbreak, so they would not have considered it a major event and adopted it as a template for COVID-19. Conversely, social resistance to mask and vaccination mandates during the present pandemic has been stronger and more sustained in many Western countries than in Singapore.

The answer to the question must be as simple as it is unabashedly generic. Lessons and insights drawn from the past cannot be applied elsewhere without recognising the context. This is why our study of the past for Singapore begins and finishes with itself, rather than another country. Our work is an attempt at contextualisation: to demonstrate how researching the past can be useful in understanding the present and preparing for future pandemics in a specific time and place. This is another way of saying that the general lessons we distil for our city-state are meant to raise further questions and ideas about having to adapt these lessons and make the best pandemic plan possible. There are perhaps universal lessons of history, but these will inevitably be general ones that have to be adapted to the local context. Contextualisation is also a question on the basis of policymaking. Whether Singapore's experience is useful elsewhere is a question for another country's leaders, subject experts and general population to decide. Hopefully, it will include a historical survey of pandemics in that country.

COVID-19 will not be the last pandemic of the 21st century. As the world (including China from December 2022) attempts to live with the disease, we recently saw outbreaks of another infectious disease caused by a different virus in several countries: monkeypox. Unlike the last decades of the 20th century, infectious diseases will likely remain on the public health agenda in the years to come. The call for interventions through the lenses of the humanities and social sciences is but a response to this fact. History is one of the tools the policymaker and epidemiologist have at their disposal to mitigate the effects of the next pandemic, but it is among the most neglected. This has to change and it begins with recognising that pandemics are part of human history.

The change will also have to come from deep within the academy. It entails a fundamental and parallel shift in how professional historians regard their craft and audience, which must now include stakeholders outside academia. In Singapore's universities, most academics in the humanities and social sciences do not work on local topics, while those who do typically frame their work with an academic audience in mind. Other countries may differ depending on how they have assessed or nurtured the relationship between academic research, social issues and policymaking. But it is not unlikely that many historians, in Singapore and elsewhere, are presently ill-prepared to consider the practical ramifications of their research. In the era of COVID-19, it is imperative that historians embrace their social role and address the concerns of broader audiences.

# Notes

1 K.T. Goh, *Epidemiological Surveillance of Communicable Diseases in Singapore* (Tokyo: Southeast Asian Medical Information Centre, 1983).
2 E.H. Carr, *What Is History?* (London: Penguin Books, 1987), 2nd edition, p. 68.
3 While a post-colonial government usually refers to the end of colonial rule, Singapore became a self-governing state under a popularly elected government in June 1959. At this point, the country could be said to be post-colonial in terms of domestic affairs, including health policy.
4 Goh, *Epidemiological Surveillance of Communicable Diseases in Singapore.*
5 James Francis Warren, *Rickshaw Coolie: A People's History of Singapore, 1880–1940* (Singapore: Singapore University Press, 2003).
6 James C. Scott, *Weapons of the Weak: Everyday Forms of Peasant Resistance* (New Haven: Yale University Press, 1985).
7 Carr, *What Is History?*, p. 86.

# The Authors

**Dr Kah Seng Loh** is a historian of Singapore and Director of Chronicles Research and Education, a research consultancy. He is interested in all things that happened in the history of the city-state and the lives of its people. His books include *Squatters into Citizens: The 1961 Bukit Ho Swee Fire and the Making of Modern Singapore* (NUS Press 2013); *Tuberculosis – The Singapore Experience, 1867–2018: Disease, Society and the State* (Routledge 2020); and *Theatres of Memory: Industrial Heritage of 20th Century Singapore* (Pagesetters 2021).

**Dr Li Yang Hsu** is an infectious diseases physician who currently serves as the Vice Dean of Global Health at the Saw Swee Hock School of Public Health. He has been on the frontlines of various major epidemics and outbreaks in Singapore, starting from SARS in 2003. He is deeply interested in all historical facets of medicine, particularly with regards to infectious diseases in Singapore. He is co-author of *Tuberculosis – The Singapore Experience, 1867–2018: Disease, Society and the State* (Routledge 2020).

DOI: 10.4324/9781003384014-14

# Bibliography

**Archival Sources**

*Britain*

CO 273 Straits Settlements Original Correspondences.
CO 275 Straits Settlements Sessional Papers, 1855–1940.

*Singapore*

Health Department (HD).
Ministry of Health (MOH).
Singapore Improvement Trust (SIT).
Singapore Municipality.

**Email Correspondence with Authors**

Allen, David. 30 June 2019.
Chew, Suok Kai. 3 July 2019.
Ho, Lai Peng. 9 September 2019.

**Oral History Interviews**

*By Authors*

Chen, Jing. 26 August 2021.
Chew, Suok Kai. 13 December 2018.
Chowdhury, Ripon. 30 August 2021.
Goh, Kee Tai. 16 February 2017.
Gomez, Dorothy. 29 May 2019.
Hossain, Zakir. 10 July 2021.
Hsu, Li Yang (with Kymelya Sari). 5 August 2019.
Lee, Lawrence. 11 August 2021.
Leo, Yee Sin. 10 June 2019.
Leo, Yee Sin. 25 August 2021.
Lim, Jayne. 29 September 2021.
Lydia. 5 September 2021.
Mak, Kenneth. 13 August 2021.

Monteiro, Edmund. 11 December 2018.
Mujiati, Siti. 20 July 2021.
Muralidharan, Letchumanan11 August 2021.
Navato, Robina. 13 November 2021.
Nisha, Akhterun. 11 March 2019.
Ong, Biauw Chi. 16 August 2021.
Ooi, Peng Lim. 6 June 2019.
Purnamasari, Endah. 29 August 2021.
Roiles, Heidee. 17 October 2021.
Rubel, Fazley Elahi and A.K. Zilani. 6 September 2021.
Sahib, Shafiq. 30 September 2021.
Singh, Harbhajan. 21 March 2019.
Soon, Margaret. 26 August 2021.
Tan, Chorh Chuan. 4 August 2021.
Tang, Zuoting. 20 November 2021.
Thirupathi, Jajala and Noelle Heng. 25 July 2021.
Toh, Paul. 4 June 2019.
Tong. 27 September 2019.

### By Oral History Centre, National Archives of Singapore

Lim, Kok Ann. 3 February 1993.
Monteiro, Edmund Hugh. Reel 12, 11 November 1997.
Monteiro, Edmund Hugh. Reel 7, 24 October 1997.
Ng, Lee Kar. Reel 1, 16 March 1982.
Sayampanathan, Sathiamoorthy Ramalingam Dr. Reel 7, 26 August 1999.
Teo, Choon Hong. Reel 2, 16 September 1983.
Teong, Eng Siong. Reel 1, 1 February 2002.

### Published Sources

Beyond Social Services, *Mind the Chasm: COVID-19 & Deepening Inequalities in Singapore* (Singapore: Beyond Social Services, 2021).
Beyond Social Services. *'People Give, Just Take and Eat': Food Insecurity and Food Aid in a Public Rental Neighbourhood in Singapore* (Singapore: Beyond Social Services, 2021).
Beyond Social Services. *Stretched at Work, Stretched at Home, Thinking Twice Before Seeing Doctor: Healthcare Capacities of Lengkok Bahru Residents* (Singapore: Beyond Social Services, 2021).
Chowdhury, Ripon. Facebook post, 23 April 2020, www.facebook.com/sta ywithMWS/posts/664083137504192
City Council, *Annual Report* (CCAR).
Department of Social Welfare. *Five-Year Plan* (Singapore: Government Printing Office, 1949).
Goh, Chok Tong. Singapore government press release, 'Fighting SARS Together', 22 April 2003.
Hossain, Zakir. 'First Draft'. *ArtReview*, https://artreview.com/the-poetry-of-singap ore-migrant-workers/
Humanitarian Organisation for Migration Economics. *COVID-19 Impact Report 2020* (Singapore: HOME, 2020).

Jarman, Robert L. (ed.). *Annual Report on the Administration of the Straits Settlements, 1858–1859* (Archive Editions, 1998), various volumes.

League of Nations Health Organisation Eastern Bureau. *Report on Study Tour of Quarantine Officers in Eastern Ports* (26 June–8 August 1930) (Singapore: 1930).

Medical Department, *Annual Report* (MDAR).

Ministry of Education. *Education Policy in the Colony of Singapore: Ten Years' Programme Adopted in Advisory Council on 7th August, 1947* (Singapore: Government Printing Office, 1948).

Ministry of Health, *Annual Report* (MOHAR).

Ministry of the Environment, *Annual Report* (ENVAR).

*Official Reports of the Singapore Parliamentary Debates* (Hansard).

Ong, Ye Kung. *Speech at COVID-19 Multi-Ministry Taskforce Press Conference*. 24 August 2022, www.moh.gov.sg/news-highlights/details/opening-remarks-by-minister-for-health-mr-ong-ye-kung-at-COVID-19-multi-ministry-taskforce-press-conference-on-24-august-2022/

Proceedings of the Legislative Council of Singapore. *The Medical Plan for Singapore*, 18 May 1948.

Simpson, W.J. *Report of the Sanitary Condition of Singapore* (London: Waterlow & Sons, 1907).

Singapore General Hospital. 'Never Again', 29 June 2022, www.sgh.com.sg/news/lighternotes/never-again

Singapore government press statement. 'Singapore Gives Australia Advice', 31 May 1957.

Singapore Health Department. *Annual Report* (thereafter SHDAR) 1952.

Singapore Improvement Trust. *The Work of the Singapore Improvement Trust 1927–1947* (Singapore: Singapore Improvement Trust, 1948).

Singapore Municipality. *Administration Report* (SMAR).

Singapore Statutes Online. *Infectious Diseases Act 1976*, https://sso.agc.gov.sg/Act/IDA1976

Singapore. *Master Plan* (Singapore: Government Printing Office, 1955–1958).

Singapore. *Master Plan: Report of Survey* (Singapore: Printed at Government Printing Office, 1955).

Straits Settlements Quarantine Inquiry Commission. *Proceedings of the Commission Appointed to Inquire into the Working of the Quarantine and Prevention of Diseases Ordinance in the Settlement of Singapore, in the Colony of the Straits Settlements* (Singapore: Government Printing Office, 1912), 2 volumes.

Tan Tock Seng Hospital. *The Silent War, 1 March–31 May 2003* (Singapore: Tan Tock Seng Hospital, 2004).

The Birds Migrant Theatre. Facebook page, www.facebook.com/profile.php?id=100057598802984

TWC2. 'COVID-19 crisis at Jalan Tukang dormitory – some immediate comments from TWC2'. 15 October 2021, https://twc2.org.sg/2021/10/15/COVID-19-crisis-at-jalan-tukang-dormitory-some-immediate-comments-from-twc2/

TWC2. 'Government announces new standards for control of virus, packaged as new dorm standards'. 30 September 2021, https://twc2.org.sg/2021/09/30/government-announces-new-standards-for-control-of-virus-packaged-as-new-dorm-standards/

新加坡万事通. 12 October 2021. https://mp.weixin.qq.com/s/zvkKy9TzCHN7bdEG0F-J4w

**Newspapers and Periodicals**

*BBC.*
*Channel NewsAsia* (CNA).
*Daily Advertiser.*
*Epidemiological News Bulletin* (ENB).
*Lat Pau.*
*Malaya Tribune.*
*Mid-Day Herald and Daily.*
*Mid-day Herald.*
*New Nation.*
*Rest of World.*
*Rice.*
*Sin Chew Jit Poh.*
*Sing Po.*
*Singapore Daily Times.*
*Singapore Free Press.*
*Singapore Monitor.*
*Singapore Standard.*
*Straits Echo.*
*Straits Observer.*
*Straits Times Overland Journal.*
*Straits Times.*
*Syonan Shimbun.*
*The Singapore Free Press and Mercantile Advertiser.*


**Books, Articles and Unpublished Theses**

'Editorial: Cholera Outbreak'. *The Singapore Medical Journal*, Vol. 4 No. 3, June 1963, pp. 52–54.
'Epidemiological Bureau at Singapore'. *British Medical Journal*, 20 June 1925.
'Historical Synopsis of Preventive Medicine in Singapore'. *The Malayan Medical Journal*, 1930, pp. 97–102.
'Remembering: A Straits Times SARS Special'. *Straits Times.* 22 July 2003.
Amrith, Sunil S. *Decolonising International Health: India and Southeast Asia, 1930–65* (Basingstoke, Hampshire: Palgrave Macmillan, 2006).
Anderson, Warwick. *Colonial Pathologies: American Tropical Medicine, Race, and Hygiene in the Philippines* (Durham: Duke University Press, 2006).
Arnold, Catherine. *Pandemic 1918: Eyewitness Accounts from the Greatest Medical Holocaust in Modern History* (New York: St Martin's Press, 2018).
Arnold, David. 'Pandemic India: Coronavirus and the Uses of History'. *The Journal of Asian Studies*, Vol. 79, No. 3,August 2020, pp. 569–577.
Arnold, David. *Colonising the Body: State Medicine and Epidemic Disease in Nineteenth-Century India* (Berkeley: University of California Press, 1993).
Bardhan, P.N. 'Notes on Etiology and Diagnosis of Influenza'. *Malayan Medical Journal*, October 1937, pp. 114–115.
Barr, Michael and Carl Trocki (eds). *Paths Not Taken: Political Pluralism in Postwar Singapore* (Singapore: NUS Press, 2008).
Barr, Michael D. *Singapore: A Modern History* (London: I.B. Taurus, 2019).

Bevoise, Ken De. *Agents of Apocalypse: Epidemic Disease in the Colonial Philippines* (Princeton: Princeton University Press, 1995).

Bishop, George D. 'SARS: A Psychological Perspective'. In Tommy Koh, Aileen Plant and Eng Hin Lee (eds). *The New Global Threat: Severe Acute Respiratory Syndrome and Its Impacts* (Singapore: World Scientific Publishing, 2003), pp. 209–220.

Braddell, Roland St. John. *The Lights of Singapore* (London: Methuen, 1947).

Brazelton, Mary Augusta. *Mass Vaccination: Citizens' Body and State Power in Modern China* (Ithaca: Cornell University Press, 2019).

Brooke, G.E. 'A System of Intelligence as a Handmaiden of Hygiene'. *The Malayan Medical Journal*, 1926.

Brooke, G.E. 'Excursion to the Quarantine Station at St. John's Island'. *Journal of the Malayan Branch of the British Medical Association*, No. XI, 1922–1923, pp. 37–38.

Brüssow, H. and L. Brüssow. 'Clinical Evidence that the Pandemic from 1889 to 1891 Commonly called the Russian Flu Might Have Been an Earlier Coronavirus Pandemic'. *Microbial Biotechnology*, Vol. 14, 2021, pp. 186–170.

Carr, E.H. *What is History?* (London: Penguin Books, 1987), 2nd edition.

Centre for Liveable Cities. 'The Sanitation System in Singapore'. *Infopedia*, https://ere sources.nlb.gov.sg/infopedia/articles/SIP_2020-02-06_113509.html

Chang, Jiat-Hwee. 'Tropicalising Technologies of Environment and Government: The Singapore General Hospital and the Circulation of the Pavilion Plan Hospital in the British Empire, 1860–1930'. In Michael Guggenheim and Ola Söderström (eds). *Reshaping Cities: How Global Mobility Transforms Architecture and Urban Form* (London: Routledge, 2010), pp. 123–142.

Chase-Levenson, Alex. *The Yellow Flag: Quarantine and the British Mediterranean World, 1780–1860* (Cambridge: Cambridge University Press, 2020).

Chew, Nicholas Wuen Ming. *Psychological Distress and Coping in Severe Acute Respiratory Syndrome.* Unpublished thesis, Faculty of Medicine, National University of Singapore, 2004.

Chok, Stephanie and Isaac Neo. 'Crisis and Inequality: Social Protection Gaps in Pandemic Singapore'. Forthcoming book chapter.

Chua, Mui Hoong. *A Defining Moment: How Singapore Beat SARS* (Singapore: Ministry of Information, Communications and the Arts, 2004).

Daniels, C.W. 'The Diffusion of Disease'. *Journal of the Malayan Branch of the British Medical Association*, December 1905, pp. 26–27.

Dehner, George. *Global Flu and You: A History of Influenza* (London: Reaktion Books, 2012).

Deurenberg-Yap, M. L.L. Foo, Y.Y. Low, S.P. Chan, K. Vijaya and M. Lee. 'The Singaporean Response to the SARS Outbreak: Knowledge Sufficiency Versus Public Trust'. *Health Promotion International*, Vol. 20 No. 4, June 2005, pp. 320–326.

Dixon, Alec. *Singapore Patrol* (London: Harrap, 1935).

Dobbs, Stephen. *The Singapore River: A Social History 1819–2002* (Singapore: Singapore University Press, 2003).

Doraisingham, M. 'Preventive Measures with Special Reference to Quarantine'. *The Medical Journal of Malaya*, Vol. 11 No. 1, September 1956, pp. 76–80.

Doraisingham, M. 'The Immune Reaction as a Measure of Immunity to Small-Pox'. *The Medical Journal of Malaya*, Vol. 1 No. 4, June 1947.

Echenberg, Myron. *Africa in the Time of Cholera: A History of Pandemics from 1815 to the Present* (Cambridge: Cambridge University Press, 2011).

Fang, Xiaoping. *China and the Cholera Pandemic* (Pittsburgh: University of Pittsburgh Press, 2021).

Fawcett, Bill. *Doomed to Repeat: The Lessons of History We've Failed to Learn* (New York: William Morrow, 2013).

Furnivall, J.S. *Colonial Policy and Practice: A Comparative Study of Burma and Netherlands India* (Cambridge: Cambridge University Press, 1948).

Furtado, Peter (ed.). *Plague, Pestilence and Pandemic: Voices from History* (London: Thames & Hudson, 2021).

Geno-Oehlers, Jillian. *The Water Supply of Singapore*. Unpublished academic exercise, Department of Geography, University of Singapore, 1966.

Giles-Vernick, Tamara and James L.A. Webb Jr. (eds). *Global Health in Africa: Historical Perspectives on Disease Control* (Athens: Ohio University Press, 2013).

Gill, D.H.S. *A Study of Small Pox Vaccination of Infants in Singapore*. Unpublished dissertation for the Diploma in Public Health, University of Singapore, 1963.

Gilmour, C.C.B. 'Bubonic Plague, Rats and Fleas in Singapore'. *The Malayan Medical Journal*, Vol. IX, 1934, pp. 177–181.

Goh, Chor Boon. *Technology and Entrepôt Colonialism in Singapore, 1819–1940* (Singapore: Institute of Southeast Asian Studies, 2013).

Goh, K.T. *Epidemiological Surveillance of Communicable Diseases in Singapore* (Tokyo: Southeast Asian Medical Information Centre, 1983).

Gordon Smith, C.E. and W.G. Thomson. 'An Outbreak of Influenza due to Type B Virus in a Residential Boys' School in Malaya'. *Medical Journal of Malaya*, Vol. 10 No. 4, June 1956, pp. 332–337.

Gordon Smith, C.E. 'International Spread of Virus Diseases with Special Reference to Malaya'. *Medical Journal of Malaya*, Vol. 10 No. 4, June 1956, pp. 63–68.

Harari, Yuval Noah. 'The World after Coronavirus'. *Financial Times*, 20 March 2020, www.ft.com/content/19d90308-6858-11ea-a3c9-1fe6fedcca75

Harari, Yuval Noah. *21 Lessons for the 21st Century* (London: Jonathan Cape, 2019).

Hell, Stefan. 'The Singapore Bureau: Lessons from Asia's First Early Warning System for Epidemic Diseases'. *New Mandala*, 6 May 2020, www.newmandala.org/singapore-bureau/

Ho, Khai Leong. 'SARS, Policy-making and Lesson-drawing'. In Tommy Koh, Aileen Plant and Eng Hin Lee (eds). *The New Global Threat: Severe Acute Respiratory Syndrome and Its Impacts* (Singapore: World Scientific Publishing, 2003), pp. 195–208.

Honigsbaum, Mark. *The Pandemic Century: A History of Global Contagion from the Spanish Flu to COVID-19* (London: W.H. Allen, 2020).

Hsu, Li Yang, Loh Kah Seng, Deborah Ng and Margaret Soon. *Documenting Middleton Hospital, Communicable Disease Centre and the Medical Heritage of Singapore*. Heritage Research Project Final Report for the National Heritage Board, 2019.

Huff, W.G. 'Entitlements, Destitution, and Emigration in the 1930s Singapore Great Depression'. *The Economic History Review*, Vol. 54, No. 2, 2001, pp. 290–323.

Huff, W.G. *The Economic Growth of Singapore: Trade and Development in the Twentieth Century* (New York: Cambridge University Press, 1994).

Ibrahim, Yasmin. 'SARS and the Rhetoric of War in Singapore'. *Crossroads: An Interdisciplinary Journal of Southeast Asian Studies*, Vol. 18, No. 2, 2007, pp. 90–119.

Iriye, Akira. *Global Community: The Role of International Organisations in the Making of the Contemporary World* (Berkeley: University of California Press, 2002).

Jayakumar, Balakrishnan. *The Singapore Water Supply, 1819–1945: The Evolution of a Governmental Responsibility.* Unpublished academic exercise, Department of History, Faculty of Arts & Social Sciences, National University of Singapore, 1989.

Johnson, Niall. *Britain and the 1918–19 Influenza Pandemic: A Dark Epilogue* (London: Routledge, 2006).

Kadri, Z.N. 'An Outbreak of "Hong Kong flu" in Singapore'. Part 1-Clinical Study. *Singapore Medical Journal*, Vol. 11 No. 1, March 1970, pp. 30–32.

Kanagarayer, K. 'Some Observations on Differential Diagnosis in the Tropics'. *Malayan Medical Journal* V, 1930, pp. 36–38.

Kisacky, Jeanne. *Rise of the Modern Hospital: An Architectural History of Health and Healing, 1870–1940* (Pittsburgh, PA: University of Pittsburgh Press, 2017).

Kolbert, Elizabeth. 'Pandemics and the Shape of Human History'. *The New Yorker*, 6 April 2020, www.newyorker.com/magazine/2020/04/06/pandemics-and-the-shape-of-human-history

Kratoska, Paul H. *The Japanese Occupation of Malaya and Singapore, 1941–45: A Social and Economic History* (Singapore: NUS Press, 2018), 2nd edition.

Kwa, Chong Guan and Joey Long. *Water: A Precious Resource for Singapore* (Singapore: Public Utilities Board, Singapore, 2002).

Kwa, Chong Guan, Derek Heng, Peter Borschberg and Tan Tai Yong. *Seven Hundred Years: A History of Singapore* (Singapore: National Library Board, Singapore: Marshall Cavendish Editions, 2019).

Lachenal, Guillaume and Gaëtan Thomas. 'COVID-19: When History Has No Lessons'. *The History Workshop*, 30 March 2020, www.historyworkshop.org.uk/COVID-19-when-history-has-no-lessons/

Lee *et al.*, Vernon. 'Influenza Pandemics in Singapore, a Tropical, Globally Connected City'. *Emerging Infectious Diseases*, Vol. 13 No. 7, July 2007, pp. 1052–1057.

Lee, Grace O.M. and Malcolm Warner. *The Political Economy of the SARS Epidemic: The Impact on Human Resources in East Asia* (London: Routledge, 2008).

Lee, Kuan Yew. *From Third World to First: The Singapore Story 1965–2000: Memoirs of Lee Kuan Yew* (Singapore: Singapore Press Holdings: Times Editions, 2000).

Lee, Pheng-Soon. 'SARS – Lessons on the Role of Social Responsibility in Containing an Epidemic'. In Tommy Koh, Aileen Plant and Eng Hin Lee (eds). *The New Global Threat: Severe Acute Respiratory Syndrome and Its Impacts* (Singapore: World Scientific Publishing, 2003), pp. 273–282.

Lee, Y.K. 'Smallpox and Vaccination in Early Singapore (Part I) (1819–1829)'. *The Singapore Medical Journal*, Vol. 14 No. 4, December 1973, pp. 525–531.

Lee, Y.K. 'Smallpox in Early Singapore (Part II) (1830–1849)'. *The Singapore Medical Journal*, Vol. 17 No. 4, December 1976, pp. 202–206.

Lee, Y.K. 'Smallpox in Early Singapore (Part III) (1850–1859)'. *The Singapore Medical Journal*, Vol. 18 No. 1, March 1977, pp. 16–20.

Lee, Y.K. 'Smallpox in Early Singapore (Part IV) (1860–1872)'. *The Singapore Medical Journal*, Vol. 18 No. 2, June 1977, pp. 126–135.

Lee, Yong Kiat. *The Medical History of Early Singapore* (Tokyo: Southeast Asian Medical Information Centre, 1978).

Leong, Laurence Wai-Teng. 'Walking the Tightrope: The Role of Action for AIDS in the Provision of Social Services in Singapore'. In Gerard Sullivan and Laurence Wai-Teng Leong (eds). *Gays and Lesbians in Asia and the Pacific: Social and Human Services* (New York: Haworth Press, 1995).

Leung, G.M., S. Quah, L.M. Ho, Ho S.Y., Hedley A.J., Lee H.P. and Lam T.H. 'Community Psycho-Behavioural Surveillance and Related Impact on Outbreak Control in Hong Kong and Singapore during the SARS Epidemic'. *Hong Kong Medical Journal*, Vol. 15 Suppl. 9, 2009, pp. 30–34.

Liew, Kai Khiun. 'Terribly Severe Though Mercifully Short: The Episode of the 1918 Influenza in British Malaya'. *Modern Asian Studies*, Vol. 41, No. 2, March 2007, pp. 221–252.

Lim, Poh Lian Dr. 'Emerging Infections and CDC'. In Communicable Diseases Centre, *100 Years: A Commemorative Publication for the Communicable Diseases Centre* (Singapore: Tan Tock Seng Hospital, 2007).

Lim, Vivien K.G. 'War with SARS: An Empirical Study of Knowledge of SARS Transmission and Attitude Toward Working with SARS Victims Among Singaporeans'. Research paper #03–15, Faculty of Business Administration, National University of Singapore, 2003.

Lloyd Davies, T.A. and Rosemary Mills. 'Survey of Sickness in Singapore, with Notes on Births, Deaths, Handicapped Persons, Puberty, Menopause, Immunisation, Incidence of Cough and Adoption'. *Medical Journal of Malaya*, Vol. XV No. 3, March 1961, pp. 117–156.

Loh, Kah Seng and Hsu Li Yang. 'The Origins of Singapore's Communicable Disease Centre: Hanging Fire'. *Kyoto Review of Southeast Asia*, No. 26, November 2019, https://kyotoreview.org/issue-26/the-origins-of-singapores-communicable-disease-cen tre-hanging-fire/

Loh, Kah Seng and Kai Khiun Liew (eds). *The Makers and Keepers of Singapore History* (Singapore: Ethos Books and Singapore Heritage Society, 2010).

Loh, Kah Seng and Li Yang Hsu. *Tuberculosis – The Singapore Experience, 1867–2018: Disease, Society and the State* (New York: Routledge, 2020).

Loh, Kah Seng. *Making and Unmaking the Asylum: Leprosy and Modernity in Singapore and Malaysia* (Petaling Jaya: SIRD, 2009).

Loh, Kah Seng. *Squatters into Citizens: The 1961 Bukit Ho Swee Fire and the Making of Modern Singapore* (Singapore: NUS Press, 2013).

Manderson, Lenore. *Sickness and the State: Health and Illness in Colonial Malaya, 1870–1940* (New York: Cambridge University Press, 1996).

May, Ernest R. *Lessons of the Past: The Use and Misuse of History in American Foreign Policy* (New York: Oxford University Press, 1973).

Menon, K.U. and Goh K.T. 'Transparency and Trust: Risk Communications and the Singapore Experience in Managing SARS'. *Journal of Communication Management, Vol. 9 No. 4*, 2005, pp. 375–383.

Menon, N.K. 'Some Medical Aspects of Local Defence'. *Journal of the Malayan Branch of the British Medical Association*, Vol 5. No. 1, June 1941, pp. 19–24.

Middleton, W.R.C. 'The Working of the Births and Deaths Registration Ordinance'. *The Malaya Medical Journal*, July 1911, pp. 33–50.

Moore, Donald. *Far Eastern Journal* (London: Hodder and Stoughton, 1960).

Narayanan, Darshana. 'The DangerousPopulist Science of Yuval Noah Harari'. *Current Affairs*, July 2022, www.currentaffairs.org/2022/07/the-dangerous-populist-science-o f-yuval-noah-harari

Neustadt, Richard E. and Harvey V. Fineberg. *The Swine Flu Affair: Decision-making on a Slippery Disease* (Washington DC: National Academies Press, 1978).

Nixon, Kari. *Quarantine Life from Cholera to COVID-19* (New York: Tiller Press, 2021).

Ooi, Peng Lim, Sonny Lim and Suok Kai Chew. 'Use of Quarantine in the Control of SARS in Singapore'. *American Journal of Infection Control*, Vol. 33 No. 5, June 2005, pp. 252–257.

Parry, Quah. *A Study of Quarantine Services in Singapore Today*. Unpublished dissertation for the Diploma in Public Health, University of Singapore, 1971.

Photovoice SG (ed.). *Inter-views: A Photovoice Collection* (Singapore: Photovoice SG, 2013).

Pirie, N.W. 'Radiation and Influenza Mutation'. *Lancet*, 15 June 1957.

Polu, Sandhya L. *Infectious Disease in India, 1892–1940: Policy-Making and the Perception of Risk* (New York:Palgrave Macmillan, 2012).

Rahim, Lily Zubaidah and Michael D. Barr (eds). *The Limits of Authoritarian Governance in Singapore's Developmental State* (Singapore: Springer Singapore, 2019).

Reid, Anthony. *Southeast Asia in the Age of Commerce, 1450–1680* (New Haven: Yale University Press, 1988, 1993), 2 volumes.

Rodan, Garry. *The Political Economy of Singapore's Industrialization: National State and International Capital* (London: Palgrave Macmillan UK, 1989).

Rogaski, Ruth. *Hygienic Modernity: Meanings of Health and Disease in Treaty-Port China* (Berkeley: University of California Press, 2004).

Saw, Swee Hock. *The Population of Singapore* (Singapore: Institute of Southeast Asian Studies, 1999).

Scharff, J.W. 'The Growth of Public Health Services in Singapore in Relation to Preventive Medicine in War Time'. *Journal of the Malayan Branch of the British Medical Association*, Vol 3. No. 3,December 1939, pp. 339–348.

Scott, James C. *Weapons of the Weak: Everyday Forms of Peasant Resistance* (New Haven: Yale University Press, 1985).

Strahan, J.H. 'Reflections on the Course of Preventive Medicine in Malaya'. *The Medical Journal of Malaya*, Vol. 2 No. 4, June 1948.

Tambyah, P.A. 'The Nipah Virus Outbreak: A Reminder'. *Singapore Medical Journal*, Vol. 40 No. 5, 1999, p. 329.

Tambyah, Paul Ananth. 'The Infection Control Response to SARS in Hospitals and Institutions'. In Tommy Koh, Aileen Plant and Eng Hin Lee (eds). *The New Global Threat: Severe Acute Respiratory Syndrome and Its Impacts* (Singapore: World Scientific Publishing, 2003), pp. 243–272.

Tan, Chorh-Chuan. 'Public Health Response: A View from Singapore'. In Malik Peiris, K.Y. Yuen, A.D.M.E. Osterhaus andK. Stöhr (eds). *Severe Acute Respiratory Syndrome* (Malden, MA: Blackwell Publishing, 2005), pp. 139–164.

Tan, Chorh-Chuan. 'SARS in Singapore – Key Lessons from an Epidemic'. *Annals – Academy of Medicine Singapore*, Vol. 35 No. 5, May 2006, pp. 345–349.

Tan, Dora S.K. 'A Review of Virus Infections of the Respiratory Tract'. *Medical Journal of Malaya*, Vol. XIX No. 3, March 1965, pp. 201–212.

Tan, Joo Lin. *A Review of the Singapore Quarantine Services*. Unpublished Master of Science dissertation, University of Singapore, 1979.

Tan, Sumiko (ed.). *In This Together: Singapore's COVID-19 Story* (Singapore: Straits Times Press, 2022).

Tarling, Nicholas. *Imperialism in Southeast Asia: 'A Fleeting, Passing Phase'* (London: Routledge, 2001).

Tay, Catherine Swee Kian. *Infectious Diseases Law & SARS* (Singapore: Times Media, 2003).

Tay, Joanne, Yeuk Fan Ng, Jeffery Cutter and Lyn James. 'Influenza A (H1N1–2009) Pandemic in Singapore – Public Health Control Measures Implemented and Lessons Learnt'. *Annals – Academy of Medicine Singapore*, Vol. 39, 2010, pp. 313–324.

Teo, Joel. 'Singapore Legal History of Water: The Municipal and the Singapore Story – Past, Present and Future'. *Singapore Law Review*, Vol. 24, 2004, pp. 22–51.

Teo, Peggy, Brenda S.A. Yeoh and Shir Nee Ong. 'SARS in Singapore: Surveillance Strategies in a Globalising City'. *Health Policy*, Vol. 72 No. 3, 2005, pp. 279–291.

Tharoor, Ishaan. 'How Epidemics Have Changed the World'. *The Washington Post*, 8 March 2020, www.washingtonpost.com/world/2020/03/06/how-epidemics-have-changed-world/

Tosh, John. *The Pursuit of History: Aims, Methods and New Directions in the Study of History* (London: Routledge, 2015), 6th edition.

Trocki, Carl A. *Opium and Empire: Chinese Society in Colonial Singapore, 1800–1910* (Ithaca, NY: Cornell University Press, 1990).

Turnbull, C.M. *A History of Singapore, 1819–1988* (Singapore: Oxford University Press, 1989), 2nd edition.

Warren, James Francis. *Rickshaw Coolie: A People's History of Singapore* (Singapore: Singapore University Press, 2003).

Weber, Ian, Tan Howe Yang and Law Loo Shien. '"Triumph over Adversity": Singapore Mobilises Confucian Values to Combat SARS'. In John H. Powers and Xiaosui Xiao (eds). *The Social Construction of SARS: Studies of a Health Communication Crisis* (Amsterdam; Philadelphia: John Benjamins, 2008), pp. 145–162.

Yeoh, Brenda S.A. *Contesting Space in Colonial Singapore: Power Relations and the Urban Built Environment* (Singapore: Singapore University Press, 2003), 2nd edition.

Yin-Coggrave, M. and Z.N. Kadri. 'Type B Influenza in Singapore'. *Singapore Medical Journal*, Vol. 6 No. 2, June 1965, pp. 71–74.

Yin-Murphy, M. 'An Outbreak of "Hong Kong flu" in Singapore'. Part 2-Virological and Serological Report. *Singapore Medical Journal*, Vol. 11 No. 1, March 1970, pp. 33–37.

Yong, Ed. 'How Did This Many Deaths Become Normal?'. *The Atlantic*, 8 March 2022, www.theatlantic.com/health/archive/2022/03/COVID-us-death-rate/626972/

# Index

For Product Safety Concerns and Information please contact our EU
representative  GPSR@taylorandfrancis.com
Taylor & Francis Verlag GmbH, Kaufingerstraße 24, 80331 München, Germany